IRISH CULTURE AND COLONIAL MODERNITY 1800–2000

From the Famine to political hunger strikes, from telling tales in the pub to Beckett's tortured utterances, the performance of Irish identity has always been deeply connected to the oral. Exploring how colonial modernity transformed the spaces that sustained Ireland's oral culture, this book explains why Irish culture has been both so creative and so resistant to modernization. David Lloyd brings together manifestations of oral culture in the nineteenth and twentieth centuries, showing how the survival of orality was central both to resistance against colonial rule and to Ireland's modern definition as a post-colonial culture. Specific to Ireland as these histories are, they resonate with post-colonial cultures globally. This study is an important and provocative new interpretation of Irish national culture and how it came into being.

DAVID LLOYD is Professor of English and Comparative Literature at the University of Southern California.

IRISH CULTURE AND COLONIAL MODERNITY
1800–2000
The Transformation of Oral Space

DAVID LLOYD

CAMBRIDGE
UNIVERSITY PRESS

32 Avenue of the Americas, New York NY 10013-2473, USA

Cambridge University Press is part of the University of Cambridge.

It furthers the University's mission by disseminating knowledge in the pursuit of education, learning and research at the highest international levels of excellence.

www.cambridge.org
Information on this title: www.cambridge.org/9781316614853

© David Lloyd 2011

This publication is in copyright. Subject to statutory exception and to the provisions of relevant collective licensing agreements, no reproduction of any part may take place without the written permission of Cambridge University Press.

First published 2011
First paperback edition 2016

A catalogue record for this publication is available from the British Library

Library of Congress Cataloguing in Publication data
Lloyd, David, 1955 Dec. 20–
Irish culture and colonial modernity 1800–2000 : the transformation of oral space / David Lloyd.
p. cm.
Includes bibliographical references and index.
ISBN 978-1-107-00897-7 (hardback)
1. National characteristics, Irish.   2. Ethnicity–Ireland.
3. Oral tradition–Ireland.   I. Title.
DA925.L57 2011
941.508–dc23   2011020304

ISBN 978-1-107-00897-7 Hardback
ISBN 978-1-316-61485-3 Paperback

Cambridge University Press has no responsibility for the persistence or accuracy of URLs for external or third-party internet websites referred to in this publication, and does not guarantee that any content on such websites is, or will remain, accurate or appropriate.

*For Robert Oliver Villiers Lloyd
and Joan Hilliere Langrishe Lloyd
in memory*

Contents

List of figures		*page* viii
Preface and acknowledgements		ix
	Introduction: a history of the Irish orifice	1
1	Irish hunger: the political economy of the potato	19
2	Closing the mouth: disciplining oral space	49
3	Counterparts: the public house, masculinity and temperance nationalism	85
4	'Going nowhere': oral space in the cell block	116
5	The breaker's yard: from forensic to interrogation modernity	166
6	On extorted speech: back to *How It Is*	198
Notes		221
Bibliography		262
Index		279

Figures

1. Ordnance Survey map of Kiltarsaghaun townland, 1840 — *page* 72
2. Ordnance Survey map of Kiltarsaghaun townland, 1889 — 74
3. Aerial photograph of Clare Island, *c.*1960 — 75
4. Aerial-view plan of HM Prison The Maze, showing the layout of the H-Blocks — 128
5. Plan of a typical H-Block in the Maze Prison — 129

Image credits:

Figures 1–3 are adapted from *Atlas of the Irish Rural Landscape*, ed. F.H.A. Aalen *et al.* (Cork University Press, 1997), by kind permission of the editors.

Figure 4 is reproduced from *Envisioning Landscape: Situations and Standpoints in Archaeology and Heritage*, ed. Dan Hicks *et al.* (Walnut Creek, CA: Left Coast Press, 2008), by kind permission of the editors.

Figure 5 was adapted by Samuel Pauwels Lloyd from *Nor Meekly Serve My Time: The H Block Struggle, 1976–1981*, ed. Brian Campbell *et al.* (Belfast: Beyond the Pale, 1998), by kind permission of Mike Tomlinson.

Preface and acknowledgements

On one of the last occasions that she was able to leave home, my mother decided to come to a lecture I was giving on the Irish Famine, a lecture that would become the first chapter of this book. Settled at the front of the lecture hall, she asked me once again:

>'What are you lecturing on?'
>'On the Famine,' I responded.
>'How's that?' she queried. 'You weren't there, were you?'
>'No,' I acknowledged, 'but I've read a lot about it.'
>'Is that right?' she said. 'But then, I wasn't there either.'
>She hesitated.
>'Or was I?'

It would be easy to dismiss that query as the quirk of an ageing person's failing memory. But then, it seems to me now to mark a proper uncertainty, an uncertainty as to the extent to which a past we did not live still marks us, marking us through stories heard and unheard, through – perhaps above all – apprehensions and reflexes that may not even be the matter of relation or record. Before anything we have read and thought, and even before anything we may wish to acknowledge, an inarticulate stratum of attitudes and responses shapes, like an unseen geological formation, the ways we are in the world.

Such responses are often formed against the grain. It was from my mother, a stubborn defender of English values and Anglo-Irish mores, that I learnt my first smattering of Irish idiom, from 'a-hain' to 'a-shay', from an *amadhain* to an eejit. It was from my father, a chemist by training and an inveterate rationalist, that I learnt, on country walks or long drives, the first elements of a fairy lore: of thorn trees, fairy rings and fairy paths; or why the half-ruined cottage still stood, though roofless, next to the new one out of respect for the household gods; or how honeysuckle should never be brought inside the house. It was my father who cursed beneath his breath, on holidays in Donegal, those 'born-to-rule voices' that carried across the bay, yet listened daily to the BBC and sent me off to British schools.

I dedicate this book to the memory of my parents, who unwittingly taught me to inhabit the contradictions of a settler colonial mentality in a post-colonial society, and who taught me to love much before I could begin to understand it.

This book has been all too long in the making. The list of debts that I have accumulated along the way is correspondingly lengthy but also full of the memories of spontaneous talk and the brilliant insights of others. The germ of this book came from a lecture by Seamus Deane at the University of California, Berkeley, in the course of which he remarked on the melancholy cast of post-Famine Irish culture. Not only to this aside, but moreover to the richness and complexity of his thinking about Ireland and modernity I owe, as do so many Irish scholars, an incalculable debt.

So much of this book was first unfolded in lectures or seminars that it would be impossible to acknowledge every one or every comment that has helped me to new insights. However, my thanks are due in particular to the faculty and students of the University of Notre Dame's Keough-Naughton Graduate Seminar in Irish Studies and especially to Kevin Whelan, whose several invitations to deliver talks and participate in conversations that would shape this book were an invaluable stimulus to its composition. Conversations indeed have been vital to the making of this book, much of its basic research having taken place, as is only fitting, less in the library than in the pub. For their kindness, wit and erudition I have to thank many Irish scholars: Luke Gibbons, whose generosity and knowledge have been unfailing; Breandán Mac Suibhne, whose acute insights and archival wealth often seemed inexhaustible; Angela Bourke, Vincent Cheng, Joe Cleary, Margaret Kelleher, Heather Laird, Laura Lyons, Amy Martin, Conor McCarthy, Sarah McKibben, Victor Merriman, Emer Nolan, Lionel Pilkington, John Waters, Clair Wills and Trisha Ziff may not even recall all the ways in which they have contributed to this book. I have been no less fortunate in my readers, whose comments on multiple drafts of this work have been invaluable to me in conceptualizing and rethinking it at various points along the way: my thanks here are due especially to Eyal Amiran, Anne Banfield, Tadhg Foley, Avery Gordon and Mark Quigley, as well as to the anonymous and generous readers for Cambridge University Press. To Peter D. O'Neill I owe not only an excellent index, but many years of conversation, friendship, wit and wisdom.

My thinking in this book has also continually been informed by friends and colleagues outside of Irish studies, whose theoretical and historical insights have posed me with the constant challenge to reconceive Irish history and culture from new perspectives. I am especially grateful for the conversation and the work of Eduardo Cadava, Dipesh Chakrabarty, Peter Linebaugh and Neferti Tadiar. Colin Dayan has been an almost daily inspiration and encouragement in the last couple of years of writing as well as providing a model of conceptual imaginativeness and engaged scholarship through her own work. Working with Carolyn Cartier on a series of events on Space and Culture at the University of California crucially advanced my conceptualization of oral space and taught me the importance of the 'spatial turn' in cultural studies. Bi-annual meetings with the Subaltern–Popular Workshop at the Universiy of California, Santa Barbara for the past five years furnished the indispensable intellectual community within which to experiment with ideas and engage in constructive critical thought. I am grateful to Swati Chattopadhyay and Bhaskar Sarkar for organizing these events and to all the participants in those workshops for innumerable insights and frequent occasions for laughter. Over the years I have been sustained too by the friendship and conversation of many whose work and insights have often informed this book obliquely but no less valuably: Fred Moten, Rei Terada, Denise da Silva, Ian Balfour, Lily Cho, Nasser Hussain, Marjorie Perloff, John Rowe, Andrew Aisenberg, Pani Norindr and Marina Perez de Mendiola. Sam and Talia Pauwels Lloyd have continually and graciously reminded me of the most important things over the years, even when my work has taken me away, physically and mentally, from their side.

Above all, I am grateful beyond measure for the companionship of Sarita Echavez See, whose spirit and humour, consummate readings and brilliant map-making have accompanied and sustained me through the completion of this work.

The research for and writing of this book has been generously supported by the following fellowships:

Research Fellowship, Center for Interdisciplinary Research, University of Southern California, 2004;

Senior Faculty Fellowship and Visiting Distinguished Professorship of Irish Studies at the Keough-Naughton Institute for Irish Studies, University of Notre Dame, 2008;

National Endowment for the Humanities Research Fellowship for 2008–2009.

Earlier versions of some of the chapters of this book have been published in the following locations. My thanks are due to the editors and peer reviewers for valuable feedback and comment:

Chapter 1:
'The Political Economy of the Potato', *Nineteenth-Century Contexts* 29.2 (2007).
– reprinted in Keith Hanley and Greg Kucich, eds., *Nineteenth-Century Worlds: Global Formations Past and Present* (London and New York: Routledge, 2008).
'Mobile Figures', *Vectors: Journal of Culture and Technology in a Dynamic Vernacular* 2 (Fall 2005), online: http://vectors.iml.annenberg.edu/index.php?page=7&projectId=54.

Chapter 2:
'The Memory of Hunger', in Tom Hayden, ed., *Irish Hunger: Personal Reflections on the Legacy of the Famine* (Boulder, CO: Roberts Rinehart, 1997).
'The Memory of Hunger', in David L. Eng and David Kazanjian, eds., *Loss: The Politics of Mourning* (Berkeley: University of California Press, 2003).

Chapter 3:
'Counterparts: *Dubliners*, Masculinity and Temperance Nationalism', in Rosemary George, ed., *Burning Down the House: Recycling Domesticity* (Boulder, CO: Westview, 1998).
– reprinted in part in Derek Attridge and Marjorie Howes, eds, *Semicolonial Joyce* (Cambridge University Press, 2000).
– longer version reprinted in Krzysztof Ziarek and Seamus Deane, eds., *Future Crossings: Literature Between Philosophy and Cultural Studies* (Evanston, IL: Northwestern University Press, 2000).

Chapter 4:
'The Myth of Myth', in Danny Morrison, ed., *Hunger Strike: Reflections on the 1981 Hunger Strike* (Dingle: Brandon Books, 2006).

Introduction: a history of the Irish orifice

> This is the loop, the pole
> Bread travels along.
> We have these mouths
> damage stretches.
>   John Wilkinson[1]

With the remarkable consistency that suggests that they are distorted forms of knowledge, stereotypes of the Irish cluster around the things we do with a single orifice, the mouth. They turn on what goes into and what comes out of that singularly labile orifice, and does so to excess. We drink too much and talk too much, at times even too well: we sing and we blather, bawl as we brawl and wail as we grieve. Given to verbal play, we excel in invective; rumour still circulates more rapidly than the daily press, just as subversion was fanned by word of mouth and the Republican ballad. But excess is counterpointed by lack: we starve in the Famine and hunger-strike in prison, and at times relapse into an ambiguous and melancholy silence. Irish silence and the Irish smile – the closed mouth and the disingenuous grin – are construed as dissimulating, subversive, unstable.[2] The paradoxes proliferate: 'stretched by damage', Irish mouths are injured by mental and physical privation but they are, for all that, the loose-lipped organs of excess, subversion and an often counterfactual cultural resistance. The history of this Irish orifice is that of multiple attempts to discipline it, taming its excesses and regulating its disrespect for the proper spaces and times of speech and performance, ingestion and utterance. It is the history of attempts 'to control a strange bodily economy in which food, drink, speech, and song are intimately related'.[3] But it is also the history of the living on of an unruly oral space even in the very architectures and disciplines of modernity, from the pub to the prison cell, and of its resistance to the effort to contain it.

The present book is about a range of Irish bodily practices, about the formation and disciplining of the Irish body at disjunctive but subterraneously intersecting moments. But while it analyses a certain set of bodily practices, it does so through the one that is uniquely privileged in relation to the Irish, the mouth. The mouth organizes the perception and articulation of the Irish body to an unremarked but nonetheless striking extent, as for psychoanalysis the penis organizes psychic comportment both temporally and in terms of the spatial distribution of the apperceived body. Likewise, and like the penis in its symbolic status as the phallus, the mouth performs a double role, being the site simultaneously of actual practices and of symbolizations through which the motions and functions of the other members or organs are endowed with meaning. Thus, for example, it is obvious that Irish violence has always been associated with Irish drinking and Irish rhetoric, whether invective or subversive speech. The flying fist and the loose lip are an inseparable couple. Less apparently, however, Irish violence is already an *effect* of the oral space whose recalcitrance to modern disciplinary institutions was always coded as unruly and insubordinate. Even before it erupted as an act considered violent, Irish orality appeared from the perspective of the colonial state to be a manifestation of violence that determined how specific Irish practices were read.

These considerations offer peculiar insights into the ways in which biological markers of identity function in the case of the Irish. Much has been written on the ways in which Irish racial difference was constituted and apprehended. That the Irish were considered to be racially alien by the English and generally as racially inferior is hardly in dispute. What has been hard to account for is how a people who had, as Charles Kingsley famously remarked, 'skins ... as white as ours' could appear to be so racially distinct as to merit colonization and subordination by means not dissimilar to those employed to rule Indians or Native Americans.[4] In the absence of any salient phenotypical or other biological markers, cultural historians have emphasized the ways in which Victorian racial pseudo-science deployed such modes of classification for the Irish as 'prognathism' or the 'index of nigrescense', all of which now bear a somewhat hallucinatory aura. But in the case of the Irish, it may be that racial difference is principally determined not by markers like skin colour or facial features that supposedly offer themselves to immediate visual recognition, but by the largely non-visual signifiers of orality.[5] Visually unremarkable as it is, what the mouth *does* and what is done in or with it – in a peculiar blend of activity and passivity, introjection and projection – is what marks Irish difference. The very lability of the mouth as signifier, the uncertainty as to the register in which it signifies or as to the way it inserts the subject in the world, accentuates by embodying the racial difference that it symbolizes: the fluctuating, inconsistent nature of the Irish themselves. If, as Hiram Perez has suggested, one of the most powerful ways in which the processes of racialization operate is through the reduction of the being of the racialized to the spectacle of a single organ in an 'unremitting cultural fixation', in the case of the Irish, that organ would be the mouth.[6] The mouth is the privileged corporeal signifier of Irish racial and cultural difference.

That the mouth organizes the apprehension of Irish bodily practices within oral space does not, of course, mean that other Irish corporeal practices are consigned to irrelevance. It is, rather, that their meanings are distributed in relation to orality and to the cultural complexes it sustains and they are read in that context as markers of racial difference. If this focus on the mouth defines Irish practices as *racial* effects, it has had a no less powerful role in the constitution of Irish gender differentiation. Gender is never determined by biological sex difference, which only appears as the natural foundation for distinctions that are, in the fullest sense, performative.[7] In Ireland, as I argue in Chapter 3, the performance of masculinity turns to a singular degree around a specific oral practice, drinking, and a set of oral practices that are articulated with it, most notably story-telling and verbal play. This is by no means a 'transhistorical' constant of Irish gender norms, but a new mode of performance that emerges in the cultural conditions of post-Famine Ireland that followed from the demise of one form of oral space and the migration of some of its practices into the regulated spaces of modernity. By the same token, the reconstitution of Irish masculinity and the regulation of proper gendered spaces that was undertaken by Irish nationalism generated a set of prohibitions and exhortations that focus on the unruly mouth. The oral thus stands as the most resonant metonym for Irish bodily culture and for the distinctive matrix of habits and practices that marks Ireland's colonial difference.[8]

In significant though by no means all respects, Ireland's remained an oral culture long after the rest of Western Europe had made the transition to the culture of print capitalism. At the same time, Ireland's was also a highly literate culture. It was a chirographic culture at a very early period, and affected by a vigorous print culture not much later than England itself. In the wake of successive conquests, respect for written culture remained strong even among the poorest Irish and was possibly even amplified by the strictures on the education of Catholics imposed under the Penal Laws in the eighteenth century.[9] Orality in Ireland is not a mode of existence that is surpassed and supplanted by literacy and the modes of living it presupposes and sustains. Orality implies, rather, a complex interaction of spaces, an intersection of oral and literate modes, each surviving in peculiar ways within the other and even preserving the other's life within itself. Folklorists and others have written voluminously about the ways in which the products of a highly literate culture – those of the Gaelic bards, lawyers and historians as well as poets – were transmitted in fragmentary and distorted forms, though sometimes with remarkable recall, through Irish oral culture. Much has been done to document, translate and transmit the records and archives of those traditions. This book addresses another aspect of orality than its artefacts: it is about ways in which the persistence of the oral within and alongside the institutions and practices of a literate and bureaucratic colonial society impacts the peculiar forms of modernity in Ireland. It is about the ways in which the spaces and practices of oral culture are represented and targeted by the colonial state and it is about the recalcitrance and even the more or less articulate resistance that the oral poses to the imposition of a homogenizing colonial culture and its values; it is about the ways in which the oral lives on, both in and through the intimate damage that colonialism inflicts.

This book is not, therefore, a history of the achievement or failure of a normative transition, the movement from orality to literacy as a component of the modernization of a society. It is not, indeed, a history at all, if what that term implies is a continuous narrative or a narrative of continuities and evolutions. As a study of the transformation of Irish oral space, it seeks to reflect on the *discontinuous*, on the suppression, displacement and unexpected re-emergences of oral practices and spaces in the very processes and institutions of modernity. For if the oral survives, and survives as the form in which Irish cultural difference is registered, it lives on above all as a certain transgressive disposition of both material and psychic space. In focusing on the spaces of Irish orality – corporeal and social – this book takes the mouth as a metonym around which, with possibly unique cultural force, various sets of bodily practice are distributed in both their uncertain disciplining and their unruly eruptions. It offers, in consequence, a counter-historical thesis about the insistence of a spatiality that defies historicist logic. Accounts of oral and literate cultures tend to be driven by a deeply historicist norm: literacy replaces orality in the progress of human kind, producing the conditions for increasingly complex mental processes and social differentiations of practice and function. It subtends what modernization theory regards as the divisions of spheres and of labour essential to modernity. Literacy induces individuation and interiorization, putting an end to the communal forms of oral culture. Literacy brings with it, above all, the historical consciousness within which its own developmental suppositions can be thought at all.

From the perspective of that historical consciousness, the oral signifies the pre-modern, the primordial, and is associated with myth and folklore, forms of consciousness that lack historical sense and imply the absence of a notion of change over time if not, indeed, an inveterate resistance to progress and development. A heady cascade of associations follows from such premises with remarkable consistency: the oral is reproductive rather than productive; it rapidly becomes feminized, summoning up old crones and kitchen tables, connoting subjection to natural cycles and atavistic beliefs and impulses. Fundamentally conservative, orality is simultaneously the domain of dark and turbulent forces, whose chaos is the effect of non-differentiation and indistinction. The oral is the clearest manifestation of a domain under the sway of the *pathological* in the strict sense in which Kant deploys it in the *Second Critique*: for him, the pathological is the realm of the subject subjected to nature and to history, as it is to its own impulses and desires. It thus designates a negative and inadequate way of being in the world, although – as I argue in Chapters 5 and 6 – what he terms the pathological might equally be seen as the very condition of life-in-common, the shared constitution of needing, suffering, desiring human bodies. From both a Kantian and a historicist perspective, however, orality shelters the unemancipated subject while literacy is the condition of possibility for discrimination, reflection, interiority, development: the categories of the ethical and fully historical subject of freedom. In its own way, psychoanalysis repeats such judgements: the oral is the first relation of the infant to an undifferentiated world of object-cathexes, symbolized in the first instance by the mother. Oral fixation signifies regression: the development of interiority, of the ego and the superego, obeys the hierarchy of the senses that aesthetic philosophy had already defined as dividing those in which the subject dissolves into its objects – touch, taste, smell – from those in which it is distanced – hearing and sight. This hierarchy of the senses in the oedipal drama parallels and rests on a map of the body's orifices that is disposed on a temporal axis, from the oral to the anal to the genital and finally to the scopic register that determines the castration complex and the movement of internalization that institutes the superego or the subject's relation to the paternal law. Thus the sight of the woman's orifice, read as a tale of lack, spells the onset of the castration complex and opens onto the inner silent voice of the superego, just as the lack embodied in the oral gives way to the inwardness and historical consciousness of the literate.

Against such insistent and mutually reinforcing historicist paradigms, I focus here on the oral *space*: on the material and social space that sustains a culture that has been understood predominantly as oral, in difference from modern, literate culture; on the ways orality in culture imagines and uses space. The spatial form that offers the initial paradigmatic instance of oral space is the *clachan* or rundale system of land use and dwelling that in the nineteenth century furnished colonial improvers and reformers with the necessary index of the irrationality of Irish agricultural practice and ways of life. Already little more than a vestige of older forms of communal land-holding, and by no means ubiquitous throughout Ireland, the *clachan* nonetheless came to symbolize the habits of work, sociality and culture that had to be extirpated in order for the Irish to be civilized. Regarded as primitive by the colonial administrator and the political economist, it was rather an instance of what I have elsewhere termed the *non-modern*, living on through and in relation to modernity, coeval with it but not subsumed by it.[10] Increasingly subdivided into smaller parcels on account of colonial dispossession, the arcane and higgledy-piggledy jigsaw of land distribution in the outfield was matched by the disorderly proximity of remarkably populous 'villages' in the pre-Famine townlands.

But it was not only this impenetrable and apparently chaotic use of material space that English administrators and landlords longed to subject to capitalist rationalization and uniform, abstract measure. It was also the cultural and even affective space that it sustained. No less scandalous to their minds than the patchwork of land held in common was the unruly mixing of labour and leisure, of marketing and dancing, of music and mourning, that thrived there. The proper separation of spheres into public and private, labour and recreation, economics, religion and politics that modernity prescribes was long resisted in Ireland – as, to a lesser extent, it was among the pre-industrial working classes in Britain up through the 1840s.[11] This resistance to the rationalization of space, both in relation to the disposition of properly bounded and stable units of land-holding and in relation to the differentiation of spheres according to their proper activities, correlated to what was perhaps the most scandalous aspect of Irish 'character': its apparent emotional instability. The cliché that the Irish appear with 'a tear and a smile' is a sentimental vestige of a censorious judgement on what was observed to be their propensity to fluctuate rapidly between contradictory states of emotion, from joy to sorrow, from laughter to anger, in a sudden leap and without transition. It is the affective correlative of the 'through-otherness' of Irish material and cultural space, a practice of emotional performance that does not obey the ever more rigorously demarcated compartmentalization of affective display that characterizes nineteenth-century English emotional comportment. Irish emotional oscillations, manifest in their political agitations as in their more intimate sorrows or pleasures and indifferent to the decorum of public or private space, corresponded to a diffuseness of boundaries that was an offence both to propriety and to the emerging norms of a well-regulated civil society. The labile mouth, conduit of drink and speech, mourning and mockery, blarney and wailing, food and laughter, was the constant metonym for the peculiarly physical performance of Irish emotion and its intimate intersection with consumption and expression. If a tight-lipped queen clad in mourning became the symbol of a society that increasingly divided – and concealed – the domestic interior and its feminized affects from the practical, masculine world of public affairs and economic activity, the Irish wake and its cloaked keener would become the sign of Irish unruliness, with its peculiar and promiscuous mixing of grief and merriment, wailing and drinking, excessive consumption and seditious complaint.

The terrible silence that fell over the land in the aftermath of the Famine and its catastrophic depopulation spelt, if not the end, then the decay of the wake and the associated practice of keening. Both the Famine and the clearance of the land that ensued were determined by a governmental discourse of political economy that regarded the cultivation and consumption of the potato rather than grain as a major impediment to the development of capitalist agriculture and the English model of a division of social classes into landlord, capitalist farmer and labouring proletariat. Wheat required a quite specific division of both labour and space: the extensive farmland, the division of production between agricultural labourers, the farmer, the corn-factor, miller and baker, and eventually the industrial workforce in the cities that would consume its final form, the wheaten loaf. It implied networks of transportation, processing, a capacity for storage, centralization and distribution, the division of country and city – and, with the repeal of the Corn Laws in midcentury, the division between the metropolis and its colonial 'bread baskets'. The humble potato, on the other hand, defied both transportation and lengthy storage, being too heavy and moist for either. It could not be processed but would be consumed, as it was grown, locally. Its prodigious reproduction on small and even relatively infertile plots enabled a more or less subsistence economy and the remarkable subdivision and reclamation of marginal land that supported the rapid increase of the Irish population from the mid eighteenth century down to the 1840s.

What the Irish put into their mouths as much as what – seditious, witty or cajoling – came out of them was thus targeted by political economy for destruction. The lumpish potato became the index of and the metaphor for Irish recalcitrance to capitalism – a recalcitrance that was proving contagious as the Irish, in another offence to proper bounds, migrated to Britain and mingled among the no less dispossessed English, Scottish and Welsh workers, spreading political dissent and alternative political imaginaries. The potato sustained and was sustained by the spaces of an oral culture that proved a resistant alternative to the processes of capitalist rationalization that enforced dispossession and expropriation through the enclosure and consolidation of land. Accordingly, it was programmed for uprooting even before the Famine re-ordered history by seeming to demonstrate the inevitable failure of the evil root and of the unruly ways of living it enabled. The first two chapters of this book describe the concerted assault on Irish oral space and its alternative possibilities, an assault focused by the catastrophe of the Famine. The first, on political economy and the potato, recounts the perspective of the colonial state at a signal moment in the formation of its institutions for an industrial capitalism to which Irish ways posed a scandalous and dangerously infectious alternative. The second, on the forms of Famine-era oral space, takes, rather, the perspective of those who went down beneath the force of the modernizing project: not only the Irish cottiers whose oral culture resided in the space of the *clachan*, but the Irish and British Chartists who found in a modified form of Irish ways a possible if last ditch alternative to industrial wage labour.

The trauma of the Famine, which accelerated the destruction of the *clachan*, must be registered not only in terms of the cultural damage it inflicted but also in terms of those cultural elements that escaped destruction. To fail to do so is to rationalize Irish history in ways that its singularities constantly elude. We can comprehend this by grasping how the relation to damage as *loss* is counterpointed always by the persistence of damage as a mode of *memory*. Precisely because it is not a form of erasure or supersession, damage itself becomes the locus of survival, the pained trajectory of what lives on and, moreover, continues to resist incorporation. The question in relation to our memory of hunger, which is the Irish version of a question that always insists for the decolonizing process, is how such a resistance to incorporation, articulated through the vertiginous ambivalences of damaged cultural forms, counts its psychic and corporeal costs. More importantly, how can such a reckoning lead us to transform the very damage that seams our survival and our difference into something more than survival, into alternative modes of living?

The space of orality not only embodied a set of material relations, but also contained a distinct set of social and cultural possibilities – *other* human potentials realizable solely through spaces different from those of capitalist modernity. Because they spoke to the needs, pains and pleasures of the 'pathological subject', their contours could never be entirely erased. They migrated into the other, modern space-times that emerged in their wake; they did not disappear, nor did they get subsumed. What Henri Lefebvre understands as the space of practice – 'the practico-sensory realm, the body, social-spatial practice' – cannot finally be reduced to the abstract, frictionless space dreamed of by capital, 'and hence new, spatial contradictions arise and make themselves felt'.[12] Oral practices live on athwart the institutional spaces of a modernizing Ireland – both the governmental institutions of the colonial state and the new political and civic agencies of anti-colonial nationalism – and their survival is inseparable from the emergence of those spaces and the differentiations they seek to impose on Irish culture.

The following chapters accordingly explore the ways in which that space lives on parasitically within the architectures and compartments of modernity. Oral space does not persist intact, though it has always been known that elements and fragments of oral culture have shown a remarkable capacity to survive, like shreds of some viral DNA, in ballads, stories and music as in a propensity for conversation and spontaneous rhetorical play. To the frustration of both colonial and nationalist authorities, such forms retained an inexpungible capacity to reproduce and disseminate memories of resistance at moments of disturbance and insurrection. Yet not only the contents, but even the *structures* of oral space find ways to live on in damaged and distorted forms and in doing so continue to represent material sites of recalcitrance and resistance both to the disciplines of labour and to the governmental institutions of the state. In doing so, they continue to confound the boundaries that divide public and private, proper and improper, in singular and persistent ways. They furnish what we can call counter-modern spaces and practices, captured and determined by the institutions of modernity, yet preserving and refunctioning elements of the non-modern that remain recalcitrant or antagonistic to the disciplines of capitalist labour or state formation.

For all its preoccupation with Ireland's phenomenal capacity for reproduction, the discourse on the Irish in the mid nineteenth century shows a remarkable absence of any developed conception of gender differentiation. Perhaps because the Irish tended to be perceived as an undifferentiated and mobile mass, spreading rhizomatically like the potato itself, no extended discourse on gender seems to have developed in or on Ireland, at least until Matthew Arnold and others began to characterize the Irish, or the Celt, as an essentially feminine race in the 1860s. In response to this no less undifferentiated judgement, nationalists sought to produce rigorous models of gender differentiation that could oppose Irish masculinity and feminine domestic virtue to English colonial rule. I argue in Chapter 3 that this attempt to produce gendered norms and gendered divisions of social space was inseparable from another dimension of the oral and its spatialization. The intended production of gendered space, the division between a feminine domestic and a masculine public and economic sphere, found itself in competition with another performance of Irish masculinity: *drinking*. Peculiarly, it may be thought, given the long-standing acknowledgement of Irish sexual repression, the formation of gendered space in Ireland may have less to do with the disciplining of the sexed body than with the negative and productive regulation of another space of Irish orality. Indeed, as Richard Stivers has persuasively argued, the emergence of a sexually conservative and celibate culture in post-Famine Ireland, which has often been understood in relation to new patriarchal practices of land-holding and transmission, was positively enabled by the emergence and celebration of bachelor drinking customs that drew from older forms of reciprocity and moral economy and adapted them to new institutions and social relations.[13] Temperance nationalism targeted the ambiguous space of that performance, the public house, but was never able to overcome its perdurability as a site where the practices of an oral culture lived on. James Joyce remains that space's most trenchant participant ethnographer. Both *Dubliners* and *Ulysses* furnish maps of urban spaces where oral practices associated with and probably derived from rural culture persist in forms remarkably akin to those of the *clachan*, even if the location and context are utterly different. In the urban pub stalks the ghost of the oral culture that the Famine liquidated, just as Joyce's representations of Dublin's wounded masculinity are haunted by fragments and textures of another sociality and its mores – treating, singing, mingling. Indeed, Joyce is remarkably attuned to the peculiar intersection of utopian desire and psychic damage that is played out in such sites and for which the homosocial pleasures of drinking furnish so rich an instance. His work also allows us to perceive the ways in which oral space, together with its values and practices, lives on, even as it is transformed and regulated in modern times and urban locations, in ways that suggest the discontinuous and lateral trajectory of its movement across time.

The counter-modern recalcitrance of drinking culture both to labour and to state-oriented nationalism occupies the regulated and licensed space that urban modernity has demarcated for pleasures that were once part of a less formally segregated interchange of labour and recreation. Other institutions of modernity sought to overcome Irish unruliness with an even more fully regulated ordering and division of space. Foremost among these was the prison, whose cellular disposition of space – though neither unique nor original to Ireland – became a model for English penal reformers by the 1870s. Corresponding uncannily with the division of rural space into isolated and bounded farms, the cellular space of the Irish convict prison emerged in the immediate wake of the Famine. Both rational orderings of space had as their aim the improvement of the Irish people. If one had silence as its effect, the other used silence as its instrument. The very architecture of the cellular system of imprisonment imposed silence and reflection as a means to produce the conforming interiority that its separate yet serially identical cells connoted. This penal attempt to regulate Irish disorder and criminality on a *national* scale was unprecedented elsewhere in the United Kingdom, despite earlier experiments with cellular prisons at Millbank and Pentonville, and was inseparable from the no less unprecedented national system of policing that came into being in Ireland after 1815.

Nothing marks the colonial nature of the British state in Ireland more than these nationally organized disciplinary institutions and the virtually continuous Coercion Acts – declarations of emergency – by which nineteenth-century Ireland was controlled. Such was the failure of hegemony – or 'improvement' – that coercion became the norm.[14] Almost from the start, the prison became a principal site of political contestation and an institution within which the modes of resistance to the colonial state were developed, articulated, communicated and symbolized. It is no accident that Irish resistance has so often been articulated through the image of the incarcerated body, since the very practice of confinement was always about the criminalization and reform of an Irish body understood to be almost primordially alien and recalcitrant to the 'civilizing process'. And, if 'separation' and silence in the cellular prison were seen to be the means to induce the reformation and the individuation of the political representatives of collective insubordination, it is hardly surprising that orality should become one privileged mode through which resistance to the modern prison regime is over and again played out.

Chapter 4 argues that the architecture of the modern cellular prison in Ireland materially embeds a recollection of the very oral space and practices of resistance it was meant to contain. The cell operates as a kind of memory chamber for what defies and ultimately exceeds its space. Apprehended within the long genealogy of cellular imprisonment in Ireland, the political struggles of Armagh Gaol and the H-Blocks in the Northern Irish Troubles can be understood as a counter-modern reactivation of the spaces of oral community within the modern structures that were designed to contain and destroy them. By the same token, the extended no-wash protests – more than the hunger strikes that succeeded them – effect an undoing of the hierarchical disciplining of the body and its orifices that defines the civilizing process. Prison struggle thus exemplifies to the full the ways in which orality persists as an unsubsumed counter-space of modernity. In this sense, indeed, the oral represents entirely the meaning Henri Lefebvre gave to that concept – though the dynamics of colonial space were far from his concerns: '[A] counter-space can insert itself into spatial reality: against the Eye and the Gaze, against quantity and homogeneity, against power and the arrogance of power, against the endless expansion of the "private" and of industrial profitability; and against specialized spaces and a narrow specialization of function.'[15] Precisely what Irish oral space represented – defiance of the rational division of spheres and functions, of economic and governmental logic, of individuation and enclosure – becomes reanimated in the absolute and punishing enclosure of the cell block. The vulnerable pathological body in all its unruliness operates (again in Lefebvre's terms) as 'a *differential* field' within the compartmentalized spaces of the prison regime and rediscovers there the political meaning of life in common. This body is not, however, the 'total body' of Lefebvre's conception. It is, rather, the body that rediscovers its own spatiality and discontinuity in the form of a 'body full of holes' even as it explores and exploits the physical cracks and fissures of the 'total institution' that is the prison.[16] Much as the public house becomes the site for the regulations of oral practice that then, metonymically as it were, channel the production of gendered spaces and bodies, so in the prisons the reconstitution of an oral space of resistance becomes the medium for a thorough-going mobilization of the body as a network or relay of orifices and secretions.

Introduction 13

The forms of state that developed in Ireland, including national penal and policing systems as well as a range of governmental institutions from the national schools to the ordnance survey and the census, came into being long before they were replicated in Britain itself. In this respect, Ireland's paradoxically precocious modernity actually appears typical of colonial state formations: in similar ways, police and educational systems that were developed in India and Africa would also eventually 'come home' to the metropolis.[17] The process by which the colony constituted the laboratory for state forms that would later be introduced into the metropolis or imperial core was not one that ceased after the colonial heyday of the nineteenth century. On the contrary, that process not only continues but has even intensified in the present, as the state of emergency that was the norm for the colonial world has morphed into the unlimited state of siege that is the global 'war on terror'. Once again, Ireland has been one crucial conduit for this movement. During the 1970s, Northern Ireland became the laboratory for modes of 'enhanced interrogation', as some now euphemistically term such methods of torture, during which experiments with the techniques of sensory deprivation were systematically conducted on internees swept up in extensive military dragnets. Internment itself was a technique of surveillance and data-harvesting that had already been deployed in other British counter-insurgency campaigns in colonies like Malaya, Aden and Kenya. The peculiarity of Northern Ireland was that it represented a colony formally incorporated into the metropolis: it was, as Patrick Carroll has termed Ireland in an earlier period, 'the doorstep colony of England'.[18] The techniques of surveillance, incarceration and interrogation, enabled by the Special Powers Act that had been in force in Northern Ireland virtually continuously since its foundation, heralded the gradual formation of the 'strong' or security state that is increasingly the norm for what were the liberal democracies.

Just as the nineteenth-century forms of statecraft developed in Ireland to break its recalcitrant social and cultural formations were gradually adopted in Britain, so in the present era the techniques of the biopolitical state that were tested in Northern Ireland's counter-insurgency campaign furnished a basis for the material and legal infrastructure of new forms of control that are virtually global in their reach. The governmental institutions of nineteenth-century Ireland targeted not merely the dissident practices of revolutionary nationalists, but a whole set of cultural formations and practices. Likewise, the significance of the transfer of counter-insurgency techniques and technologies into the fundamental infrastructure of the state signals not merely an extension of policing in a restricted sense, but a further transformation of the role and idea of the state and of the cultural imaginaries by which its subjects are interpellated. Chapter 5 argues that the relationship between the citizen-subject and the liberal state could be represented by the archetype of urban modernity, the *flâneur*-detective, while the late-modern strong state finds its correlative figuration in the torturer–tortured couple. Where the most imaginative critic and historian of modernity, Walter Benjamin, descries the paradigm of the *flâneur* in the poetry of Charles Baudelaire, the outlines of this new, late-modern archetype are foreshadowed in the oral balladry of Republican prisoner, Bobby Sands. As the scenario of torture – once concealed within the recesses of the colonial apparatus or of racial policing – becomes an open secret, the citizen is repeatedly invited to imagine him- or herself in one of the complementary roles of torturer or tortured. A shift in subjectivity occurs that corresponds to the shift from the biopolitics of the liberal welfare state to that of the neo-liberal security state. In an era of newly intensified accumulation, the exigencies of control and coercion of the security state reconfigure the apparatuses of the liberal state that emerged from the processes of enclosure and expropriation that Marx recognized in post-Famine Ireland. In both eras, the violence of accumulation targets, as Rosa Luxemburg saw, not simply the material goods, but even the cultural formations, 'the social and economic ties' of the dispossessed.[19] The colonial counter-insurgency laboratory of Northern Ireland prefigured this re-formation of the state. In it, the regulation of oral culture and its paradoxically vociferous unreadability was replaced by the violent coercion of speech as a means to penetrate the opaque ethnic enclaves that were the residues of a colonial regime of domination and discrimination. The grilling of the nineteenth-century Irish peasant by the landlord that Hugh Dorian describes in Chapter 2 was systematized in the interrogation centres of Northern Ireland in 1972.

In a profound sense, modern Irish literature has always been highly attuned to the workings of the biopolitical state, from the writings of Irish political prisoners like John Mitchel or O'Donovan Rossa to their successor, Oscar Wilde in his 'The Ballad of Reading Gaol'; from Yeats's fascination with the possibilities of eugenics to Joyce's constant recurrence to the biopolitics of birth, living and death in the colonial metropolis of *Ulysses*. Samuel Beckett's work, for all the critical effort to celebrate its aesthetic purity, is no exception. His awareness of the anti-colonial wars in Ireland, the anti-fascist resistance in France and the decolonizing struggle in Algeria informs his work with an apprehension of the general failure of the liberal model of subjecthood that would later become manifest in the transition to the security state. To a remarkable and largely unrecognized extent, Beckett's work is obsessed with scenarios of torture and interrogation and with the coercion of 'extorted speech'. Chapter 6 argues that his last extended prose fiction, *How It Is*, written in the midst of vexed public debates in France about the use of torture in Algeria, renders an uncompromising critique of liberal subjecthood from the perspective of the oral pathological subject and its undisciplined orifices. Its vision of 'life in common' can only be articulated from the negative space of wretchedness and deprivation and through the deconstruction of the aesthetic and political supremacy of the abstract 'subject of freedom'. Yet its rigorous performance of the 'tortured–torturer' couple finally opens the possibility of reimagining the pathological subject, so disparaged by post-Kantian ethics, as the body of need and desire upon which a renewed notion of the commons might be asserted.

The unrelenting ugliness of *How It Is*, with its creatures crawling through the mud and its breathless, unpunctuated and utterly *oral* spasms of prose, corresponds to what Lefebvre describes as the resistant '*texture* of space'. That grainy texture is constantly articulated with the 'violence that is inherent in space', as an abstract conception of space – that of capitalism and the modern state – strives to subdue the irreducibility of the 'practico-sensory realm'.[20] What I have sought to render in the notion of an *oral space* is the resistance of certain forms of cultural and physiological practices of pleasure, desire, affect, and even of need and grief, to the rationality of the modern state. This space of the 'Irish orifice' is not an alternative abstract space, not a pure alterity that exists outside of modernity or in some ideal location sheltered and preserved from the destructive inroads of colonialism or capitalism. It is, rather, a *counter-space* of modernity, or what Lefebvre describes as a 'differential space', one that potentially represents, even under conditions of rationalization and discipline, 'the seeds of a new kind of space'.[21] As a 'differential space' it marks a kind of social friction that can only become apparent in relation to an emerging conception of masterable abstract space – the space of uniform mapping and of movements of commodities and labour, of capital flows and exchanges.[22] In this respect, Ireland represents a prefigurative instance of what social geographers have come to understand after David Harvey as 'space–time compression', although in an antithetical sense.[23] In the term space–time compression, Harvey conceptualizes the approximation of frictionless space newly enabled by containerization and the deregulation of financial capital, as well as by the acceleration of means of transportation or monetary transfers. These have had the effect of shrinking the spatial distance that separated centre from periphery, the colonial power from its colonial territories. But already in the nineteenth century the close geographical relation of Ireland to England signalled the uncanny presence of the colony, represented as the lagging instance of past social formations, in the temporal present of the metropolis. Ireland, in other words, prefigured the ways in which, in post-modern capital, non-modern colonial cultures are brought into disturbing proximity with the metropolitan culture of the former imperial powers, creating there spaces of counter-modern disjunction and recalcitrance.

This phenomenon, which Homi Bhabha has described as the effect of 'disjunctive time' when it 'comes home' to the imperial nation, is the very condition of possibility of what Harvey has designated the regime of flexible accumulation.[24] In contradistinction to the era of Fordism, neo-liberal capital lays hold of the labour power of social and cultural formations globally that have not undergone the transformations that theorists of capitalist modernization from Karl Marx to Karl Polanyi considered as the prerequisites for proletarianization and citizenship. These are, in fact, the economic conditions of colonial capitalism reconstituted in the era of post- or neo-colonialism. While on the one hand they deliver ever more vulnerable and unorganized sectors of young and female labour to the violence of capitalist exploitation, on the other they furnish the means to unexpected and highly differentiated modes of resistance. In this respect, differential spaces maintain the irreducibility and the friction that abstract space has always sought to flatten and overcome. What I designate the Irish space of orality is an instance of such recalcitrant difference, not only at the moment in which it was targeted for destruction, but also in the numerous forms in which, transformed and distorted by the regulative institutions of modernity, it finds ways to live on and reinvent resistant practices. If, in Lefebvre's terms, differential space represents the ways in which abstract space 'carries within itself the seeds of a new kind of space', I argue here that in fact the architectures of modernity everywhere retain the residual and potentially emergent spectres of those they were intended to contain. To adapt a formulation of Neferti Tadiar's, 'the seeds of the future may have long incubated in the everyday practical memories we carry within us', not only 'in our literature', but in the very architectures that seem the most representative sites of modernity: prisons, pubs and even, it may be hoped, schools.[25]

As a space of friction rather than abstraction, as a space that embodies the circuitous and discontinuous living on of practices scheduled for annihilation, and not the ideal space of imaginary or imaginable relations, the space of orality is without doubt a utopian projection. But it is not *utopianist*, in the sense that utopia originally designated a non-existent geography of rationalized space, conceived in the governmental imagination of Thomas More and satirized in the fearful and genocidal reason of Swift's Houyhnhnmland. Rather, the utopian promise of oral space lies – as I argue of the H-Blocks – in the defiance of historicist or developmental temporality that transforms the 'nowhere' of utopia into a space of possibility defined by the indeterminacy of its 'going nowhere'. It is never the space of rational progression, of the subsumption of useful particularities into exchangeable commodities, or of the development of cultural traits into universal instances. The utopian is not imagined wholesale as a frictionless space of rational intercourse defined by sameness and regularity, but is projected from the damaged conditions of actual human existence as the realization of abundance out of scarcity and of fulfilled pleasure out of the partial, threatened, yet irreducible pleasures of the present. This is a utopia imagined out of the recalcitrant and uneven intuitions of a possible life in common that are afforded by actual, material communities, every one of which is less than it desires and more than the logic of development can acknowledge. Such a utopian longing, embedded as it is in the texture of actual locations and in the granular historicity of survival, is utterly at odds with the utopianist or settler colonial logic that declares the condition of an always future promised land to be the *terra nullius* of a landscape cleared of its obstinate populations and reduced to the blank slate of abstract, functional space.

As against such conceptions of space remade and renewed in subjection, conceptions that are ultimately theological if not theocratic, I posit the possibilities of recalcitrance that are embodied in the needs and desires of the pathological subject. Precisely at a moment in which the logic of privatization – or what Harvey terms 'accumulation by dispossession'[26] – seeks to appropriate what remains of the commons, the significance of the radical but subterranean tradition that has always predicated life in common on the rights of the needing, desiring body has never been more apparent. The liberal subject, the abstract subject of freedom, is the product and the beneficiary of what we might call the 'second commons': of those institutions of the state that furnish welfare, education and public services in compensation for the rights of commons that were expropriated and privatized in the long history of the capitalization of social life. In face of the erosion and deliberate destruction of that 'second commons', and in face of the violent appropriation of what remains of the commons itself – goods such as oil and, most saliently now, water – an alternative politics based on what Lefebvre calls the body as 'differential field' stakes its claims.[27] That body is not the transhistorical biological entity, but the culturally specific, historically transforming and contested locus of need and desire, divided in itself by the contradictions between its desires and the disciplines that shape it. Its claims are those of affective possibilities and of cultural potentials whose unfolding has been suspended or limited by the homogenizing drive of the capitalist colonialism in relation to which it is shaped anew as resistance. Its potentials are not the petrified remainders of economic and social forces that have consigned them to irrelevance if not oblivion, but unsubsumed resources for alternative imaginaries, drawn not from abstract principles but from the damaged and disregarded forms of 'useless' life. In the unusable may lie the elements of a life that cannot be subjected to the false universality of exchange. As Tadiar puts it of a different but not incomparable context of 'creative restitution', such elements 'can become the very means to realize as yet untried, if not unimagined, viable, just modes of social life'.[28] In the Irish context, oral space is an instance of the unsubsumable, sensuous and culturally determined practices that not only 'appear to fail' but have always appeared as impediments to the achievement of an abstract and homogenizing state of domination *or* emancipation. They defy, to paraphrase Fanon's still luminous formulation, every unilateral declaration of universality.[29] This book is dedicated to the hope that the implosion of neo-liberalism and of the predictably short-lived Irish economic boom, the ill-conceived and ill-fated 'Celtic Tiger', may foreshadow a creative restitution of the utopian potentials lodged in Irish oral space, and not the consolidation of a permanent emergency whose latest avatar is the global security state.

CHAPTER I

Irish hunger: the political economy of the potato

> The language used by some writers on the subject of the potato would not be more adequate, if, as Judge Longfield somewhere remarks, potatoes ate men instead of feeding them.
>
> J.E. Cairns [1]

I

The story of the Great Hunger or the Irish Famine is all too well known. But even at the risk of redundancy, it is still worth rehearsing what appear, after the upsurge of research of the last decade or so, to be the facts of the case. The Famine, which commenced in 1845 with a failure of the potato crop and recurred over large parts of the country until 1851, was the greatest demographic catastrophe in European history. At least one million people died of starvation and a further million left the country, inaugurating a trend of massive emigration that continued unabated until nearly the end of the last century. The Famine was thus directly responsible for the disappearance of at least one-quarter of the population, estimated in the British census of 1841 at 8.1 million. The vulnerability of the Irish population to such a subsistence crisis was occasioned by the very abundance of the potato, which was capable of remarkable reproduction on poor and marginal land, with the result that a family could subsist for almost the whole year on the yield of a one-acre plot. Dispossessed by settler colonialism of the more fertile lands and driven onto the bogs and mountainsides, the Irish poor had developed what is now understood to be a sophisticated and ecologically inventive means of survival on the basis of the potato crop. They had succeeded time after time in reclaiming marginal land in the most inhospitable regions of the island, especially along the western seaboard.[2] Despite regular but generally short-lived and localized failures of the potato crop, the success of the Irish in cultivating this root had enabled both a high rate of population increase and the progressive subdivision of land-holdings. This system of potato cultivation on small, rented plots, combined with occasional labour on larger farms for low wages or for payment in kind, was known as cottierism.

Several factors contributed to the subdivision of holdings. Principal among these had been the expropriation since the seventeenth century of agricultural land by large landowners who tended, through the medium of the infamous 'middlemen', to extract increasingly high rents in a system that became known as 'rack-renting'. By the mid nineteenth century, the picture of the absentee landlord living in London on rents extracted from an increasingly penurious Irish peasantry was complicated by a new tendency towards 'improvement', or the rationalization of agriculture along capitalist lines.[3] Improvement envisaged the consolidation of land-holdings into larger farms on the English model, the concomitant enclosure of all but the most marginal wasteland, the turn to less labour-intensive grain farming and grazing, and the eviction of the small-holding tenants. These landless tenants in turn placed further pressure on the dwindling areas of cultivable land, with the consequence that the highest rural population densities were concentrated on the poorest land. Two further factors facilitated this peculiarity of Irish demographic patterns: first, both the paucity of capital required by the cottier, who needed only to purchase or borrow seed potatoes and a spade to lay down a crop, and the relative ease and informality with which a family holding could be subdivided enabled early marriages and child-bearing. Early marriage and high rates of reproduction were the norm in pre-Famine Ireland to an extent almost unimaginable from the perspective of the highly conservative rural society that rapidly developed after 1850. Second, there persisted, in adapted forms and principally in the more impoverished areas of the western seaboard, an older Gaelic system of communal land-holding known as *clachan* or rundale. This form of land-holding ensured that most tenants would have access to a variety of land types, from the higher reaches of the mountain where a few sheep might be grazed to the more fertile patches where potatoes or, on occasion, oats could be cultivated. Given the high degree of subdivision, the *clachan* system came to entail patchwork patterns of land-holding within which pieces of any family's holdings could be scattered in tiny plots across a neighbourhood without apparent logic and certainly without any attempt at consolidation. The *clachan*, though confined to certain specific regions of Ireland, came nonetheless – as we will see more fully in the next chapter – to symbolize the irrationality of Irish ways to colonial improvers oblivious to the actual inventiveness and sophistication of its practices.[4]

The desire to rationalize or 'improve' Irish agricultural practices and Irish character was theorized and driven by political economy. Thomas Boylan and Timothy Foley have amply documented English efforts throughout the nineteenth century to disseminate political economic doctrine in Ireland with a view to economic improvement and political pacification. Political economy, whose interventions were always linked with the framing of policy, aimed at the transformation, and not merely the description, of the condition of the Irish.[5] Indeed, classical political economy was less an economic doctrine than 'the governmental discourse of the modern world', offering, 'through a new representation of the economy ... a new definition of the state's legitimacy, of its role and of its relation with citizens'.[6] In Ireland, that 'new definition' involved both the successive attempts to give British rule legitimacy and the no less crucial delegitimation of Irish cultural formations that were deemed recalcitrant to a rational political economy. In this struggle over legitimacy, the terms of British political economy shifted decisively in order to take account of Irish differences while, in turn, British prescriptions led to the emergence of new Irish social formations that remained out of kilter with British norms. Irish conditions were at once the object and the test of political economic theory. Its inability to accommodate those conditions to its theoretical assumptions led by the end of the century to the displacement of 'political' by 'national' economy, the latter emerging with the gradual recognition of the necessity to take into account the disparate forms and practices of regional and local economies. Where many Famine-era political economists and administrators influenced by them rejoiced in the 'providential' effect that catastrophe had in clearing the land of a surplus population and making way for 'capitalist farming, on the English model',[7] others drew more durable lessons that implicated both Ireland and economic theory. John Stuart Mill's solution to the overpopulation and under-employment of Ireland, which he began to develop in his *Morning Chronicle* editorials during the Famine itself, drew heavily on proposals already circulating in Ireland and recommended the introduction of peasant proprietorship. The establishment of a peasant proprietary, he believed, would set to work the 'magic power' of property. Mill's proposals, which finally bore fruit in Gladstone's Land Acts in the 1860s and 1870s and in a small farm economy ironically very different from English models, aimed at the 'moral improvement' of the Irish by redirecting them onto what was beginning to be seen as the normal path of economic and social development.

The Irish economist, Mill's disciple J.E. Cairnes, spelt out more explicitly the developmental function of peasant proprietorship. 'It would seem', he argued, 'that, in the progress of nations from barbarism to civilization, there is a point at which the bulk of the people pass naturally into the peasant proprietor condition.'[8] Pointing out that that stage in England 'seems to have been about the end of the fifteenth century', Cairnes asserted that 'into this phase of industrial existence the Irish people have never passed'.[9] The Irish character was thus caught in a historical time lag, consequent on Irish under-development in comparison with a more advanced English agricultural and industrial economy. Peasant proprietorship, as Cairnes conceived it more frankly than Mill, was a kind of mechanism for the production of individuality, which evolved from 'joint ownership' under the 'primitive communism' of tribal societies through 'a process of "gradual disentanglement of the separate rights of individuals from the blended rights of a community"'.[10] In this new, liberal dispensation of political economy, the Irish in the nineteenth century were already subjected to programmes of development that are all too familiar to us now from the experience of the former colonial world.[11] The Famine thus belongs in a historical structure of longer duration that David Scott has described, in a different context, as that of 'colonial governmentality', a regime that aimed at *'the systematic redefinition and transformation of the terrain on which the life of the colonized was lived ... so altering those* conditions as to alter fundamentally that character [of the colonized] in an improving direction'.[12]

The theory that underlay this new conception of economic development can aptly be termed 'historicist'.[13] Unlike classical political economy, which posited universally valid laws, the historicist theory of economic development assumed that material conditions, social forms and moral character unfolded together. Over time, the self-dependent possessive individual emerged along with capitalist rationality and a sense of property rights. The interventions of policy could be shaped in Ireland, as in India, to further this end. Historicist economics thus aligned the legitimation of a new form of liberal or hegemonic state colonialism with the logic of history itself. As a history of transitions between states or conditions, it was entirely adapted to negotiate the 'transitional moment' in British colonialism that the Famine appeared to mark. More liberal than orthodox political economy in its acceptance of Irish differences from England, it was in certain ways even more rigid in its outlook. In some respects, as we shall see, the desire of classical political economists to establish and maintain universal economic laws led them to glimpse, however indirectly, the challenge Ireland posed to their assumptions. They reacted with palpable anxiety to what they saw as a threatening alternative with contagious effects on the British working classes. Historicism, on the other hand, understood Irish differences to represent no more than a different stage on a single historical trajectory and, while it generally eschewed coercion, offered all the more powerful instruments for the transformation of Irish ways and the justification of colonial rule.

Ironically, this 'historicist' economic theory that came into being across the period of the Famine has continued to shape the ways in which that event is remembered and contextualized. For all that we have learnt of the causes and the mismanagement of the Famine, it is still hard to find a historian who does not seek to redeem the catastrophe by casting it as an inevitable Malthusian disaster that ultimately made way for the modernization of the Irish economy. It was equally hard not to read in the commemorations of the Famine in the 1990s the attempt to lay to rest at last the ghosts of that demographic disaster so that Ireland could move on to take its place psychically as well as economically among the developed industrial nations.[14] Such thinking is saturated with the assumption that there was in fact no viable alternative to the advent of modernity and the capitalist mode of production and that the Irish who died or departed during the Famine were the inevitable victims of an ineluctable historical process. It takes colonialism at its word, so to speak. But at the time Ireland seemed to present intractable anomalies that political economy was unable to accommodate precisely because, if only for a moment, they represented the outlines of viable alternatives to a capitalist economy that had not yet achieved the unquestionable dominance that now seems so foregone a conclusion.[15]

In thinking about the Famine, it is thus crucial to dispense with the satisfactions of hindsight in order that its apparent inevitability should not structure in advance our attempts to comprehend not simply *what* happened but what *meanings* circulated around the event.[16] With hindsight, indeed, the Famine appeared to be the inevitable consequence of an excessive Irish population that depended perilously on a single crop: it is one of those singular accidents that reorganizes the preceding and subsequent constellations of events into a predetermined pattern, thus coming to seem the only possible occurrence. It is accordingly all the more important to reopen the indeterminate constellations of discourse and practice out of which that event condensed; constellations in which there lurked, and are still discernable, the spectres of other possibilities. For the materialist cultural historian, the actual outcome of multiple social vectors is often less important than the swirling eddies of possibility out of which that outcome emerged. The Famine makes that archaeological process all the more difficult. Its terrible death toll hangs over any attempt to comprehend it, adding, as it were, the moral force of commemoration to the dismal appearances of historical determinism. Furthermore, the archive to which one must turn for evidence about the condition of the Irish is so unrelievedly negative about the social and cultural formations that went down in the event with such seeming inevitability that it appears to justify their fate. Only by pulling apart the logic of events in a way that attends to the sense of crisis they provoked and the material and discursive turbulence their presence stirred up can we return a degree of agency to the impoverished Irish who have been seen almost exclusively as the passive victims of the Famine. Only thus can we restore to the past the possibilities drained from it by historicism.

II

The two principal anomalies that British economists and administrators encountered in Ireland may be summed up as land and population, the related and recurrent objects of colonial governmentality. Each posed the fundamental problem of reproduction, in the double sense of Ireland's apparently prodigious capacity for sexual reproduction and its tendency to reproduce social formations that were tenaciously recalcitrant to capitalist economic and political transformations. In the intimate connection between the material conditions that sustained the prodigious reproduction of the Irish poor and the reproduction of a culture enabled by those conditions lies the significance of Irish hunger.

Contrary to what has often been assumed, the inevitability of a devastating famine in Ireland was by no means self-evident to contemporary observers. Even though the declining rate of population increase prior to the Famine may not have been apparent to contemporary observers, the size of the Irish population does not seem to have been perceived as presenting what we might think of as a 'Malthusian' crisis.[17] It was not a given that the Irish population had reached some critical point that made disaster inevitable. Writing some ten years after the publication of his *Essay on the Principle of Population*, Thomas Malthus was less concerned with the imminence of famine than with the potential political exploitation of religious distinctions and other discontents. His attitude to Irish population growth in 1808 seems, with post-Famine hindsight, almost sanguine:

> Although it is quite certain that the population of Ireland cannot continue permanently to increase at its present rate, yet it is as certain that it will not suddenly come to a stop. Mr. Newenham, assuming that it will go on for some time, at least, as it has done of late years, supposes that the country will contain 8,413,224 inhabitants in 1837; and enters into an elaborate calculation to show that it is fully capable of maintaining such a number ... [W]e feel confident, that a much greater population might in time be supported in that country if potatoes continue to be its staple food.[18]

Malthus concluded the Irish population would continue to grow for quite some time and that the problems the English faced with Ireland lay rather in the potential disaffection of a possible '*twenty millions* of people' than in the imminent prospect of their starvation.[19]

Malthus's prognosis for Ireland was thus far from 'Malthusian' as that expression is generally understood.[20] Nonetheless, it was typical and possibly seminal in setting the terms for the response of political economists to Ireland's prodigious capacity for reproduction. This response had less to do with hunger and distress than with the social and political impact on Britain of an increasing Irish population with cultural habits that were not only alien but in many respects antithetical to the values that a burgeoning capitalism needed to reproduce in its own working classes. We may say that the problem of Ireland was paradoxically not scarcity, but *abundance*: abundance of population and abundance of the means to support that population, an abundance notoriously supplied by the potato. The infamous Irish 'poor mouth', *an béal bocht*, was at the same time a mouth that was all too full. It was the spectre of abundance, rather than that of distress, that haunted political economy and made Irish conditions a scandal in theory and a nightmare for practical policy. In that sense, the event of the Famine was a godsend not only to the administrator but to the theorists too, apparently confirming precepts whose predictive validity had been made questionable by the condition of Ireland. The image of Irish misery in the first half of the nineteenth century is so self-evident to us at this point that it is easy to overlook how earnest and arduous the production of that image actually was. To say so is not to minimize the actual hardship of the Irish poor nor to idealize their conditions, but rather to interrogate how the meaning of those conditions was produced and transformed, both differentially, in relation to the condition of their British counterparts, and in conformity to the emerging theory and governmental discourse of political economy.

We can trace the changing signification of Irish wretchedness, and the counter-image of Irish abundance and contentment, through the shifting evaluation of the potato in classical political economy. In *The Wealth of Nations*, Adam Smith famously attributed the health and beauty of the Irish poor in London to their consumption of potatoes.[21] More remarkable to us now is that Smith's evaluation of the social effects of the potato's dissemination as a staple was unhedged with anxiety:

Should this root ever become in any part of Europe, like rice in some countries, the common and favourite vegetable food of the people, so as to occupy the same proportion of the lands in tillage which wheat, and other sorts of grain for human food do at present, the same quantity of cultivated land would maintain a much greater number of people, and the labourers being generally fed with potatoes, a greater surplus would remain after replacing all the stock [capital] and maintaining all the labour employed in cultivation. A greater share of this surplus, too, would belong to the landlord. Population would increase, and rents would rise much beyond what they are at present.[22]

Smith thus accurately foresaw the capacity of the potato not only to reproduce labour but also to enable the reproduction and increase of capital in the form of surplus value, a fact that made possible the extraordinary depletion of capital from nineteenth-century Ireland by the system of rackrenting. What he did not foresee was that this 'primitive' accumulation of capital could lead to a crisis of over-population that would affect the United Kingdom as a whole.

Arthur Young, travelling in Ireland at virtually the same moment, was, if anything, even more convinced of the positive qualities of the Irish labourers' mode of life. Not only were the Irish physically healthy, 'as athletic in their form, as robust, and as capable of enduring labour as any upon earth', they were moreover better off in real terms than their English counterparts:

That the Irishman's cow may be ill-fed, is admitted; but, ill-fed as it is, it is better than the no cow of the Englishman; the children of the Irish cabbin [sic] are nourished with milk, which, small as the quantity may be, is far preferable to the beer or vile tea which is the beverage of the English infant; for nowhere in a town is milk to be bought ... The crop of potatoes, and the milk of the cow is more regular in Ireland than the *price* at which the Englishman buys his food.[23]

Young's assessment of the benefits to the Irish of a largely non-monetary subsistence economy is the antithesis of later political economists' desire to see the Irish develop a cash economy. For Young and Smith, the nutritional advantages of the potato were morally indifferent and even productive of superior health and contentment. But for later economists, the potato seemed irrevocably connected to moral and political as well as economic characteristics that were expressed in Irish recalcitrance to capitalist development. The potato soon ceased to be just one crop among others and became the root of Irish evil. The trajectory that leads us from Malthus to Charles Trevelyan, Treasury Secretary and chief administrator of Famine relief, culminated in the latter's brusque expostulation: 'what hope is there for a nation that lives on potatoes?'[24]

Writing some three decades after Smith, Malthus began to descry in Ireland the first results of that nutritional experiment, and though the final outcome remained a matter of speculation, it was a speculation considerably more anxious:

> It is the first and only country that has yet fully taken to a species of food, which, at the most, requires only one third of the land necessary to yield the same nourishment in wheat. Its effects, hitherto, have been truly astonishing; and in its future progress, it may be expected to produce proportionate results. We should not wonder if Ireland were destined to become an instance of the greatest density of population yet known in the world: and it has sometimes struck us as possible, that the prodigious physical force thus created in a particular country, might, like the standing armies introduced into modern Europe by France, occasion the adoption of the same system in neighbouring states. We own that we do not contemplate such a change as favourable to the happiness of mankind.[25]

Malthus was writing in the midst of the Napoleonic wars, and at a time of consequent agricultural prosperity. Accordingly, his concerns are principally political and military rather than economic. It was this contingent set of circumstances, however, that led him to sketch a seminal if speculative correlation between the material and social conditions that the potato as a staple produced and its reproduction of a determinate set of cultural and political characteristics. The 'political degradation' of the Irish had made them resort to the potato, and if the outcome of the Napoleonic wars were to be 'the establishment of universal despotism', other nations might well emulate them. 'Improved forms of government' would, on the other hand, habituate the 'lower classes' to a better quality of food, which would in turn attach them to a 'superior political condition'.[26]

Malthus's arguments established the matrix of terms in which Irish conditions would continue to be addressed: the role of the potato in sustaining 'a rapid increase in population'; the potato as indelibly linked to Irish poverty and a pool of surplus labour; the need to convert the population to a diet of 'wheaten bread' like that of their English counterparts;

and, not least, the relation of these factors to the problem of forging possessive individualism in a political culture that seemed to oscillate between anarchy and political despotism. Malthus had come to conceive that a people's diet, not only in quantity but also in kind and quality, determined more than their mere numbers. It underlay the reproduction of their habits of life. Consumption of the potato as the staple food permitted the astonishing rate of reproduction of the Irish population; more dangerously, it sustained their cultural tendencies against individuation and their inclination towards economic and political dependency. And in a transitional moment, when the outcome of the war remained uncertain, the troubling possibility was that Ireland's conditions rather than England's might represent the horizon of the future.

Malthus thus established the anxious terms in which the 'Irish question' was mapped, politically, economically and culturally for most of the nineteenth century. They functioned as a virtual rhizome, at whose metaphorical root lay the potato, which continually connected those distinct domains and led to their incessant confusion. In tracking their permutations, however, we should not lose sight of the persistent if occluded fact that to the practical, legislative or administrative problems the colony posed to British rule, there remained attached the spectre of the threatening alternative that Ireland presented to the unfolding hegemony of a capitalist economy and its gradually emerging state formation. Negatively as it was and had to be represented, insistently as Irish misery replaced the fleeting glimpse of Irish contentment, the shadow of an unruly Irish surplus persisted in summoning up an otherness, recalcitrant and inassimilable, that threatened constantly to overwhelm the discursive and political boundaries that were produced to contain it.

For political economy, it was in the first place the sheer surplus of Irish *population* that scandalized. The problems it posed were at once practical and theoretical. The practical problems are well documented. In Ireland, numerous inquiries into the conditions of the poor culminated in the new Irish Poor Laws, establishing the national network of Poor Law Unions and workhouses that so notoriously and so soon collapsed during the Famine. Irish poverty had always threatened to overwhelm the institutions established to contain it and the financial resources that maintained them. That story has been told in such detail elsewhere as not to need rehearsing here.[27] Generally, however, the failure of the Poor Law institutions and supplementary measures during the Famine has been ascribed to the application in relief policy of the more or less scientific principles of political economy, usually encapsulated as 'laissez-faire'. Though there is some truth to this argument, what has not been sufficiently emphasized is the fact that even before the Famine, and not only during the unfolding of its horrific effects, the theoretical terms of political economy constantly veered to a moral and cultural rather than 'purely economic' rhetoric when confronted with Irish conditions. Far from maintaining the principle of laissez-faire, economists consistently advocated modes of interference guided by their theories and directed at the economic and moral improvement of the Irish. The very alterity of the conditions they contemplated threw into relief the failure of political economy to accomplish its scientific ends in separation from the ideological and cultural formations that were secreted in its universal laws.

J.R. McCulloch spelt out the problematic nature of Irish reproduction in a way that encapsulated the line of orthodox theory that ran from Malthus to Nassau Senior and McCulloch himself. In the course of his discussion of wages he makes the distinction between 'the Market or Actual Rate of Wages' and 'the Natural or Necessary Rate of Wages'. The market or actual rate is that which actually obtains at a given moment in any country or locality and is based on the proportion between population and available capital: the more the available capital, the larger the wage fund; the greater the labouring population, the more draw on that wage fund and the lower wages fall.[28] By this Malthusian logic, over time the labouring population should stabilize into equilibrium with the available capital. The demographic logic here assumes, however, a fundamental 'natural or necessary wage', the lowest subsistence that the labourer can or will accept.[29] As McCulloch admits, however, there can be, despite the name given to it, no 'fixed and unvarying' natural rate of wages. It is determined, as Adam Smith claimed, by 'not only the commodities that are indispensably necessary for the support of life, but whatever the custom of the country renders it indecent for creditable people, even of the lowest order, to be without'.[30] In this acknowledgement, the notion of a universally identical 'race of labourers' begins to succumb to the problematic prospect of cultural differences that are rapidly racialized. The question of demography, the mere biological reproduction of that race of labourers, is intimately bound up with their cultural reproduction, with 'custom', 'decency' or cultural formation. The economic reproduction of capital depends on cultural reproduction, both of labour, with its various skills and disciplines, and of the habits of consumption that encourage the circulation of commodities. Thus a purely economic theory collapses into the political and cultural anthropology that had always secretly underwritten it.[31]

Malthus had assumed that the Irish rate of population increase would be 'retarded' either by Irish poverty or by an elevation in their living standards and expectations, such that their 'necessary wage' would rise.[32] But Irish reproduction defied the laws of political economy and continued to increase despite the notorious and frequently lamented lack of capital available in the country. Numerous factors ensured that Ireland lacked the capital necessary for the development or 'improvement' of its undoubtedly rich natural resources: on the one hand, the dearth of skilled labour and the supposed insecurity of a country troubled by agrarian unrest and urban combinations prevented investment of new capital, while on the other, capital constantly drained away, directly in the form of rent paid to absentees and indirectly through the export of unworked produce. Nassau Senior's essay on the condition of Ireland in 1843 summarized these problems, dividing Ireland's evils into the 'material' and the 'moral': 'The material evils are the want of Capital, and the want of small Proprietors. The moral evils are Insecurity, Ignorance, and Indolence.'[33] Proposing for Ireland the standard prescription, the establishment of an English-style capitalist farming, he acknowledged that in the present state of Ireland, the only means to achieve that end would be 'the introduction of capital from abroad'. Yet, he continued, 'there is something in the institutions of Ireland, or in the habits of her people, which deters British capital from one of its most natural, and apparently one of its most productive employments'. Thus Ireland's 'Moral evils ... exclude the remedies for her Material evils'.[34] Those moral evils lay principally in the Irish refusal of law, or, more accurately, in their adherence to a principle of counter-legality, 'a rival law, with rules and sanctions of its own'.[35] The vicious circle that resulted was evident to Senior, illustrating 'how insecurity occasions want of capital – how want of capital occasions idleness and misery – and how idleness and misery lead to turbulence and insecurity, until the result is a circle of calamities, each in turn creating, aggravating, and recreating the others'.[36]

Senior proposed a series of practical remedies, from the suppression of agrarian unrest and combinations to the endowment of the Catholic Church and the extension of the fledgling national school system. Both his analysis and his remedies were typical. The projects of government were in some sense continuously directed towards remediating Ireland's 'material and moral evils', whether through the coercive apparatus of the paramilitary national police force, established in 1814, or through the medium of a national school system aimed at improving the skills and the 'moral character' of the people, or even through the later but associated attempts to clear the 'surplus' population by assisted emigration and the regulation of the land system. For all that, the enormous excess of the population over the available capital, and the capacity of that population to subsist and even to thrive, defied the logic of a political economy. Both the existence of the population and its subsistence, miserable as it was, outside the laws of capitalist economy posed a theoretical problem for political economy that was intrinsically linked to the practical problems it posed for the disciplinary apparatuses of the state.

In face of these intractable anomalies, political economy veered into moral or cultural evaluations that were quite explicitly racial. Even Senior's relatively measured analysis invoked the problem of the Irish moral character. McCulloch expounded more vehemently the effects of Irish immigrants, 'the outpourings of this *officina pauperum*', on the English and Scottish 'necessary wage'. His terms were by no means unusual:

> Had we only to deal with the poor of Great Britain, means for their improvement might be devised with comparative facility; but, unluckily, we have also to deal with the poor of Ireland; and the degraded state of the latter, their improvidence and recklessness, make the expectation of their improvement alike feeble and remote. In the meantime, however, they are impelled, partly by the impossibility of providing for themselves at home, and partly by the temptation of comparatively high wages, to emigrate in vast numbers to this country … Certainly, however, few things could exercise so destructive an influence over the condition and prospects of the English and Scottish labourers. Their forethought and industry have, in fact, tended rather to facilitate the invasion of this pauper horde, than to improve their own condition. Their wages have been reduced by the competition of famished serfs cast upon our shores; and, what is still worse, their tastes and opinions in regard to what is necessary for their subsistence have been lowered by the contaminating influence of example, and by familiar intercourse with those who are content to live in destitution and misery. It is difficult to see how, with the existing facilities of communication between the two countries, the condition of the working classes in them should not be pretty much approximated; and there is much reason to fear that, if left to itself, the equalization will be brought about by the degradation of the English and Scotch rather than by the elevation of the Irish.[37]

The rhetorical excess here, the very surplus of its repetitions and its prolixity, matches the surplus of the 'pauper horde'. It is as infected rhetorically by its vision of the Irish invasion as British workers are by the 'contaminating influence' of their savage example.

A comparable rhetoric of contamination echoed throughout nineteenth-century Britain in dire warnings about the effects of the Irish that mobilized a matrix of economic, cultural and biopolitical topoi with steady consistency. McCulloch's remarks are a virtual transcript of the medical and educational reformer James Kay, writing in 1832:

> Ireland has poured forth the most destitute of her hordes to supply the constantly increasing demand for labour. This immigration has been, in one important respect, a serious evil. The Irish have taught the labouring classes of this country a pernicious lesson. The system of cottier farming, the demoralization and barbarism of the people, and the general use of the potato as the chief article of food, have encouraged the population in Ireland more rapidly than the *available* means of subsistence have been increased. Debased alike by ignorance and pauperism, they have discovered, with the savage, what is the minimum of the means of life, upon which existence may be prolonged. The paucity of the amount of means and comfort, *necessary for the mere support of life*, is not known by a more civilized population, and this secret has been taught the labourers of this country by the Irish. As competition and the restrictions and burdens of trade diminished the profits of capital, and consequently reduced the price of labour, the contagious example of ignorance and a barbarous disregard of forethought and economy, exhibited by the Irish, spread.[38]

Kay's antagonism to these Irish migrants, with its analogies of savagery and barbarism, of nomadic hordes threatening to destroy settled and domesticated civilization, was in turn taken up and amplified by the more notoriously racist and anti-Irish polemicist, Thomas Carlyle:

> Crowds of miserable Irish darken all our towns. The wild Milesian features, looking false ingenuity, restlessness, unreason, misery and mockery, salute you on all highways and byways ... He is the sorest evil this country has to strive with. In his rags and laughing savagery, he is there to undertake all work that can be done by mere strength of hand and back; for wages that will purchase him potatoes ... The Saxon man if he cannot work on those terms, finds no work. He too may be ignorant; but he has not sunk from decent manhood to squalid apehood: he cannot continue there. American forests lie untilled across the ocean; the uncivilized Irishman, not by his strength, but by the opposite of strength, drives out the Saxon native, takes possession in his room. There abides he, in his squalor and unreason, in his falsity and drunken violence, as the ready-made nucleus of degradation and disorder ... We have quarantines against pestilence; but there is no pestilence like that; and against it what quarantine is possible? ... The time has come when the Irish population must either be improved a little, or else exterminated ... In a state of perennial ultra-savage famine, in the midst of civilization, they cannot continue.[39]

For all its ferocity, Carlyle's racism only elaborated a well established matrix of axioms on the Irish: their excessive reproduction, the backwardness or savagery of their moral character, the threat their incivility poses to British norms and, at the root of it all, their dependence on the potato.

The pattern that Mary Poovey has noted in James Kay, his tendency to domesticate or obscure Irish difference and simultaneously to distance them into radical alterity, bound the scientific discourse of political economy to the extravagant racial typologies of mid-Victorian social critics.[40] In some respects, these are the familiar tropes of nineteenth-century colonial discourse and for Carlyle, at least, the link between the Irish and the newly emancipated black populations of the West Indies could not have been clearer: eating potatoes and eating what he called 'pumpkins' fixed the Irish and the ex-slaves in a common oral state of backwardness and indolent moral laxity.[41] In the case of the Irish, however, that overarching paradigm of savagery and backwardness was overlaid by an insistent pattern in which the catachrestic affirmation of the stereotype – the same, but not quite – was maintained in relation to its reverse – other, but not quite.[42] Even in the historicist accounts of Irish otherness, newly emerging in Mill and Cairnes, that reversible, specular oscillation is maintained in a dual form: the same but not yet; belated but coeval. In this complex of proximity and alterity, anteriority and contemporaneity, the Irish remained troublingly inassimilable for the dryest political economy as for the most assured liberal historicism.

Evidently, the proximity of the Irish was in the first place geographical – not only was Irish poverty massed a mere day's travel across the Irish Sea from the imperial capital, the migrant Irish already constituted, according to McCulloch, 'from a fourth to a third part' of Britain's urban population.[43] That geographical proximity and the consequent intermingling of Irish, Scottish and English bodies and cultural practices (interestingly, the Welsh are never mentioned) precluded the possibility that removal in space could stand for the removal in time that colonial 'savagery' or 'barbarism' normally signify. On the contrary, and unlike the case of other colonial nations at the time, Ireland's coevality with the metropolis was manifest in their constant and persistent presence, both spatial and temporal. The oral space of the Irish, their habits both of consumption and of utterance, intermingled with the increasingly bureaucratized, institutional space of an emerging industrial and colonial state, marking the disturbing presence of the time of the other.

As the presence of another time in the present, the Irish posed a problematic counter-example for political economy's insistence on the relationship between its laws and 'human improvement', between the development of capitalism and the inexorable advance of civilization. In a peculiar sense, the Irish represented the simultaneity of, rather than the historical lag between, different moments of social formation; more precisely, they represented the interpenetration of the most advanced capitalism with those other and recalcitrant formations that continually emerge at the interface of the modern and the non-modern, as its incommensurable by-products rather than its pre-history.[44] The incommensurability of the social forms that emerged out of Irish 'nomadism' with those of industrial capitalism was an anomaly that could still only be cured by the governmental intervention of modern institutions. Political economy, reformulated for the colonial sphere as a discourse of development, would take up anew the task of transforming the cottier into a modern subject and of shaping the institutions that task would require. Its project was to transform the threatening *presence* of Irish differences into a product of their backwardness, thus occluding the 'infectious' alternatives they represented. The destructive reshaping of Irish space and modes of living that that improving project required and the peculiar ways in which the recalcitrant and utopian horizons of Irish oral space lived on against the expectations of historicism are the concern of the next chapters.

III

Even as the Irish called forth all the emergent institutions of governmentality, summoning into being the formations of the modern state itself, they simultaneously generated a far less stable, and far more anxious, *figural* productivity, analogous in its effects to the materially infectious example that English social critics dreaded. The figural instability of the Irish again and again undoes in critical ways the attempts of both orthodox and historicist economic discourse to fix them metaphorically in temporal or spatial otherness. If the movement of the tropes that attach to Irishness at this period is often hard to follow, it may be because the threatening dissolution that the Irish seem to embody enters into the discourse about them, constantly dissolving the opposition between fixity and mobility through which the Irish oscillate. On the one hand, the Irish are fixed: embedded, as peasants, in restricted and local horizons; stuck at a backward moment in time, tradition- and custom-bound and incapable of development; bogged down in a subsistence agriculture that does not allow for the circulation and the mobility of the market. On the other hand, the Irish are disturbingly mobile, in their prodigious surplus exceeding their proper boundaries, spilling into Britain itself, a still semi-nomadic 'horde' of paupers, that seems to swirl and eddy in perpetual migration through the Empire. But their mobility is also in their relation to more conceptual and more intimate spaces – they embody the lability of an oral culture, transgressive of proper spaces and relations of space and social organization, indifferent to the proper times and places of emotional display. As we shall see in the following chapter, this mobility or spatial dissoluteness infects their domestic architecture and their collective living, from the rundales of Connaught to the slums of Manchester, undermining the spatial and moral orders that British capitalism and the state are slowly accomplishing with their own domestic populations.

Irish mobility and lability infect, to use a recurrent figure, both the contiguous populations of Britain and the discourses that seek to represent, diagnose and contain them. The Irish, as Carlyle angrily registers, trouble the regime that anchors utterance in truth as much as they do the regime of labour and domestic order: 'A people that knows not to speak the truth, and to act the truth, such people has departed from even the possibility of well-being. Such a people works no longer on Nature and Reality; works now on Phantasm, Simulation, Non-Identity.'[35] The elements of Irish material conditions thus become refigured as their essence, an essence that is their instability, and, at the same time, the metonyms of Irishness become its metaphors, collapsing a fundamental rhetorical axis of distinction. The three most recurrent and intimate signifiers of Irishness in this nineteenth-century British discourse, each defined by its relation to Irish orifices, share the peculiar trait of dissolving into one another and challenge every attempt to hold them apart: the potato, pestilence, or 'miasma', and dung.

We have seen that the gradual accretion of negative connotations around the potato long pre-dated the Famine. What was regarded by Arthur Young and Adam Smith in the late eighteenth century as merely one staple among others slowly transformed into the root cause of Irish evils, moral and material. The pun is ineluctable and tracks the transformation of the potato from an object of consumption to a virtual subject with agency. It is, in the first place, the remarkable reproductive capacity of the potato that sustains the no less prodigious reproductive capacity of the Irish. By the same token, its very abundance permits the subdivision of the land that perpetuates and exacerbates the systems of conacre and cottierism. But gradually its capacity to sustain a population greatly in excess of available capital and, in doing so, hindering every attempt to consolidate small plots into larger holdings, makes the potato appear as in itself an opponent of capitalism. Rather than being merely a starch analogous to grain crops – known generically as 'corn' – and even nutritionally superior to some, such as oats or barley, the potato becomes the antithesis of corn. The transformation of the Irish from potato-eaters to corn consumers becomes the primary project of English administration and has ramifications that extend far beyond what the Irish put *into* their mouths to the whole intricate network of oral culture that the potato sustains.

While Malthus, Senior, McCulloch and other political economists had all noted the effect of the potato on population increase and low wage rates, it was Charles Trevelyan who provided the most thorough-going exposition of this opposition between the social effects of the potato and those of wheat. His prescription for Ireland was simple: the transformation of a potato economy to one based on grain and cattle grazing. But, as always, this policy was predicated on the moral as much as the material effects of the potato as opposed to those of corn. It is no accident that the commodity that for so long provided political economists with the measure of value, with all the ambiguities as to the moral or material valence of that term, was corn. For corn is the foundation, not only of the material reproduction of the labouring classes, but of the reproduction of a capitalist agricultural system as a whole. It is, in the first place, a commodity that could be both stored and transported, not merely consumed on site but exchanged over long distances. As the orthodox Irish economist Archbishop Richard Whately almost incidentally pointed out, the transport of wheat from country to city by corn factors is what enables the progress of capitalism at all: the defence throughout the Famine of the much-maligned corn dealers is, in effect, the defence of the most fundamental precondition of capitalism.[46] The efficient production of grain requires, furthermore, the concentration of land and workers, thus enabling capitalist agriculture and the division of labour together with the intricate social relations and class formations these assume and enable. The long process in England and elsewhere of the enclosure of the commons and the displacement of agricultural labour to form an urban proletariat – still ongoing even as Trevelyan wrote – was founded on a corn-producing agriculture.

Corn is at once, like money, the commodity par excellence and the medium and support of commodification. It circulates, flowing from the rural site of abundance to the urban site of potential scarcity, and in doing so its very circulation enables the reterritorialization in the division of labour of those whom its large-scale production has displaced. From text to text of political economy, the corn dealer, as the medium of this circulation, is the recurrent figure of the merchant capitalist, through his self-interested activity performing the magic that equilibrates demand and supply. For Whately, he is the epitome of the 'invisible hand' or the agent of Providence, the evidence of how 'what may be called the *instincts of Man* lead to the advancement of society'.[47] Alexander Somerville, anti-Corn Law journalist and working-class political economist, expends pages of his *Letters from Ireland during the Famine of 1847* combating the popular detraction of corn factors, even sketching a novel to reveal their virtues and to redeem them from William Carleton's satiric portrait of Darby Skinacre in *The Black Prophet*.[48] The corn factor is the heroic protagonist of the political economists' social history, bearing and advancing wealth and civilization.[49]

What is at stake here is, of course, the opposition between political economy and a moral economy that had, as E.P. Thompson first showed, a long tradition among the poor in Great Britain and Ireland.[50] In Ireland, that moral economy was also an alternative economy that was deeply embedded in the opposition of the potato as means of subsistence to corn as commodity. The potato is the antithesis of corn in almost every respect. Unlike corn the potato is not conducive to storage or long-distance transportation. As Trevelyan remarked: 'The potato cannot be stored, so that the scarcity of one year may be alleviated by bringing forward the reserves of former years, as is always done in corn-feeding countries. Every year is thus left to provide subsistence for itself.'[51] Disabling attention to the future, the critical horizon of capital, the potato is equally a crop confined to its locality: 'the bulk of potatoes is such, that they can with difficulty be conveyed from place to place to supply local deficiencies, and it has often happened that severe scarcity has prevailed in districts, within fifty miles of which potatoes were to be had in abundance.'[52] The bulk and slowness of the potato, again, defies that other critical capitalist virtue, speed of movement across space. Dependent on a food that thus lacks marketability, that cannot effectively be circulated as a commodity, the Irish fail to enter into the Empire-wide market for commodities: 'Their ordinary food being of the cheapest and commonest description, and having no value in the market, it gave them no command of butcher's meat, manufactures, colonial produce, or any other article of comfort or enjoyment.'[53] Both domestic and class distinctions are erased and dissolved:

> The domestic habits arising out of this mode of subsistence were of the lowest and most degrading kind. The pigs and poultry, which share the food of the peasant's family, become, in course, inmates of the cabin also. The habit of exclusively living on this root produced an entire ignorance of every other food and of the means of preparing it; and there is scarcely a woman of the peasant class in the West of Ireland, whose culinary art exceeds the boiling of a potato.[54]

Where, for Arthur Young, seventy years earlier, the spectacle of the Irish meal of potatoes, feeding pigs, hens and children, beggars and cottiers alike, seemed a picture of contentment and abundance, the famous Irish pig in the kitchen is now the figure of the impropriety of Irish domestic habits, a symbolic confusion of domestic species and spaces.

Finally, in the absence of capitalist farming, social relations on a larger scale are themselves dissolved into what Karl Marx would describe as the 'idiocy of rural life', which Trevelyan envisaged as a state of mere savagery and indolence, culminating in political disaffection:

The relations of employer and employed, which knit together the framework of society, and establish a mutual dependence and good-will, have no existence in the potato system. The Irish small-holder lives in a state of isolation, the type of which is to be sought for in the islands of the South Sea, rather than in the great civilized communities of the ancient world. A fortnight for planting, a week or ten days for digging, and another fortnight for turf-cutting, suffice for his subsistence; and during the rest of the year he is at leisure to follow his own inclinations, without even the safeguard of those intellectual tastes and legitimate objects of ambition which only imperfectly obviate the evils of leisure in the higher ranks of society. The excessive competition for land maintained rents at a level which left the Irish peasant the bare means of subsistence; and poverty, discontent, and idleness, acting on his excitable nature, produced that state of popular feeling which furnishes the material for every description of illegal association and misdirected political agitation. That agrarian code which is at perpetual war with the laws of God and man, is more especially the offspring of this state of society, the primary object being to secure the possession of the plots of land, which, in the absence of wages, are the sole means of subsistence.[55]

The relentless negativity of Trevelyan's description of the condition of the Irish potato-eaters and their oppositional culture invokes and brings together all the strands of political economy's ultimate antagonism to the potato and its material effects, lending to that antagonism the forceful appearance of a truth confirmed by the fatal consequences of the Famine. But again, we must be careful not to allow the only apparent inevitability of that event to structure likewise our judgement of the social formations that the eventual subsistence crisis was deployed to destroy. As Kevin Whelan and others have shown, the popular response to the Famine was, however fatalistic and chastened, no less a lament for a culture that thrived on the abundance of the potato and the complex social life that it sustained.[56] Paradoxically, that abundance and the alternative lifeways it permitted – rendered negatively as the counter-law of agrarian outrage or the anti-individualistic 'old barbarous Irish tenure called

Rundale'[57] – impelled the antagonistic evaluation of Irish culture and of the potato that was at once its condition and its metaphor.

Indeed, the constancy with which the potato slips from being a metonym for the Irish to being a metaphor for them reveals the extent to which the *discursive* event of the Famine belongs with a longer-lasting and incessant effort to apprehend the incomprehensible, a lawless or antinomian culture whose norms and values cannot be represented in the conceptual systems, economic or social, that are to hand. Out of that incommensurability an 'Irish crisis' emerges that is as much rhetorical as it is governmental and that takes on the problematic features of ideology in general – being at once effective and contradictory, stereotypically fixating and uncontrollably generative.

As the potato moves from being the more or less contingent staple of the Irish to appear as the root of their moral and material evils, so too its properties transfer. Like the potato, the Irish are rooted to the local. They partake of the potato's fecundity and indifference to soil types, reproducing seemingly without labour and on the most unpromising waste land. The very mass of the potato that makes it so recalcitrant to transport and exchange becomes for the British the signifier of the 'masses' of the Irish, that 'helpless mass of famine and disease', that 'mass of poverty, disaffection and degradation without a parallel in the world'.[58] They form a mass of properties without subjects, without subjectivity, as they are a mass of persons without property.[59] The potato, unable to enter into an economy founded on the work of abstraction and exchange, is the emblem of a people in turn incapable of abstraction and exchange, the twin foundations of representation and subjecthood. Marx's famous dictum on the French peasantry who form a mass of 'homologous magnitudes, much as potatoes in a sack form a sack of potatoes' is all the more fecund for the Irish.[60] A collectivity of mere contiguities, never rising to the level of a representative abstraction, the Irish are the type of metonymy metaphorized by the potato. Metonymy is the very form of their collectivities and of the uncanny mobility that belies their appearance of stolid, stupid fixity. Their movements are characterized like the potato by a rhizomatic, lateral transmission that is profoundly antithetical to the centralizing and subjectifying desire of the state that emerges to confront them. This characteristic of the agrarian movements from the 1780s through the 1830s was constantly noted by observers, a capacity to communicate from neighbourhood to neighbourhood without the need for centralized organization. Constantly the effect of Irish movement, whether in migration or in subversion, is described as *contagion* – another metaphor for a metonymic movement — contagion that spreads diffusely, seeping from place to place like the airborne blight itself, transforming the solid bulk of the potato into a liquid mass of suppurating rot.[61]

And so too the Irish are a rotting, fluid mass, are the 'pestilence', in Carlyle's term, from which they suffer and which they transmit. Although in fact the cholera which caused James Kay's moral panic passed first from English to Irish ports, that and the other epidemics that flourished fatally in the Famine years were already and constantly associated with the migratory Irish masses and with the filth and ooze of the slums in which they perforce congregated, in Britain and further afield.[62] Drawing extensively on, and endorsing, passages from Kay and Carlyle already cited above, Friedrich Engels added his own prejudices to their associations of the Irish with filth:

> Filth and drunkenness, too they have brought with them. The lack of cleanliness, which is not so injurious in the country, where population is scattered, and which is the Irishman's second nature, becomes terrifyingly and gravely dangerous through its concentration here in the great cities. The Milesian deposits all garbage and filth before his house door here, as he was accustomed to do at home, and so accumulates the pools and dirt-heaps which disfigure the working-people's quarters and poison the air.[63]

For both Kay and McCulloch likewise, it was not only the literal contagion that the Irish communicated, but also the social and moral, the cultural effect of their contiguity with the Scottish and English working classes that was at stake. 'Such a people', Carlyle in turn fretted, 'circulates not order, but disorder, through every vein of it', nicely condensing economic and biological metaphors.[64] In accord with the medical understanding of the time, which had yet to attribute epidemics to the isolatable agency of distinct microbes, the Irish were not seen as individual agents communicating specific diseases, any more than they were understood as articulating any actual anti-capitalist or otherwise dissident ideology, for all the activism of Irish workers in Chartist and other radical movements of the moment.[65] They spread, as McCulloch put it, 'a contaminating influence of example', rather than engaging in organized political activity — though why their example should have been so seductive and contagious to their British counterparts is rarely addressed.[66] Their morally corrupting example operated like the 'miasma' that was thought to be the medium that communicated disease, circulating and penetrating bodies, 'poisoning the air' like the odour or stench that was the almost material signifier of its invisible motions and with which, accordingly, it was often confused or identified.

The contaminating effects of odour transfer from their source that is not a subject as an unindividuated fluid mass, incapable of restraint and transgressive of boundaries. It is a quasi-corporeal emanation that invades and infects other bodies, at once sensibly and imperceptibly, transferring its properties from one body to another. It is at once intimate and alien, an internal sensation that is apprehended as the invasive mark of otherness. Odour operates as at once a mode of abstraction from the body that is its origin, and as a material parody of abstraction, resisting fixity and identification. If, as both Alain Corbin and Dominique Laporte have argued, the policing of odour is at once the governmental concern of the centralizing state and a key factor in the separation of the deodorized private space from the promiscuous and malodorous public spaces of labour and crowds, the filthy Irish, circulating odour and disease, are no less the figure for the undifferentiated mass that government seeks to individuate and subjectify.[67] They present at once the problems of hygiene and of moral education. Discursively, however, their restless circulation works uncontrollably as a parasitic parody of the very dominant representations that seek to hold them in place. Literally reeking of the sweat of labour and the fetor of poverty, the Irish are the odour of abstraction, the insistent and material remainder of the processes that seek to unleash for capital the mass of human energy that takes the form of value-producing abstract labour. They are both the product of the process that unleashes labour as such from concrete work, Marx's 'real labour of men', and its recalcitrant and unruly counterpart, the mass without which the refined distinctions of abstraction are unthinkable.

One further figure for Irish filth links the pervasiveness of odour and miasma to the bulk of the potato: dung. No traveller in Ireland ever failed to note the ubiquity of the peasant's dunghill and its immediate proximity to the cabin door. There were, of course, good material reasons for both the existence of the dunghill and its closeness to the cabin. As a striking handbill of 1831 put it, 'The greatest part of a Poor Man's Treasure is his Dunghill'.[68] Dung fertilized the potato field, without which the 'Poor Man' and his family would have starved; it was frequently the means to reclaim waste and barren land and its closeness to the cabin door bespoke the real value it embodied and the peasant's fear of the loss of this indispensable supply of what was, in effect, their only capital, or 'treasure'. Dung was the means to the reproduction of the peasants' life and an intrinsic element of the culture that it reproduced. As Whelan comments: 'The dung heap beside the door was not, as casual observers all too frequently asserted, a symbol of indolent slatterliness, but of persevering industry. In the absence of artificial fertilizers, natural ones were valuable.'[69]

For all the material rationality of the accumulation and the placement of the dunghill, foremost in the English observer's mind is its association with the foul odour of the miasma and the disease it spreads. Somerville's remarks, though those of a former ploughman accustomed to agricultural environments, are quite typical among descriptions of Irish rural settings:

All have pigs and asses in the huts with them in ordinary times. They have not all pigs now, for the food of pigs is no more; but all have dunghills and pools of stagnation in the narrow places between and at the ends of the huts, and not infrequently within them. That there should be fever and other diseases originating in filth, dampness and foul air, is only a natural consequence at the best of times. That there should be an aggravation of those diseases and death with them now, when to filth, dampness and foul air is added famine, is not to be received as a wonder, but as a natural result.[70]

Little distinction was ever made between the spectacle, odour and ill effects of the rural environment of the Irish and those of their migrant urban counterparts. The ubiquitous association of the Irish and their dung runs as deep as that with their potatoes, and has a material as well as an associative logic. Dung is that from which the potato springs and to which, as waste, surplus or residual matter, it returns. To many of the survivors of the Famine, its horrors came as a divine punishment after a season of unusual abundance in which the uneaten – and unstorable – potatoes were flung like dung on the fields.[71] Thus to short-circuit the transformation of the food substance back into the dung from which it sprang represents a sinful transgression of the boundary that symbolically separates food and life from shit and death and that holds apart the body's orifices according to their discrete functions. But it also powerfully signifies the intimacy of the relation and the ease with such a slippage could occur rhetorically.

From a quite different perspective, the dung that is always contiguous with the Irish becomes the appropriate metaphor for their excessive, redundant population surplus. Even to a sympathetic commentator, such a metaphor is ready to hand, as George Poulett Scrope in his criticism of the new Poor Law exclaims of the evicted cottiers who were 'flung away to rot on the nearest dunghill'.[72] His phrasing condenses nicely the rhetorical process by which the Irish enter a chain of associations that runs from their status as human waste to the potato to the dunghill. Elsewhere, the associations are less sympathetic and more haunted by the mobility of the dung-like masses, as was George Nicholls, architect of those same Poor Laws. As he saw it, 'a mass of filth, nakedness and misery is constantly moving about, entering every house[,] addressing itself to every eye and soliciting from every hand'.[73] Again, the circulating fluidity of Irish indigence threatens to seep across national and domestic thresholds in its restless motions. In the chain of substitutions that links the Irish to their filth, their food and their fetid odours, and in the constant transformations of these metonyms of fixity into metaphors for mobility, the discrete force of the threat they pose shadows every effort to categorize them. The image of that threat, and the turbulent eddies it produces in English discourse on the Irish, is found in the labile orifices that eat potatoes and emit dung, in the 'laughing misery' and 'squalid apehood' of the Irish migrant.

Thought incapable of participating in the economy of capitalism, too unskilled to become free labour, too tied to subsistence on the uncommodifiable potato, and, like that potato, resistant to abstraction and exchange, the mobile Irish nonetheless become the figures for a constant circulation and an incessant economy of transfers and substitutions. The point here is not simply that the idea of the Irish as external to the capitalist economy is quite false: Irish labour and Irish goods played a significant, if not a crucial role in the British and the larger Atlantic economy, and Irish under-development is always and clearly constituted in differential relation to British colonial capitalism. It is, rather, that the representations of the subaltern formations of Irish culture, representations of contagion and economic parasitism, are themselves contagious elements parasitic on and parodic of the structures of representation. It is as if, even in denying the Irish presence in the economy, the rhetorical economy of British discourses constantly takes on the very instability that it seeks to foreclose by that denial.

The Irish circulate, and with them circulate pestilence and the odour of excrement. That circulation, as it enters representation, is characterized constantly by a fluid and unstable passage between metonymy and metaphor. This tropological movement mimes, in effect, the paradoxical discursive movement of the Irish from fixity and location to migration and dissemination. No less paradoxical is the oscillation between their recalcitrant materiality and their mass mobility and uncontainable contagion. One is never entirely sure which of the axes of metonymy or metaphor they occupy, for at one moment the potato is the metonym of their dull embeddedness, the food by which they live; at another the metaphor for their reproductive surplus or for their rhizomatic movements and their unindividuated but disorganized mass. At one moment they are lodged literally contiguous to their dunghills, at the next they become a fluid dung-like substance that spreads and corrupts. The very metaphors are metaphors for metonymic movement, for migration and contagion, marking the recalcitrance of the Irish to that characteristic nineteenth-century model of assimilation and acculturation by way of 'likeness', the movement from local particularity to wider identifications that is the prelude to ethical citizenship and political representation.[74] They are the very figure of the likeness of difference, Carlyle's 'squalid apehood' that is the image of the direst falsehood, not the absence of truth but its mockery as 'Phantasm, Simulation, Non-Identity'.[75] In this incessant tropological movement, the very process of abstraction that seeks to represent, define and conceptualize the Irish, to establish their likeness and their difference, operates like an odour in relation to its corporeal origin, as an emanation that bears the corrupting trace of its materiality. Recalcitrant to abstraction and to assimilation in their cultural formations, insubordinate to capitalist ethics as to modern forms of political subjectification and organization, the Irish shift restlessly through the 'veins' of the body politic and, as figures, infect the discursive order in turn.[76]

For does this peculiar tropological circulation not share the forms of commodity circulation itself? This could scarcely be surprising, for the Irish, in their migrations, did represent that singular form of commodification, 'living labour' abstracted from locality and tradition and sold as mere 'labour-power', as Marx put it. They become abstract labour-power at precisely the moment when capitalism is most dynamically attempting to impose its own regime of abstraction, that endless tendency which is the counterpart of its relentless need to dissolve ties and melt all that is solid into air.[77] Unleashed from the soil in the continuing process of primitive accumulation that enclosure and consolidation represent, the Irish in their dissoluteness figure as the spectre of the violent dissolution of social ties that capitalism effects and seeks ideologically to rationalize. The often-remarked and terrifying dissolution of social ties the Famine effected is an intensified version of the processes of modernity that advanced at an accelerated pace in Ireland as its culture and society succumbed to the alien power of an imposed capitalism. As James Fintan Lalor was to put it in his epochal assessment of the Famine's political implications:

The failure of the potato, and consequent famine, is one of those events which come now and then to do the work of ages in a day, and change the very nature of an entire nation at once. It has even already produced a deeper social disorganisation than did the French revolution – greater waste of life – wider loss of property – more than the horrors, with none of the hopes … It has unsettled society to the foundation; deranged every interest, every class, every household. Every man's place and relation is altered; labour has left its track, and life lost its form … Society stands dissolved.[78]

If Lalor's writings gave birth to a new mode of social struggle in the Tenant's League and the subsequent Land Wars, British capital and its representatives simultaneously sought to recuperate the moment of social dissolution into what Sir William Wilde understood to be a 'transition state' in the conversion of the Irish from backward serfs to modern subjects.[79]

Materially recalcitrant to these processes, as spectral figures, as *forms*, the Irish haunt the logic of the commodity and its circulations. For the logic of the commodity itself depends upon the double axis of metonymy and metaphor, combining and distinguishing the moments of contiguity and likeness in the process of exchange. Any given commodity, that is, an item produced for exchange, involves the transformation of a specific and particular set of use values into an exchange value. That transformation takes place by way of a formal resemblance that is established as the principle of exchange itself, namely, that the articles in exchange, irrespective of their material substance or form, resemble one another *as* commodities. Corn and shirts can be exchanged because, by abstraction from their particularity as objects in use, they are alike in being objects that embody a quantity of value – that is, as Marx shows, they embody comparable quantities of abstract (or commodified) labour. This we can conceive of as the metaphoric axis of exchange, insofar as – as in metaphor – the commodities are brought into identity in certain of their properties while the remainder that constitutes their differences is held in abeyance.

At the same time, however, the process of exchange itself sets up a potentially vertiginous and infinite series of substitutions and displacements that are metonymic in form and depend on the regime of differences. We can exchange corn for shirts, and shirts for spices, and spices for cotton or guns or opium, each for each, because they represent different use values and can be placed in contiguity with one another on the market. This metonymic axis of exchange is an endless chain of displacements and is the motor of political economy's pursuit of a single measure of value that will anchor the apparently ceaseless and bottomless movement of exchanges – the pursuit of a metaphor for metaphor itself. But, we may note, this endless series of metonymic substitutions is driven by the metaphoric movement that brings different and otherwise incommensurable use values into contiguity *as* commodities. The moment of abstraction that enables exchange, the moment of metaphorization, simultaneously dissolves back into the material abyss of metonymy. While money functions as the ultimate metaphor-commodity in exchange, it remains nonetheless, as labour itself does, a commodity. The series that Marx expresses in *Capital* as CMC, the metamorphic series of exchanges of commodities for money for further commodities, remains the serial metonymy that drives capitalism's own restless and destabilizing movements.[80]

If labour becomes the measure and origin of value, establishing value as an effect of production rather than exchange, it seems to do so by naturalizing the origin of value in the human body and its exertions. Yet, as the fluctuating relation in political economy between the 'market or actual' and the 'natural or necessary' rate of wages indicates, labour itself is recognized to succumb to commodification: it is, as Marx grasped, the commodification or abstraction of labour that enables the difference between the labour embodied in the commodity and its price on the market to be extracted as surplus value.[81] Abstract labour, indifferent to the particular mode of real labour engaged in any productive activity, reduces all work to a moment of identity or equivalence. Yet at the same time, the abstraction of labour as a commodity unleashes labour from the particularity of its tasks into the endless series of substitutions that are the mark of its reduction to equivalence. In the calculation of capital, the labour which produces corn is equivalent to that which spins cotton or forges iron, precisely insofar as it is commodified. In this vertiginous displacement of labour as a commodity, political economy confronts, as a discourse, the spectacle of ceaseless displacement that the dynamics of capital inflict on the social body, the effect of a discursive and material instability that is, as the *Communist Manifesto* insisted, at once the fascination of capital and the source of its contradictions and antagonisms.

The Irish, whose unskilled, mobile labour is in one sense the most abstract, appear both within and without the system of British capital. From one perspective, the labour that is reproduced in the form of the potato economy is *not* equivalent to capitalist labour in general. It is inconvertible, literally failing to enter the exchanges of the money economy, and its rhythms and practices – epitomized for Trevelyan in the 'lazy bed' in which the potato was planted – encourage indolence rather than capitalist discipline.[82] From this perspective, Ireland is marginal to capitalism, a country and an economy yet to be developed and subject to coercive intervention to draw it into the larger industrial economy of Britain and the world. It is, simply, spatially peripheral as it is temporally backward and its spaces, as we shall see, embody a temporality – that of orality – which defies capitalist logic and the rationalizations of space and function it dictates. Its prodigious surplus population is a waste matter that flows through the economy, generated by the scandalous abundance of the potato, infecting all with its contagion as it 'circulates ... disorder'.

Yet it is this very circulation of the Irish, enabled by their contiguity with Britain, that sets in play a contrary movement in which the Irish appear as all too mobile within and all too contemporary with British capitalism whose logic they infect precisely because of their uncanny resemblances. Apparently incapable of using money, of engaging in abstraction or exchange, they circulate nonetheless like money itself, or like an abundance of cheap goods whose surplus – like the surplus of labour that the Irish indeed are – floods the market and degrades its values. They are the mobile counterpart of the money that has been racked from them in the form of rent, that displaces them from the land that has been expropriated from them in the violence of primitive accumulation. The refuse of the system, the dung that must be set aside in discrete invisibility, they return at once as the spectres of primitive accumulation that haunt the extraction of surplus value and as the figures of 'filthy lucre' itself, of the age-old association between dung and money. The paradoxical embodiment of the disembodied, the insistence of the non-modern at the heart of the modern, these figures of 'degradation and disorder' circulate through English writings from Malthus to Kay and from Kay to Carlyle and McCulloch, and even to Engels and Marx. In a peculiar way, their circulation knits together the modern discourse of the social, left to right, in a common desire to discipline this wild counterpart of the capitalist economy. Theoretical and governmental discourses are as one in the need to contain the Irish, to civilize and modernize them, to harness their energies for either capitalist or revolutionary projects, and it is this anxiety as to the uncontainable circulation of bodies that a vigorous capitalism unleashes for which the Irish mouth, in its consumption and in its utterances, in its lability and its mobility, has become the most eloquent figure, at once metaphor for and metonym of the recalcitrant body.

Figures of a spatial and temporal fixity that is nonetheless in perpetual displacement, the Irish spectres that haunt the nineteenth century embody the paradoxical effects of accumulation. They bear one non-modern social formation, considered backward and savage, into the presence and the present of another that represents itself as advanced and rational. But in this transition, impelled by the unbinding energies of primitive accumulation, from one place into another they also transform their non-modern practices into counter-modern dissonances within the capitalist system they at once serve and challenge with infectious alternative possibilities. For what the Irish embody is not, in fact, simply a social formation lagging in the past of modernity and waiting on development, as historicism would have it. It represents, rather, a different social imaginary *in* the present and *for* the future. At the heart of an emerging capitalist state characterized by an ever more rigorous division of labour and spheres, by a rationalization of spaces according to the activities and attitudes proper to them, the Irish transgress spatial and discursive boundaries with their insistent mobility. But they also infect those regulated spaces with another conception of space, one that appears to be a zone of confusion and non-differentiation, of lability and inconsistency. That space, in which the cultural difference of the Irish is so persistently articulated, is the space of orality.

CHAPTER 2

Closing the mouth: disciplining oral space

I

Sinéad O'Connor's still haunting track, 'Famine', opened with the uncanny sound of a dog howling.[1] The sound remains uncanny for several reasons. It is impossible to tell if the howl is of hunger, grief or some condensation of the two; it is difficult to determine whether the sound we hear is actually a dog's howl or a human imitation of the sound, a difficulty which in itself opens the uncanny domain where the human and the natural converge and mimic one another; this animal lament accentuates the absence or the silence of what properly should be the sound of human mourning: it is as if the field of human society itself has been decimated to the extent that all that remains of its domestic and affective fabric, for which the memory of the dead is an indispensable thread, is this anguish of the domestic animal on the verge of reverting to its wildness. 'Mouths biting empty air', these sounds of dogs howling insist disturbingly on the question as to what issues from the empty mouth, what speech follows the horrors of famine, what mourning can work through the memory of mass destruction.

These are, of course, among the themes that Sinéad O'Connor pursued, insisting on the repression of the memory of the Famine in subsequent Irish culture, connecting this with our deeply embedded habit of disavowing the personal and cultural damage that is in part the legacy of our colonial past, and demanding that we learn to grieve in order to heal. In relation to this demand, her stated understanding of herself as a contemporary 'keener' was entirely apposite and invoked a motif that we will return to later.[2] In its demand for accountability to and mourning of the victims of the catastrophe, 'Famine', indeed, pre-empted the upsurge of historical and cultural work that responded to the 150th anniversary of the Great Hunger. The enormous volume of new and nuanced research of the last decade-and-a-half has enriched and complicated our narratives of the Famine era, but even now it would be too soon to say that new knowledge or richer understanding has finally laid our ghosts to rest, allowing us to move on, satisfied that in mourning we have worked through and out the damage of a colonial past. For ghosts are not merely the tattered remnants of our unpacified history, the unquiet afterbirths of historical trauma. They may also represent the survival, in unexpected times and places, of unexhausted possibilities, of potentials that exceed the confines of common sense or verisimilitude.[3] Their manifestation is often in those strangely familiar motifs, excessive and recurrent, that are contained in but not by the historical record and to which we give the name of the uncanny.

Thus the uncanniness of the dog's howl lies not only in its immediate effects on the hearer. For if the sound is quite literally haunting, that is surely because it picks up and foregrounds a complex of representations of the Famine and its psychological effects that echoes through virtually every account, journalistic, historical and fictional. It is as if we had always heard it. In account after account of the Famine, the terrible silence of the land is counterpointed by the sound of wailing or howling, a sound that seems undecidably human or animal. The silence is at once the silence of depopulation and the silence of a traumatized culture; the wail is the almost animal wail of despair and passivity before a catastrophe that seems to exceed comprehension and reduces the human to the mere form of living being. Wordless, the wail is also anonymous, without any distinct agency to utter it: as a recurrent motif in representations of the Famine, it marks simultaneously the dissolution of the Irish as subjects of their own culture and history and the historical emergence of a new kind of Irish subject whose elements are in many respects still with us and which embodies a peculiar weave of memory, damage and modernity.

The sense of shock at a catastrophe epochal in its implications is clear in a celebrated account of the Famine's effects written in its immediate aftermath:

The 'land of song' was no longer tuneful; or, if a human sound met the traveller's ear, it was only that of the feeble and despairing wail for the dead. This awful, unwonted silence, which, during the famine and subsequent years, almost everywhere prevailed, struck more fearfully upon their imaginations, as many Irish gentlemen informed me, and gave them a deeper feeling of the desolation with which the country had been visited, than any other circumstance which had forced itself upon their attention.[4]

In his 1889 memoir of life in North Donegal, former school-master Hugh Dorian gave a participant's account of the effects of the Famine from a perspective far closer to the peasantry. But he too emphasizes the terrible silence of the Famine years and the common fate of human and animal:

> A mournful silence, no more friendly meetings at the neighbours' houses in the afternoons, no gatherings on the hillsides on Sundays, no song, no merry laugh of the maiden, not only were the human beings silent and lonely, but brute creation also: not even the bark of a dog nor the crowing of a cock was to be heard – and why? These animals had nearly all disappeared.[5]

Dorian's virtually verbless syntax and exhausted run-on sentences are saturated here with the people's loss of agency and community in the Famine years and with a sense of paralysis whose correlative is this loud silence that descends in the wake of catastrophe.

Half a century later, Liam O'Flaherty picks up the powerful acoustic image of wailing in his description of the advent of the blight, and with a similar sense of its vocalizing of despair and paralysis:

> Towards the north, in the direction towards which Thomsy pointed, Mary and the old man saw people looking over fences, just as they themselves were doing. The people had begun to wail. In this wailing there was a note of utter despair. There was no anger in it, no power, not even an appeal for mercy. It was just like the death groan of a mortally wounded person, groaning in horror of inevitable death.
> 'It's the blight,' Mary whispered. 'Oh! God in Heaven!'
> ... Mary turned away from the fence as he approached. She began to walk back to the house.
> The wailing was now general all over the Valley.[6]

In a more recent account that likewise draws on contemporary testimony, Thomas Gallagher produces a no less graphic account of the anguished response to the blight:

> Unlike the previous year, when large areas in both the north and south were unaffected, the blight this time spread to every area in so short a time that a kind of wailing lament rose throughout the country wherever neighbours gathered ... Keeners at a wake could not have sent up more varieties of anguish and despair than did these Irish families at the sight of their entire year's food supply being destroyed.[7]

Examples of the recurrence of the motif of wailing and its relation to the passivity of the afflicted Irish peasantry could be multiplied indefinitely and with a regularity that suggests that we have to do here not merely with dramatic effect but with a discourse that once again constitutes the very meaning of the Famine as a cultural rather than a natural phenomenon. Unlike the discourse of political economy discussed in the previous chapter, this appears less as a discourse of mastery and rule than one infused with a sense of shock and marked by the ceaseless displacement of loss. And yet, as O'Connor's 'Famine' aptly captured, there is something in this discourse that registers the unnaturalness of the silence, its discursive production as both an index of loss and, yet more disturbingly, as a guarantee of the finality of the transformation that the Famine and its administration violently achieved. The unwonted silence of the post-Famine Irish marks their shaken entry into modern times.

So much was grasped already at the time. Neither the cultural constitution of the Famine's meaning nor the shock that accompanies it are in any simple way a retrospective construction: the counterpoint of silence, wailing and passivity was clearly quite available to contemporary observers and embedded in the most immediate representations of the catastrophe. Among the most powerful of such observers was William Carleton, not least on account of his intimacy with the peasant culture from which he had emerged. His 1847 novel, *The Black Prophet*, though ostensibly about an earlier famine, was written explicitly to alert an English reading public to the horrors of starvation and accordingly records the Famine's effects in painstaking detail:

> In all these acts of violence [the food riots that occasionally broke out] there was very little shouting; the fact being, that the wretched people were not able to shout, unless on rare occasions; and sooth to say, their vociferations were then but a faint and feeble echo of the noisy tumults which in general characterize the proceedings of excited and angry crowds ... The ghastly impressions of famine, however, were not confined to those who composed the crowds. Even the children were little living skeletons, wan and yellow, with a spirit of pain and suffering legible upon their fleshless but innocent features; whilst the very dogs, as was well observed, were not able to bark, for, indeed, such of them as survived, were nothing but ribs and skin. At all events, they assisted in making up the terrible picture of general misery which the country at large presented. Both day and night, but at night especially, their hungry howlings could be heard over the country, or mingling with the wailings which the people were in the habit of pouring over those whom the terrible typhus was sweeping away with such wide and indiscriminating fatality.[8]

That Carleton's novel aimed to reach a British public does something to explain the emphasis of his representations of the starving people, which underplayed the rage that was often expressed in popular attempts to halt the daily export of foodstuffs from the country throughout the Famine years. To gain their sympathy, Carleton minimized the anger and resistance among the poor and, throughout the novel, represented the Ribbonmen as a minority of misguided agitators.[9] Unlike O'Flaherty, who provided a sympathetic narrative of resistance in *Famine*, Carleton emphasized the passivity and patience of the population.

In such a context, the wailing of the Irish, not unlike their silence, becomes the sign of their helplessness in face of the 'fatality' of the Famine. But the association of the Irish with 'wailing' is not new: it is at once continuous with and, in the context of Famine narratives, transformative of one of the most perdurable topoi of pre-Famine English representations of Ireland's cultural peculiarities, 'keening'. Scarcely an English traveller's account of Irish social customs fails to discourse on the singularity of this practice and in the period immediately prior to the Famine, when Ireland had become both a principal locus of post-Romantic tourism and a major site of political concern for the Empire, keening became a crucial index for an emergent ethnographic discourse on the Irish national character. As a phenomenon through which the strangeness of Irish customs and values was articulated, keening focused a profoundly ambivalent matrix of responses to pre-Famine Irish culture, at once fixing that culture in its primitive incivility and giving rise to disturbance and uncertainty. Reading the discourse on keening carefully situates within a deeper history the association of the Famine and wailing and furthermore contributes to our understanding of the ongoing cultural transformation within which the Famine was a critical turning point.

The American traveller Mrs S.C. Hall's description of a not uncommon scene of annual hardship and shortage in West Cork around 1840 indicates that the relationship between hunger and keening was already well established before the Famine:

At Bandon we beheld a melancholy scene – several carts returning to their homes in the country, which they had quitted in the morning with money to procure food, but compelled to go back without it. Women and children accompanied them with loud cries; literally 'keening', as if they were following a corpse to its place of rest.[10]

Generally, however, keening was recognized prior to the Famine as a practice specifically related to mourning for the dead, which is why it became the focus for discourse on the strangeness and dangers of Irish emotion. Descriptions of the practice by English or American writers hesitate between the recognition of its professional and often formulaic nature and its appropriation as a sign of Irish subjection to and indulgence of violent and unpredictable emotion. That emotion in turn becomes the index of Irish political and cultural instability. Another account by Mrs Hall, this time of a funeral or wake in Kerry, begins by acknowledging the organized and ritual nature of the practice:

> The women of the household range themselves at either side [of the corpse], and the keen (*caoine*) at once commences. They rise with one accord, and, moving their bodies with a slow motion to and fro, their arms apart, they continue to keep up a heart-rending cry. This cry is interrupted for a while to give the *ban caionthe* (the leading keener) an opportunity of commencing. At the close of every stanza of the dirge, the cry is repeated, to fill up, as it were, the pause, and then dropped; the woman then again proceeds with the dirge, and so on to the close.[11]

For many observers of the keen, part of the difficulty of comprehending it lay in the apparent contradiction between its wild extemporaneity and its formulaic aspects or, to put it otherwise, the difficulty lay in comprehending the performance of emotion.[12] The sinister connotations of keening that such difficulties gave rise to were often condensed with the fact that the professional keener generally was – or appeared to be – an old woman: 'The keener is almost invariably an aged woman; or if she be comparatively young, the habits of her life make her look old.'[13]

In Thomas Crofton Croker's account of 'Keens and Death Ceremonies', the uncertainty that attaches to the figure of the keener attains a peculiar intensity that is inseparable from his difficulty in determining the political significance of Irish cultural practices. In this description of the funeral procession for a member of an old Gaelic family, he oscillates between an understanding of the keener's expression as spontaneous, 'dictated' by grief and therefore one with the natural sublimity of the scenery, and the acknowledgement of her professional status:

> The vast multitude approaches, winding through some romantic defile, or trailing along the base of a wild mountain, while the chorus of the death-song, coming fitfully upon the breeze, is raised by a thousand voices. On a closer view, the aged nurse is seen sitting on the hearse beside the coffin, with her body bent over it; her actions dictated by the most violent grief, and her head completely enveloped in the deep hood of her large cloak, which falls in broad and heavy folds, producing altogether a most mysterious and awful figure ...
>
> The Irish funeral howl is notorious, and although this vociferous expression of grief is on the decline, there is still, in the less civilized parts of the country, a strong attachment to the custom, and many may yet be found who are keeners or mourners for the dead by profession.[14]

The mystery of what lies beneath the voluminous cloak, the impenetrability of this quasi-supernatural figure who seems at once decrepit and powerful, rapidly becomes the allegory for the secret circulation of sedition for which both the keen and its language become the 'cloak': 'Keens are also a medium through which the disaffected circulate their mischievous principles, and this they do without much attempt at concealment, the Irish language being a sufficient cloak for the expression of seditious sentiments.'[15]

Yet it is less the concealed content of the keen that gives rise to disturbance than the *form* itself, which stands as a striking instance of Irish cultural difference from the English. Like the ambiguously canine or human howl, and perhaps as its prototype, keening enters as an unsubsumed motif into these literary representations, which seek to convey and to interpret an oral and performative practice that exceeds their comprehension both literally and figuratively. One might say, indeed, that the formalized repetitiveness that appears to connote the contradictory status of the keen as spontaneous or 'dictated' *artifice* enters into the very form of its representations. The almost generic recurrence of the same observations, focusing on the same salient and anomalous elements of the practice, gave rise to a subgenre of Irish writing with all the consistency and regularity of a discourse. For that discourse, it was not simply the seditious sense of Irish sentiments that was at stake, but the nature of Irish 'sentiment' itself, which was so deeply recalcitrant to anglicization.

It is well known that Irish emotional or sentimental characteristics were subjected to a considerable labour of investigation and interpretation in the course of the nineteenth century. This labour was continuous in many respects with the long-standing English discourse on Irish violence and incivility. But it received added impetus from England's political difficulties with Ireland after the Union of 1800, particularly in relation to the desire to integrate Ireland politically and economically into the Empire, and was, further, formalized by the emergent science of ethnography and its inquiries into national and racial character. The political and ethnographic impulses were synthesized in Matthew Arnold's *On the Study of Celtic Literature* which, appearing twenty years after the Famine, gave canonical expression to the idea of the 'sentimentality' of the Celtic nature and of the relation between Irish culture and grieving.[16] Arnold's work, which drew on other European Celticists like Ernest Renan and Henri Martin, can be seen as a critical moment in the long trajectory of a steadily transforming discourse on the Irish emotional economy, for which the shift from the performance of grief in the often-seditious keen to the fatalistic wail of the famine-stricken peasantry is one crucial marker.

The force of Arnold's argument was that the alternately feminine and childlike or turbulent sentimentality of the Celt, which was so ineffectual in political and economic spheres, would find its cultural value only when supplemented and disciplined by Anglo-Saxon steadiness and when taken up into the larger and emerging unity of an English empire. For Arnold, the disposition of the Irish belonged in the longer narrative of a developing English civilization that constantly assimilated cultural difference to itself, and his argument thus partook of the transition from absolutist to historicist notions of racial difference that we have traced in the case of economics in the previous chapter. This temporal framework sought to dissipate anxiety over the apparent incommensurability of Irish and English cultural forms, while its assertion of the Celtic propensity for mourning naturalized the defeat of Irish culture as the expression of an ethnic predisposition.[17] As this narrative took shape, the shift from keen to wail doubtless signified the transition from sedition or outcry to fatalism and, as we shall see, to melancholy. Wailing is the disciplinable remainder of keening.

At the same time, however, the predominantly temporal framework within which ethnic characteristics were disposed for Arnold was counterpointed by what we might describe as a spatial economy with regard to the strangeness of Irish sentimentality. For that sentimentality involved not merely grieving but also transports of joy and especially rapid transitions from one state to the other. The Irish emotional economy was envisaged as the 'maniacal' obverse of the 'dullness' of the Anglo-Saxon; it manifested the characteristics that Norbert Elias discerned in the personality of pre-modern Europeans. For Elias, such 'fluctuation' was typical of the disposition that preceded the regulation of emotion by the 'civilizing' process as the centralized political state and its corresponding 'civility' emerged in Europe: 'The personality, if we may put it thus, is incomparably more ready and accustomed to leap with undiminishing intensity from one extreme to the other, and slight impressions, uncontrollable associations are often enough to induce these immense fluctuations.'[18] This connection of the emotionally consistent or regulated personality with the forms of civility reminds us that in the tradition of representations of Irish character, discourse on the 'fluctuations' of Irish emotion embedded a system of political and moral judgement within ethnographic description.

Accordingly, the proximity of emotional traits that colloquial whimsy still designates 'the tear and the smile' figured in proto-ethnographic discourse prior to the Famine as an index of impropriety. Impropriety has reference not simply to the moral codes of bourgeois civility as such, but to the spatiality and the timing of emotional display. It is not just that the performance of emotion is itself an affront to the assumptions of an English observer for whom the authenticity of emotions such as grief is inseparable from privacy and inwardness, but that within the economy of Irish emotional expression, the site of grieving is not necessarily separated, either temporally or spatially, from that of 'merriment' or pleasure. The long civilizing process, in which the forms of emotional display and 'fluctuation' that Elias describes yield to a demarcation of proper spheres for distinct emotions and the eviction of sentiment from public space, thus appears scandalously unrealized in Ireland. The famous wake is the recurrent scenario where the consequent sense of acute cultural alterity is staged. The impropriety of Irish conduct is displayed at once in the fluctuations between emotional states and in the absence of marked distinctions between discrete spaces each of which is 'proper' to a certain display of emotion or topic of conversation. Thus Hall's description of funeral ceremonies that we began to quote above continues as follows:

> During the pauses of the women's wailing, the men, seated in groups by the fire, or in the corners of the room, are indulging in jokes, exchanging repartees, and bantering each other, some about their sweethearts, and some about their wives, or talking over the affairs of the day – prices and politics, priests and parsons, the all-engrossing subjects of Irish conversation ...
>
> It is needless to observe, that the merriment is in ill keeping with the solemnity of the death chamber, and that very disgraceful scenes are, or rather were, of frequent occurrence; the whiskey being always abundant, and the men and women nothing loath to partake of it to intoxication.[19]

Multiple transgressions of the proper disposition of spaces are in evidence here: the boundaries between pleasure and pain, mourning and levity, are fluid; what began as a gendered division of the chamber between 'wailing women' and bantering men clearly dissolves as the women enjoy in equal measure the spirits that undermine propriety; and the mouth itself, the privileged site of oral culture, becomes the unstable and indifferent locus of intoxication and sedition, laughter and lament.

We will return to this ambiguous territory of the mouth later, noting only how charged this orifice is for the ambivalent representation of Irishness: the site at once of fluent speech and secretive silence, lament and laughter, intoxication and hunger, guile and guilelessness, and of the slippage between them. This disturbing observation of the spatial instability of Irish emotion has to be resituated on the temporal axis of ethical judgement and transformative prescription. For, as in the economic domain, the moral censure that attaches to the unsettling contiguity of Irish emotional states is embedded in a historical logic whereby English commentators seek to locate and stabilize their Celtic others in relation to their own sense of cultural and political modernity. Croker's judgement of the Irish character is not untypical:

> The rough and honest independence of the English cottager speaks the freedom he has so long enjoyed, and when really injured his appeal to the laws for redress and protection marks their impartial and just administration: the witty servility of the Irish peasantry, mingled with occasional bursts of desperation and revenge – the devoted yet visionary patriotism – the romantic sense of honour, and improvident yet unalterable attachments, are evidence of a conquest without system, an irregular government, and the remains of feudal clanship, the barbarous and arbitrary organization of a warlike people.[20]

This appeal to the constitutional legality that guarantees the English spirit of independence as against the 'barbarous' irregularity and the local and affective attachments of its subject peoples would become the staple of the liberal version of British imperial discourse throughout the nineteenth century. What it implied was the necessity for English interventions to bring subject peoples like the Irish to the point where they could become political subjects in a modern sense, capable of self-submission to the *regularity* of law and of attachment to abstract principles rather than to sentimental affective ties.[21]

This British political project was, of course, inseparable from an economic judgement as to the moral character of the Irish that turned on their perceived incapacity for sustained labour. We have seen this assumption about the Irish circulating through the discourse of political economy in connection with the Irish disrespect for property to which their lack of propriety was clearly tied. In the proto-ethnographic discourses of the period, what was at stake was a racial typology expressed as 'character'. Croker's comments are again typical:

> The present Irish character is a compound of strange and apparent inconsistencies, where vices and virtues are so unhappily blended that it is difficult to distinguish or separate them. Hasty in forming opinions and projects, tardy in carrying them into effect, they are often relinquished before they have arrived into maturity, and are abandoned for others as vague and indefinite ... The virtues of patience, prudence, and industry seldom are included in the composition of an Irishman: he projects gigantic schemes, but wants perseverance to realize any work of magnitude: his conceptions are grand and vivid, but his execution is feeble and indolent: he is witty and imprudent, and will dissipate the hard earnings of to-day regardless of to-morrow: an appeal made to his heart is seldom unsuccessful, and he is generous with an uninquiring and profuse liberality.[22]

Given the insistent blendedness of their character, its oscillation from state to state, what the Irish appeared to lack were precisely the virtues, political and economic, that would permit the development of Ireland into a modern nation. Within the emerging historicist terms of English colonial discourse, Ireland's backwardness was understood as the effect of their fixation at an earlier historical stage, that of feudalism, out of which English political modernity had already emerged. Ireland lay on the same historical time-line as England, just as they were spatially contiguous, and only a time-lag divided them. It was this lag that English reform intended to make up. Politically, the systematic extension of English law and education would lead the Irish from affective attachments to the feudal clan to rational submission to abstract principles.[23] Economically, as we have seen, reform meant either the subjection of the Irish to English capitalist norms, or, later, their gradual development through rudimentary forms of ownership into economic subjects: the Irish incapacity for sustained labour or 'the virtues of patience, prudence, and industry' would be overcome by the discipline of political economy.

To invoke this economic project at once obscures and reveals the fact that what was at stake was producing not merely a new set of psychic and ethical dispositions, or even a new 'social body', but in a quite immediate sense a new physical economy, a new spatiality for the Irish body. Culturally, the political and economic projects required the reorganization of Irish space and the disciplining of their mouths. If the former was in part realized on the land in the wake of the Famine, the terrible silence that was registered as that catastrophe's cultural consequence was the all too apposite metaphor for the destruction of Irish oral culture and the social spaces that sustained it. The ambiguous, mobile and threatening keen was replaced by the monovalent, fatalistic and reassuringly defeated wail whose legibility was the prelude to new forms of subjection. The zones of the new body on which Ireland's possible development was predicated were so deeply reordered as to transform a body that had been the synchronous site of contiguous and shifting affects into a disciplined body, one habituated to the differentiation of space into the public and the private, the rational and the emotional, the proper and the improper. This involved, as Seamus Deane has put it, 'an attempt to control a strange bodily economy in which food, drink, speech and song are intimately related'.[24] The developmental projects of political economy, articulated at the level both of individual subjects and of the social or cultural whole, also aimed at a thorough-going reorganization of Irish space, the spaces of body and affect as much as the spaces of social intercourse and economic activity. This entailed, along with the many other modes of discipline characteristic of modernity, the attempt to impose a distinctly modern hierarchy of the senses for which the eye and ear, the most distanced and objectifying of organs, represented the privileged vehicles of culture while those senses that mingle the body with its objects, touch and smell and taste, remained tied to the suspect domain of the unruly body.[25]

Above all, the moral discipline that sought to transform the shiftlessness of the Irish who were 'regardless of to-morrow' into prudence and economy required the subordination of that most undisciplined of Irish orifices, the mouth. The impropriety of the Irish was consistently located in the laxity of their mouths as sites of consumption and rhetoric, input and output. They could be rectified by a new morality that would cure Irish hunger – and close Ireland's empty mouth – by targeting oral culture and alcohol, the inveterate causes and symptoms of Ireland's backwardness. That the moment of the Famine is generally regarded as that of the final and irrevocable demise of the Irish language is only one index of the ensuing assault on what had become an oral culture. Although it is possible to account for that demise in terms of the mass emigrations that took place mostly from predominantly Irish-speaking areas, or in relation to the pragmatic realization of those who remained that their children's survival depended on proficiency in English, there is little doubt as to the equal impact of the post-Famine traumatization of a whole culture on the loss of the language.[26]

The precipitous decline of Irish at the time of the Famine may well have fed a popular belief that the Famine was in some respect a punishment for the speaking of the native language. Nor is this understanding of the Famine as punishment an entirely superstitious or fanciful supposition on the part of Irish people. As we have seen, the legitimation of British administrative practice throughout the period lay in the intersection of the pragmatic logic of political economy, for which the Famine represented a unique opportunity to clear the land of its redundant population, and the assertion of a providential design to punish the Irish for their cultural profligacy. From another perspective that we will explore further here, the Famine did indeed result from the loyalty of the Irish to spaces and mores that were anathema to British propriety.[27] In a very profound sense, the Famine was an experience of punishing social and cultural discipline against which no protest availed. And it is impossible to separate this sense of discipline from either the advent of a new Irish subjectivity or the concomitant freezing of the practice of keening that had once combined its mourning with its protest against the conditions that occasioned it.[28] This encryptment of Irish culture, the closing of the mouth or biting down on the traumatic sense of loss that haunts it, furnishes some explanation of the intense strain of melancholia in Irish post-Famine culture: a mourning that cannot be spoken remains incomplete and unworked-through.[29] But that is not the whole story. In other respects, the effect of the destruction of the spaces of Irish orality meant not the silencing but the displacement of its practices into the spaces of modernity itself, with the result that Irish modernity is unusually seeded with oral elements, and not only in its celebrated literary loquacity. Some of those spaces, and the peculiar resurgence in them of spectres of an older orality, will be explored in subsequent chapters.

This emphasis on the *spatial* formations that sustain oral culture is intended as a corrective supplement to the almost exclusively temporal axis along which what is understood as the transition from orality to literacy has generally been rendered. In a way that largely replicates the developmental or progressive schemata that emerged in mid-nineteenth-century colonial historicism, orality has been understood as a stage antecedent to literacy in the gradual evolution of increasingly sophisticated human civilizations. As one of the foremost scholars of orality and literacy, Walter Ong, has put it:

Since at least the time of Hegel, awareness has been growing that human consciousness evolves ... Modern studies in the shift from orality to literacy and the sequels of literacy, print and the electronic processing of verbalization, make more and more apparent some of the ways in which this evolution has depended on writing.[30]

In this historicist schema, writing is bound up with the advent of interiority and a more self-reflexive consciousness and is opposed to the 'communal structures' of what are implicitly earlier phases of human sociality:

The evolution of consciousness through human history is marked by growth in articulate attention to the interior of the individual person as distanced – though not necessarily separated – from the communal structures in which each person is necessarily enveloped ... The highly interiorized stages of consciousness in which the individual is not so immersed unconsciously in communal structures are stages which, it appears, consciousness would never reach without writing.[31]

Not only is the narrative of transition and evolution related within a historicist framework, literacy itself is the condition of and identified with historical consciousness itself: 'The concept of an era', Jack Goody remarks, 'is not the kind of thing that develops in oral cultures.'[32] Literacy bears with it a historical frame of mind and, consequently, a sense of change through time that is unavailable to the largely atemporal oral culture.[33]

The dominant model of orality and literacy assumes, then, as Brian Street puts it, 'a single direction in which literacy development can be traced, and associates it with "progress", "civilisation", individual liberty and social mobility'.[34] Critics of this historicist assumption regarding the advent of literacy and its relation to civilization and consciousness point, as Street does, to the ideological foundations of the causal priority given to literacy, and to the fact that in most societies oral and literary modes persist in mixed and interacting ways.[35] My own point is somewhat different, however, and seeks to underscore the ways in which consideration of the temporal dialectic of orality and literacy occludes the spatial dimensions of both. Certainly it is recognized that the advent of literacy impacts the disposition of space. As Ong puts it of early literacy textbooks, 'the material was organized spatially in itself and in the mind. Every art was in itself completely separate from every other, as houses with intervening open spaces are separate from one another, though the arts were mingled in use'.[36] The conceptual spaces of literacy are intimately connected to 'the sense of closure fostered by print' and we can recognize in the spatial disposition of the arts, as Ong's metaphor of housing suggests, the kinds of spatial disposition of disciplinary institutions at every level that Foucault famously analysed in *Discipline and Punish*. Street similarly notes both the effect of 'distancing' in the social functions of literate intercourse and the ways in which it assumes an implicit sense of 'boundaries' and 'mental separation' at the core of the subject's relation to the world.[37]

If literacy is a principal condition of possibility for the development of what we consider 'interiority', then we must recognize also that this spatial metaphor for consciousness belongs with a highly elaborated set of spatial givens that amount to a modern 'common sense' of space as a whole. This common sense assumes a determinate disposition of both material space and psychic or affective comportment. It assumes, for example, boundedness and closure or enclosure. The Lockean genealogy of property itself from the initial enclosure of common land signals the close alliance between the claims of property and the conventions of propriety: the 'proper' display of emotion that we have already touched on requires the psychic counterpart of the regulation of property and its boundaries.[38] Propriety requires that emotion and affect be in the first instance experienced in the interior of the subject – outward displays of emotion are suspect as insincere 'performances'. And that 'interior' presumes equally the withdrawal of the subject and the performance of 'intimate' emotions from public space into the inmost reaches of the domestic interior: we 'retire' in order to mourn. Each form of interiority is the other's metaphor. By the same token, affect has its place. Private emotions, like grief or love, personal anger or even joy, belong in the interior space of the private realm, and even there in specifically demarcated quarters. The long-standing suspicion of the crowd or mob derives in large part from the manifestation of emotion spilling over into public space, in an excess that is always read as atavistic and violent no matter how peaceful the crowd in actuality may be. Emotions do not belong in the public sphere of reasoned, dispassionate discourse, and have only a transitional or provisional place in interstitial institutions like schools, churches or indeed prisons, as we shall see in later chapters. Their function is to mediate the passage from the emotional, potentially unruly interior world of the individual subject to the public, articulate world of reason and deliberation. What has been understood as the 'separation of spheres' in modernity has its counterpart in the distribution of psychic and affective space also.

That the spatial disposition of literate modernity has achieved the status of a largely unanalysed common sense helps to explain the sense of the uncanny that was registered by Anglo-American travellers in Ireland. Irish performances of emotion in wakes, for example, or their peculiar capacity for contentment in misery or for combining labour and pleasure, could only strike the modernized observer as a bizarre and unruly lack of proper boundaries, as an unsettling fluctuation between inadequately differentiated psychic and economic states. Disciplined and trapped as they were within a subjectivity intimately formed by historicist assumptions about the nature of selfhood as about the development of society, it was impossible for them to register what they observed through anything but an imaginatively impoverished notion of Irish backwardness. For them, the Irish represented only an earlier stage of civilization, feudal or primitive, rather than a coeval alternative to their own cultural and psychic formation. Hence the uncanniness that haunted such encounters: travellers experienced Irish ways as spectres of what were for them earlier formations. If the uncanny is always 'something one does not know one's way about in', it is also that 'which leads back to what is known of old and long familiar'.[39] The uncanniness of keening is an effect of the temporal framing of modern experience, an instance of the 'return' of the primitive in the present.

It would be temptingly easy to analyse that sense of uncanniness by suggesting, for example, that what such observers were moved by was an obscure memory of their own childhood emotional states, prior to the discipline of the civilizing process. To do so, however, would be precisely to underwrite the developmental schema that framed their observations in the first place, and that relegated the Irish to the status of primitive children. Rather, we should understand the encounter as one between two incommensurable but coeval formations of material and psychic space, oral and literate, non-modern and modern. In this respect, their disturbance is related to the disturbance English political economists and social theorists felt at the contagious proximity of the 'Irish example', naturalized as racial backwardness but covertly feared as a political alternative. Accordingly, the evolutionary paradigm of the advent of literacy is of no help here, even where it registers the mixed nature of social worlds. Given the self-evidence to the modern scholar of such historicist paradigms, the space of orality can only be seen as one *lacking* features it has yet to attain, not as a present alternative conception of the world. While literacy is seen to give rise to the spatial organization of concepts and of mental life, one corresponding to the material and practical spatial differentiations of modernity, the description of the spaces of orality tends to imply only their non-differentiation and confinement within temporal and spatial localisms. Accordingly, even when it is recognized that most societies actually function through a mixture of orality and literacy, the oral element tends to be read as merely residual, rather than an active and often effectively recalcitrant counter-space of modernity. In order to elaborate an adequate picture of oral culture, we require a far thicker description of its spaces and practices and of the dynamic interface between literate and oral formations.

II

Something of the lability of Irish oral space, a lability that we have seen to be symbolized by that most Irish of orifices, the mouth, can be grasped from the descriptions of keening. So too can the unease that Irish practices of consumption and expression aroused. The post-Famine shock at the depopulation of Ireland resounds against the pre-Famine experience of population density on every scale. Not only was Ireland as a whole populated with virtually twice the numbers that it would contain for the century-and-a-half after the Famine; the spaces of oral culture seem to have been characterized furthermore by a willing pursuit and enjoyment of crowding. That crowding was already a feature of pre-Famine villages. E. Estyn Evans, the foremost historian of the rundale system, notes that:

Travellers a century or so ago tell us that villages with 50 or 60 houses were not uncommon ... The houses were clustered without plan or order (and never strung together end to end) generally in some sheltered hollow in the richest part of the townland, thought they might be disposed along a road with some semblance of regularity.[40]

Elsewhere, he cites a resonant metaphor for these unruly clusters of houses that seemed as if they had fallen 'in a shower from the sky'.[41] The close proximity both of dwellings in relation to one another and of people within them sustained an intimate oral culture and the 'promiscuity' that English observers found so scandalous. Rather than inhabiting discrete spaces devoted to one or other kind of sanctioned activity or mode of expression, the press of Irish bodies in contiguous space enabled rapid transitions of emotion and rhetorical mode and the undisciplined unfolding of argument, banter, joking and invective.

Hugh Dorian provides a detailed picture of such an evening gathering or 'throng' in a house in the village of Doaghbeg, Co. Donegal:

> Here a more important scene was enacted, that is to say the introduction and discussion of politics, and as it was always so well known to the neighbours from information got through the scholars, when and where the [school]master should be billeted for that night, so it happened long before darkness set in that some of these men who had a considerable distance to go were to be seen making headway to the place of rendezvous.
> This early start was a wise thought on their part and very necessary too, as well to avoid the inconvenience arising from the darkness as to have a chance of a sitting place secured in the house of meeting, of what may be called a parliament house on a small scale; in the event of, or expectation of a throng, more speed was put on so that the house was invaded and seats taken up long before the arrival of the master and his guide.[42]

There ensues a night of conversation whose topics range from local incident to 'the more serious discourses – the deep subjects' of history, politics and prophecy, much of it directed against the British colonial regime. Such spaces and rituals of nightly discussion were led by the schoolmaster and the local 'wiseheads', constituting an interface where literacy and orality meet. Many of the participants were accustomed to read books and newspapers, others were illiterate, but relied on remarkable feats of memory. Dorian's extended description of these meetings over several chapters testifies to their significance to the people while his own style, oscillating rapidly between the comic or satirical and the solemn, bears the impress of the peculiar mix of discourses that informed these oral 'parliaments'. Yet there was a level of serious discussion maintained, guaranteed, no doubt, by the direct impingement of the politics of dispossession on their own lives. Oral or literate, Dorian suggests, the Irish peasant knew how to interpret – or 'read' – his reality: 'The Donegal peasant has got all the historical learning he requires; he has his ancestors' history open before him every day he rises; it is exhibited in the large characters – the ocean, the mountains and his own state of poverty – and if he reads anything he must read how it is that he is there and why.'[43] The close association between dispossession and the desire for knowledge, however unsystematically transmitted, underlay the crowded spaces Dorian describes, the houses 'filled with anxious listeners, many of whom had neither stool nor chair to rest upon, so glad were they to be within hearing distance' and 'overcrowded so much that many in the rear had to stand and lean one against the other'.[44]

Against such a picture of Irish sociality, its density and noise, the approach of the peasant to the great house is thrown into stark relief, highlighting the terror that the silence and empty space of such houses, erected as symbols of domination achieved through ordered space, could induce:

To the complaints of some he [the Anglican cleric] would promise amendment, and in cases more difficult or seemingly so he ordered the applicant to appear before him at his own residence on a certain day and hour, a task which some of them would sooner not perform or have to undergo, for the reason that the noise of their footsteps on the gravel walk on approaching the half-door was a terror which made the frame tremulous, heating the blood in the first instance, but which soon runs chilly and cold through fear.

These trials partly overcome, a big mastiff, basking on the steps before the door is to be approached, who fails to show pity, and after that was to be encountered the trying, the venturesome attempt at pulling the bell-handle, and another electric shock ran through the frame as the clinking was heard from the inside, and soon a servant in livery, 'the butler', appears – who between contempt and anger manages to control himself within the bounds of a few questions in an angry tone.[45]

This intimidating approach to the great house seems to have composed a conscious function of their architecture and disposition, their isolation and elevation dominating both the landscape and the peasantry whose humiliation was integral to the maintenance of the colonial regime of distance and separation. At Strokestown House in Roscommon, for example, labourers, servants and tenants were obliged to approach the house to work or pay rent though a tunnel or sunken path, thus emphasizing their unsightliness and literalizing their subjugation. Dorian, indeed, reads the spatial terrors of the great house as a deliberate preliminary to interrogation, unfamiliarity and disorientation functioning as a kind of technique of 'sensory deprivation and over-stimulation' all too familiar to the contemporary reader:

> Now inside the hall, the door closes, but the captive's breathing seems to be faltering, the doctor understands as much and walks instantly on some pretension into another room for a little, leaving the terrified bashful creature to have a view at the weather glass, the papered walls or other curious things surrounding him, and so the sufferer's breathing returns more natural. The 'master' returns and his questions are entirely foreign from what was expected and different from the original petition, and the poor tenant is drifted into matter which he had no notion of but, trembling, he tries to give satisfactory answers to everything asked of him.
>   By such means, by such traps as these, the clergyman – the petty landlord – the wolf in sheep's clothing – in a very short time knows the history of every man and of everything in the place.⁴⁶

Dorian, who as a school-master moved between the oral and the literate communities and embodied their mixing, is an extraordinary observer of the phenomenology of social space and of the dynamics of the colonial regime. His mapping of the divide between the architecture of the colonizer and the intimate spaces of the colonized lucidly anticipates Frantz Fanon's analysis of the Manichaean and compartmentalized world of the colony, where the spacious ease and orderly streets of the colonizer confront 'a world without spaciousness' where 'men live … on top of each other, and their huts are built one on top of the other'.⁴⁷ Yet his analysis is far more intimate with and sympathetic to the denizens of the *clachan*. The isolation of the great house from the people obliges the master's interrogation of the tenant, estranged as the colonizer is from the 'occult spaces where the people dwell', to paraphrase Fanon.⁴⁸ The alienation of the great house, with its gravel surround and spacious vestibule, not to mention its guard dog and empty interior, is counterpointed by the dense clusters of houses that compose the village: 'so many and so closely packed were the dwellings that a stranger on entering the village would have [to make] a scrutinizing survey and withal be under the necessity of the direction of the guide to make his way to the occupier of a certain dwelling whom he wished to visit.'⁴⁹ The crowded embrace of these intimately 'knowable communities' defies colonial surveillance – and indeed, much of the chapter 'Villages' concerns the villagers' evasion of the intrusions of those twin arms of the colonial regime, the police and the bailiffs. We confront in the opposition of these two spaces a graphic architectural representation of what Robert Scally has nicely described as 'Divergent mental geographies, one graphic and the other oral, [that] governed the use of land simultaneously'.[50] Not only divergent, these geographies were deeply inimical to one another, and the process of modernization, or 'improvement', was aimed at extirpating the vulnerable spaces of the oral community as incompatible with the rational compartmentalization of labour and other human practices.

Noting that the 'absence of any discernible plan ... led visiting critics to regard the clachan as a reflection of the disordered Irish mentality', Estyn Evans has characterized both the spaces and the practices of Irish oral community with the colloquial term, 'through-otherness'.[51] 'Through-otherness' refers of course to the higgledy-piggledy arrangement of houses or cabins in the *clachan* and to the confused and parcelled holdings that constituted the porously bounded out-field, lands shared over time in increasingly complex distributions of good and bad land, upland for sheep and lowland for rushes, for example, that enabled the self-sustaining community to ensure a modicum of subsistence. As Scally puts it:

Traditional forms of cooperation among neighbors in labor and land-holding, like *meitheall* [shared or communal labor] or 'cooring', joint holdings in both land and animals, and 'booleying' [transhumance] were also adaptable to the struggle with scarcity and, perhaps equally as important, they could help to restrain the annual panics and the inevitable internal squabbling and 'defections' that came with them.[52]

The practices of the *clachan* were, in other words, pragmatic means to survive the depredations of a colonial settlement. But through-otherness can also aptly describe the mingling of different kinds of activity in the same space – the mingling of labour and pleasure, of work with drinking and song, that was to become anathema to the economically rational British and their index of the obdurate contentment of the Irish. Dorian again describes such mingling of work and pleasure, though at a moment when those traditions had already been to some extent appropriated by the bailiff in the form of 'duty days':

Word was passed round by the overseers and idlers that as soon as the turf would be all gathered in and the stack completed, the sports, that is to say the *races*, would commence. This induced all who were fond of the sport to work and make all others work and drive harder, and so by united exertions long before the time of the setting sun, men and horses were encamped on the 'strand', not indeed before the surrounding hillocks were already crowded with spectators, young and old from all directions far and near, to witness the sports.[53]

Dorian continues to describe the assembly of an ad hoc market-place on the strand, including both a licensed drinking tent with its written sign and a shebeen lurking in the margins, bearing witness to the mixture of commerce and pleasure, legality and customary practices, literacy and orality. Clearly such practices of mingling labour and enjoyment were not aimed at the maximization of efficiency, or at the rationalized division of labour that contemporary projects of improvement required. The *clachan*, with its apparently irrational and inefficiently confused divisions of space that resided in a principle of the commons and in popular memory rather than in written deeds and contracts, was anathema to the modernizing improver. It sustained an alternative ethic and a conception of life in common which, however diminished and impoverished by centuries of colonialism and dispossession, still had the power to embody a potentially contagious defiance of capitalism's logic at a time when capitalism itself was not yet assured of its inevitable dominance.

The contours of an oral culture are determined by the intermingling of its spaces and its practices. The typical figures of orality – rumour, noise, commotion – that signify its lability and unruliness from the perspective of the modern state connote equally the transgression of boundaries, the leakage of sound as material and as excessive signification out of its proper domain.[54] No wonder that the Irish wake, with its performance of laughter or banter, drinking and sedition in the place of mourning, and keening in the public place of sociality, became the type of such impropriety. That impropriety is spatial in a double sense. Psychically it refers to the unsettling lack of proper boundaries between different kinds of emotion – sorrow and outrage, mourning and mirth – or different kinds of utterance – personal grief and political complaint or jest – in the same place and at the same time. Materially, it designates the simultaneity of incompatible functions and practices in the same space or in close proximity to one another. Later, as we shall see, the separation of drinking from both politics and work became another crucial 'improving' project.

The condition of possibility of such impropriety is the mingling of bodies, and not just emotional states, in the same space. Accordingly, the logic of improvement aimed above all and in the first instance at the redistribution of Irish space. Asenath Nicholson's otherwise sympathetic account of Ireland in the Famine years constantly recurred to this need to reorder Irish domestic space: 'If', she exclaimed, 'sixty-two mud-wall huts … look a little untidy in an isle where castles and rich domains dot the green surface, why not substitute the comely cottage?'[55] Her account of Lord Hill's improvements at Gweedore, Co. Donegal, emphasized that this redivision of space and the establishment of proper, surveyed boundaries was the foundation of his scheme of improvement. It would eventually lead the Irish natives to become consumers of commodities and small proprietors in the gradual victory of what she clearly understood as a civilizing process whose sign for her was the emergence of the well ordered domestic space. The primitive if hospitable Irish were to become, through the reorganization of their social space, modern and properly bounded subjects, humans rather than savages. Through her enthusiasm for the project, nonetheless, the intensity of the resistance to the destruction of the *clachan* still speaks eloquently:

> The next difficult work was to place each tenant on his own farm and to do this every land-holder was served with notice 'to quit'. A surveyor had drawn maps, the tenants were assembled, and, the new allotments made according to his rent, all previous bargains were adjusted to mutual satisfaction. But the final allotments of land took three years to settle: they must look over the new farms, all in one piece, and cast lots for them ...
>
> When the houses were set up anew upon the farms, Lord George thought it advisable to have a few ten-acre farms fenced in on the wasteland. This was instantly opposed, for they did not want these divisions occupied, as by so doing it would thin out the crowds and break up the clanship too much. They would not be hired to make the ditches, and a 'fearless wanderer' could only do the work. Though sods of turf were hurled at him he kept on, but the contest was so sharp that it was settled at last by two policemen at night, who frightened away the assailants who had assembled to 'settle' the ditch. Peace was concluded, ditches were made, premiums were offered for the best specimens of clean cottages, which now had chimneys and windows, whitewashed walls, suitable beds and bedsteads, crockery and chairs, and the *manure heap* at a respectable distance, and all bearing the appearance of comfort.[56]

Lord Hill's improvement by consolidation and by the more geometric disposition of the small farms on his estate was being replicated during and after the Famine throughout Ireland. In Baltiboys, Co. Wicklow, for example, Mrs Elizabeth Smith, wife of the local landowner, recorded the gradual eviction of small-holders, the landless labourers and 'small tenants'. Her 'stated goals of depopulation and consolidation' were largely achieved as a result of the Famine, by way of deaths and assisted emigration, and were by no means untypical of developments throughout the country.[57] Depopulation approximated the dream of restoring a *terra nullius*, eviction and clearance of the cottiers aiming 'to remove all evidence of their existence, creating a *tabula rasa* on which a more orderly plan could be drawn'.[58]

The steady destruction of the *clachan* was, for all the inconveniences and conflicts endemic to it, profoundly resisted by those who dwelt in it. Nicholson was not alone in registering the commitment of the Irish to defending their practices and spaces. This resistance, it seems, was not solely about property or land rights, but about the specific forms of sociality that the *clachan* sustained. As Estyn Evans remarks,

we must recall the extreme reluctance with which the system was abandoned, the social benefits it conferred on members of the kin. The reforming landlord, Lord George Hill, comments that 'the pleasure the people feel in assembling and chatting together, made them consider the removal of the houses, from the clusters and hamlets in which they were generally built to the separate farms, a great grievance.' Another writer gives as the basis of the tenants' grievance, 'the recollection of nights of social concourse, of aid in sickness, of sympathy in joy and sorrow, of combined operations of defence against bailiff or gauger.'[59]

That other writer, Sir William Wilde, writing in 1853, captured better the complex social system and its integration of affect, political resistance and welfare that made the *clachan* worth defending and a grief to lose. As Breandán Mac Suibhne and David Dickson note, its destruction spelt the demise of the bearers of an oral tradition and of the complex of social relations it sustained and depended on:

The footloose people 'removed' by the Famine and its aftermath had included some of the most vital agents of cultural reproduction – fiddlers and pipers, singers and storytellers, hedge-schoolmasters, herbalists, wise women and, ironically, the prophecy-men themselves; and, above all, the Famine had reaped a swathe of the elderly, the great interpreters and adapters of tradition. The transformation of the landscape also had had a disheartening effect. The rundale 'villages' had been convivial stages for song, story, music and dance and conducive sites for the formation of hurling teams and harvesting parties.[60]

It is this adherence to a whole, complex set of social expectations and commitments, undergirded by the specific spaces that enabled the flourishing of an oral community with all its ramifications, that gets simplified into the British understanding of the Irish cottier's tenacious if primitive belief in common property in the land. It was an adherence to far more than common property, a struggle for the survival of a life in common which, preserved in and through scarcity, nonetheless maintained its utopian horizon in the vision of a life in common predicated on a shared abundance. The resistance to the destruction of the *clachan*, hampered as it everywhere was by poverty, isolation and eventually famine, was the crucible in which later struggles, like that of the Land League and eventually the largely rural war of decolonization, were forged and tested.[61] But the idea of a life in common, bound up with the persistence of an oral community and its practices, lives on in less dramatic ways also, in the dispersed and displaced, informal and ingrained habits of mind and of daily life that constitute the often still recalcitrant formations of Irish culture.

Figure 1 Ordnance Survey map of Kiltarsaghaun townland, 1840

In the course of the nineteenth century, the visible patterns of land use and distribution changed markedly in the struggle over improvement and land tenure, as any overlay of the familiar small but more or less geometric fields on the motley jigsaw of *clachan* and outfield dramatically displays. Yet Irish land-holding never entirely attained the projected capitalist rationality of English models: Irish recalcitrance in the form of what was understood as an obstinate adherence to the commons produced rather a mode of small-farm peasantry that ultimately furnished 'the nation-building class' and counterpointed the large cattle-grazing farms that otherwise dominated a depopulated landscape.[62] This new, often rigidly stone-walled closure of rural space and the scattering of small cottages at considerable distance from one another spelt the break-down of oral 'through-otherness' and the close and crowded proximities that enabled it (Figures 1, 2 and 3). Post-Famine space and its new enclosures offer a psychic as well as a cadastral map of Irish transformations, one so familiar that its features have come to seem traditional and even 'essentially' Irish. The segmentation of the land into such discrete parcels, the distancing of former communities into isolated homesteads, and not only the catastrophic loss of population to famine, disease and emigration, subtended the melancholy silence of the nineteenth-century landscape. But that process of enclosure and fixed partitioning of space accompanied a partially achieved inner partitioning of the Irish psyche: the encryption of memories of the Famine, the closing of the labile mouth and its disciplining, the decline of practices like waking and keening that were the indices of a less proper sociality, accompanied a new and melancholy sense of propriety and punishment. As Kevin Whelan notes, 'A certain amount of iron entered the Irish soul in the Famine holocaust'.[63]

These dour consequences of the Famine's destruction were anticipated even as it ended. Writing at a moment he recognized to be 'a transition state', Sir William Wilde in 1851 powerfully and at length recorded the process of destruction of Irish popular culture that the Famine entailed and its intricate relation to the troubled silence with which this chapter opened. The fatal effects of the Famine were, for him, inseparable from the inroads of the modern institutions of a governmentality guided by political economists, to which, as we have seen, the transformation of subsistence crisis into catastrophe were largely due. Wilde's painful lament is worth quoting at length:

The great convulsion which society of all grades has here lately experienced, the failure of the potato crop, pestilence, famine and a most unparalleled extent of emigration, together with bankrupt landlords, pauperizing poor-laws, grinding officials, and decimating workhouses, have broken up the very foundations of social intercourse, have swept away the established theories of political economists, and uprooted many of our long-cherished opinions ... The hum of the spinning wheel has long since ceased to form an accompaniment to the colleen's song; and that song itself, so sweet and fresh in cabin, field, or byre, has scarcely left an echo in our glens, or among the hamlets of our land. The Shannaghie and the Callegh in the chimney corner, tell no more the tales and legends of other days. Unwaked, *unkeened*, the dead are buried, where Christian burial has at all been observed; and the ear no longer catches the mournful cadence of the wild Irish cry, wailing on the blast, rising up to us from the valleys, or floating along the winding river, when

> 'The skies, the fountains, every region near,
> Seemed all one mutual cry.'

Figure 2 Ordnance Survey map of Kiltarsaghaun townland, 1889

... In this state of things, with depopulation the most terrific which any country ever experienced, on the one hand, and the spread of education, and the introduction of railroads, colleges, industrial and other educational schools, on the other, – together with the rapid decay of the Irish vernacular, in which most of our legends, romantic tales, ballads, and bardic annals, the vestiges of Pagan rites, and the relics of fairy charms were preserved, – can superstitious practices continue to exist?

But these matters of popular belief and folk-lore, these rites and legends, and superstitions, were after all, *the poetry of the people*, the bond that knit the peasant to the soil, and cheered and solaced many a cottier's fireside. Without these, on the one side, and without proper education and well-directed means of partaking of and enjoying its blessings, on the other, and without rational amusement besides, he will, and must, and has in many instances, already become a perfect brute.[64]

Figure 3 Aerial photograph of Clare Island, c.1960

Wilde presciently understands the Famine as a social trauma whose costs are to be redeemed by the governmental institutions of modernity, not least by education and by a distinct sphere of recreation ('rational amusement') that will henceforth be kept separate from that of labour. On the very threshold of Ireland's modernization, he momentarily grasps the ways in which modernity both creates and exploits the catastrophes that dissolve one formation of society in order to impose a new direction upon it. Of course, for Wilde the folklorist, doctor and man of letters, the memory of the culture that has gone down in the Famine will become part of the repertoire of knowledge, the 'rational amusement' of the 'properly educated' and 'well-directed' modern Irish subject, a tradition that will be the object of aesthetic pleasure among the traces of a history that has moved on. A similar elegiac sense of the past, and a conviction of its melancholy residues, notoriously left its mark on the Irish literary tradition.[65]

III

But such forms of memory, related as they are to the elegiac aesthetic of modern ethnography, do not monopolize the possibilities of remembrance, powerful as their effects may have been.[66] Given the erasure even by nationalism itself of the culture and spaces of Irish subalternity, it is perhaps salutary to end this chapter by resurrecting one moment at which Irish customs and practices were actually apprehended as the bases for potentially viable alternatives to industrial capital. As we have seen, the effort to inculcate in the Irish a respect for property was intimately linked to the need to instill capitalist labour discipline and the desire to produce for and participate in a market economy. Irish recalcitrance to those ends was embedded in the forms of land-holding and subsistence economy that the potato crop enabled. Irish food ways sustained an alternative economy and an alternative culture, a culture of orality based on contiguity and proximity rather than abstraction and circulation. Until the catastrophe of the Famine and the massive proliferation of images of destitution and misery, the predominant construction of Irish conditions and habits had to a considerable degree emphasized the indecent phenomenon of Irish *contentment.* As one Ordnance Surveyor put it in the 1830s: 'An apathy and indifference to the accumulation of wealth seems to pervade almost the whole population, apparently happy and contented with their condition and nearly upon equality with each other. They evince no ambition or desire of independence.'[67] Despite the cultural antipathy of such observers to the lack of a work ethic among the Irish, it is clear that they saw in the cultural formation that allowed such contentment a provocative if bewildering counter-principle to the inculcation of capitalist values. As we have already seen, the anxiety of social reformers and political economists is not that the English working classes will be repelled by Irish savagery, but that they will be infected or seduced by their example. But we need to be careful not to allow, once again, the image of the Irish as passive bearers of an infection to obscure the possibility that the anxieties that attended Irish migration were political in the fullest sense.

Even down to the present, historical accounts of Irish labour in Britain are marked by an eloquent contradiction. On the one hand, in continuity with the terms used by Victorian writers, the Irish migrants are depicted as a circulating mass of unskilled and socially and politically backward labour, 'a turbulent mass of starvelings' as English labour historian G.D.H. Cole described the London Irish of the 1830s.[68] In such representations, the Irish – backward, peasant interlopers in the more advanced urban centres of industrial Britain – are responsible not only for 'undercutting English standards' of wages and living, but for retarding political development with their non-modern habits and susceptibility to demagoguery.[69] At the same time, it is noted by almost all labour historians that the Irish often represented the most advanced and radical elements in the burgeoning labour movement. This was so not only among the leadership and the intellectuals of the Chartists, with figures like Bronterre O'Brien and Feargus O'Connor, but also among the lower echelons of the movement. Eric Hobsbawm speculates, all too briefly, that the radical contribution of the Irish may have derived from their lack of investment in British social institutions.[70] Perhaps a more positive way to describe that lack of investment is the suggestion that the Irish migrants brought with them an alternative conception of social institutions, or a conception of an alternative to the degradation of urban industrial life that was derived from their own experience of small-holding husbandry in collective relationships, however impoverished, that systems like rundale sustained. There is no doubt that the Irish practices underlying such a conception of a transformative alternative to industrialism and private ownership were widely seen as in potentially revolutionary antagonism to the regime of capital: every inquiry into Irish conditions and virtually every political economic text asserts as much. Even the liberal John Stuart Mill expostulates on the 'essentially anarchical system' that is cottierism, much as Malthus some forty years earlier had predicted the socially subversive potential of Irish culture.[71] The rhetoric of moral infection appears in this context as the displacement of a not unreasonable fear of a quite articulate political contagion, a contagion that manifested itself time and again between English radicals and Irish Republicans, Chartists and Repealers, socialists and Fenians, from the 1790s to the 1860s.

The clearest instance of the convergence of an English Spencean radicalism with an Irish Republican agrarianism appeared in the Chartist Land Plan of the 1840s. Advocated by Feargus O'Connor, son of a radical United Irish family and possibly a former associate of the Whiteboys, the plan sought to resettle working-class families on collectively purchased land in communities of Chartist smallholders. It was explicitly based on Irish models.[72] Historians have tended to be sceptical as to the practicality of the plan as a whole, and especially of the possibility that settling families on four-acre plots would furnish them with sufficient means to life. O'Connor himself wrote the manual on small farms and spade-husbandry which accompanied the plan, published first as a series of articles in the Chartist newspaper, the *Northern Star*, and then collected in a small book. His estimates of the productivity of the suggested four-acre plots per family seem to be projected from the even smaller acreage on which Irish families survived.[73] While the assumptions of the English historians tend to be based on the large wheat-producing farms familiar to them, his proposal was expressly based not only on the Irish practice of spade tilling, but also on the extensive, though not exclusive, cultivation of potatoes. While critical of 'the exclusive use of the potato as an article of food' in Ireland, O'Connor continued to see the potato as 'indispensable to the complete working of the small farm system, and … peculiarly adapted to spade husbandry'.[74] O'Connor, in part through experiments on his own farm in Ireland, in part through observation of the cottiers, had grasped that the combination of spade cultivation and the potato crop was capable of redeeming waste land and increasing its fertility.[75]

At the same time as he prized the potato and made it the foundation of the Land Plan, O'Connor critiqued the overvaluation of wheat, tying its domination of agriculture precisely to its serviceability as a storable and transportable commodity that we explored in the previous chapter:

If I was to classify the produce of the land according to the relative value of the several crops, I certainly should not have given the preference to wheat, inasmuch as, in my opinion, it is less profitable than many other crops. However, the notoriety that it has obtained as an article of importance in the money-market in consequence of our artificial mode of life, as well as the necessity for its general use as an article of food, and which latter necessity arises merely from the fact that wheat can be preserved for many years, while the working classes generally would not be so dependent upon it for support if they had a sufficiency of land whereby their food might be diversified, and good substitutes found in many, very many things, which, however, being for the most part perishable, cannot be brought into the wholesale market as competitors against wheat, which will keep for many years in stock if well made and well thatched, and for many more if kiln-dried and well managed in the warehouse.[76]

O'Connor's critique of the relation of wheat to the capitalist division of labour did not aim at substituting the monoculture of the potato for the political economic hegemony of grain, but at the diversification of working-class food within a context of reclaimed abundance.[77] Rather than attributing Irish poverty to the culture of the potato, O'Connor anticipated Mill and others in arguing vigorously for fixity of tenure and deriving Irish immiseration from the growth of large farms:

> As it is necessary that I should answer the sophistries of those ignorant parties who would urge the state of Ireland in opposition to the small farm plan, I may here remind them that every advance in the large farm system has led to increased pauperism in Ireland, while it has contributed to an increased glut of Irish labourers in the English market … [I]t should be understood that that my system of small farms would be incomplete unless based upon the principle of a real 'fixity of tenure'; the want of which in Ireland operates more injuriously against the small farmer than it does against the large farmer.[78]

In fact, O'Connor's Land Plan, though advocated in England for the English working classes, had its place among a long series of works proposing fixity of tenure as a solution for Irish misery and unrest, from William Conner to Isaac Butt, which eventually converged with those of Mill and Gladstone.[79]

O'Connor's Land Plan was, thus, not a reproduction of the *clachan* as such, but a projection from its communal, non-capitalist forms into the conditions of small-holding as an alternative to capitalist labour. Those elements of the *clachan* that owed their features to immiseration – the through-otherness of tiny segments of communal land reclaimed from otherwise useless terrain, the monocultural crop, the crowding – give way to a more expansive vision of the 'mutual dependence' of small rural communities, predicated on O'Connor's long-standing belief in 'the poor man's right to an abundance of everything'.[80] Unlike the English advocates of fixity of tenure, therefore, O'Connor aimed neither at the pacification of Ireland nor at the eventual evolution of capitalist farming through peasant proprietorship. Rather, the Land Plan represented a radical alternative to the emerging system of industrial capitalism and had both an immediate practical element and a utopian dimension.[81] In consequence of personalized attacks upon it and upon O'Connor himself by other Chartists like Bronterre O'Brien and Robert Gammage, one of Chartism's earliest and most influential historians, the Land Plan has been much misunderstood and pilloried as impractical and distracting from the goals of the movement.[82] More recent assessments, however, have clarified that O'Connor's scheme did not aim to return all the urban and manufacturing working classes to the land, but rather to raise the general level of wages by reducing the surplus labour pool at a time of general economic crisis and providing a comparative measure of the value of labour. By furnishing those workers who might otherwise form part of the 'surplus' pool of labour with an alternative, and by demonstrating the productivity of the independent small farmer's work, O'Connor aimed 'to establish the real value of labour in the natural labour-market, below which the labourer will not work in the artificial market'.[83]

But there was also a utopian element to the Plan that exceeded its immediate practical import. In every detail, that utopian aspect can be seen to have been projected out of Irish conditions: from the size of the farms to the value placed on the potato as the foundational crop, from the emphasis on spade-husbandry rather than ploughing to the proposal for the building of clay cabins on each plot, O'Connor draws on his experience of Irish cottiers and their modes of subsistence on the most marginal land and under the worst of conditions.[84] It is not that he seeks to reproduce those conditions in England; it is rather that he projects from their forms of survival a utopian model based on the transformation of their conditions of scarcity into those of abundance. Again and again, he insists that the misery of the Irish does not derive from their mode of life but from their oppression and exploitation. What they furnish is the grounds for a belief in an alternative to capitalism which, as we have seen, political economists and politicians feared that the Irish did indeed represent. O'Connor thus inverts the political rhetoric that uses Irish misery as a means to castigate Irish ways and draws from their forms of living a critique of what both English and Irish workers had suffered, 'the havoc, the desolation, the persecution, and wholesale murders committed by the capitalists in England'.[85] This is perhaps nowhere clearer than in O'Connor's approach to labour. While recommending a fundamentally Republican principle of tenure and cooperation – 'the co-operative system of labour with individual responsibility and possession' – that resembles the collectivity of the *clachan*, he estimates the system as a whole would permit a family to support itself on 180 days' labour.[86] The notorious idleness of the Irish and their contentment in the face of scarcity converts here into an anti-capitalist principle of freedom from labour. Long before the passage of the 10 Hours Act, at a time when six days' labour per week was the norm, O'Connor's Plan proposes a vastly reduced subjection to work within a calculus of abundant sufficiency.

While O'Connor's scheme could in some ways be considered 'the most extended development of the principle of Chartist self-provision, promising not only escape from the wage contract but also total independence from all the subordinating relationships of capitalist social life', it was not what later historians would consider a 'socialist' alternative.[87] The Plan was not an attempt at land collectivization or nationalization nor, above all, did it propose that working-class emancipation could only come about by way of embracing and passing through the capitalist means of production. It was not in this sense a 'progressive' project. It can better be understood as a leftist Republican alternative to a capitalism that had yet to achieve uncontested dominance, and as a utopian projection from Irish cultural and economic formations that had long resisted the regime of capitalist modernity that sought to extirpate them. In that respect, it belongs with traditions of Irish radicalism that emerge from agrarian traditions of resistance and re-emerge in popular movements like Fenianism and in the predominantly syndicalist Irish labour agitation of the late nineteenth and early twentieth century. Alien to the socialist and Marxist politics that arose in the urban industrial centres of Britain and Northern Europe, the radicalism of Irish traditions has remained largely illegible to them.[88] That illegibility has contributed to the negative historical assessment of the Land Plan and to scepticism as to its potential as an alternative to capitalist social relations.

Opinion at the time was divided, but certainly tended to take the scheme rather more seriously. Mill considered it both sound and viable, and even recommended it as a model for peasant proprietorship in Ireland.[89] Others, and in particular those associated with the advocacy of free trade and anti-Corn Law agitation, were profoundly antagonistic. Alexander Somerville, the Radical journalist who travelled in Ireland in 1847, used the occasion of the Famine to launch a vehement and extended attack on the Land Plan in his *Letters from Ireland*, erroneously fearing it to be a covert prelude to 'the Chartists' "true" aim of land nationalisation and the confiscation of property'. He evidently perceived the Irish example that lay behind this radical project and exploited the catastrophe of the Famine to undermine public support for it.[90] The British government in turn clearly took the plan seriously enough to mount a steady war of attrition on it through largely legal means that eventually destroyed it. As Eileen Yeo put it, in her study of the legal manoeuvres of the government:

The Chartist search, over ten long years, for an adequate and legal form of national organization reveals what a potent shaping and ultimately deforming influence the State was, whether it was showing an iron fist, as custodian of public order suppressing Chartist militancy, or wearing a velvet glove, as framer of legislation giving legitimacy and protection to selected forms of working-class association. The land scheme collapsed, exhausted by its attempts to clear the hurdles of the law and debilitated by internal difficulties.[91]

In the wake of this defeat, the tenor of the attack on the plan shifted from scepticism as to its practical viability to the more ideological ground of the historical impropriety of the plan as an alternative to industrial capitalism. The tragic coincidence of the failure of the Irish potato crop with the defeat of Chartism and its alternative visions led to the common assessment that both Irish ways and Chartist radicalism were inevitably doomed to historical obsolescence. The Famine, appearing in retrospect as a predictable catastrophe caused by doomed social conditions, in some ways sealed the triumph of the historicist approach that was emerging at that very moment and that received, as we have seen, a major impetus from the anomaly of Irish conditions. Accordingly, an alternative that drew on those conditions suffered a simultaneous and thorough defeat.

Antagonism to the Land Plan continued to be couched for over a century in the terms of this unexamined historicist logic. Cole is both typical and summary of this tendency:

The basic truth was that, in the 'thirties and 'forties, capitalism was a rapidly developing system which was in a position to increase the total wealth of the country at an unprecedented rate. Its possibilities, so far from being exhausted, were immense; and the leaders of capitalist industry possessed the ruthless confidence of men assuredly advancing towards new triumphs of productive technique. Anything which endangered these developments was, to their minds, anti-social and unprogressive; and though many of them had democratic sympathies, they would stand for nothing that would check the speed of economic advance. They were right in saying that, if the workers would but abide patiently the passing of the immediate crisis, and await the blessings which would follow upon the repeal of the Corn Laws, much of the prevailing misery would disappear, and the real standard of living would rise – provided that they were allowed to have their way in opposing all artificial restrictions on the pace of economic advance.[92]

From this perspective, O'Connor's plan can only seem a nostalgic and distracting dream for the working classes 'of escape into the blessed country which they idealized from their own memories of childhood or their parents' tales'.[93]

Dorothy Thompson's critique of this kind of evaluation of Chartism and the Land Plan focuses sharply on the historicist fallacy and valuably questions its thesis as to the inevitability of capitalism's triumph:

Those aspects of the Chartist movement which were based on the defence of 'artisan values' – the independence of the craftsman, his control over his personal environment, the defence of craft standards – or on the desire felt by many factory workers to leave the industrial districts and join communities of rural or semi-rural producers, are seen as backward-looking, peasant-inspired, and are often blamed on the Irish origins of Feargus O'Connor. In this socialist

teleology, many of the most highly-charged and powerful impulses behind the protests of the common people are seen as manifestations of 'false consciousness'
...
To the people in the manufacturing districts of Britain in the earlier nineteenth century, however, the truths of political economy were not self-evident. Experience of industrialization in other parts of the world since has shown that there is not a single unique road along which industrializing nations must travel. If we are to listen sympathetically to the voice of Chartism, we should perhaps set aside some preconceptions about historical absolutes and listen to the contemporary debate without being too fixated on our *ex post facto* knowledge of its outcome.[94]

The historicist commitment to progress bows to the verdict of the 'actually existing' at the cost of imposing a singular and determinate teleology on the past and, in doing so, betrays the struggles of the past to realize alternative possibilities, grounded as they were in the social and cultural formations that were the available and often fertile resources of anti-capitalist movements.

Like the actual alternative practices that were its kin if not its model, the Land Plan went down to an orchestrated historical defeat. But the defeat of any given alternative may entail not so much its silencing as its survival in the encrypted forms of the popular memory, from which it emerges again as a differently articulated and newly oriented ideology. Only the most extravagant stretch of the imagination could trace in the actual conditions of the Famine-era peasantry, in the *clachan* or cottierism, a realized alternative to either a semi-feudal colonialism or industrial capitalism. That is not the argument pursued here. But these modes of quite material survival, forged in the damaged conditions of a colonized and ravaged people, gave rise to popular practices of the commons that embodied a conception and an 'ethic' of mutuality, of hospitality and of 'indifference to the accumulation of wealth' that was admitted to be inassimilable to the capitalist principles in whose name its destruction was undertaken. In the wake of that destruction, the reformation of the Irish by the inculcation of the virtues of political economy or domestic propriety was counterpointed by a mutation of that alternative conception of the social, preserved and transformed by both the memory and the continuing practices of colonial domination. After the Famine, in the persisting social struggles against eviction and exploitation that inform the Land War, Fenianism and the syndicalist traditions of the Irish labour movement, an alternative memory of the past was mobilized, nurtured by oral practices that lived on in the very spaces that were designed to suppress them. That memory, inscribed in the very material institutions of modernity, proved capable of apprehending in the damaged past a repertoire of unrealized possibility rather than the outlived prehistory of the present. In her back-handed elegy to the Irish tenantry of Gweedore, written even as they and the spaces that had sustained their culture were being subjected to rationalization and 'improvement', Asenath Nicholson inadvertently captured that non-linear process of survival, the living on of oral practices in other spaces:

> The Rundale system, when disturbed, brought new difficulties to these people; it broke up their clusters of huts, and the facilities of assembling nights, to tell and hear long stories; and they must tumble down their cabins, which were of loose stones; and the owner of the cabin hired a fiddler, which no sooner known, than the joyous Irish are on the spot. Each takes a stone or stones upon his or her back (for women and children are there). They dance at intervals – the fiddler animates them on while daylight lasts, and then the night is finished by dancing.[95]

In the very moment of its 'disturbance', the oral culture took its staggered flight into the space of the improvement that intended to suppress it. We may retrieve there a figure for the ways in which that oral culture would re-emerge, bearing both its 'joyous' potential and its damage, as a subversive and unruly survivor in the recesses of the architectures of modernity.

CHAPTER 3

Counterparts: the public house, masculinity and temperance nationalism

I

The post-Famine Irish landscape offered a melancholy vista. The division of large parts of a once densely populated land into small farms and isolated homesteads perpetuated the silence that followed on mass death and emigration. As many have noted, the Irish rural scene that is so often taken to be traditional was in fact the product of the latter half of the nineteenth century, as both the British administration and Irish nationalists struggled over the fate of the land and the intractable differences between Irish and English relations to land and property became encoded as marks of the antagonism of Celt and Anglo-Saxon, colonized and colonizer. Even in the wake of land settlements predicated on the idea that security of tenancy would develop a capitalist sense of property and work, Irish material and cultural formations swerved away from the norms assumed in English notions of modernity and 'improvement'. The enclosure of the Irish commons and the destruction of the *clachan* eventually took forms that were not anticipated by British political economists or administrators at the time of the Famine. Ireland's economy remained predominantly agricultural, but deviated from the pattern of landlord, capitalist farmer and labouring proletariat that Charles Trevelyan and others had hoped to induce. The small family farm rather than the large capitalist enterprise emerged as the dominant form of land-holding, while grazing rather than grain production became the principal agricultural activity. In cultural terms, the most striking impact of the Great Hunger and of the post-Famine emergence of these small family holdings was the institution of primogeniture and its concomitant effects: an economically prudent emphasis on late marriage on the part of the oldest son and high rates of migration or emigration on the part of younger children. Gone was the simple subdividing of rented plots or the expansion of cultivation onto more and more marginal land; gone with them the early marriages and high rates of reproduction. The Irish population remained, in consequence both of massive emigration and of late marriage, astonishingly stable for well over a century, scarcely ever exceeding four million and eliciting gloomy speculation on the 'vanishing Irish'.[1] Notoriously, these new social conditions helped to produce a singularly conservative and sexually inhibiting form of Catholicism, which emphasized celibacy and modesty and the increasing segregation of the sexes into separate spheres.

These demographic and cultural patterns are well documented and have been much discussed, both in scholarly study and in literary and other aesthetic works. It would seem as if the enclosure of those vestiges of the commons that sustained the space of Irish orality, together with the traumatic catastrophe of the Famine that brutally consolidated the transformation, led also to the closing of that most labile orifice, the Irish mouth. Sealed like a crypt around the unspeakable disaster of mass death and dispossession, the Irish mouth bit down on the melancholy remainders of a once vital oral culture. The word, as Patrick Kavanagh was to put it, had become clay, and that within 'the grip of irregular fields'.[2] The division of physical space into bounded parcels resonates in psychic space also, establishing new thresholds and barriers in the material and imaginary life of the subject. Almost by definition, modernization – even in the anomalous trajectories that it took in colonial spheres like Ireland – requires the division and regulation of space. In this, as we have seen, it seeks to contain and subdue the spaces and practices of orality that are characterized by a much greater degree of mixing and by the transgression of what are, from the perspective of modernity, proper psychic as well as material boundaries. The modern subject, disciplined to inhabit and to move among the discrete spaces of civil and political society, can only regard the formations of pleasure and pain that an oral culture exhibits as unruly and, inevitably, backward, as formations that await corrective development into the full, critical consciousness that modernity and literacy bring with them. Understanding development as the instrument that raises an oral culture from its embeddedness in the indistinction of an atavistic or mythic bog, that subject cannot easily grasp the damage that modernization as a process inflicts. Nor, committed as s/he is to the idea that progress entails letting go of the past, can s/he conceive of the ways in which the practices and affects of oral space may in fact survive the damage inflicted upon it. Yet perhaps, as Kavanagh also puts it, 'some of the saga defied the draught in the open tomb / And was not blown'.[3] Something lives on in and through the encryptments of damage.

It is to the peculiar ways in which orality lives on even in damaged forms and even in the form of damage that this chapter is dedicated. No stereotype more closely links the Irish with an oral practice than their association with drinking. It is a complex stereotype, in that what began as a 'negative identity' has proven capable of being 'transformed into a positive group identity'.[4] Such a transformation is not merely irrational defiance. It retains the trace of modalities and sites of pleasure for which drinking may merely be the metonym. Drinking was, as we have seen already, an entirely adequate signifier for oral culture and its practices: itself a form of oral consumption, it also occasioned and embodied the lability of the oral. It promoted an indecorous mingling of affect and a promiscuous interpenetration of spaces even as its ingestion in the mouth relayed with utterances that made that orifice the medium of unseemly emotional display or improper and seditious speech. Drinking was the synecdoche for the wake as the wake was the synecdoche for the improprieties of Irish culture as a whole. As such, both are the indices of the modes of contiguity between pleasure and pain, merriment and mourning, damage and survival, that seem to be inseparable features of the oral. Intrinsic characteristics of the pathological subject, played upon by the impulses of need and desire, these volatile affects obey a different logic than is dictated by modernity.

And yet, recalcitrant as drinking is to the capitalist disciplines of labour and to the ethical formation of the modern subject, it is a practice that was gradually regulated and incorporated by modern institutions. Targeted, as we shall see in greater detail, by successive waves of the temperance movement, and by a series of governmental initiatives like licensing and the limiting of hours of business, drinking became one of the objects of modern discipline.[5] At the same time, into the times and spaces of its regulation, into the public house with its licensing hours and the enclosure that made it a public space with private features, drinking bore with it some of the habits and codes of other times and places. It is one of the singular modes in which oral space lives on with all the ambiguities of damaged pleasure. In one respect, it may have been a paradoxical aid to the transformation of the values and mores of rural society, adding a further twist to the paradoxical forms in which Ireland modernized. Richard Stivers argues that the emergence of what he terms 'avunculate' bachelor drinking groups in post-Famine Ireland was crucial in forging a new mode of celibate masculinity that both compensated for and enabled the imposition of stricter sexual mores and the circumscription of male access to land. Stivers claims plausibly that one can trace 'a historically specific type of Irish male drinking for the period from the 1870s through the 1930s, though its beginning can be dated to the 1840s and the rise of a new Irish family system'.[6] He goes on to argue that 'hard drinking' represented a form of 'cultural remission, that is, a release from the difficulty of adhering to the dominant symbols of the culture by which personality is socially constructed. It was a release from sexual puritanism'.[7] At once an expression of and an antidote for economic and emotional anomie, drinking rather than sexuality became the principal site for the performance of masculinity. Increasingly practised within the closed space of the public house, this new mode of masculine drinking contributed to the restriction of the more fluid and gender-mingling forms of pleasure characteristic of the *clachan* and of customs like wakes and 'duty days'. Male hard drinking was a formation determined by a specific form of modernization that overtook post-Famine Ireland. But it was also a means by which certain practices customary in the less spatially and occupationally segregated oral culture were transmuted within the institutional architecture of modernity. In practices like treating or the round system that reflect a surviving moral economy, as well as in specific oral performances like storytelling and banter, the non-modern pleasures of oral space continue to haunt the public house.

This chapter explores the peculiar ambiguities that emerge from the paradoxical function of drinking as a means of enabling modernization that nonetheless retains certain practices of an oral culture whose formations have always been problematic if not recalcitrant for capitalist modernity. In drinking and its regulated spaces, the non-modern enters into modernity, bearing with it rhythms, pleasures and claims to a different moral economy that at times constitute a counter-modern set of practices. Damaged and damaging as they are, these represent – in ways common to all the partial pleasures that live on in the pathological body – the utopian projection of alternative desires that cannot be fully realized within the enclosure of regulation and the restrictive disciplines of labour and exchange. Perhaps perversely, I would read in Irish drinking and its performances of a masculinity defined otherwise than by paternity, labour and economic prudence, not just a delusory compensation for anomic life, but a deliberate interruption of the constraining rhythms of modernity by something akin to what Paul Gilroy has defined, in the context of the music of the Black diaspora, as a 'counterculture of modernity'. In its performance, Gilroy claims:

The wilfully damaged signs which betray the resolutely utopian politics of transfiguration ... partially transcend modernity, constructing both an imaginary and anti-modern past and a postmodern yet-to-come. This is not a counter-discourse but a counterculture that defiantly reconstructs its own critical, intellectual, and moral genealogy in a partially hidden public sphere of its own.[8]

In the 'partially hidden public sphere' of the public house, something also goes on that is difficult for discipline to recuperate fully and which stands as the sign of desires for another future that is not convertible into the temporal logic of historicism. Not quite amounting to a 'counterculture', its counter-modern elements retain the projected imagination of unruly pleasures as old and as out of place as the medieval Land of Cockaigne, as askew to normalized temporalities as the carnival and the wake. Stivers recognizes that even in the potential self-destructiveness of Irish intoxication there lay historically a form of rebellion against English rule and the civilizing process it imposed. Citing Horkheimer and Adorno, he sees in intoxication a rebellion against the path of 'obedience and labor' that modernity prescribes as the way to happiness; even the 'dread of losing the self and of abrogating together with the self the barrier between one-self and the other life ... is intimately associated with a promise of happiness that threatened civilization in every moment'.[9] A sign of the irrevocable destructiveness of that civilizing process and of resistance to it, drinking embraces the damage with the pleasures it occasions in defiance of a rationality whose irrational destructiveness is not apprehended in memory alone, but in the very diminished forms of life that its spaces and rhythms require.

Surprisingly, given the centrality of drinking to Irish culture, we lack an extensive historical or ethnographic literature on its social history or on the spaces of consumption – the shebeens, spirit grocers, ale-houses, taverns and public houses – that represented different modes and eras of regulation.[10] Least of all do we have any systematic account of the differential relationship of the pub and the practices it houses to the spaces of work and politics, domestic and public life, that were simultaneously emerging in nineteenth- and early-twentieth-century Ireland. Yet the pub and its pleasures permeate the fictional literature as well as memoirs and autobiographies in ways that generally suggest how inseparable the oral practices of drinking and eloquence are in the Irish cultural imaginary. Literature is not empirical history and yet for that very reason may more effectively put in play the complex constellations of labour and affect, pain and pleasure, public and private space that compose the daily life of a culture, in all its contradictions and undercurrents. For turn-of-the-century Ireland, there is perhaps no more deliberately diagnostic literary work than James Joyce's *Dubliners* which offered almost programmatically an 'anatomy', to borrow Cheryl Herr's rich term, of colonial Irish culture.[11] Central to Joyce's representations of Dublin life, and integrated with its religious, political and commercial life, is Irish drinking as it takes place in private houses, political meeting rooms, hotels or public houses. More than any writer in any genre, in texts paradoxically imbued with and structured by orality, Joyce captures the symbolic resonances of Irish oral culture as it survives in the modern colonial city, in drinking, eating, singing and, notoriously, in talking. The caustic naturalism of the stories is saturated with his awareness of the anomie – or 'paralysis' – that afflicts the colonized, the 'gratefully oppressed', as he refers to the populace at one point.[12] That emphasis, in keeping with Joyce's own, has generally been the focus of critical readings of the volume. In what follows, however, I want to track though one story a different trajectory, the peculiar dialectic of pleasure and damage, resistance and dependence, that Joyce anatomizes in Irish drinking and in Irish politics and culture as a whole.

II

The man returned to the lower office and sat down again at his desk. He stared intently at the incomplete phrase: In no case shall the said Bernard Bodley be... and thought how strange it was that the last three words began with the same letter. The chief clerk began to hurry Miss Parker, saying she would never have the letters typed in time for the post. The man listened to the clicking of the machine for a few minutes and then set to work to finish his copy. But his head was not clear and his mind wandered away to the glare and rattle of the public house. It was a night for hot punches. He struggled on with his copy, but when the clock struck five he had still fourteen pages to write. Blast it! He longed to bring his fist down on something violently. He was so enraged that he wrote Bernard Bernard instead of Bernard Bodley and had to begin again on a clean sheet.

He felt strong enough to clear out the whole office single-handed. His body ached to do something, to rush out and revel in violence. All the indignities of his life enraged him ... Could he ask the cashier privately for an advance? No, the cashier was no good, no damn good: he wouldn't give an advance ... He knew where he would meet the boys: Leonard and O'Halloran and Nosey Flynn. The barometer of his emotional nature was set for a spell of riot.[13]

In this brief scene from the story 'Counterparts', Joyce draws out the complex rhythms of alienated labour in early-twentieth-century Dublin, linking the repetitive functions performed by the legal clerk Farrington with his sensation of humiliation, frustration and rage. Male rage and violence at the conditions of a specifically *literate* work in an office with which, apparently, his very bodily frame is at odds, are counterpoised with the heterotopic oral space of the public house, with its odours and sensations and the prospect of homosocial conviviality and even misrule or 'riot'. As the story unfolds, Farrington indulges in a brief witticism at the expense of the Northern Irish head of this clearly British firm, in consequence of which he is further humiliated by having to make a public apology; later, in the pub, as the story is retold and circulated, the humiliation is erased and the scene becomes one in which Farrington figures as momentary hero. But as the evening progresses, Farrington is again humiliated, this time by an English actor whom the 'boys' meet, who sponges off them and then defeats Farrington in an arm-wrestling contest: both his own and the 'national honour' he is jocularly called on to defend are tarnished. Returning home, raging, his money spent, his watch pawned, his thirst unslaked, he finds the house dark, his dinner cold and his wife out at chapel. The story concludes with him savagely beating his son who pleads for mercy with the promise that he will 'say a Hail Mary' for his father.

This spare and desolate story, together with many others in *Dubliners*, is bitterly diagnostic of the paralysis of Irish men in colonial Ireland, of their alienation and anomie that is so often counterpointed by drinking and violence. As is so much of Joyce's work, it is also profoundly suggestive as to the disposition and practices of gendered social spaces in early-twentieth-century Dublin: spaces of work, leisure, domesticity and religion. As much as anything, it is indicative of the troubled nature of the intersection of these spaces, of their antagonism and contradictory formations. In what follows, I want to situate 'Counterparts' in relation to the gradual and complex emergence of specific forms of colonial modernity in late-nineteenth- and early-twentieth-century Ireland and to the sites of 'counter-modernity' that seem simultaneously to be engendered and in which many of the practices of orality live on in an altered and newly regulated space. In particular, I want to follow the story's suggestion in exploring the forms in which Irish masculinity was deliberately and programmatically being reconstituted by Irish nationalist movements at this moment. The story implies equally the recalcitrance presented to such projects by constructions of masculinity in a popular culture that continued to value oral performativity. Much remains to be done by way of producing a 'gender history' of Irish social spaces and their refiguration within nationalist as well as colonial projects of modernization. What I hope to do here is suggest the singularity and unevenness of the ways in which Irish culture enters modernity, and the complexity of the historiographic project that we require in order to grasp the implications of such singularity. Not the least of the complications of that history is to write back the *oral* into the narrative of both gender and ethnic formations that — however characteristically 'Irish' they were seen to be — nationalism itself sought to transform in an improving direction.

The problematic status of the nationalist project of modernization is in evidence in Ireland as generally among third world nationalisms. It is evident both in relation to the philosophical foundations of modernity from which largely it derives and in relation to the cultural formations of the colonized society as these emerge in time with, but yet athwart, modernity. The problematic nature of nationalist projects has been more fully elaborated elsewhere and can be briefly summarized here. Nationalism is deeply informed, and yet simultaneously judged lacking or 'secondary', by the twin concepts of autonomy and originality that furnish the regulative norms for virtually every level of modern society: for the individual, for culture as it emerges as a separate or distinct sphere, and for each of the increasingly differentiated social spaces of civil society. In its drive to produce or capture the modern state, the nationalist project in its turn must pass by way of the reproduction of such autonomous domains. At the same time, the legitimacy of the call for independent national statehood must be founded in the establishment of the cultural difference of the nation or people, a difference necessarily derived from the traditions of the people that are distinct from those of the dominant or colonial culture. In this way, the claim to autonomous statehood is founded in the originality of national identity, yet in an identity whose configurations derive from the elements of society that have, in some sense, survived the inroads of colonial modernity, that are the formations of non-modernity. Often, indeed, those cultural elements are actually and actively residues of the non-modern, sites of resistance not only to colonialism but also to modernity even in its nationalist version. Nationalism proceeds, furthermore, by the direct politicization of cultural institutions: that is, where it is the function of aesthetic culture in dominant societies discretely to form subjects for the state, under the conditions of insurgent nationalism, cultural forms are directly endowed with political significance.[14] Culture cannot be either disinterested or autonomous, but is openly subordinated to the political projects of the nationalist movement.

But nationalism's relation to tradition is no less refractive and problematic. For what, through a rigorous process of selection, canonization and fetishization, gets called 'tradition' in relation to modernity emerges as such in the very recalcitrance of popular practices to colonial modernity.

These practices prove to be no less recalcitrant to nationalism insofar as it is itself devoted to modernization as the very condition of state formation. In particular, popular practices tend to be resistant to the cultural disciplines that seek to forge the formal citizen-subjects of political modernity that the nation state requires to constitute its people. Accordingly, in its drive to produce subjects to be citizens of the nation that has yet to come into being, nationalism seeks to refine its own version of national culture out of the heterogeneity of popular cultural practices, modernizing and regulating what survives in the form of cultural difference. This is understood, of course, as an attempt to overcome the damage inflicted by colonialism: it is the function of national culture to produce national subjects as empowered agents against the heteronomy and the paralysis of the colonized culture and to restore the wholeness of a fragmented society. If the desired independence of the colonized nation is preceded by the attempt to produce independent subjects, all too often the traits and practices of the 'traditional' and largely oral culture bear with them the marks of what nationalists, like the colonial administrators and travellers before them, regard as the fatal 'dependence' of the native. Quite as much as the colonial state, but with a necessarily higher degree of ambivalence, the nationalist movement regards the oral space and its practices with suspicion, and often animosity, as signs of backwardness and impediments to state formation. Hence the nationalist invention of tradition is always a function of selection.

In this respect, the function of the icons selected as representative of tradition – whether national heroes or aestheticized natural or artefactual objects – is not merely inspirational. They are symbols which, by virtue of their participation in the original and – in its occluded depths – continuous life of the people, represent the virtual nation that has yet to be realized. Symbolism endows the fragmentary and not always consistent remains of popular culture with the ideal unity that the nationalist project requires. Around these symbols the aesthetic formation of the citizen subject takes place. Tradition becomes, in this refined form, the means by which the nation accedes to modernity. But tradition itself, as Frantz Fanon vigorously argued in *The Wretched of the Earth*, thus becomes the paradoxical enemy of the popular culture wherein the cultural difference of the colonized persists in its embedded resistances, its unevennesses and its perpetual transformative adaptations.[15] It is this problematic and doubled relation to its own modernity and its traditionalism that makes nationalism, in Partha Chatterjee's memorable phrase, at once 'a different discourse, yet one that is dominated by another'.[16]

A principal means by which nationalist movements declare their cultural distinctiveness from the dominant power and engage in the refinement of popular culture is manifest in a certain 'transvaluation of values' undertaken generally in the early stages of anti-colonial mobilization. This transvaluation involves the inversal of stereotypes by which the colonizer has marked as inferior the signs of the colonized's cultural difference. Perhaps the most famous instance of this process is that of the Negritude movement among Francophone blacks of which Fanon writes extensively and with some critical sympathy. Negritude, which begins by inverting such stereotypes as black 'passion' or 'primitiveness', or the propensity for rhythm, into the signs of a less alienated connection to the natural world than that of the European, of an essential fullness of life rather than the abstraction of modernity, eventually becomes for Fanon the index of a fetishizing fixation on the 'native' and a consequent disavowal of the actual condition of the black intellectual.[17]

Irish cultural nationalism at the turn of the century engaged in a reversal of stereotypes akin to and in anticipation of the Negritude movement. Thus, for example, the notion of Irish factionalism, based in an inveterate attachment to clan or family rather than to the abstract forms of law and state, became the sign of an indomitable resistance and of a spirit of loyalty capable of attachment to the nation. It formed, no less, the foundations of a masculinity that would be transformed and disciplined through institutions ranging from sports clubs to paramilitary movements. The famous quality of 'sentimentality' was recast as the foundation for piety and for an empathetic moral identification with the oppressed, while even the stereotype of a racially determined backwardness became the index of Irish distaste for mechanical English modes of modernity and the grounds for an alternative conception of the modern. It is important to emphasize this point, since it was rarely the case, even in such ardent defenders of Gaelic tradition as Douglas Hyde, that Irish nationalists sought to go against the current of history: it was an alternative modernity rather than the restoration of old forms that nationalists sought, even as they appealed to traditions. The transvaluation of the stereotype at once recognized it as a form of knowledge, predicated on the apprehension of a difference, and converted its meaning in relation to the possibility for modernization. Celticist nationalism engaged in the revalorization of social or cultural traits whose material conditions of possibility it in fact sought to eradicate. In this respect, Irish nationalism continued, even in its transvaluative efforts, the diagnostic motifs produced by colonial ethnography and redeemed them by obedience to the historicist logic that allowed cultural difference to exist only insofar as it could be subsumed into development or modernization.

But in certain cases, both reversal and eradication are attended with peculiar difficulties. This is evidently the case with that most common and perdurable of stereotypes of the Irish, their propensity for drink and drunkenness. The reasons for the difficulty that nationalism found in dealing with the possibility that drinking represented an engrained ethnic trait were at once logical and cultural. Logically, it is difficult to conceive of a reversal of intemperance, though its eradication was all too readily advocable. For, though in different forms, drinking is the effect of a prior cause, whether that cause be seen, as we shall see, as colonialism or ethnic predisposition. Unlike sentimentality, it is not an essential characteristic whose valence only is in question; it is a metonym for Irishness that can be disavowed, suppressed or denied, but not inverted or transvalued. Even where attempts were made to convert the phenomenon of drinking into a perversion of native 'hospitality', drinking remained an ever possible effect of that trait, not its obverse: as Weathers, the English actor in 'Counterparts', slyly remarks, 'The hospitality was too Irish'.[18] Culturally, it remains even now the case that drinking practices furnish a critical site for the performance of Irish masculinity and ethnicity, an actuality so embedded that any national movement that attempted to overlook this phenomenon would have been obliged to disavow a profoundly significant popular mode of articulating cultural difference. Furthermore, as we shall see, the practices that cluster around drinking retain many of the recalcitrant features that made the space of orality problematic for improvers: it intersects all too easily with labour time, defies the logic of economy and accumulation, and, of course, intrinsically sets in play the lability of the Irish orifice. As I shall be suggesting, it is in the attempt to transform the terms of Irish masculinity, rather than to transvalue the stereotype, that nationalism backhandedly acknowledges the significance of this cultural trait while at the same time necessarily suppressing the counter-modern implications of drinking practices themselves. But this may be because of a third difficulty that attaches to nationalism's relation to drinking, which is that drinking itself may be seen as an allegorical figure for nationalism. That is, like nationalism, drinking represents the imbrication of resistance with dependence: as a practice which refuses the values of the colonial economy, values of labour, regularity or thrift, in favour of an alternative mode of homosociality, drinking resists the incorporation of the colonized culture into the colonial enterprise; as a practice that entails debt as well as psychic dependence, it is at once the cause and effect of an individual and national lack of autonomy. It is, to paraphrase Chatterjee, a practice of difference, but a dependent one.

We will take up this line of argument again momentarily. But the acknowledgement that drinking practices constitute a site for the performance of masculinity raised a second stereotype that proved no less difficult for nationalists to reverse, that is, the famous 'femininity' of the Celt. The notion of an essentially feminine Celtic nature emerged in the writings of philologists and ethnographers in the nineteenth century and, like that of the lamenting Celt, received its clearest and most widely disseminated formulation in Matthew Arnold's *On the Study of Celtic Literature* (1867): 'the sensibilty of the Celtic nature, its nervous exaltation, have something feminine in them, and the Celt is thus peculiarly disposed to feel the spell of the feminine idiosyncracy; he has an affinity to it; he is not far from its secret.'[19] But it is important to note that the stereotype of the feminine Celtic nature was constituted within a matrix of stereotypes that intersected, on the one hand, with a corresponding set of stereotypes about the 'feminine idiosyncracy' and, on the other, with the set of stereotypes that constitute the 'ungovernable and turbulent' Irish as the proper objects of Anglo-Saxon discipline within the Empire. Both stereotypes succeed in *racializing* the common characteristics of what, as we shall see, Kant terms the 'pathological subject'. By the same token, they *pathologize* what are perceived to be Irish characteristics. The femininity of the Celt is a function of his 'receptivity', of a certain more or less passive submission to impulse, whether the impulse of unreflective personal inclination or the impulse of external influence of nature or society. It is the very foundation of Celtic sensibility, and Arnold's only wish is 'that he [the Celt] had been more master of it'.[20] The lack of ethical self-mastery explains the possibility for the convergence of apparently incompatible stereotypes, of feminine sensibility with the violent turbulence that, especially in the proliferating caricatures of simian Irish terrorists that stemmed from the Fenian campaigns of the 1860s, dominated popular images of the Irish in late-nineteenth-century England.[21] An unmastered sentimentality founded the political servility of the Celt no less than his aesthetic hypersensitivity. The Celt's 'unpromising political temperament' required its complement in Anglo-Saxon rule just as, within the gradually consolidating domestic ideology of Victorian Britain, woman's private sentimental morality required regulation by male civic virtues.[22] This novel stereotype of the Irish as 'essentially feminine' was thus at once transitional and wishful. On the one hand, it took the older stereotype of the Irish as savage or barbaric that travellers like Thomas Crofton Croker circulated before the Famine and formed a new matrix of elements that allowed them to appear as truly susceptible of assimilation and improvement; on the other, it contrasted the Irish mode of femininity, in its potential for turbulence and violence, with the orderly feminine space of British domestic ideology which, indeed, Irish violence helped to consolidate.[23]

Rather than a transvaluation, this unpromising stereotype required eradication through a series of projects that were directed at the reconstitution of Irish masculinity. I use the term reconstitution advisedly, in order to suggest that what was at stake was not merely assertions of Irish manliness in denial of the stereotype, but a more or less systematic attempt to reproduce in Ireland a modern division of gendered social spheres within which the image of a masculine civic or public sphere could be reframed in opposition to a privatized feminine space.[24] The nationalist modernization of Ireland was inseparable from its project of masculinizing Irish public culture and regulating a feminine domestic space; a project, as I shall suggest, that to a very large extent runs against the grain of both cultural and material popular practices. This was so, because nationalism at once accepted the colonial stereotype of 'turbulent' Irish masculinity and sought to respond by transforming Irish masculinity into 'governable' forms that would found an independent state formation.

In the first place, there seems little doubt that we are dealing here with the emergence of something new in Irish culture. For the apparently self-evident assumption that masculinity is properly defined and differentiated by its opposition to femininity was by no means a given earlier in the century. For Young Ireland nationalists in the 1840s, 'manliness' as an ethical and political disposition of the subject was properly opposed not to womanliness but to slavery, the ultimate index of subjection. The autonomy of the politically free citizen and nation was opposed to the absolute instantiation of heteronomy, the slave. Thus Thomas Davis, in an essay entitled 'The Young Men of Ireland', addresses the problems of moral corruption in a colonized society:

A Frenchman, M. De Beaumont ... has discussed the character of our People ... and he has discussed it with severity and beauty. He has attributed the 'dark vices' of the Irishman to that part of him which is the making of Englishmen – to that part of him which is a slave. If he be improvident and careless, it was because there was no use of accumulation under the eyes of English avarice; if he be 'ireful' and vindictive, it is because 'six hundred years of hereditary slavery, physical suffering, and moral oppression, have vitiated his blood and tainted his habits' ... The vices of Irishmen are of English culture; their virtues are of the homegrowth of the heart – the nation's heart – 'that recess where tyranny has vainly endeavoured to force an entrance; which has remained free from every stain; that part which holds his religion and his charities.'[25]

A series of oppositions structures this passage: between slavery and moral manliness; between 'English culture' and Irish nature; between the alien and tyrannical rule of the colonizer and the besieged home/body of the Irishman, between the healthy and the 'vitiated' body. What now seems surprisingly undeveloped is an opposition between a distinctly feminine space for Irish culture that is to be protected or liberated by manly resistance. On the contrary, despite the implicit feminization of the inviolate 'recess' that resists the invader, the Irishman is himself the site of division between a contingent outer world that is subject to slavery and an intimate and essential inner world in which the moral constitution of manliness itself is preserved. The project of Young Ireland is, in a sense, to expand that inner space in order to take back the 'part' that is enslaved, to make the slave moral that he might be free. We can perhaps throw the distinctiveness of this formulation into greater relief by comparison with Chatterjee's discussion of 'the nationalist resolution of the woman question' in Bengal. There, in the context of the material domination of British colonialism, a discourse emerges which asserts the superiority of Indian spiritual values while acknowledging the material superiority of English civilization. Even as Indian men are obliged to function in the public world of the British Raj, the feminized domestic space is constructed as that of the preservation and reproduction of inviolate Indian spiritual values.[26] Clearly, Davis's formulations place the division rather within the Irish male body and psyche, at most foreshadowing the divide between the feminine domestic and the male public spheres which, as we shall see, emerged in Ireland in ways very different from those Chatterjee analyses in Bengal.

By the turn of the century, however, a fundamental shift had taken place in nationalist discourse such that a major component of its rhetoric involved the proper distribution of opposed male and female spaces and practices. The conditions for this shift were numerous, but we can cite several relevant ones here. First was, no doubt, the simple fact that the abolition of slavery diminished the force of the very common analogy between the conditions of the slave in the southern states of the United States and those of the Irish poor. Second, the emergence into prominence in the second part of the nineteenth century of a powerful Victorian discourse on domestic ideology had been made possible by the productivity of British capitalism and the extension of the middle-class domain of the private family home among the skilled working classes. This ideology doubtless provided the model with which a modernizing nationalism sought to compete. Third, the intervention of a new racial discourse on the Irish, which asserted their femininity as part of the set of characteristics that makes them incapable of self-government, demanded a response in the form of remasculinizing the Irish public sphere.

We can identify two distinct but interlocked modes of response to the feminization of the Irish during this period. The first can be seen as a celebration of those elements of Irish culture that could be identified in certain ways as feminine. In general, the stereotype of femininity became attached to those survivals of a Gaelic culture that came to be seen as the domain of folk or peasant society. Oral space was thus recreated as feminine space. As is well known, the Irish Literary Revival and the Gaelic League's project to restore the Irish language was predicated on a massive effort to collect, catalogue, disseminate and refunction Irish folklore. This project required the translation of oral cultural elements into the forms of print culture, and, in powerful if inadmissible ways, foregrounded the opposition between the modernity of the collectors and their public and the pre-modernity of the folk. But the gathering and rationalization of a body of materials that included fairy and folk tales, superstition and rural religious practices, and records of medical and other lore was shadowed equally by an implicitly gendered division. It is not for nothing that, although many of the storytellers and informants were men, the figure of the old woman as repository and transmitter of folk culture dominated and continues to dominate the folkloric imaginary. The space of the Irish peasantry came to seem at once pre-modern and feminine; in its conversion and refinement into a coherent body of tradition, it was subjected to the labour of modernizing nationalist men. At the same time, the tone of the collector was familiarly elegiac: these represented, as Sir William Wilde already forecast in 1851, the records of a dying civilization that nationalism itself had displaced, even though neither fact could be fully acknowledged. In the new dispensation, the feminine oral tradition was absorbed into the foundations of a virile Irish modernity. Yeats's famous distinction between the moon of folk culture and the sun of an aristocratic literary culture was only the most notable expression of such an attitude.[27] And if the newly feminized oral culture was absorbed, it proved harder to contain: as we will see in the next chapter, it retained the oral space's dangerous inassimilability and became the recurrent locus of turbulent projections. Associated with the no less feminized domains of blood and kinship, the oral was also understood to be the reservoir of violence and myth. Paradoxically, however, the feminine was at the same time in the process of being domesticated, literally in the form of a newly demarcated set of domestic spaces that became the woman's proper domain. Within that space the oral – in the form of the prototypical elements of maternal reproduction and nurture – was relegated to its proper modern reserve, the space of actual childhood that became the analogue for the figurative space of the 'childhood of the race' that needed to be outgrown.

This ambiguous celebration of the 'feminine' elements of Irish folk culture and the coeval emergence of domestic space were both counterpointed by and captured in a vigorous project aimed at the reconstitution of Irish masculinity. Given the recent context of counter-insurgency discourses, wherein it is all too often assumed that anti-colonial violence stems from the aberrant 'hypermasculinity' of the Republican 'physical force' tradition, it is important to recognize that military nationalism was not the only expression of this project of remasculinization. Not only in the paramilitary organizations that found legitimation in the traditions of the United Irishmen and Young Ireland as well as the Fenians, but equally in a whole range of closely articulated civic and cultural organizations, institutions and practices did this project emerge. Paramilitary displays constituted only one mode in a larger effort to recapture the public sphere as the site for the performance of Irish masculinity. They belonged in the context of linked endeavours that sought to redefine the public sphere in relation to the simultaneous production and protection of a distinctive Irish private or domestic sphere. Their disciplinary formations were linked, similarly, to the attempt to transform the 'turbulent' Irish male body, whose habits were the end result of colonialism, into a disciplined and moral labouring as well as fighting body, one on whose productivity the future prosperity of the nation might be predicated. These political and economic projects were triangulated and, at the turn of the century, explicitly linked with the cultural projects that found expression in the literary revival, the national theatre and the Gaelic league. Such emergent institutions of cultural nationalism were no less concerned with the production of a new Irish masculinity and had at their core the project of organizing Irish political desire around feminized symbols of the nation which represented the objects of a heterosexual male devotion.[28] There was, as I shall argue more fully later, a profound connection between the symbolist poetic mode, no less manifest in Patrick Pearse than in the Yeats of around 1904, and the transformations and regulation of social space that a modernizing nationalism required.

The projects of this modernizing nationalism met in every domain a deep material and cultural resistance. The desire to produce an Ireland whose foundations lay in a feminine domestic space was at best utopianist in a country where a large proportion of the most exploited work force was female, both in the industrialized and semi-industrialized cities of Belfast and Dublin, and in rural areas where much female labour was unpaid and unacknowledged. It was equally unrealistic in a country where in urban centres there was a constantly acknowledged drastic shortage of dwellings, leaving whole families to inhabit single rooms in Dublin's notorious tenements, and where in rural society small family farms continued to require the labour of the whole extended family unit.[29] It also came up against an increasingly organized social resistance to the new post-Famine patterns of both industrial and agrarian labour, especially in the form of a syndicalist labour movement whose agenda was by no means always congruent with or subordinated to nationalist mobilization, and which forged its own version of engagement with capitalist modernity. These struggles and resistances, of course, produced the contestatory field of possibilities within which Irish nationalism took shape. But there was another mode of resistance to official nationalism that I would term recalcitrance and which drew on cultural practices that were at once embedded in the popular imaginary and incompatible with nationalist canons of tradition and moral citizenship. Those practices were problematic, as I have already suggested, precisely because they represented, alongside nationalism, significant sites for the performance of cultural difference that could not simply be erased or disavowed and, like nationalism itself, adaptive accommodations to the destructive inroads of colonial modernization.

In what follows, then, I want to focus on the cultural significance of drinking in Ireland and its rendering within nationalist discourse as a problem of intemperance. My focus is not on what we would now call alcoholism, though that is ineradicably one aspect of an anomic culture within which dependence itself constitutes a form of resistance to incorporation by antipathetic social norms.[30] I want rather to approach drinking practices more widely as these are embedded within a whole matrix of behaviours that are the recalcitrant effects of modernity itself. That is to say, Irish drinking is not to be seen as the residue of pre-modern, pre-industrial practices, nor as in any simple way congruent with, for example, working-class drinking in modern industrial societies in general, but rather as itself transformed and reconstituted in relation to an emergent modernity as an element of disciplined but unincorporated cultural difference.[31] It is a manifestation of the non-modern practices of oral culture transformed into the counter-modern practices of oral space in modern times.

III

Let us proceed by way of a brief history of temperance movements in nineteenth-century Ireland. Prior to the 1830s, temperance work was principally undertaken by dissenting Protestants, whose campaigns were largely conducted against intemperance as an individual matter and without reference to the larger social conditions that might have contributed to excessive drinking in Ireland. In fact, to the contrary, their views tended rather to assume that the reputed turbulence of Irish society derived from intemperance rather than to understand that both drinking and unrest might stem from social conditions. In this connection, it is perhaps important to note that the evil was primarily understood as binge drinking, occasional excessive drinking at fairs or other social gatherings, sometimes referred to as 'circumstantial' rather than habitual drinking.[32] The problems caused by intemperance were thus associated with what might be called a 'spasmodic' theory of social violence, whereby the poor Irish were understood to be reactive and effectively passive in relation to their conditions. As Elizabeth Malcolm notes, the growing antagonism to Irish drinking was not focused on alcoholic consumption alone, but partook of the larger assault on Irish popular cultural practices in the nineteenth century: 'Attacks on popular culture launched in the early nineteenth century, and especially attacks on wakes, patterns, and fairs, almost invariably singled out drunkenness and fighting resulting from drunkenness as among the main abuses needing to be stamped out.'[33] By the same token, as we began to see in previous chapters, Irish drinking was also inseparable from habits of mixing drink and work, leisure or pleasure and labour, in ways that were coming to seem incompatible with a well disciplined capitalist workforce. Moreover, many quasi-ritualistic practices of the workplace, such as occasions for treating or 'fines' paid in alcohol, were deeply associated with guild traditions and with the urban and rural 'combinations' that Nassau Senior and other economists abhorred in Ireland.[34]

The first mass movement for temperance was instigated by the Capuchin Father Mathew in the 1830s and 1840s. This movement, which for the first time drew mass Catholic support, was nonetheless largely in accord with Protestant assumptions that the control of intemperance was a means to regulate and diminish social disorder. Father Mathew's campaign deliberately sought not only to avoid party politics, but also to condemn membership in 'secret societies', those agrarian organizations whose role in defending the material supports of subaltern oral space were recognized by even so respectable an observer as Sir William Wilde.[35] In this respect, the temperance movement, even in its relatively short-lived incarnation prior to the Famine, must be seen not as an attempt to control drinking alone, but as a further antagonist of the non-modern oral space in which drinking was articulated with other customary practices.[36] It was among the various nineteenth-century movements and governmental interventions that targeted Irish oral culture in the broadest sense in the name of 'improvements in morals and the cultivation of people's minds'. As Asenath Nicholson saw the break-up of the *clachan*, so Father Mathew saw temperance as '"humanising" and "elevating" the Irish people'.[37] Where for political economy the potato was the root of Irish evils, for the temperance crusade, alcohol was to blame for social unrest and poverty. It was cause rather than symptom. Father Mathew's work accordingly continued to emphasize individual reform and drinking itself rather than any genetic connection between larger social ills and intemperance. That connection was, however, directly made by the Young Ireland movement, which endorsed Father Mathew's campaign but did seek, in correspondence with their larger derivation of Irish social problems from British rule, to connect the regulation of intemperance with its roots in the social and economic conditions of the Irish poor.[38] The abortive uprising of 1848 and the effective dissolution of Young Ireland interrupted the development of this understanding of intemperance, which was not to find full force again until the end of the century.

By the 1880s and 1890s, a new convergence had become possible between the Irish Catholic Church, the resurgent nationalist movement and the cause of temperance. The increasingly unchallenged authority of the Church, which may be seen to have gradually emerged as a kind of shadow civil society in nineteenth-century Ireland, made it possible for priests to articulate an ever more uncompromisingly nationalist position, one that supplanted an earlier sense of institutional dependence on the British state. The concern of the Church with combating intemperance and with the general moral reform of the Irish accordingly coincided with a new political militancy. Within this new formation, the earlier concern with individual reform was linked to a vigorous rejection of English stereotypes of an essentially bibulous Irish race and an uncompromising attribution of intemperance to the effects of British rule:

How many Englishmen ever reflect that England is responsible for [the] intemperance of the Irish? Our Celtic ancestors were a very temperate people before the English landed on our shores ... It was only after they had lost their independence that this vice broke out among the Irish; and when we take into consideration all that they suffered from English tyranny during the last seven hundred years, can we be astonished that they turned to drink?[39]

Intemperance was thus no longer seen as the symptom of an internal racial organization already given to modes of dependence that fit it only for the external discipline of British rule, but as a synecdoche for the larger effects of that rule on the Irish body and the Irish psyche. Colonialism was a kind of intoxication of which intemperance was one among many effects. Accordingly, intemperance and political dependence stood in a reversible relation, such that the eradication of intemperance would lead to the eradication of British rule and vice versa. Hence emerged the celebrated slogan, 'Ireland sober, Ireland free'. In this respect, we may note again the difference from what Chatterjee analyses in the Bengali context. For in Ireland, the assumption was that the Irish body and spirit are indeed *both* already contaminated by the effects of British rule, so that private no less than public life required a process of 'detoxification', a process which Douglas Hyde in another context termed 'deanglicisation'.[40]

Accordingly, the work of temperance nationalism became inseparable from the production and dissemination of a vigorous domestic ideology which strove to establish the well regulated feminized home as the counterpart to a reformed masculine labour and saw both as the foundation of a reformed and independent nation state. Typical in its pedagogical insistence was Revd J. Halpin's *Father Mathew Reader on Temperance and Hygiene*, a text intended for school use, which makes quite explicit the connections between the reform of men for public duties, the feminine sphere of the domestic and the home as foundation for society:

For the homes make up the nation; and as are the homes, so will be the nation itself. Whatever wrecks the home wrecks the nation as well ... Now, what destroys the home more surely and more quickly than intemperance?[41]

If intemperance unfits man for the discharge of his duties, how much more truly does it unfit woman for hers? What is to become of her home and her domestic duties – the care of her children, for instance, in the exercise of which so much depends for society itself as well as for the family? As the nation depends on the homes, the homes depend on the mothers that reign there.[42]

All women can, each in her own sphere, give good example ... We must be very practical here. In the first place our Irish women are blamed for their cookery, or rather for their ignorance of cookery. And it is said that a better knowledge of that 'lost art' would half solve our drink question in Ireland.[43]

Yet more than all this may woman do for temperance. She can make the home attractive and sanitary, and even beautiful; yes, beautiful, for even the humblest and poorest home may be made beautiful and attractive in its way and measure, and all that a home should be, by a tidy thrifty and intelligent woman ... Well, there is a rivalry between the home and the public-house; and if the home is to prevail it must have something attractive about it; something better than disorder and dirt, untidy children and an ill-tempered wife.[44]

Halpin's linked concern not merely with temperance but with the inculcation of 'domestic economics', with hygiene, cookery and beautification, marks this and texts like it as part of a larger project of modernization which, in its desire to regulate the feminine domestic sphere, established domestic economy as a foundation for the national or political economy. Indeed, at moments it curiously echoes Trevelyan's Famine-era contempt for the women of the west whose knowledge of cookery did not extend beyond the boiling of a potato. It is not so much a discourse about the repression of an evil, drunkenness, as it is about the reconstitution of the social formation and the establishment of the domestic sphere as the counterpart to an invigorated masculine public sphere of economic and political labour.

Inasmuch as 'there is a rivalry between the home and the public-house', we can understand the public house to be no less a rival to the public sphere. It constitutes a third term whose very name marks its ambiguous location. As observers of working-class drinking always understood, it was a rival to the home in providing an alternative space for male conviviality, leisure and community, one not yet subordinated to the regulations of private domesticity and, accordingly, 'public'. Indeed, Malcolm argues that 'working-class men consciously went to the pub to escape their homes and families' and that 'in the countryside particularly', pubs 'were regarded as second homes by their customers'.[45] At the same time, it rivalled the public sphere insofar as it constituted a space for the dissemination of news and rumour, for the performance of a heterogeneous and largely oral popular culture, and, indeed, for the organization and dissemination of dissent, sedition and resistance. But it was no less a recalcitrant space, the site of practices that by their very nature rather than by necessary intent were out of kilter with the modern disciplinary projects. Certainly the pub in Ireland was subject, from the mid nineteenth century on, to a regulatory process that embraced drinking houses from shebeens and spirit grocers to public houses themselves, and that defined the nature of the pub as a social institution very different from the taverns of an earlier time.[46] But as a site which was irrevocably a product of modernity in its spatial and its temporal demarcations and regulations, in its relation to the increasingly disciplined rhythms of work and leisure, it was nonetheless a site which preserved and transformed according to its own spaces and rhythms long-standing popular practices of orality that would not be incorporated by discipline: treating or the round system; oral performance of song, story and rumour; conversation itself which becomes increasingly a value in a society ever more subject to the individuation and alienation of the worker within the system of production.[47] It may be seen as a crucial site of counter-modernity.

In this respect, then, the pub was no less a rival to the linked set of national institutions which came into being alongside and in relation to temperance nationalism, and often under the auspices of the same figures: the Gaelic Athletic Association (GAA), the Gaelic League, the Irish Literary movement and the National Theatre, and the various paramilitary movements. At the same time as such institutions often expressly sought to provide an alternative to drinking as the predominant form of male recreation, they strove to produce a public sphere cleansed of the intoxicating influence of English culture and commodities. As Archbishop Croke, first patron of the GAA, put it: 'England's accents, the vicious literature, her music, her dances, and her manifold mannerisms ... [are] not racy of the soil, but rather alien, on the contrary to it, as are for the most part, the men and women who first imported and still continue to patronise them.'[48] Yet it is clear that these various institutions sought equally and no less importantly to constitute an alternative, nationalist civil society alongside the institutions of the colonial state, in the anticipation of an independent national state with its own civic institutions. Their function was not only to propagandize and disseminate nationalist ideology, it was also to produce formally a counter-hegemonic set of articulated but autonomous spheres which could perform the modernizing functions of education, recreation, political organization and opinion formation by whose means the national citizen would be formed. The public house not only rivalled such institutions, then, it troubled their intents. It was a site of the performance of a profoundly heterogeneous popular culture, one inflected, as the 'Sirens' chapter of *Ulysses* alone might suggest, by European opera, English music hall, nationalist balladry, gossip, irreverence and humour, all of which was intrinsically recalcitrant to nationalist refinement. At the same time, it was, even in its demarcation as a distinct space, internally resistant to differentiation: it was a crucial site not only for the mixing of cultural elements but for the intersection of functions, leisure and work, politics and religion, literature and orality, public life and a kind of domesticity.⁴⁹ It is the locus of cultural differences and heterogeneities with which nationalism perforce intersected but which it could not fully incorporate.

Nationalism, as we have seen, requires the establishment of cultural differences from the colonial power in order to legitimate its own claims to statehood, but the cultural difference it requires must, in order to fit with its modernizing drives, be a difference contained and refined into the canonized forms of tradition. The civil institutions of national modernity work off but also against the grain of popular cultural practices through which the heterogeneous, unrefined and recalcitrant modes of cultural difference are continually constituted and transformed. We can situate Irish drinking as one element in a matrix of such historically shifting cultural differences, differences of practice and social form that prove unincorporable either by colonial or by nationalist modernity and that remain accordingly ungathered by history, as a kind of dross or irregularity of which neither sense nor use can be made. What is intended here is thus not the ideal form of pure and originary difference towards which an extreme traditionalist and separatist nationalism might tend; it is rather that mode of constant differentiation, refraction and refunctioning that occurs in the encounter between the evolving institutions of colonial modernity and the adaptive spaces of the colonized culture. What determines cultural difference is not its externality to modernity, nor the persistence of a pre-modern irrationality, but rather the mutually constitutive relation between the modern and the non-modern that emerges in the counter-modern spaces of modernity itself. The temporal structure within which the colonized culture emerges in its difference is not that of a movement from an origin which is interrupted by and then assimilated into a more developed, more powerful state, nor that of the recuperation of an authentic and ultimately unbroken tradition within the revivalist logic of nationalism. It is, rather, the structure of the eddy by which Walter Benjamin redefines the processes of origination:

Origin [*Ursprung*], although an entirely historical category, has, nevertheless, nothing to do with genesis [*Entstehung*]. The term origin is not intended to describe the process by which the existent came into being, but rather to describe that which emerges from the process of becoming and disappearance. Origin is an eddy in the stream of becoming, and in its current it swallows the material involved in the process of genesis.⁵⁰

The cultural forms of the colonized do not simply disappear; in the turbulence of the encounter with colonization, they become something other that retains the traces of the violence of that encounter, preserving it in the very form of a persistent damage, and yet survives. Survival in this sense is a mode of adaptation that is often more resistant to than acquiescent in domination, a 'living on' that is not about the preservation or fetishization of past forms but nonetheless refuses incorporation.[51] This unevenly distributed relation of damage and survival forges the recalcitrant grain of cultural difference.

The problematic status of Irish drinking has over and again to do with what has always seemed to the modernized eye the improper confusion of spaces and practices. One instance of this is evident in the arguments for licensing and regulation of drinking to separate work time from leisure or drinking time, and to end such practices as paying workers in public houses. This was, as Roy Rosenzweig points out, the ubiquitous concern of industrial societies, but it may be that the uneven penetration of rationalized capitalist modes of labour in Ireland permitted the persistence of mixing labour and pleasure to a greater degree than elsewhere.[52] Similarly, particularly in rural districts, the overlap between public and domestic drinking, between the shebeen and the private dwelling, and the persistence of customs like the wake and the *ceilidh*, spelt a culture spatialized in ways not only different from those that were coming to be regulated by state law and religious dictate, but in ways increasingly seen to be improper. Unlike the public house, these oral spaces of popular drinking were clearly not segregated by gender and indeed could involve whole communities: there is little to suggest the homosociality of drinking practices at least prior to the Famine.[53] At the same time, these were the spaces often regarded as giving material expression to the fluctuations of Irish 'sentimentality': as we have seen, wakes, in particular, which had always been suspected by English observers, were the object of increasing censure by the Catholic Church as the century progressed, not least because of their improper display and mixing of lament and keening, laughter, social criticism and satiric, often impious, invective, all under the influence of drinking.

What each of these instances figures is the persistence and complexity of a culture of orality, in the fullest sense, alongside, inflecting and inflected by a modern state and print culture. What orality here signifies is not so much the modes of transmission of a non-literate society or even the oral artefacts and materials that formed the objects of folklore collections, as the modes of sociality and bodily practice that are embedded in oral space.[54] The improperly differentiated functions of the mouth and the tongue are the indices of a disturbing cultural difference that thrives in the pub as in the shebeen or at the open-air fair with which it continued for a long time to intersect, despite decades of governmental regulation of those spaces.⁵⁵ In this respect, the pub is the sublimation, the *Aufhebung*, not the destruction, of oral space and its unruliness. Mouths that imbibe drink and utter sedition, nonsense, lament and palaver are the figure for an absence of distinction and for the borderless contiguity of social and psychic or emotional spaces, wherever drink is taken. Looseness of the tongue makes of it an insubordinate and virtually separable autonomous organ, one that is closely associated in Joyce's 'Counterparts' with the recalcitrance and the pleasures of the drinker:

… almost before he was aware of it, his tongue had found a felicitous moment …
   He had made a proper fool of himself this time. Could he not keep his tongue in his cheek?
   The bar was full of men and loud with the noise of tongues and glasses.⁵⁶

Within the emergent modernity of Dublin in the early 1900s, the pubs that Farrington repairs to constitute heterotopic sites where drinking is articulated with a whole set of other cultural practices that functions as an Irish mode of counter-modernity. The pub is, indeed, the type of such spaces. Like the prison (as we shall see), the pub is indubitably a site of regulation and control, a space into which modernity extends its discipline and, what is more, one that contributes to the constitution and enforcement of a newly gendered space in Ireland: even more than the homilies of the priests or the exhortations of temperance nationalists, by shaping a material and partly sanctioned space in which specific cultural practices could live on, 'the rise of the pub played a part in separating the sexes and confining the woman to a purely domestic role'.⁵⁷ Indeed, as Stivers argues, the emergence of bachelor drinking culture in post-Famine Ireland, devoted as it was to male hard drinking, actually served to consolidate the new rural culture of primogeniture, celibacy and late marriage. Yet it is precisely this fact that made the public house a potentially alternative space for homosocial conviviality that operated outside the norms and rhythms of alienated labour or the hierarchies of the workspace that impinge on Farrington's daily life. Outside, but nonetheless constrained and defined in relation to those rhythms and norms, drinking functions as a transgressive negation. The public house as alternative space was already defined by licensing hours as a space of leisure that no longer intersected intimately with the rhythms of work: 'The creation of the pub and the suppression of other venues led to a shift in drinking from outdoors into the confined and regulated space of the government-licensed drinkshop.' There, 'in a clearly designated and controlled space', the consumption of alcohol during the day had become marked as the sign of indiscipline and anomie; its pleasures are tainted and secretive as Farrington's furtive work-time drinking exemplifies.[58]

The public house, with its traditions of treating and oral exchange, equally abutted the theatre that had become marked as the domain of English incursions and commodification, but was accordingly under contestation as a possible site for the redefinition of Irish masculinity and femininity.[59] The figure of Weathers, arriving in the pub with his sexually charged female companions, condenses that displacement and contamination of Irish male pleasure by its rivalrous counterpart, and the English actor's victory over Farrington is doubly humiliating, expressing not only a breach in his performance of masculinity, but his inferiority within a colonial hierarchy and the consequent endangerment of his spaces of pleasure. Within the unforgiving laws of commodity exchange, drinking is only notionally a space of reciprocity: defiant of the logic of the cash nexus as a cultural survival like treating may be, modernity makes of it an accumulation of debt.[60] Having pawned his timepiece to subvent the evening's drinking, as if in revolt against the clock that has marked his entrapment, Farrington nonetheless ends his evening penurious and on the edge of a fatal economic dependence that matches as it is produced by his alcoholic dependence. His outlet is to bring home the violence he could not express at work: the story concludes with a brutality that, for all its vigour, is no less paralysed insofar as it is issueless and doubtless the source of its own repetition, generation after generation. Ironically, the 'spell of riot' that he craved in the office finally makes its appearance in the domestic space where he feels equally trapped. But his violence is not one in which he can revel: like drinking itself, the violence of fair and pattern has been contained within a new and constraining space of modernity, the feminized domestic space that is the counterpart and rival of the public house.[61]

As if to open yet one more triangle of competing institutions, Farrington's rage is provoked in part by his wife's absence when she is out at chapel, another ambiguously regulated and intermediate space of Irish modernity that lies between the private and the public. As much recent feminist scholarship suggests, the Church and its philanthropic missions furnished not only a site of patriarchal discipline and containment, but also a vehicle through which women, otherwise increasingly confined to the domestic sphere, could enter into public life.[62] Ironically, the Church, not unlike the public house, furnishes both a 'rival to the home' and a space within which, in richly complex ways, practices of oral culture live on. It is remarkable to what an extent Joyce's stories in *Dubliners*, not only 'Counterparts', but also 'A Little Cloud' or 'Grace', for example, are attuned to the structure of this peculiar rivalry of colonial-modern spaces, even if he shows little sympathy for the actual experience of women in the Church and highlights instead the paralysed predicament of his male protagonists. The homosocial context of the pub remains the site in which he explores the survivals of oral space and their contradictions most lucidly.

Read in this way, 'Counterparts' stages drinking as a dangerous and unstable instance of damage and survival within and athwart the terrain of modernity. To be sure, drinking represents the recalcitrance of Irish orality against the alienating rhythms of labour, against the regulation and division of time and space characteristic of modernity. It is no less opposed in this to the domestic than to the workspaces of modernity, and is by no means the site of a sentimental celebration of hearth and home against economic rationality and calculation that structures domestic ideology as a function of capitalist modernity. Yet the containment of drinking within the spaces of modernity makes of it the locus of a damaged masculinity, predicated on the recalcitrance of an anomie that constantly swallows up any articulation of resistance that might emerge there. Shot through with the paralysis of anomie, drinking repeats, at the level of the individual, the violent colonial apparatus of humiliation, with its system of economic and cultural dependence. In this, I have already suggested, drinking is, as Joyce clearly grasped it, the shadowy figure of nationalism's own articulation of resistance and dependence: drink, not temperance, is nationalism's counterpart.[63]

IV

And yet, as so often in Joyce, something escapes the dismal sobriety of this logic.

Let us return to the scene from 'Counterparts' with which we opened. It is a scene of writing in which, as Farrington repetitively, absently, copies over a document, the materiality of the letters ('B...B...B') separates out from the sense of the phrase. In his very frustration and alienation, and in his mild inebriation, something detaches itself from sense. That something is the senseless yet sensuous repetition of an oral and aural material, almost literally a babble, an infantile ba-ba-ba that – with the power of an automatism – leads the copier to write awry. In this scene, Farrington is copying a document known in legal parlance as a counterpart: a copy torn off from the original in such a way that, when the two are brought together, the copy authenticates the original. The counterpart of the title refers, then, not only to rivalry, but to secondariness, imitation, but in a way that disturbs the hierarchies of originality. If we consider nationalism as a rival of the imperial state, it is also its counterpart in the second sense, its dependent or secondary copy. But its repetition constitutes not simply a difference, capable of rehierarchization, but a deviation of sense. This deviation is, I would argue, into the space of a cultural difference that is not caught in the logic of opposition.

This deviation is no less a deviation from what were, around 1900, the givens of nationalist aesthetics, with its emphasis on the representative function of the symbol. The counterpart as document is identical to the symbol in its etymological derivation, from the Greek *symbolon*:

Symbola were pledges, pawns or covenants from an earlier understanding to bring together a part of something that had been divided specifically for the purpose of later comparison ... A coin could be a *symbolon*. Indeed, *symbola* were often 'halves or corresponding pieces of [a bone or] a coin, which the contracting parties broke between them, each keeping one piece.'[64]

But this etymological derivation, grounded in the transition from preliterate signs to literate contracts, highlights the extent to which the contemporary meaning of the symbol deviated from its own original. The *symbolon*, like the counterpart, is an allegory: it is in a relation of contiguity to what it represents rather than being a part of it. But precisely what activates the nationalist political possibilities of a post-Romantic definition of the symbol is its conceptualization as a representation that participates in what it represents, as a particular that is part of the whole for which it stands. The landscape may be a symbol of nature or natural process because it is already a part thereof; the national martyr or poet is the symbol of the nation for whose virtual existence he stands because he already belongs to it as part of it. The temporality of symbolism entails the transformation of a merely contingent relation to the nation into a representative function. We might describe this as a series of rhetorical transformations: from the metonymic (Leopold Bloom's 'I'm Irish; I was born here') to the synecdochic ('I participate in the nation as a particular instance or member of the whole body politic') to the metaphoric ('I represent the nation because my essential qualities are those with which an Irish subject should identify'). It is a tropic movement that educes generality out of particularity and contingency and its mechanism is desire, in the sense that Yeats understood his early cultural nationalist work to have sought to 'organize' the desire of the nation around certain symbols.[65] In its effort to mobilize a unifying desire, nationalist symbolism is directed against the fragmentation and dispersal of the body and the social space of modernity and towards a suturing of the individual body in itself and with the nation as a whole.

Joyce's *Dubliners* is structured rather around what he describes as the epiphany, an epiphany secularized beyond the account that Stephen Dedalus gives of it in *Stephen Hero*. There, the epiphany at first appears as a still auratic translation of the religious epiphany, the moment of the manifestion of the divine in the worldly; in effect, as a symbol in which the particular undergoes a transubstantiation into an illumination of the transcendent:

> By an epiphany he meant a sudden spiritual transformation, whether in the vulgarity of speech or of gesture or in a memorable phrase of the mind itself...
> First we recognize that the object is one integral thing, then we recognize that it is an organized composite structure, a thing in fact: finally, when the relation of the parts is exquisite, when the parts are adjusted to the special point, we recognize that it is that thing which it is. Its soul, its whatness, leaps to us from the vestment of its appearance. The soul of the commonest object, the structure of which is so adjusted, seems to us radiant. The object achieves its epiphany.[66]

But even in this description, saturated though it is with the young Joyce's Aquinian aesthetic vocabulary, something moves beyond the symbolic, auratic register and closer to the form of the profoundly secular and *aural* epiphanies that he collected in his notebooks and which came to inform the work of *Dubliners*. For the epiphanies of Joyce's work, as opposed to those of Stephen's theory, are dedicated less to the symbolization of the real, its transumption into representation, than to a certain metonymic singularity. They are also, for the most part, not the visual objects his language of appearance might suggest, but overhearings, the fragments of oral events that hang in the air or in the ear. As such, they are dedicated to a presentation of the 'whatness' of the thing that is achieved, as this passage intimates, by way of an extreme degree of internal, aural intensification that ensures their detachment from rather than their representation of that of which they are a part. Their objective epiphany is not matched by a subjective revelation, but rather by a sense of estrangement or alienation. The intensified moment, like Gabriel Conroy's glimpse of his wife standing on the stairs *listening* to distant music, in fact refuses to be a symbol of something and embeds instead a profound resistance to incorporation, a recalcitrant particularity that refuses to be subsumed into the narrative of representation.[67] It is, as a diagnostic moment structured around its internal relations, closer to the 'alienation' of Bertolt Brecht's later tableau or gestus.

In Stephen's analogy, what is emphasized in the epiphany is its effulgence of spiritual radiance: an auratic light emanates from and detaches itself from the transubstantiated object. As Joyce writes of the effect of *Dubliners*, it is not so much an *aura* that detaches itself from the object as an *odour*: 'It is not my fault that the odour of ashpits and old weeds and offal hangs around my stories. I seriously believe that you will retard the course of civilisation in Ireland by preventing the Irish people from having one good look in my nicely polished looking-glass.'[68] Odour is for Joyce the aura that escapes the representation of the object, that is suspended above it as its ineffable trace. Insofar as it is also distasteful, it implies the status of a counter-aesthetic. What is implied here is the inseparability of the odour from a project of rigorous mimesis, the juxtaposition of a project of specular revelation, predicated on visibility and illumination, with an unprojected effect of that mimesis, its counter-sense. The celebrated 'scrupulous meanness' of the style of *Dubliners* invokes a naturalism that refuses the incorporative desire of either symbolism or realism that would be the privileged modes of a bourgeois nationalism. It is devoted to the mimesis of a paralysis that suspends action outside the teleological drive of representation: it refuses to redeem colonial paralysis by subordinating it to a transformative sense of history. Instead, the diagnostic mimesis of paralysis produces a suspension of sense issuing in this odour that hangs around these stories. The odour is a counter-sense made possible by the very rigour of the sense on which Joyce's mimesis of colonial Dublin insists.

We can understand the relation between odour and mimesis as constituting a double track of signification. Within the track of mimesis, which is still subject to a moral and formative intent, narrative itself becomes over and again suspended in paralysis. In that paralysis, we are to decipher the dysfunctional contours of colonial Dublin, the ineluctible determination of material and psychic conditions, repetition and the inhibition of the will. The sense of the narratives in this register is overwhelmingly that of the vacuity of narrative itself where nothing moves. And yet that very suspension of narrative in paralysis releases an odour whose sense has nothing to do with paralysis, which does not even seek to effect or justify things in the registers of moral or political agency. We have seen already how the odour associated with the nomadic Irish operated both as the material trace of their abstracted labour power and as the disturbingly mobile sign of their materialization 'out of place' in Britain. Here in Joyce, odour is again a trace that survives the passing of the body, but as the circulation of stories in the public house detaches itself from the violence and repetition of the narrative to constitute less a determinate engagement with the real than a repertoire and a rehearsal of alternatives. This realm of possibilities is not legitimated by its realization in the actual but sets off eddies in the forward-moving stream of a historicized temporality. Joyce suggests to us, as does Fanon, that in the sites of an apparent suspension of historical motion are the grounds for possible counter-histories. For with the counter-senses that these eddies preserve, a materialist historiography must go to work, tracing over and again the alternative resources that are the emanations of the damage taken up in every living on. If the odour that hangs around the stories recalls the miasmatic odour of the migrant Irish, counterpart of their supposed fixity in time and space, it is also an abstraction, a sublimation of the material that moves and circulates in excess of closure and determination, and yet goes nowhere, neither in space nor in time. A smell has no direction. Odour is, in that respect, the allegorical counterpart of the oral and the aural, an evanescent material trace that insists on returning and yet remains unavailable for historicist logic: it is the spectre, the revenant, that returns to haunt the spaces of modernity. That it goes nowhere even as it continues to return is, we will see, the index of its utopian potential.

CHAPTER 4

'Going nowhere': oral space in the cell block

I

The events surrounding the struggle of Republican prisoners in Northern Ireland for political status, from the mid 1970s to the hunger strike of 1981, have a logic to them that unfolds with a seemingly inexorable fatality. In the wake of violent police reactions to the Civil Rights movement of the late 1960s, conflict in Northern Ireland rapidly escalated from street protests into organized armed struggle. The British Army initially responded to the conflict in a framework based on colonial counter-insurgency campaigns it had fought elsewhere in the post-war period, including Malaysia, Kenya and Cyprus, campaigns in turn partly shaped by previous insurgencies in Ireland. Among the strategies adapted from those 'low-intensity' campaigns was internment, implemented in Northern Ireland in August 1971. Numerous suspected Republican activists were incarcerated, including some who were neither paramilitaries nor, in many cases, politically involved at all. Most internees were subjected to 'in-depth' interrogation, a practice examined in the following chapter, and committed to extended incarceration without trial. The number of internees eventually reached more than 2,300.

On account of the counterproductive politicizing effect of such mass intrusions, predominantly into Catholic and nationalist communities, British policy-makers increasingly turned to using the courts as a means of convicting and confining those suspected of terrorist offences. Whereas internment indirectly recognized the colonial nature of the conflict, use of the court system began the gradual effort to recast it as a law-and-order problem. Nonetheless, between 1972 and 1975, as a result of a hunger strike by Republicans, paramilitary prisoners were granted 'Special Category' status. Effectively recognizing the political motivation of their offences, and therefore the political nature of the conflict, Special Category status allowed for the segregation of prisoners in separate compounds according to their ideological and organizational affiliations and for free association within the compounds. These conditions permitted education and training to take place alongside sporting and other recreational activities.[1] The prison regime of the camps at Long Kesh, colloquially known as the Cages, also recognized the command structure of the paramilitary organizations. In 1976, however, the British government radically changed its counter-insurgency policy in Northern Ireland, and decided to regard all terrorist acts as ordinary crimes rather than as politically motivated offences. The policy of 'criminalization', which belonged with a larger strategy of seeking to 'normalize' life in Northern Ireland and to cast the violence as an apolitical question of law and order, was clearly designed to delegitimate the IRA and other paramilitary groups and to deny the colonial roots of the conflict. Men convicted in the special or Diplock courts from 1976 were to be incarcerated as ordinary criminals in the purpose-built Maze Prison at Long Kesh, a complex of cellular blocks that became known as the H-Blocks on account of the way in which the wings were arranged around a central administrative 'bar'. Women were held in the older cellular prison at Armagh where they were, as in other female prisons, allowed to wear their own or civilian-type clothing.

Republican prisoners immediately determined not to recognize their criminalization. The male prisoners refused to wear the prison uniform and were locked in their cells naked apart from the towels or blankets that they wrapped around themselves. In order to break the prisoners' resistance, the prison authorities attempted many strategies of humiliation, including obliging prisoners to go to the canteen naked or to stand naked outside the governor's office. The casual and systematic violence of the warders meant that movement in the wings, to use the bathrooms or go on visits or medical checks, became the occasion for harassment, beatings and intrusive bodily searches, including the infamous and brutal mirror searches of the prisoners' rectal passages and other orifices. Eventually prisoners refused to leave their cells and went on the 'no-wash' protest (often known as the 'dirty protest'). When warders began to empty their chamber pots onto their bedding, prisoners resorted to emptying them out of their windows. When these were blocked up, they would empty them under their doors at night. Eventually, they were forced to dispose of their excrement by smearing it on the walls of their cells rather than allowing it to accumulate in corners. In the course of the 'blanket' and no-wash protests, the prisoners managed to gain considerable control of their cell blocks, being held in de facto segregation from both Loyalist prisoners and the non-political offenders, known as

'Ordinary Decent Criminals' or ODCs. They negotiated with prison officials only through their Block and Wing Officers Commanding (OCs) and, despite the appalling conditions in which they lived, organized political and language classes and other forms of recreation within their wings, while continuing to communicate and strategize with the IRA command. In Armagh, women prisoners, though allowed to wear their own clothes, also went on a no-wash campaign in February 1980 in protest against violent strip-searching conducted by or in the presence of male warders.

These conditions continued until late 1980 when H-Block prisoners decided that their protests were failing to gain sufficient public awareness and escalated their protest by adopting the tactics of the hunger strike. The first collective hunger strike in December 1980, joined by three women in Armagh, appeared to achieve the majority of the prisoners' demands and was called off when one striker was in danger of dying just as negotiations were being accomplished. However, British authorities reneged on the understandings that were reached, believing that they had broken the prisoners' resolve, and in March 1981 the prisoners began a second hunger strike, planned in a different and unprecedented way. Rather than striking en masse, volunteers went on strike serially, at regular intervals, thus ensuring that there would be a continuous 'conveyor belt' of dying prisoners if authorities refused to yield. In a radical break with the Republican tradition of refusing to recognize the British parliament, the National H-Block–Armagh Committee put forward Bobby Sands, the leader of the strike, as a candidate in the April by-election in Tyrone, listing him on the ticket as a 'political prisoner'. Unexpectedly he not only won the election, but did so with an overwhelming majority of nationalist votes, which signified an unanticipated moment of unity between Republican Sinn Féin supporters and the 'constitutional' nationalists who tended to support the Social Democratic and Labour Party (SDLP). Sands's death in May 1981 was met with world-wide protest and was followed by the deaths of nine more strikers before family members began to call them off the strike when they lapsed into coma, thus effectively breaking its momentum. Although the negotiations around the hunger strike ended in compromise, gaining the prisoners most of their demands short of official political status, Sands's election victory and the international recognition that it brought to the prisoners was understood to have gained them the political legitimacy that they sought, not only in Ireland but – perhaps more importantly – with the Irish community in the United States.

Some thirty years after the protests of political prisoners against their criminalization in the H-Blocks and Armagh culminated in the 1981 hunger strike, the history of those events continues to be enshrouded in the haze of myth. I do not mean by this the mythic narratives that Irish Republicans are so often assumed to have perpetrated, but the mythic framework that has been projected upon them by journalists and historians alike. As so often, where understanding meets its own conceptual limits, recourse to mythology takes its place. Social critics, historians or journalists, limited by rigid categories and ideological assumptions from grasping new forms of struggle and resistance, fall back on the ascription to those whose acts they do not understand of a consciousness outside the pale of modernity and civility. Those being the terms that legitimate the state, whoever opposes the state must be consigned to the pathology of pre-modern modes of thinking. Myth represents the primal violence and disorder that the state, with its therapeutic force, comes to cure. Violence is not a product of the coercive dynamics of the state but the atavistic response of those who have yet fully to enter the condition of modernity.

To understand social conflict in these terms is not an innocent act. The mythologization of struggle, its rendering in terms of 'blood sacrifice' or primal rite, is the mystifying counterpart of criminalization. Both practices partake of a counter-insurgency discourse that seeks to locate the roots of violence in the pathological state of individuals and communities rather than in the economic and political inequities that the state itself maintains and reproduces. Against the 'normalized' good conduct of the citizen, resistance manifests the symptoms of an aberrant pathology: if, on the one hand, popular culture provides the image of the 'godfathers of violence', the terrain of myth furnishes the terms by which the mentality of Republicanism becomes 'atavistic', primitive and reactionary.[2] Mythological analysis furnishes the deep structure of motivation that underlies and belies any claim on the part of the Republican movement to represent a radical and socially progressive tendency. In this respect, the ascription of mythological thinking to Republicanism is more insidious than the effort to criminalize it: its function is to insinuate that, beneath whatever progressive rhetoric the Republican articulates, there lurks a deeper reactionary tendency. That tendency is, by the nature of mythic motivation, scarcely conscious: it is a drive unsusceptible to argument or discussion, and thus beyond the pale of civil society.

Although it was probably an essay on Yeats and fascism by Conor Cruise O'Brien, written on the eve of the fiftieth anniversary of the Easter Rising, that crystallized revisionist efforts to recast the history of Republicanism, the clearest statement of the connection to be made between Republican violence and mythological thinking was Richard Kearney's 'Myth and Terror', published in *The Crane Bag* (a journal not itself shy of indulging in mythic thinking and formulations like 'the Irish mind' or 'the Irish psyche').[3] Appearing in 1975, the essay anticipated the advent of the prison struggles and the British campaign of 'criminalization' that impelled them, and offered a 'deep structural' account of 'terrorism' that would supplement the political, economic and historical analyses then available, all of which risked acknowledging the material grounds for the Republican insurgency. In fact, presented as a modest supplement to more socially grounded analyses of the Northern Irish conflict, Kearney's 'mythological perspective' rapidly came to supplant them, claiming to provide 'a sort of depth-hermeneutic which would be capable of detecting the more occult motivations operative in Ulster terrorism'.[4] Inevitably this uncovering of the determining 'cultural deep-structure' tended to displace prior 'orthodox interpretations', making them more or less epiphenomenal, determined by rather than determining the nationalist movement's 'mythical-nucleus'. It was as if this mythological deep-structure acted as a kind of symbolic grammar that determined and constrained the acts and statements of Republicanism.

Several further assumptions flow from this assertion of a cultural deep-structure. The first and foremost is that Republicanism is a phenomenon without effective history, that its forms and practices remain the same across generations, manifesting always and everywhere the same 'mythological essence': the Fenians, the Irish Republican Brotherhood, Patrick Pearse and Thomas MacDonagh, presumably the Republicans throughout the period from 1922 to 1969, all recur to and draw from the same mythological figures and motifs as Kearney assumes drive the Provisional IRA in the 1970s. The symbolic core of those motifs is the blood sacrifice – the idea that the land can only be restored to fertility by being watered by the blood of young men. Terror is thus in the first place intimately bound for Kearney to the symbols of Republicanism, within which the baroque imagery of Catholicism fuses with a primordial Celtic mythic nucleus to produce a quasi-religious imperative for blood-letting as an ongoing means of purification and restoration. From such a perspective, the analogues between Republicanism and fascism follow almost inevitably.

But terror is deeply entwined with this putative mythological essence of Republicanism not only by virtue of its sacrificial content but also through its *forms*. The appeal to myth collapses historical process into mere immediacy. Myth pre-empts history: 'the "mythic" recourse to miraculous powers of transformation is primarily motivated by the apparent occlusion of all normal channels for effecting political change *in* history ... a certain *fatalism* is inherent in all mythic invocations of the Past.'⁵ Immediacy manifests itself in a double form. In the first place, it is the immediacy of a revolutionary terror that seeks to anticipate, to pre-empt, the historical process of change, and, moreover, the transformation of popular consciousness, by symbolic rather than strategic or tactical acts of violence. Such critiques of terrorist violence go back to Hegel's analysis of the French Revolutionary Terror and maintain their force in Marxist critiques of terrorism even now. But immediacy also manifests itself in the evacuation of historical process and its reduction to recurrent manifestations of the same mythic content: history becomes the eternal repetition of the same cycle of sacrifice and rebirth. As Kearney puts it:

By means of such periodic blood-letting, the cult enables man to violently pre-empt history. It empowers him to give the lie to the intractable world of fact, sanctioning his accession to a mythic world where different laws apply and where he may be relieved of all the onerous inconveniences which bear him down.⁶

Myth accordingly appears as a means to escape, but insistently commits the subject to repetition. Those who seek to escape their history, one might say, are doomed to repeat it.

Mythological thinking is, then, the recourse of those incapable of taking effective measures to change their conditions and is deeply related to a sense of historical impotence: 'The experience of terror central to myth – and particularly the myth of sacrifice and renewal – is perhaps most plausibly explained in terms of a community's original experience of total impotence before a cruel and ineluctable destiny.'⁷ Myth is thus the expression of a collective sense of victimhood, the recourse of those who are not fully the agents of their own existence. Myth, to close the circle, is the expression of those who are subject *to* rather than subjects *of* their history: what is at first understood as a *motif* becomes a *motivating force*. History's victims, unable to take control of their own destinies, are unconsciously driven by mythic forces that they are impotent to control. Once more, if in a new vocabulary, the uncivil Irish appear as the embodiment of pathological subjecthood.

Of course, a deep irony underlies Kearney's approach. In unfolding his analysis of the mythic drives that supposedly motivate contemporary Republicanism and make of terrorism a pathological and reactive response to victimhood, he neglects to observe that he is captured by the very irrationality of the mythic structures he pretends to critique.

For his argument to have validity, Kearney must assume that the deep-structure of the 'mythic nucleus' is in fact an effective underlying motive force in contemporary Ireland. In thus taking myth at its own word, so to speak, he in his own turn short-circuits historical process, reducing the long and highly differentiated history of Republicanism to the eternal manifestation of the same mythic motifs and the history of the present to a manifestation of deep mythological powers. The further contradictions that ensue from this are manifold. But the failure to acknowledge so glaring a contradiction at the heart of the method of analysis itself indicates the degree to which the critic has baulked at any serious attempt to understand the dynamics of conflict in the North: mythic explanation, projected onto what he fails to grasp in its historical dimensions, itself pre-empts and mythologizes history.

This fact has not prevented Kearney's essay from providing a kind of explanatory template for writings about the hunger strikes. Emblematic of these, and perhaps the most widely circulated and cited, was journalist Padraig O'Malley's *Biting at the Grave*, which stands as an index of the extraordinary extent to which discussion of the prison protests, both in Ireland and across the Atlantic, was saturated by the kind of psychomythological analysis that Kearney articulated. O'Malley's initial rhetorical questions so set the terms of his reportage that they more or less predetermine the answers his investigation will come up with:

Who were we, I wondered, who could incubate and breed such merciless young who would prefer to do right by denying life instead of affirming it, whose sense of victimhood had become such an integral part of their personality that they needed to affirm it by destroying identity itself? And who were they, I wondered, who could harden themselves to abandon life with a casual disregard for the terminal consequences of their actions, eyes fixed on a star in a galaxy of patriot-ghosts imploding in their imaginations, their bodies sacrificial offerings to the glutinous [*sic*] gods of a degenerative nationalism, minds impervious to the importunings of those who did not inhabit their closed universe.[8]

The terms are precise and damning in advance: victimhood, sacrifice, 'patriot-ghosts'. What the hunger strikes bring out, for O'Malley, are 'the psychic undercurrents of religion and tribe' and 'the ancient mythologies carefully nurtured for decades, an idea of Ireland imbued with memory traces of blood sacrifice'.[9]

Almost all accounts of the H-Block struggles, whether journalistic, historical or ethnographic, have tended to follow remarkably similar lines and manifest two basic tendencies. Either they focus on the contemporary conditions of the struggle, the dynamics of the prison regime and the prisoners' situated tactics of subversion and legitimation, or they foreground the long history of Republican prison protest and understand the H-Block campaign as an extension of that earlier history, to the extent of descrying in it, as Kearney and O'Malley do, some kind of mythic recurrence of the Eternal Same. But even those whose focus is most resolutely on the contemporary dynamics tend finally to converge with this mythic tendency. Allen Feldman, whose invaluable *Formations of Violence* insists on 'the modernist [sic] character of political violence in Northern Ireland, despite all popular and easy characterizations of this situation as an archaicized religious or tribal conflict',[10] nonetheless relapses into the interpretive language of myth and eschatology in face of the prison struggles. For Feldman, the hunger strike is the culmination of the prison protests and a return from defilement to the sacral, a 'ritualized circuit travelled by the hunger striker from agency of political violence to incarceration-criminalization, to biological defilement, to purifying sacrificial death and political sacralization'.[11] This kind of anthropological interpretation of the prison experience rests on the unexamined assumption of a prior Republican ideology of martyrdom, circulating before and outside the prisons, that is uncritically drawn from revisionist accounts of the history of the movement. Similarly, Begoña Aretxaga, in her pioneering ethnography of gender relations in Northern Ireland, insists on the fundamentally ahistorical and anti-enlightenment character of the Republican ideology that informed the prisoners:

History as a succession of events is not conceptualized by Republicans as a linear progression. Such a conception is after all the enlightened optimism of imperialism. Set *against* the colonial power of Britain, history appears to Republicans as a succession of stages each representing the same drama in different times. Chronology provides the scenario for a recurrent transcendent theme – colonial oppression and national freedom – that in turn endows with meaning the inchoate feelings of dispossession.[12]

Historical consciousness, the index of modernity, thus appears as if frozen, or paralysed, by the pathologizing effects of colonialism. Over the long duration, temporality offers not historical change and transformation, but the eternal recurrence of the same: the colonial pathology is internalized and manifests itself in the playing out of mythological structures, the expression of a resentment that never comes to analytical consciousness but remains always 'inchoate'.

The mythic hypothesis that underlies so diverse an array of interpretations of Republican violence in general and the prison protests in particular nonetheless unwittingly sheds light on one of the persistent mysteries of the literature on Northern Ireland: the relative occlusion of the experience of the women incarcerated in Armagh Gaol. This occlusion, indeed, parallels what Aretxaga observes – the silence of the community about their protests and the reluctance of the IRA leadership to allow them to proceed.[13] Aretxaga attaches this silence to the negative taboo on menstrual blood that the women were obliged to smear on the cell walls during their no-wash protest, but it is possible to see in blood a more productive relation to myth and to the pathologization of the prisoner. As I will argue at greater length, the interpretation of political motive as mythic motif serves to pathologize the male prisoners and thus replicates the aims of the prison regime itself. The aim of the prison is to break the prisoner's will, reducing his unruly freedom to the dependence and subjection of a pathological body. But, as Mary Corcoran has shown, the penal regime as a gendered structure regards the female prisoner differently, as always already a pathological creature in need of a different mode of psychic and physical intervention.[14] That a priori pathologization of the female offender by the disciplinary institutions of the state parallels the process we have already observed, the gradual tendency to relegate the oral, or the traditional, to the realm of the feminine, where it connotes a turbid mix of superstition and myth – indices, in other words, of the woman's subjection to nature, impulse and biology. The figure of myth *is* woman, from the aged keener to the 'grannies of hate' that haunt the tabloid press. As Adorno and Horkheimer argue in their genealogy of myth and reason,

> man as a ruler denies woman the honor of individualization. Socially, the individual is an example of the species, a representative of her sex; and therefore male logic sees her wholly as standing for nature, as the substrate for never-ending subsumption notionally, and of never-ending subjection in reality. Woman as an alleged natural being is a product of history, which denaturizes her.[15]

Menstrual blood is the corresponding sign of that pathological subjection to the realm of natural cycles and the pre-civic bonds of reproduction and kinship. It becomes the debased signifier of the historically produced mythic world that the state comes to oppose and redeem, while the disgust that it elicits becomes the index of the state's own mobilization of mythic violence and irrationality. But, as I will suggest, the assumption of the pathological nature of the female prisoner, of which blood is the sign, also undercuts her attempt to use the pathological body, in the way male prisoners did, as a means to negate the prison regime. The gendered regime of the prison prevents an equivalent mode of struggle in Armagh and the H-Blocks.

If I defer at this point the further discussion of this impasse, it is because the condition of possibility for the almost ubiquitous recurrence of the same mythic model of analysis in accounts of Republican prison protests lies in an impoverished historical approach to both Irish anti-colonial movements and colonial penal systems. Already committed to demonstrating the atavistic nature of a nationalist ideology, recent Irish histories have reduced those movements to a series of statements abstracted from any consideration of the material and structural history of the state apparatuses in relation to which those movements were formed and transformed. A peculiar set of disjunctions emerges even within what are otherwise the most attentive ethnographic and historical accounts. This disjunction lies not only between the interpretative frameworks and the prisoners' own accounts, which singularly and consistently lack any sustained basis in Catholic attitudes or even in Republican traditions. It also appears between the painstaking anthropological elaboration of the dynamics of the prisoners' corporeal resistance to the prison regime, on the one hand, and the account of their ideological and emotional motivations on the other. The one appears inseparable from a Foucaultian understanding of the disciplinary and penal formations of modernity, the other to reside in the ahistorical terrain of myth. What we still lack is a historical approach that links the situated dynamics of the prison protests to the longer history of incarceration, civil and political, in Ireland and Britain, and to the legacy of former prison struggles that is articulated in the very architecture of the prison itself. In such an account, the evolving spatial organization of the prison and its regimes of regulation and control is understood not as a fully articulated modern apparatus that comes to contain and discipline anti-modern subjects and their atavistic practices, but as a set of structures that have emerged in time with and in response to prior modes of resistance and thus retain, as it were, a memory of the past. Within that emerging set of structures, the prisoners' resistance at any given moment is situated and has a more or less transformative effect on the penal regime and on the larger social and cultural meaning of incarceration.

It is this dialectical relation between the corporeal practices of the prisoners and the spatial regime of the prison that Mary Corcoran emphasizes in one of the few studies of the prison struggles that takes the longer historical formation of the modern carceral system into account. Invoking 'Foucault's concept of *productive power*, with its emphasis on the agency of the suppressed, the dispersal of conflict across different points of a social field, the subversion of institutional closure and the subsequent disruption of historically determined outcomes', Corcoran equally attends to the circumscribed nature of the struggle, its *relational* and *situated* dimensions: the latter are determined not only by the play of power and counter-power within the contemporary institution, but by the representations of the prisoners and the formation of their conditions. These have a longer historical trajectory that shapes expectations and responses as well as the possible tactics through which prisoners' agency can be articulated.[16] Prison struggle is not the encounter between a fixed prison regime and the obdurate resistance of prisoners motivated by an inert ideological commitment; it is both spatially and historically determined, on the one hand by a structure and regime that 'remembers' the past modes of resistance that it was designed to contain, on the other by the agency of prisoners who may in turn recall past struggles but also respond pragmatically and situationally to the current conditions that constrain their practices of resistance. Each continues to transform the other and every dimension of the struggle and of the regime's response – spatial, historical, ideological or representational – signifies within and beyond the prison walls.

II

'Every H-Block contains ninety-six single cells separated into four wings of twenty-four.'[17] This simple statement of the spatial organization of the H-Blocks already condenses every dimension of its significance (Figures 4 and 5). Under the new regime of criminalization of political offenders, the principal object of incarceration was separation. This demanded the breakdown of the collective system of the 'cages' at Long Kesh, which in their spatial organization and self-governing regimes recalled the familiar POW camps of Colditz and *The Great Escape* and signified the status of internees as political prisoners. The cellular system was a spatial means to destroy the Republican community in the jails. By the same token, the separation of political prisoners into separate cells, above and beyond the outward signs of their having to wear prison uniforms or mingle with ODCs, signified criminality in and of itself, and in a way that was distinctively modern. That distinctive modernity lay both in the definition of criminality and in the direction of its 'cure', in the diagnosis of an improper or failed moral development on the part of the criminalized that would be countered and ameliorated by the isolation and individuation of the prisoner. In the context of insurgency, the diagnostic implication of cellular imprisonment was clear and was entirely in keeping with the pathologization of Republicanism in the counter-insurgency discourse of mythic motivation: both implied the atavistic motivations of political resistance and the need for the institution of a civilizing process that would individuate the prisoner, emancipate him or her from unhealthy collective identity, and inculcate a modern, self-disciplined critical consciousness in place of tribal affiliations and violent impulses. The very appearance of the prisoner in a cell immediately indicated his or her criminality, represented as an object of the state's therapeutic care, rather than as a member of a self-organizing, mutually responsible political community. The intimate relation between the cellular system and its significance and the counter-insurgency discourse that circulated around it with reciprocally reinforcing effect set the terms for the conduct of the struggle and for the contested meanings that it generated.

Both the cellular system of the H-Blocks and the performative structure of the counter-insurgency discourse are embedded in the longer history of penal institutions in Britain and Ireland. From the late eighteenth century, penal doctrine in England as in the United States increasingly emphasized the reformative capacity of the prison over either the spectacular forms of corporal and capital punishment that Foucault famously detailed at the beginning of *Discipline and Punish* or the presumably deterrent horrors of open-space prisons like the infamous Newgate, where prisoners of all kinds and classes mingled in almost carnivalesque anarchy.[18] The mingling of young and minor offenders with hardened criminals in such prisons was increasingly understood as producing a kind of criminal infection or contamination such that communication of any kind among prisoners came to be seen as intrinsically suspect.[19] Thus the isolation of prisoners from one another became the desirable precondition for their moral reform. The new architecture of the prison, constructed around rows of separate, individual cells, emerged in time with a novel emphasis on the corrective capacity of the prison system.

From the late eighteenth century on, 'England moved perceptibly but falteringly toward a new prison system based upon privacy, reformative discipline, and the psychological transformation of the self in the cell'.[20] The so-called 'separate system' relied not only on the architectural and psychic isolation of the prisoners to create the conditions for reflection, prayer and remorseful repentance, it sought actively to *break* them. It was intended in the first place to break the *will* of the prisoner as a precondition for reform:

Penal discipline finds the will vigorous, but vicious, propelled powerfully, but lawlessly. It is this vicious activity that is subjugated by protracted seclusion and wholesome discipline ... The will is subdued ... bent or broken, and the moral

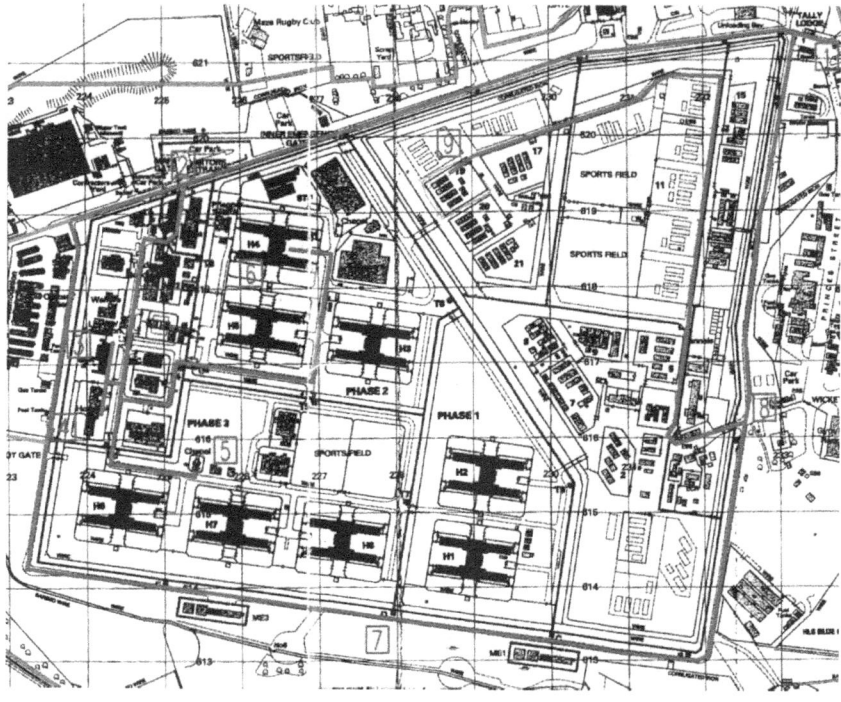

Figure 4 Aerial-view plan of HM Prison The Maze, showing the layout of the H-Blocks

character is ... made plastic by the discipline ... The will is bent in its direction; it is broken in its resistance to virtue, its vicious activity is suppressed only to leave it open to the control of better motives.[21]

Solitary confinement was no less directed at breaking the prisoner's ties to what was increasingly seen as the malignant and contagious culture of the convicts and substituting individuation for community: 'Solitude cut the offender off from his false community.'[22] The enemy of reform was 'the autonomy of prisoner culture'[23] that thrived in the shared spaces and assemblies of the congregate or gang system; it was countered less by educative or religious intervention than by the rearticulation of penal space through 'a physio-centric design that separated every body with stone'.[24] Architectural space became the privileged means of producing the psychic effect of reform. For architects like William Blackburn, the friend of penal reformer John Howard, 'rationally organized space ... would foster

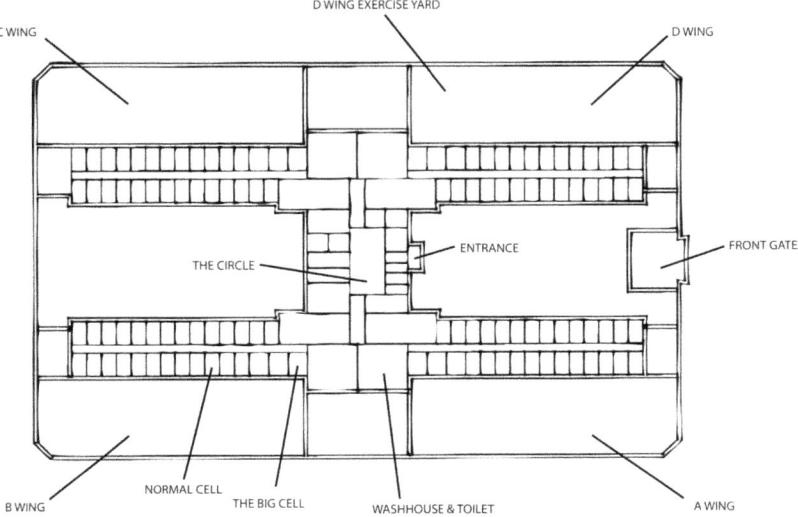

Figure 5 Plan of a typical H-Block in the Maze Prison

the development of reason and self-regulation in its inmates' and 'the main task of architecture ... [was] the regulation of human sociability'.[25] What was planned, if only relatively rarely carried out in such prisons as Pentonville and Millbank, was in effect a spatial map of individuation. The serial array of cells in formally repeated wings and blocks would ensure the isolation of the prisoners from one another and constitute the conditions for silent introspection and the unhindered interventions of warders, clerics and philanthropists.

The prison architecture that emerged from this conjunction of a discourse on the reform of the criminal and a new conception of penal space were quite distinct from the Panopticon advocated by Jeremy Bentham that Foucault considered the model for punitive surveillance. Reformers emphasized the goal of separation even to the extent of frustrating the ends of surveillance, impeded as those would be by the linear corridor and the closed door that sealed the prisoner from contact with other prisoners. Individuation and isolation, as preconditions for reform of the self, were the principal aims and the closed cell became the analogue of the discrete and autonomous individual, arrayed in contiguity and equivalence alongside his fellows. In place of the direct exposure to visibility implied by the panoptical model, the surveillance of the prisoner was mediated through an architecture that submitted him to an intense form of serialization in which he became no more than 'one digit in an aggregable series'. The spatial form of the prison thus anticipated the prisoner's reinsertion after his individualizing reformation into an outer world reordered no less on a principle of seriality, the governable world of the modern nation state within which '[t]he particular always stood as a provisional representative of a series'.[26]

In practice, however, the realization of the cellular 'separate system' was constantly hindered by numerous factors, ranging from the recognition of the enormous psychic damage exacted by extended periods of virtually complete isolation to the lack of centralization of the British prison system, together with the intractable fact 'that the number of convicts [was] too overwhelming for the means of proper and effectual punishment'.[27] This combination of factors either caused or was supplemented by a swing in penal ideology back to the ideal of retributive or deterrent punishment through hard labour, including the enforcement of the treadmill in the 1865 Prison Act.[28] Accordingly, already by the 1870s, reformers were obliged to emphasize once again the virtues of a modified cellular system. Thus William Tallack, secretary of the penal reform association, the Howard Society, prepared a critical report on the British and Irish penal system in 1872. He lamented the undermining of the separate system that isolated convicts only at night by the gang or congregate system that brought them together to labour by day:

Prisoners congregated at work together in silence, represent a great day school in which cunning – how to outwit the watchers – is the only lesson learnt *by heart*. Besides the frequency of punishment, and duplicity fostered in evading it, a third objection is, *the expense of superintendence*. More warders are required than under any system, fruitless as their surveillance is after all; and this is the fifth objection, that *the end is not accomplished*. Prisoners do communicate, to their mutual and serious disadvantage.[29]

The mixed system that had emerged in the haphazard and localized penal administration hindered moral improvement and prevented efforts to educate convicts, above all by failing to ensure the prescribed silence through which the psychological effects of prison were to have been achieved. 'Prisoners *do* communicate.' Against it, Tallack advocated a modified version of the separate system that had depended on extended and total isolation, advocating instead a cellular system which recognized the inhumane effects of total isolation and accordingly 'in its perfection, implies total separation, both by day and night, from *other prisoners only*, but frequent daily communication with instructors, prison officers, or philanthropic visitors'.³⁰

Tallack relied on the examples of European prisons, especially in Belgium and Holland, for his models of the cellular system. Other reformers, however, found a model closer to hand. Mary Carpenter, educationalist and prison reformer, published in the same year a pamphlet entitled *Reformatory Prison Discipline, As Developed by the Rt. Hon. Sir Walter Crofton, In the Irish Convict Prisons*, a work intended for circulation at the same Prison Congress as Tallack's own report.³¹ Like most reformers, her assumption was that 'the very worst men are capable of transformation into self-supporting members of society' and that accordingly, '[t]he object of Prison Discipline is to transform offenders into honest self-supporting men and women'.³² Carpenter opposed the use of coercive force as contrary to the very principles that prison discipline is ideally designed to inculcate – 'industry, self-control, and self-reliance' – but held that 'the will of the individual should be brought into such condition as to wish to reform, and to exert itself to that end, in cooperation with the persons who are set over him'.³³ To her, the Irish Convict System, as designed by Sir Walter Crofton, Chair of the Irish Convict Prisons Board from 1854 to 1862, represented the ideal means to effect such transformation and 'to facilitate the absorption of the well-intentioned convict into the labour market'.³⁴ A 'stage system' of reformatory discipline, it involved an initial period of absolute isolation in virtually complete silence, accompanied by a minimal diet and hard labour in the form of picking oakum. This stage was deliberately designed to have 'a depressing influence on the minds of those men' and it is clear that Crofton and Carpenter understood intimately the psychological effects of what we would now call extended 'sensory deprivation'.³⁵ By the end of three months, in most cases, it was anticipated that 'the idler will generally have learned to associate industry with pleasure'.³⁶ This severely penal stage was followed by a second stage in which the convict was permitted to engage in more vocational forms of labour, to undergo instruction and to mix with other prisoners. During this stage, the convict was subjected to a system of marking, according to which his progress was measured and his conduct assessed, good conduct leading to advancement, recalcitrance to demotion, in a series of steps towards a third or intermediate stage. In this, the convict 'graduated' to an open system prior to release, during which he was permitted to perform paid labour and returned to prison-like quarters only at night.³⁷ This system of marks was intended to persuade the convict that his moral improvement depended on his own exertions.³⁸

Through the Irish Convict System, the prisoner was ideally led from idleness and insubordination to disciplined labour and self-dependence by a combination of architecture and silence. The unruly communities that typified those 'nurseries for crime', the Associated Gaols,³⁹ were replaced by a form of cooperation in which the prisoner was voluntarily self-subordinated to discipline and capable of working outside the prison walls as part of labour gangs. In this final stage, '"Individualization" is the ruling principle', the whole system leading from anarchic association to the economic individual.⁴⁰ In other terms, we could say that the ideal of the Irish Convict System was that of a hegemonic state apparatus supplanting a coercive one – except for the fact that the outer coercive shell of the colonial state remained very much in place: as Mike Tomlinson points out, 'Between 1800 and 1921 the British Government brought in 105 separate Coercion Acts dealing with Ireland. Habeas corpus was as often suspended as in force in 19th-century Ireland'.⁴¹ In the penal system as elsewhere in Irish social life, the larger framework of an almost permanent colonial state of exception furnished the condition of possibility for the 'hegemonic' work of individual transformation and the 'civilizing process'.

Several factors, embedded in the coercive apparatus of the state, determined the emergence of a more systematic and centralized Convict System in Ireland than in Britain. As Carpenter and Crofton were quick to point out, the centralized Irish police system, and in particular its early deployment of photography as a means of surveillance and control, facilitated 'a general and uniform system of the registration of criminals' through which recidivism could be controlled and repeat offenders identified.⁴² Across the board, the colonial administration of Ireland had permitted the establishment of a linked set of disciplinary institutions, ranging from a national, armed police system that would become a model for colonial policing to a national system of education and the convict system itself.⁴³ Such centrally controlled institutional interventions in the daily life of the population, which would have been inconceivable in Britain, were crucial to the colonial project of transforming Irish conditions 'in an improving direction'.

In this respect, the emergence of the Irish Convict System was both discursively and materially an extension of the economic and social prescriptions that were instrumental in determining the course and severity as well as the outcomes of the Famine. Tomlinson notes the temporal coincidence of the Famine and the moment at which 'the Irish "convict system" was properly established and placed under central government control'. But beyond this historical conjunction, he notes the underlying economic and ideological imperatives that conjoined them:

> Just as the famine was seen by the British administration of the time as an opportunity for economic and social development – a lesson in political economy with the potential to transform a peasant, subsistence and potato economy into one based on cash and waged labour – so too was it felt that the new prisons should be places for inculcating the fundamental principles of labour and property relations amongst a rebellious peasantry.[44]

Both the criminal typology that governed the developmental schema of the staged system of imprisonment and the goal of that system, guiding the prisoner from criminality to 'industry, self-control, and self-reliance', conformed with the ways in which, as we have seen in earlier chapters, the recalcitrance of the Irish to the models of character and practice determined by political economy was represented. Carpenter's characterization of the 'habitual offenders' echoed political economists' descriptions of the asociality and the lack of 'providential forethought' of the savage and the poor Irish: 'They dislike labour of all kinds, and to supply their own wants exert themselves only by preying on the property of others. They are self-indulgent, – low in their desires, ignorant of all knowledge that would profit them, skilful only in accomplishing their own wicked purposes.'[45] This description of the habitual offender overlapped with the one she gives of the predominantly Irish slum-dwellers of cities like Liverpool and Bristol: 'They are in a state of semi-barbarism. They are slaves of their lower instincts and passions; they have no care for what does not immediately concern their present needs ... They live in a state of ignorance of all that constitutes civilized society, a practical ignorance of man's immortal nature and destiny.'[46] Criminality lay not in specific acts, but became generalized to a state of savagery that typified a class of the population, that which required intervention and development. The function of the prisons was akin to that of the newly founded industrial schools that Famine observers like Asenath Nicholson commented on, both institutions inculcating 'industry that not only rewarded but elevated'.[47] Just as the cure for the poor Irish was intended to be their transformation from propertyless cottiers whose labour was sporadic and unregulated into productive wage labourers with a respect for the rights of property and accumulation, so the cure for the criminal class lay in the transformation of the prisoners 'into honest self-supporting men and women'.

This transformative, educational drive required nothing less than a fundamental reorganization of Irish space and, where necessary, the constitution of novel spaces that would define the trajectory of this newly emergent, disciplined individual. We have seen already the process and the effects of the transformation of Irish agricultural space in the wake of the Famine, as economists and reformers like Lord Hill, J.S. Mill and J.E. Cairnes commended the decimation of the *clachan* in the interests of producing a society of small tenant farmers and gradually inculcating the values of possessive individualism. The small, bounded and consolidated holding is the imaginary spatial equivalent of the bounded individual and of a transformed conception of gender relations secured through the dominance of primogeniture; its clear demarcation, like the ten-acre holdings praised by Nicholson in Gweedore, spells the end of the 'through-otherness' of the oral community. So too the national schools that begin to dot the countryside, together with the philanthropic Industrial schools, furnish the bounded spaces through which the child of the peasant must pass on its way to becoming the economic individual.[48]

The new cellular prison is cognate both functionally and spatially with those other institutional spaces that map the becoming of the modern subject and reorganize the actual and imaginary geographies of Ireland. In some respects, it is the condensation of those other spaces, their absolute reduction to the minimal requirements of a space that separates, individuates and facilitates the carefully graduated development of the subject out of the savage. The solitude and the silence it imposes function only more discretely than the Famine to destroy the kinds of community and subjectivities that flourished in the *clachan* and to establish new norms of social and individual comportment. The terrible silence that followed the Famine reigns nowhere more intently, more meaningfully, than in the cell block. More than a mere functional apparatus of incarceration, its very form is the distillation of the meaning of those other, more commodious and less evidently coercive institutions and spaces that have so far failed to reach or failed to transform the raw material that is the inmate. The cell is the concentrated instance of the developmental project of colonial modernity. In that respect, it also partakes of the double-edged nature of that project: just as the latter, in its very claim to enact a civilizing mission, produces the Irish as its racial other even as it seeks to improve them, so the cell effectively converts a population into an undifferentiated criminal class even as it promises to individuate its inmates. In the colonial context, the general contradiction that the carceral architecture instantiates, that between the rigorous individuation of the inmates imposed by the cells and the no less rigorous reduction to equivalence expressed in their serial disposition and numeration, is also racialized. The contours of Irishness become those of criminality; to be in the cell determines that one was always already, as a racial subject, in need of the development the prison promises to effect.

The issue of imprisonment as a political terrain can therefore never be merely a question of symbolism as a mythic account of the hunger strikes and the struggles in the prisons would suggest. The contestation of imprisonment is never merely an adjunct to the 'real' political struggle that takes place elsewhere, in those sites recognized as proper to the political. For those spheres that are demarcated political are as articulated with the prison cell as they are with the spheres of schooling, of labour, of leisure. Historically, the cell represents a material apparatus of colonial modernization whose very space produces both subjects and meanings. Its aim is at once to produce subjects in conformity with the modernizing project and to induce the dissolution and forgetting of other, derogated forms of association. It is also to forestall the emergence of the new kinds of counter-modern association that the congregation of inmates from widely dispersed locations in the penal system might suggest and enable. The entry of the political prisoner into the penal system accordingly sets in play not only the question of punishment and of the legitimacy of the state's application of force, but, furthermore, the meaning and function of the cell as a productive colonial apparatus. It does so, however, at different moments in the history of the penal system and with differing tactics and effects according to the degree to which the cellular regime – always more an ideal than an actuality – has been realized or another mode of incarceration been instituted.

Between 1867 and 1871 – the very moment at which the English prison system had reverted to the model of punitive hard labour and the gang system that the prison reformers found themselves contesting anew – the Irish Fenian O'Donovan Rossa was arrested, tried and jailed for sedition in English jails. The Fenians were among the first 'terrorists', and were the earliest objects of modern forensic technologies – subjected to the first systematically gathered 'mugshots' and to a biometrics directed at the human body.[49] In their own self-definition, they were also among the first self-consciously *political* prisoners in that the conditions of their imprisonment became the stage for a performative contestation of the legitimacy of the state itself. The Fenians also transformed the prisons into a stage on which the literal 'bare human', the naked body itself, became both means to and site of struggle with the institutions and architecture of the state. O'Donovan Rossa's memoirs document the dialectic of such a struggle on the cusp of two contradictory prison regimes, between the principle of congregate labour and the principle of isolation.

As we have seen, the attempts of reformers during the 1860s to produce and institute the cellular system with its programme of isolation and individuation confronted the existent system of gang or congregate labour, a system which enabled the interaction and collective association of prisoners as a dissonant counterpoint to the prison regime. Despite all efforts to institute non-communication in the daily penal labour of convicts, the very instruments of discipline became the means to evade its ends, to assert the collectivity of the prisoners against the institutional goal of separation. O'Donovan Rossa observed this phenomenon when he was obliged to work with other prisoners on the treadmill:

> There were thirty of us in that gang, and fifteen to each side of the crank, facing those opposite. We laid hold of the iron bars, and the officer cried, 'On!' We pushed; our bodies bent; our heads came together at every revolution of the wheel; and remarks of some kind were passed. Those professionals could whisper without moving a lip or a facial muscle, and I took much interest in their flow of stories.[50]

The convicts, 'appendages of the machine', found means to 'communicate' and thereby to create provisional but effective forms of oral 'community' whose very existence, fleeting as they may have been, undermined the disciplinary ends of the penal system.

At the same time, however, that community, and participation in it, was the sign of an inveterate criminality, understood as a refusal to be subjected to the reformatory goals of the prison. Hence O'Donovan Rossa, however sympathetic to the convicts and their tactics, needed to *separate* himself from this community as a statement of his non-criminality as political prisoner. For to criminalize is to normalize within the purview of the state, to disavow the challenge that the political prisoner's existence poses to the legitimacy of the state, while for him to belong to the community of prisoners is to accept the legitimacy of his incarceration and the criminality of his acts as a Fenian. Accordingly, if the penal system is the means by which the colonial state is legitimated and through which its pacifying ends are to be achieved, the political prisoner is called to refuse both its discipline and the curative care that it offers towards these ends. To refuse a criminalization that is tantamount to the racialization of the Irish population is to name the prison as a productive apparatus of political rather than simply reformative ends.

O'Donovan Rossa was therefore obliged to use the disciplinary mechanisms of the prison and their contradictory principles against his own criminalization. Just as the convicts used the treadmill, the instrument and signifier of the congregate or 'gang' regime, as a means to reconstitute their community outside the reach of the prison regime, so O'Donovan Rossa discovered that he in turn could use the other regime of the prison, with its emphasis on separation and individuation, equally against its own ends. The very uneven and mixed introduction of the 'cellular system' meant that he was able to manipulate the contradiction between the mass incarceration of prisoners and the system's desire to individuate them. Recognizing that his 'masters' were using his association with the 'criminal' inmates as a mode of both punishment and denomination, he recognized that he had to choose separation from their 'society' not willingly but 'in opposition to the authority that would degrade a Irish rebel'.[51] He accordingly infringed regulations precisely in order to bring down the force of 'disciplinary separation' (or isolation) on himself: 'So that this was actually compelling them to do what I had asked them to do in the first place – separate me from the other convicts. My whole fight had been to require them to recognize the difference between us "politicals" and the ordinary convicts, and in the end they were obliged to do it.'[52] The 'political' thus turned the discipline and the structure of the prison against itself, even discovering that cellular separation offered him more opportunities to write. Indeed, O'Donovan Rossa's whole narrative is replete with instances of his use of the very architecture of the prison to communicate with other prisoners by tapping on walls or floors or incising roof slates that could be thrown over the walls of exercise yards; or to conceal items of contraband, such as by slipping his pen between floorboards or brickwork or hanging his inkwell outside from the bars of the cell; or to exchange confidences with other Fenians across the barriers that separated them at mass but also concealed their whisperings from the guards.[53]

O'Donovan Rossa recognized immediately that at every level – its architecture, its routines, its intrusive practices – the technology of the prison is directed at *breaking* the prisoner. Crucial in this process is the practice of strip-searching. The stripping of prisoners is in the first place an instance of biometric rationality. On several occasions, usually but not always as he was being transferred from one prison to another, O'Donovan Rossa underwent being 'measured, weighed, stripped, searched, bathed, re-dressed, shaven, shorn, and entered on the books'. The putative concern with the welfare of the prisoner's body meets here with the function of identification and control. But stripping simultaneously becomes a means of discipline and humiliation. O'Donovan Rossa instantly recognized the parallel between strip-searching and the military's 'breaking' of recruits through stripping:

> For three months, day after day, those officers put me through the same routine ... I am not overly sensitive or thin-skinned, but I own to strong feelings against my fellow man looking at me in a 'state of nature'. When I was at school, and heard boys tell tales of how men were stripped naked when they enlisted, I imagined it to be the most arbitrary outrage they could suffer, and there was little fear of my ever becoming a soldier.[54]

This is the fundamental paradox of the naked body under the surveillance of the state: that which is most intimate and 'private', most the property of the individual, the site of identification as of identity, is equally the site of the person's reduction to the unindividuated 'state of nature'. Strip-searching, like military discipline, combines in one complex the vulnerability and exposure of the individual with his reduction to mass of undifferentiated flesh: its function is identical to that of the cell, at once isolating the prisoner in his vulnerability and reducing him to an interchangeable unit in a mass.

Even this complex practice of surveillance, discipline and nakedness, however, O'Donovan Rossa managed to transform into the means to a re-differentiation of the political prisoner. At one point he responds eloquently to a prison governor who says:

> 'England has no political prisoners now-a-days. You are no more than any other prisoner here, and are treated like every other prisoner.'
>
> O'D: 'Ah, but Governor, I think you are mistaken. You don't keep the gas burning in the cell of every other prisoner all night; nor do you strip every other prisoner naked once a day; You don't take every other prisoner through wards and corridors from his day-cell to sleep in another at night; nor do you punish every other prisoner for not doing two work tasks at the same time.'[55]

The spectacle of 'unaccommodated man' became the sign of his refusal to 'accommodate' to the prison regime and therefore of his refusal to accept the state's monopoly on rights and on the right to punish and reform the dissenter into a 'cooperative' subject. The body that is deprived of all 'welfare' is the very image of the insistence on a threshold of difference from the incorporative function of the state that operates through its curative 'care'. Here the political prisoner's naked body stands as a staging of bare life, that *zoe* that Giorgio Agamben distinguishes from the *bios* of political existence as its very sill or unincorporated point of differentiation.⁵⁶ The assumption of that status by rhetorically embracing the political prisoner's state of exception vis-à-vis other prisoners is at once the refusal to be subjected to disciplinary incorporation by the state and the assertion of standing at the threshold of another political community that will accommodate this bare life.

O'Donovan Rossa's dialectical turning of both the meaning and the space of his incarceration against themselves was conditioned both by the specific contradictions of the British penal regime at the time and by the practice of holding Fenian prisoners as far as possible in segregation from one another. Denied for the most part the possibility of articulating collective resistance, he found ways instead to insert himself as a recalcitrant element into the regime and architecture of the prison and to transform the technique of punitive isolation into a means to differentiate himself as a political prisoner from those inmates whose criminality was signified by their subjection to the mass regime of hard labour. O'Donovan Rossa's prison struggle thus necessarily remained almost entirely individual and was fought out through the architecture of individuation that instantiated the ends of the cellular system. Subsequent forms of incarceration of Irish political prisoners followed a quite different spatial and penal model, obeying rather the logic of the concentration camp or the barracks than the cellular prison. Certainly in the wake of the 1916 uprising, leaders of the rebellion, including most notably Eamonn De Valera and Countess Markievicz, were imprisoned in segregated cells, but the mass of those who surrendered or were rounded up in the aftermath of the rebellion were eventually held collectively in the prison camp at Frongoch in North Wales, established on the site of a former mine works. Here, the purpose-built living huts, although their disposition in street-like rows obeyed the rigorously serial logic that typifies the disciplinary institution, created collective spaces for the assembly of the prisoners. The relative autonomy granted to the inmates to organize their own command structures and regimes of training and education was recognized to be an invaluable opportunity for the IRA.⁵⁷ Not only the regime that the camp permitted, but its very spatial layout articulated the modern 'military machine' that the IRA sought to be, a simulacrum of the military discipline and disposition developed at Sandhurst. Frongoch became, as contemporary observers already noted, 'a veritable political university and military academy' or 'a "University for Revolutionists"'.⁵⁸ But it is not only the internal disposition of space, which allowed for relatively free movement and assembly by the prisoners, that was significant in and of itself, but the fact that that space was *bounded*. A space of concentration, it succeeded in constituting a nucleus of the nation itself, confined within the finite, limited boundaries within which any 'imagined community' is conceived.⁵⁹ Its practical and its symbolic importance lay in the fact that not only did it bring members of the IRA together in a single, relatively autonomous space, but that it brought volunteers from all over the island together for virtually the first time. The camp became a synecdoche of the imagined community even as it fulfilled the practical function of unifying the organizational and doctrinal purpose of the movement across the geographical territory of the nation.⁶⁰ Unlike the cellular system, whose spatial organization expressed the subjection of the individuated prisoner to a regime of re-formation that would make of him a governable unit among many, the space of Frongoch effectively admitted the legitimacy and self-governing capacity of an anti-colonial collective.

It has often enough been noted that the compound system of Long Kesh, in which paramilitary prisoners and suspected Republicans swept up by the policy of internment were held between 1972 and 1976, resembled Frongoch. It too functioned under the political and militarized control of the paramilitary organizations, and allowed for a very large degree of association and self-education on the part of the prisoners.⁶¹ What is less often noted is the distinction between them and the ways in which their spaces functioned in relation to the internees at the specific moments in which they were incarcerated. Frongoch housed a relatively organized body of men who had been trained as recruits to the Irish Volunteers and the Citizen Army. Nothing in the writings about it suggests that the space was familiar in either its regime or its layout to either its inmates or their guards. It came into being in response to the need to intern a large number of rebels at a time when Britain was at war. Everything about Frongoch, from its construction in an old mine works to the uncertainty and flexibility of the regime, suggests its ad-hoc nature, as if the nature of such a camp was still being invented. Within that fluid structure, prisoners learnt to use the architecture and regime against their intended functions, as in the ingenious workings of the 'Republican postal system' or the use of the recesses between the hospital building and lavatories for the passage of contraband.⁶² But it is not apparent that the period of incarceration was transformative, ideologically or organizationally, for the prisoners there: at most, they 'were confirmed in the doctrine of resistance to British rule' and, as mentioned already, gained a more national sense of the movement.[63] Long Kesh, however, appears by all accounts to have had a thoroughly transformative effect on the prisoners and on paramilitary organization. The majority of those who entered were new recruits or even only Republican sympathizers without a very deep commitment to the movement, many of them probably impelled into resistance to British rule by recent events like Bloody Sunday in January 1972 or by internment itself.[64] Later leaders of the movement and the prison protests, like Bobby Sands, effectively cut their political teeth in Long Kesh. It was there that the younger generation of Provisionals, particularly the 'coffee-drinking intelligentsia' of Cage Eleven, began to study Irish, to read and explore the work of anti-colonial intellectuals like Fanon, Guevara and Cabral, and to forge a left-wing Republicanism, based on indigenous models like James Fintan Lalor, James Connolly and Liam Mellowes, against the conservative older generation. It was also there, after the experience of British in-depth interrogation during internment, that the military structure of the IRA was rethought, abandoning the locally based and easily penetrated brigade structure for the cellular system that revived an earlier Fenian model of organization, though it was probably immediately based on readings in the guerilla tactics of other anti-colonial movements.[65]

The function of Long Kesh as a 'university of revolution' was facilitated by the relative autonomy of paramilitary organizations within the prison regime that acknowledged their command structures and permitted 'freedom of association'. That regime was grounded in the signification of the spatial organization of the camp. Administratively designated 'special category' prisoners, the internees and those convicted of terrorist acts alike were effectively acknowledged to be political prisoners or 'prisoners of war' by the familiarity of the space in which they were incarcerated. It is not for nothing that Long Kesh is so often described by comparison with Second World War prison camps like Colditz or Stalag Luft which had been familiarized by film and TV. The resemblance of its barbed-wire compound and array of Nissen huts to the spaces in which British officers were held by the Wehrmacht materially produced the sense of legitimacy that the claim to 'political status' sought to confer ideologically on Republican prisoners. The architecture and historical meaning of the camp itself both enabled the collectivity of the prisoners and confirmed their status as the virtual representatives of an alternative political formation, endowing young working-class activists, whose engagement with Republican politics had largely been spontaneous and reactive rather than self-consciously reflective, with a sense of recognition and gravity.

III

The cellular plan of the H-Blocks was the architectural negation of the 'free association' of Long Kesh and the spatial correlative of criminalization. The regular, self-replicating cell-block with its individual, identical compartments, embodying a legacy of penal philosophy that had produced the criminal since the nineteenth century, was designed to isolate and individuate *as criminal* paramilitary actors who understood their operations as political. Not only the prisoner, but even his motivation was to be individualized and derationalized. The meaning of the cell block, in a paradox that has always been constitutive of the cellular system, was at once individuation and non-differentiation: the individuation of the prisoner in the cell, reduced to one criminal among others, was counterpointed by the *indifference* that the identical, serial repetition of prison cells and numerical identification imposed. In its very form, the cellular architecture of the Maze Prison signified that paramilitary prisoners were to be indistinguishable from the so-called 'Ordinary Decent Criminals' among whom they were supposed to be distributed.

Accordingly, O'Donovan Rossa's use of isolation as a means of affirming his political status was no longer available to Republican prisoners after 1976. Given the intervening history of the generalization of the cellular system as *the* form of incarceration, the cell was the mark of criminality. As Feldman points out:

> The first IRA men to enter the H-Blocks encountered a regime that refused to recognize any social unit larger than the individual inmate. The depoliticization of the paramilitary's formal penal status conversely meant his extreme individualization and a refusal on the part of the prison administration to recognize his organizational affiliation. The paramilitary's space was reduced to the prison cell, the prison uniform, the prisoner's identification number, the 'black book' (the prisoner's file), and the prisoner's interaction with prison staff.[66]

But the penal strategy of individuation and isolation is not only aimed at separating the prisoner from the organization, denying thus the political motivation of the crime and breaking the supportive ties that connect the offender to a larger collective. It also and more significantly transforms the meaning of that collective retroactively, in line with the general thrust of counter-insurgency discourse. According to the logic of individuation, if the 'cure' for criminality is isolation, the motivation for the crime, and the collective mentality that it stemmed from, must already have been pathological, such that the prisoner is diagnosed as having lacked sufficiently developed individuality. The collective is denied rational intentionality and the prisoner is rewritten as the passive victim of malevolent influence, of atavistic impulses or of a tribal mentality who can be reformed by the therapeutic regime that removes him from those pre-political influences. The hygienic architecture of 'the most modern prison facility in Europe'[67] declares in effect that the function of the prison regime is not only to punish or incapacitate the terrorist; it is to modernize him. The distribution of cellular space is the material correlative of that intent.

The political struggle of Republican prisoners was thus situated in and defined by the spatial organization of the H-Blocks. Though the initial expression of resistance to the prison regime was its first inmate, seventeen-year-old Kieran Nugent's refusal to don the prison uniform, the subsequent escalation of the blanket and no-wash protests was determined by and aimed at the transformation of the space of the prison and its meanings. There is little evidence that many, if any, of the prisoners, most of them extremely young, had much detailed knowledge of previous Republican prison struggles, apart from a general knowledge of iconic figures, nor that they had any long-term programmatic strategies of prison resistance in mind on entering the blocks:

There was a vague awareness that we were heading for some sort of confrontation, but it wasn't something which preoccupied us. I think this was partly because most of us were young and hadn't the inclination to think too far into the future ... The average age was around 19 or 20, and we were more concerned with the craic and pulling 'mixes' on each other than anything which might happen to any of us in the long distant future.[68]

Even where the prison protest was informed by Republican ideology, that ideology tended to be expressed in very general terms as being 'based on the centuries old Republican tradition which had been handed down from generation to generation' of fighting 'the jail system to maintain their identity as POWs'.[69] In any case, as Feldman argues, 'the assumption of a seamless evolutionary continuity in the development of Republican ideology and tactics obscures the particular experiential basis of their resistance and its symbolic systems'.[70] Space, rather than an ideologically preordained practice, the necessity to seize and transform the space of the prison, to refunction its meaning and workings, determined the mode of struggle and its political reverberations. And that space, in which the congealed memories of past resistances and past formations were crystallized, also unleashed the ghosts of less easily articulated presences.

The situation of the Blanketmen was almost diametrically opposed to that of the Fenians of the nineteenth century. Whereas the latter were imprisoned in relative isolation, within a very short time the H-Blocks, purpose-built for segregation, were overwhelmed by the numbers of non-conforming Republican prisoners. By early 1978, the numbers on the blanket protest had increased to 250 or more. By the time the hunger strikes brought an end to the no-wash protest in 1981, there were around 500.[71] The increasing numbers obliged the prison administration to double up prisoners, thus undercutting the goal of cellular isolation, and once again to concentrate the prisoners in blocks according to their organizational affiliations and in separation from the ODCs. Rather than imposing isolation, mass imprisonment became the means to reasserting a collective status and a degree of control over the conditions and meaning of imprisonment.

The aspect of the cellular prison's architecture that is designed to isolate the inmates from one another comes almost immediately into contradiction with its other functions: to facilitate the movement, provision and supervision of prisoners, to rationalize and homogenize their conditions, to replicate their environments in an identical series. The uniformity and seriality of the cells, as well as the gaps and fissures required for the circulation not only of inmates and warders but also of material elements essential to their well-being, such as heat and air, lent themselves to inventive forms of communication. In a way familiar from almost all prison narratives, the walls whose purpose was separation became tympani, thresholds of communication between prisoners through tapping and drumming in code. So too did the heating pipes that had perforce to run the whole length of the cell block. These also furnished more sophisticated means of communication: prisoners learnt to dig out the plaster around the pipes, thus making a series of gaps along which threads torn from blankets could be slipped, their ends lit to provide lights for rolled cigarettes that passed the whole length of the block. This was known as 'pulling the choochoos'.[72] Other techniques were also developed:

> We were now able to make contact with other cells by 'swinging the line' ... The process was simple. We tore a strip of blanket about 6 foot long and a half inch wide. On one end we tied a dead weight – a bar of soap or a tube of toothpaste – to give enough power to get a swinging action. We put it out the window and told the man in the next cell to put his hand out. Then we started swinging. When he grabbed the dead weight, the stuff – anything from a religious magazine to tobacco – was tied on at the other end of the line.[73]

Another method that made use of structural gaps in the prison's enclosure was known as 'shooting the line':

Swinging the line gave us access to everybody on our side of the wing, but not to the lads on the other side. That was the case until someone came up with the ingenious idea that would enable us to pass stuff from one side of the wing to the other. It consisted of a button taken from a prison shirt and 10–15 feet of fine wool which was used to stitch the top of the prison blankets. We tied one end of the wool onto the button. At the bottom of every cell door was a small gap through which the button would pass. It was then flicked with a plastic comb, making it shoot across the wing with the string travelling behind. After a couple of attempts we always got it close enough to the cell opposite for the man in the cell to be able to fish it in using a folded mass sheet as a hook.[74]

Prisoners even discovered that the prefabricated construction of the blocks meant that 'each dividing wall between the cells had two shackle holes that had allowed cranes to drop each pre-cast section into place when the Blocks were being built'.[75] A concerted effort to remove the plaster that filled these regularly placed holes furnished yet another set of openings for communication. Not only the ritual humiliation of the naked prisoners and the continual violence of wing changes, strip- and mirror-searching, forced washes and the random assaults by individual prison officers, but also the very architecture of the prison was designed to break the prisoners, to break their individual will to resist and to break their collective ties. As one prisoner put it, 'There was no single piece of the prison that wasn't used to break us.'[76] Accordingly, the prisoners' 'breaking down' of the prison into its multiple gaps and fissures was a means of transvaluing its space, transforming it from a hostile enclosure into an intimate tissue of openings and possibilities for connection through its blank walls and locked doors.

The prisoners' refunctioning of the architecture of the H-Blocks, discovering fractures that were the effects of the seamlessly compartmentalized yet articulated spaces it was intended to secure, had its counterpart in an analogous reconfiguration of the space of the body itself:

The H-Blocks broke all your inhibitions about your body. It made you more aware of your body. You never thought you had so much fucking space up there. You look at your body and you think it's a solid mass. I never knew anything about my body, but in the Blocks you become dead aware that you had a sphincter, a colon passage, a bowel. You never knew it before. You appreciated there was a hole in it.[77]

The 'undivided' body is the visual image of the individual as unit and integral person. The bounded and continuous surface of the body materializes the psychic boundaries of the ego, the imago formed out of the fragmentary and dispersed cathexes of the infant's multiple orifices in their relation to an as yet undifferentiated world.[78] The cell, developed as a technology for the production of the individual, is the spatial extension and container of this bounded body image. If the naked body of the prisoner in the cell appears as the absolute reduction of the human being to the condition of bare life, persisting in its condition of civil death, it is still an image of the human individual, a human at the threshold between *zoe* and *bios* from which the claim to an alternative sociality can be staked.[79] The experience of the Blanketmen exceeded this image of the integral body, disintegrating its smooth surface into the multiple cavities of its folds and orifices. The prisoners' practical use of the body as a means of transport and communication by way of its gaps and fissures corresponded with their refunctioning of the supposedly closed space of the cell into one that is riddled with holes. Both entailed a fundamental reimagination of spatial and corporeal relations. Motivated in the first instance by the need to evade the surveillance of the warders, the deployment of the inner spaces of the body constituted a space beyond the regime of the visible that the image of the solid body inhabits. The imagined 'solid thing' becomes a body full of holes.

The emergence of a radically altered image of space and the body belongs, as does the dynamic of the prison protests as a whole, with the gradual and situated escalation of the prisoners' tactics. This reimagination of the body as a network of fungible orifices was in the first place purely functional. Through a practice to which they gave the resonant name 'bangling', prisoners succeeded in deploying the interior spaces of their exposed and utterly surveilled bodies into the means of smuggling an extraordinary array of items, ranging from tobacco and cigarette papers to ballpoint pen refills and even custom-made cell radios. Contraband could be conveyed in the anus, the foreskin, the nose or mouth, even in some cases in the navel. Most important of these contraband items were the coms, messages to and from the prisoners written in minuscule handwriting on cigarette papers and wrapped in cling film. Transfer of those vital messages generally took place mouth to mouth as prisoner and visitor kissed. The disintegration of the individual prisoner's body into the array of its orifices is here supplemented by the mingling of bodies through their orifices, ensuring communication by contiguity and transfer rather than by point-to-point transmission. The function of the mouth as an organ of speech is displaced by its functions as a zone of intromission and of sexual pleasure. But these functions are in turn displaced by the function of communication in a circuit that relies on the irreducible lability of the orifice.

Thus deployed as a vehicle for communication, the interior of the body is extroverted through the openings of its orifices. So also, as both Maud Ellmann and Allen Feldman have pointed out, is the body folded outwards onto the exterior of the cell:

> In Long Kesh ... the distinction between room and person virtually disappeared, because the inmates imprisoned themselves in their own substance by caking their cell walls with excrement. Although their world had been reduced to four cramped walls, within that tiny compass self was everywhere ... for they cocooned themselves into their excremental signatures.[80]

Or, as Feldman puts it, 'the personal defilement of the state's cell rendered the latter an organic extension of the individual prisoner's body'.[81] But that extroversion of the body, like the opening of its interior spaces, ultimately exceeded a defensive or passively resistant function. The use of the body's cavities as a means of evading surveillance goes some way towards countering even as it calls forth the invasive violence of strip-searching and associated forms of brutality that breach the physical and psychic boundaries of the individual. The extroversion of the body onto the cell – the reclamation of the latter through excrement and odour – similarly defies the intent of confinement: the isolation and reduction of the prisoner. As the prisoners extend the limits of their corporeal presence to the interior walls of their cells, they not only reclaim that space from the hygienic regime of the prison, they reconstitute the interior of each cell and the series of connected cells along the block into an intimate, contiguous zone of communication. The fetid odour of the cell blocks, the reek of excrement and unwashed bodies on which every visitor or employee comments, constituted the boundaries of a virtual no-go area which warders entered only reluctantly and by which they were palpably contaminated. It functioned as a boundary wall that demarcated the retrieved space of the prisoners' reclaimed community:

> When I turned into B Wing, the smell hit me right in the face. It was unbelievably bad; it nearly made me throw up. It was like walking into an invisible wall. It was like the smell of bodies decomposing. But after a while on the Blanket I became used to the smell, though coming back from a visit I always hit that invisible wall again.[82]

The miasma of this disseminated odour marked the outer limits of the extroversion of the prisoners' bodies, constituting a kind of transcorporeal space that exceeded the bounds of the individual body and of the separate cells. Odour became the medium of an (im)material communication among the prisoners' bodies, capable of perfusing the cell walls and doors.

The cell blocks were no less pervaded by the sounds of the prisoners' voices. The intimate contiguity of the cells, designed though they were to isolate and to silence, enabled a flourishing of oral communication along each wing, especially at night after lock-down and the withdrawal of the warders to the central 'cross-bar'. Prisoners sang, recited novels or stories from memory, held political or tactical discussions and classes or *ranganna*, and learnt Irish together. Less formally, teasing, jokes and banter – the *craic* – functioned as a means to break down the boredom of constant confinement and to boost morale. This affirmation of an inner oral community, furthermore, must have maintained the Blanketmen's sense of purpose, affirming the logic of what they were doing against the deadening and dehumanizing impact of depredation and of the squalor they inhabited. An equally crucial activity was passing the news, or *scéal*, that enabled prisoners to feel connected both with the larger community of the blocks and with the outside world. It was fed by visits, conversations at mass and by bulletins picked up on the contraband radios. But the form of the passing of *scéal* is as important as its content for the ways in which it refunctioned the cellular system. Largely unwritten and unauthoritative, and subject to discussion and interpretation, *scéal* had the status of rumour or gossip and was transmitted in analogous ways. Ranajit Guha comments on rumour that, unlike the written message, it lacks 'a necessary distinction between the communicator and his audience', being rather a message passed 'from a teller to a hearer who himself becomes a teller'. It is 'not sealed off by any "final signified" emanating from a primal source', but is rather 'a chain of reactions'. Its metonymic mode of transmission – by contiguity rather than from source to receiver – resembles that of the famous chapati that circulated among Indian peasants at the time of the Mutiny or, indeed, the messages that mobilized agrarian revolts in eighteenth- and nineteenth-century Ireland. Like the miasma, it is a form of contagion that hangs, as Guha puts it, 'in the air', a phrase reminiscent of the prisoners' own expression for the movement of persons or communication through the wing: being 'on' or 'off the air'.[83] The passing of *scéal*, the transmission of the voice through and along the cells of the wing, becomes a medium that deconstructs the space of each individual cell, transforming them from isolating boxes into a communicating series. The cell as enclosure becomes rather the biological cell, subject to the osmosis of the voice, or the radio cell, the medium of transmission and reception.

The reconstitution of the cell block into a kind of oral community used the layout of the cell block in order to transform the repressive space of the prison into a zone of impenetrability, a virtual 'no-go area' where the prisoners regained a degree of autonomy. The gradual emergence of Irish, *Gaeilge*, as a medium of communication among the prisoners was crucial to shaping and maintaining a space that escaped the surveillance of the authorities: like the odour of their bodies and their cells, it constituted a kind of outer wall within which the actual walls of the cells were perforated. For those prisoners who entered the H-Blocks already knowing some Irish, it originated as an affirmation of the cultural difference that legitimated their struggle as an anti-colonial one, signifying 'a unique Irish cultural colony within occupied territory' – a 'Gaoltacht'. But that culturally and politically symbolic function was rapidly overtaken by the pragmatics of developing a medium of communication that would be obscure to the warders.[84] The emergence of H-Block Irish partook of the general condition of the struggle, its shaping in and by the conditions of the modern jail. As McKeown comments:

But just as our conditions threw up obstacles they also provoked determination and ingenuity. One crucial factor that spurred us on to overcome the difficulties was our need to be able to communicate with one another without the screws knowing what was being said. All of these conditions gave rise to the beginning of Irish language classes.[85]

Rather than an instance of cultural revivalism, the formation of the Gaoltacht was a prime instance of the 'invented tradition'. Invented traditions can have a reactionary and fetishistic function, but it is no less true that significant cultural differences can be forged, transmitted and elaborated through practices that are not merely imaginary or symbolic, but materially imbricated in the modern institutions that they negotiate. They shape space and performance in ways that often embed unwitting modes of repetition and transformation, constituting new practices out of the occluded legacy of the old, in discontinuity rather than in an ideal or 'spiritual' continuity. H-Block Irish functioned in just this way above and beyond its use as 'the "coded system" for secretive communication'.[86]

The reconstitution of an oral community within the H-Blocks, with a reconstructed Irish language as its vehicle, directly confronted the rationale and the spatial logic of the cellular system and frustrated its aim of producing the isolation and individuation of the prisoner through silence and separation. It was seen to 'break' the prison:

We changed the prison. When I first went to jail, you couldn't talk out of the door. You would get done for 'disturbing the peace of the prison.' Less than a year later we were having sing-songs out the door, giving the Gaelic lessons and the political lectures. We just broke down the whole prison discipline.[87]

Relying literally on the reactivation of memory traces both to teach and to learn the language without grammars or other texts, the Gaoltacht also unleashed traces that transcended the memory of any individual prisoner and were, rather, embedded in the architecture and function of the prison itself. Originally designed to break up the unruly assemblages and subversive communication of prisoners that frustrated the 'congregate' system of imprisonment, the rationale of the cell block was continuous with that of the project of breaking up the 'through-otherness' of the *clachan* and producing the property-owning individual through the redivision of the land into contiguous, bounded plots of farmland. Both strategies assumed the congruence of the units of a rationally organized space with the imaginary bounded body of the possessive individual, who is, in turn, the synecdoche for the body politic of the state, composed by the aggregation of those identical units. In their formal identity was grounded the possibility of the representative function of the state as the expression of the 'imagined community' within its bounded territory.

We have seen in previous chapters how the poor Irish, both in their inhabitation of spaces like the *clachan* or the English slum and in their movement through space as 'mobile hordes', posed a powerful imaginary challenge to emergent notions of governable space. Their representation as miasma, as odour and contagion, figured the breakdown of bounded spaces and bodies into porous and unstable zones that threatened the political and economic regime of a not yet entirely consolidated modern state. Their imaginary power was as much figural as material, marking the existence of a potentially contagious alternative sociality in excess of any actual prospect of successfully subverting the social order. They provoked accordingly a flood of negative typologies, at the heart of which were the twin figures of orality and dirt, both of which connoted the transgression of proper spatial bounds as well as the fundamental incivility of the Irish. Seamus Deane has noted how representations of the no-wash protest recall a much older judgement of Irish incivility, 'a four hundred year-old distinction between barbarians and civilians' which played itself out in the clash between the 'the filthy nakedness of the prisoners and the space-suited automatism of the disinfecting jailers' that seemed to represent 'vulnerable Irish squalor, impervious, impersonal English decontamination'.[88] But beyond the discursive proliferation of these counter-insurgency images of Irish incivility, the spectre of the earlier threat to the colonial social imaginary and its idea of governable space also haunts the material terrain of the blocks. This is not to suggest that in any way the prisoners saw themselves as recomposing the earlier oral community of the *clachan*, as engaging in a recovery of rural Irish traditions or even restoring its communal values. Nonetheless, precisely in and through deconstructing the prison apparatus whose forms emerged as part of a general effort on the part of the colonial state to break the recalcitrant formations of oral community, the prisoners forged a life in common that peculiarly reconfigured the underlying forms of the *clachan* as a mode of living. Breaking down the compartmentalizing boundaries of the cells that were designed to separate and individuate, they transformed the serial array of the wings into metonymic sequences of displacement and dissemination. Withdrawn from visibility and surveillance, their bodies largely out of sight of one another as well as of the warders, sound and voice became means of relay rather than authoritative utterances of individuated subjects. This transindividual soundscape became the foundation of a collective recomposition of Irish as the medium of the community, passing from one to another like a kind of contagion. It was no less the foundation of the collective project of dialogical, Freirean mutual education that profoundly marked the new forms of politicization that were to emerge from the blocks and change the direction of the Republican struggle.[89]

Such external and long-term effects of the reconstitution of orality in the blocks do not, however, render adequately the radical nature of the transformation of subjectivity that it entailed within the space of the prison and through the duration of the no-wash protest. The ways in which oral communication among the prisoners enacted an imaginary dissolution of the enclosing walls of the cell is inseparable from the effect of the dissolution of the solid, bounded body that we have already explored. Together with the inhabiting of shit-lined cells and the penetrating diffusion of odour that emanated from them, orality and the breaking-down of the bounding surface of the body into its folds and orifices constituted something yet more: an inversion of what Norbert Elias has designated 'the civilizing process', the development of forms of etiquette and self-control that accompanied the state's gradual monopoly of violence by disciplining the individual's impulses and comportment.[90] The civilizing process is not merely a matter of manners and behaviour: its gradual unfolding involves the systematic occupation and disciplining of the orifices of the human body in accord with the regime of 'propriety'. One could say, indeed, that the civilizing process involves the serial closure of the orifices and their organization into a hierarchy equivalent to the familiar hierarchy of the senses. Just as taste, smell and touch were aesthetically subordinated to hearing and sight, so the various orifices and their biological functions would be disciplined and governed by their distribution into proper spaces and times. The functions of urination, excretion and passing gas are privatized into discrete spaces; the lability of the mouth is disciplined and zoned according to the proper times and spaces for speech or for eating or drinking or for singing, as well as being subject to rules of propriety with regard to what enters and is emitted from it; even the eye and the ear are subject to controls on seeing and not seeing, weeping and not weeping, hearing and not hearing.

This system of regulation of the orifices into their proper functions and spaces is the fundamental discipline of the modern self: 'the notion of the self is founded on the regulation of the orifices', as Maud Ellmann succinctly puts it.[91] Regulation of the body not only establishes the proper spaces and appropriate times for the multiple functions of the orifices, it arrays them according to a hierarchy that maps onto a kind of metahistorical developmental schema. Grossest and lowest of the orifices are those associated with excretion and urination; above them those, the nose and the mouth, that more ambiguously mark the boundaries between inner and outer, sites of the absorption of alien matter into the self through taste and smell; highest of all, those through which the exterior enters only in the most abstract forms of light and sound, the privileged aesthetic organs of the ear and the eye. It is a schema constantly afflicted by its own instability, given that to a greater or lesser degree every orifice is afflicted with an ambiguity of function in relation to the civilizing processes, from the proverbial *inter faeces et urinas nascimur* that marks the proximity of excretion and sexual pleasure, to that most labile of orifices, the mouth, whose functions perpetually deterritorialize one another. It is, nonetheless, a schema that maps onto a universal history of civilization, distributing populations according to their location on the scale of that hierarchy.

The developmental schema of the orifice also intersects with the disciplining and formation of the psycho-sexual subject and its libidinal drives. The various erogenous zones of the body are associated in psychoanalytic theory with the *stages* of the subject's development, a development that is tied at every moment to the formation of the ethical person. The oral stage, that of the infant's narcissistic non-differentiation from its world of objects, gives way to the anal stage of negation and aggression. That in turn opens on to the genital stage, which both inaugurates the possibility of the oedipus complex with its dissolution in the internalization of the father as superego and marks the superordination of visual marks of sexual and other forms of difference.[92] In both schemata, the various zones of the body that are defined by its orifices become reordered as stages on the way to fully human subjecthood. The gradual constitution by the Blanketmen of an oral and excremental community and their discovery of the 'body full of holes' stands not merely as a defiance of the hygienic and reformatory ends of the prison, but as a dismantling of the fundamental schema that sustains it as an organ of the larger civilizing process of the colonial state. 'This continuous incompletion of the captive body in the prison', as Feldman puts it, 'its permanent liminality and fragmentation, was the precondition for cultural constitution and genesis'.[93] The opening up of the architectural spaces of the prison is inseparable from the opening out of the body into a surface across which its orifices are redistributed into a chain of dehierarchized and metonymic equivalencies. This undoing and reversal of the formative discipline of the subject through the unleashing of the orifices from their disciplinary closures doubtless accounts for the carnivalesque elements that are a constant of every narrative of the experience of the H-Blocks that follows closely the prisoners' own testimonies. It helps to explain the paradox that those who passed three or four years in the most unimaginably immiserated conditions never fail to emphasize the more than compensatory camaraderie, the *craic* whose complex play exceeded the manifestations of banter and black humour that traditionally enable the survival of hard times. The releasing of the orifices was accompanied by an unleashing of libido that became available for recathexis on the immediate community – and was expressed in laughter and exuberance.[94]

The prisoners' undoing of normative forms of subjectivity and their virtual reconstitution of non-modern modes of sociality into counter-modern practices also explains why the blanket and no-wash protests have seemed constantly to defy comprehension or even representation. There remains an 'unassimilated aspect', as Feldman puts it, citing one former prisoner:

This is what's frustrating about the H-Blocks – that people to this day don't understand what was going on in the H-Blocks. They don't even start to understand. We recognize ourselves that nobody who's not actually been there cannot know what it was like. When people ask me, I find myself at a loss for words, to find words to portray what I really felt.[95]

That peculiar triple negative perhaps best captures the involuted negation of negation that lay at the core of the prisoners' experience of the no-wash protest. Though it endured longer than any of the hunger strikes and was directly participated in by many more prisoners, its logic is usually either directly subsumed into the explanatory system of mythic self-sacrifice that is used to account for the hunger strikes or understood as an acting out of ritual defilement for which the hunger strikes became a mode of symbolic purification. Even Maud Ellmann, the least bound to mythical attribution of any commentator on the cultural meaning of the prison protests, tends to conflate the meaning of the no-wash protest with that of hunger striking as a mode of reclamation of the bounded body: 'Through the dirty protest, they were striving to reclaim their cells, just as they reclaimed their bodies through the hunger strike.'[96]

But there is a profound symbolic and practical difference between the opening of the orifices that took place in the one and the closing of the orifice in the other. The double sense of 'closure' suggests at least part of the difference. As the prisoner just cited goes on to remark, being on the blanket became 'a way of life ... It was no longer a protest with a visible end to it'. Unlike hunger striking, the no-wash protest ceased to be simply a means to an end, to the restoration of a prior state of being, such as Special Category status, or the achievement of goals legible to the world beyond the prison. It became rather a mode of living that embodied the outlines of another mode of sociality that not only defied the prison regime but actually exceeded the very terms in which the social defines and delimits the representable. In it, agency ceased to be articulated through disciplined subjects and space ceased to be determined by a set of interlocking and centred loci. The metonymic dissolution of space and subjectivity dislodged the metaphoric anchors of sense and nonsense – the figures of identity through which the dominant social imaginary is reproduced – and plunged the prisoners into an alternative collectivity of profound 'through-otherness'. The violent and intrusive assault of the prison on their vulnerable bodies, a violence directed at smashing the boundaries of their subjective defences in order to reconstitute them as disciplined subjects, was pre-empted in the unfolding dialectics of the prison struggle by a dissolution of boundaries and subjectivity that not only resisted the ends of the regime but succeeded in projecting the contours of a utopian alternative out of the damage inflicted upon them. The pathological body rather than the disciplined subject became the vehicle of a possible alternative sociality.

It is generally agreed that the prisoners recurred to the familiar strategy of hunger striking precisely because it was seen that the blanket protest 'was no longer a protest with a visible end to it'. It was 'going no where'.[97] Where the blanket and no-wash protests were articulated around the recapture and the reimagination of the space of the prison, and constituted the collective space of an alternative community, the hunger strikes were resolutely temporal acts. Not only did they have specific ends, both in the sense of their terminus in death and in that of their goals, they also sought to establish control over temporal duration – over the length of time the hunger striker endured and over the sequence though which one volunteer after another joined the 'queue' of those on the strike. With a terribly fatal logic, they unfolded the spatial seriality of the cells into the temporal sequence of individual deaths. This temporal dimension of the hunger strike has led to the common 'eschatological' interpretation of the strategy, which is read in terms of sacrifice, martyrdom and redemption. The hunger strike appears as a purification ritual after the defilement of the 'dirty protest'.[98] Drawing heavily on Feldman's 'eschatological' interpretation of the hunger strikes, Aretxaga provides a succinct summary of this mythic interpretation of the prisoners' actions:

> The prisoners endowed the transcendence of religious metaphors with historical meaning and legitimacy. The Ulster mythological warrior Cuchulain and a long list of republican martyrs were condensed in the ritual complex of Christological sacrifice ... With this profound belief in historical redemption and the emotional strength derived from religious identification Bobby Sands immersed himself in a hunger strike to death.[99]

Aretxaga's language of figurality – metaphors, condensation, identification – signals that the prisoners' shift in strategy correlated with a tropological shift from the axis of metonymy that organized the blanket protest to the axis of metaphor. Generally speaking, this shift is understood to reconnect the prisoners with the community from which they had been cut off and with whom they shared a common figurative and mythic vocabulary. As Aretxaga puts it, 'the hunger strikers seized and deployed the politics of redemptive sacrifice, pervasive in their different forms in republican and Catholic cultures'.[100] In doing so, as we have seen, the hunger strikers, and the Republican movement which they represented, are understood to present themselves as the symbols of a community with which they are consubstantial and with which they share an ahistorical, mythic consciousness – a pre-modern, archetypal mentality.

No aesthetic representation of the H-Blocks highlights the split between the formal modality of the blanket protest and that of the hunger strikes more dramatically than Steve McQueen's film *Hunger* [2008]. It brilliantly captures the brutal spatial dynamics of the blanket protest and its counterpointing stases, the stretches of boredom and stillness interrupted by sudden and extreme violence, and the interface between the technological hypermodernity of the prison's hygienic regime and its subversion by the prisoners' bodies. Yet the film's final third still casts Sands's hunger strike in the isolating glare of an almost transcendental light. The collective experience of the Blanketmen, captured in the interplay between the prisoners' naked vulnerability and their ingenuity, between intense moments of gathering at mass and the squalor and tedium of the cells, is abruptly suspended. The hunger strike itself, which was by all accounts a collective affair even in promoting the representative function of the strikers, appears only as Sands's individual sacrificial act. The intense debates among the strikers themselves, which continued for the duration of each striker's fast so long as they were physically capable of speech, are annulled, as are the regular, politically strategic visits from the blocks and from outside. The one appearance of a Gerry Adams-like visitor at Sands's bedside is muffled in the blur and buzz of his failing sight and hearing. In the intense visual purity and extremity of this final third, the emphasis falls on the loneliness of the long-distance hunger striker, meticulously and painstakingly represented breath by breath and sore by sore. The film thus wittingly or unwittingly endorses the ethical view of the priest who debates Sands's decision in what is surely among the film's *tours de force*, a daringly extended debate before which the camera remains virtually motionless for some twenty minutes. The charge that this is a sacrilegious act of suicide is borne out precisely in the erasure of its collective aspect. The strategic rationale of Sands's and the other hunger strikers' willingness to stake their lives in the battle for political status, which had become critical to the legitimation of the Republican struggle, vanishes in the undoubtedly moving spectacle of bodily decay and of the sheer individual will to undergo the agonizingly extended process of death by starvation. The hunger strike is at once aestheticized, in however cold and clinical a light, and by the same token mythologized again as an act of 'passion'.[101]

All of these interpretations of the hunger strikes tend to draw on a selection of the political icons that circulated outside the prisons with a view to drawing support, especially that of the Catholic community in the face of clerical condemnations of hunger striking, and on a small selection of Sands's own writings. They tend to overlook the far from mythic, technical and highly medicalized preparation for and conduct of the strike by the prisoners, who regularly sent out for information on the process and effects of starvation and kept as close a watch as they could on the physical statistics of each of the strikers.[102] In a more general sense, the mythical account once again ignores not only the articulation of prison protest with the conditions of the modern prison, but that of the larger campaign with the forms of the modern colonial state. In collapsing the suffering endured by the collectivity of the prisoners on the blanket protest with that endured on their behalf by the hunger strikers, such interpretations fail to observe or else misunderstand the radical shift in practice and meaning of the protests that took place as the prisoners opted for new strategies. Having evolved and inhabited a space organized around transforming the function of the intense contiguities of the cell block into an oral community mediated by the metonymies of *scéal* and *craic*, and having undergone the systematic dispersal of their body-imagos, the prisoners were obliged to pursue a quite different organizational and figural logic in committing to the hunger strike.

It is generally understood that the crucial victory of the strikers lay in their intervention in electoral politics, in the election of Sands and others that demonstrated their extensive support in the nationalist community and contested the logic of their criminalization. The mobilization of collective forces was crucial to the outcome of the strikes. What is rarely understood is that the apparently mythic logic of symbolism in fact coheres with the structures of representation of the modern democratic state. That reversion to the mode of representational politics affected the rhetoric of the hunger strike at every level. In the first place, it meant the restoration of the image of the bounded and civil body, a fact marked not only by the specific role of the individual hunger striker and the symbolism of his gradually degenerating frame, but also by the immediate cessation of the no-wash protest and the embrace of the modern, hygienic conditions of the H-Blocks.[103] The logic of representation also determined the selection of the actual hunger strikers from the pool of volunteers: they were chosen to represent the six counties of Northern Ireland and the two paramilitary movements, the Provisional IRA and the INLA, to which the prisoners belonged. This principle of selection, however, did not follow any ancient Celtic mythic symbolism connecting the dying hero's blood to the revival of the land, but obeyed the territorial and demographic imperatives of the modern democratic state for which the representative is the synecdoche of a locality and its population. It is, in other words, a mode of symbolic representation, in which the part is understood to represent the whole with which it is consubstantial, and whose logic undergirds the legitimacy and sovereignty of the modern nation-state. As the state is the expression of the sovereign people, so the individual representative is the expression of the constituency, drawn from it and speaking and standing for it. That Sands could be identified with the nationalist population, and his physical suffering be understood as the metaphor for their political suffering, obeys the logic of democratic theory and processes irrespective of the Christological or heroic figures that may have been invoked to express that relationship. It was the logic of representation, not the logic of sacrifice, that meant that his electoral victory spelt the failure of the policy of criminalization and the possibility of Sinn Féin not only claiming the legitimacy conferred by the popular vote but subsequently re-entering the political process. In a certain sense, the very suspension of the blanket protests and the move to the representative structures of the hunger strike already entailed a reorientation of the struggle away from the possibility of an alternative conception of community, however dimly apprehended its terms and contours might be, and towards a re-engagement with the rhetorical as well as the institutional structures of the state. It is for that reason that the hunger strikes, however hard it may be to comprehend the motivation or perseverance of the individuals who were willing to die, appear legible or 'make sense' in a way that the blanket protests do not. For better or worse, the consequences of that strategic decision continue to play themselves out in Irish politics.

IV

But the mythic hypothesis regarding the prison protests also finds its slender moment of truth here. What it captures is the historical role of the state in negating cultural formations that are articulated through contiguity or locality rather than through 'imaginary' relations of identity expressed in terms of abstract space and of what Anderson, after Benjamin, terms 'empty homogeneous time'. We could say, all too schematically given the perpetual incompletion of its projects, that the state seeks to displace the 'through-otherness' that characterizes the community with the symbolic identifications that mediate the relation of the individual subject with the nation; to subordinate the axis of metonymy, with its subversive and unregulated movements of contagion, rumour and dissemination, to that of metaphor that subsumes difference into identity; to supplant the modalities of the oral community with those of civil society and with the practices of written documentation and codified rationalization that sustain the governmental apparatus of modernity. Modernity thus opposes the critical historical consciousness of the state and its literate actors to the subconscious drives of myth or folklore. In suppressing equivalent if mutually antagonistic possibilities, it poses the state as the historically progressive form whose advent subsumes and overcomes the limits of its atavistic other. In the Hegelian terms that are still the rarely acknowledged legislators of the historicist model in question, the state as representative instance of the universal overcomes the law of family, kin or blood ties – that 'law of the ancient gods, "the gods of the underworld"' that remains 'a law opposed to public law, to the law of the land'.[104] Conceived in this way, the claims of the law, as the objective and mediated expression of the formal equivalence of all subjects, must overcome the 'dark gods' of the mythic underworld, and the immediate and irrational ties of ethnic or 'tribal' identity. The clan is the perpetual antagonist of an orderly civil society. If, on the other hand, we understand this Hegelian model of world historical evolution as the expression of the modern and colonial state's contingent need to eliminate all alternative forms of social or cultural relations, then it becomes clear why the discourse of counter-insurgency constantly projects onto such alternatives the connotations of tribe, myth and blood. The recognition of the state is already granted in the acknowledgement of the rationality of its terms; the counter-possibility of an alternative rationality is consigned to the fundamentally unrepresentable cusp of myth and prehistory: the pathological domain of blood that the state comes to cure.

Blood haunts the prison protests as the unspeakable mark of the unrepresentable, of an inassimilable supplement. It also marks the limit at which the blanket protest ceases to be capable of generalization. It is a striking aspect of the history of the prison struggles that the experience of the women prisoners in Armagh Gaol were for so long effectively eclipsed by the H-Block struggles.[105] There are mundane numerical reasons for this, in that the numbers of Republican women prisoners were always much smaller – a factor, certainly, in the IRA leadership's order that the women not join the hunger strikes, since their capacity to make Armagh ungovernable was correspondingly limited. The fact that the women were in any case allowed to wear their own clothing also rendered the no-wash protest a tactic directed at specific abuses rather than an ongoing strategy for contesting criminalization. Furthermore, the purpose-built architecture of the H-Blocks furnished the novel terrain for qualitatively new forms of struggle in ways that the Victorian prison architecture of Armagh could not. None of these factors, however, account fully for the inadequacy of the historical or ethnographic record with regard to Armagh or for the peculiar unease evinced especially by early chroniclers of the no-wash protests there.

The issue is blood, specifically menstrual blood. Seeking to assert that 'Armagh is a feminist issue' in the face of the feminist movement's indifference to women they saw as members of a fundamentally patriarchal nationalist movement, Derry journalist Nell McCafferty was probably the first to force the matter into the public arena. Her article opened: 'There is menstrual blood on the walls of Armagh prison in Northern Ireland.'[106] In conditions where the prisoners, reduced to the status of the bare human, could only articulate their struggle for rights and recognition through their excrement, menstrual blood became the most scandalous mark not only of abasement but of a persisting gender asymmetry. Tim Pat Coogan's otherwise largely sympathetic account admits perhaps the most unguarded reflex of the shock of that difference:

I was then taken to inspect A Wing where the dirty protest was in full swing. This was sickening and appalling.

Tissues, slops, consisting of tea and urine, some faeces, and clots of blood – obviously the detritus of menstruation – lay in the corridor between the two rows of cells ... I found the smell in the girls' [sic] cell far worse than that at Long Kesh, and several times found myself having to control feelings of nausea.[107]

Both Aretxaga and Corcoran similarly record the sense that menstrual blood was taboo specifically in its *unspeakability*. Aretxaga reads Coogan's revulsion as being 'triggered by the sight of *that* which constitutes a linguistic and visual taboo. A horror that he cannot articulate linguistically'. For her, 'menstrual blood stood as a symbol of that reality excluded from language'. At the same time, despite the cultural taboos on speaking of menstruation, blood becomes an objectification of an *inexpressible* pain, of an experience that 'eluded language': 'In Armagh jail the prisoners' pain became objectified in the menstrual blood, a complex symbol that inscribed their suffering inside the contours of what Spivak has called "the space of what can only happen to a woman".'[108] Excluded from language and yet a signifying thing, menstrual blood occupies the space of the mythic itself, on the borderline between culture and nature, law and instinct. And for both Corcoran and Aretxaga, its significance is correspondingly archetypal: it belongs, in terms drawn from Mary Douglas, on the unclean side of the division between the impure and the pure that is crucial 'in organizing ideas of savagery and civilization, establishing social boundaries, and formulating cultural classifications'.[109] This general anthropological context for the understanding of the taboo on menstrual blood is forceful, but it simultaneously tends to erase the specificity of its meaning: 'As in most cultures around the world, in Ireland menstrual blood is impure.'[110] Such levels of generality are not the only problem. Once again, the mythic hypothesis overlooks the modern construction of the phenomenon it labels archetypal – in this case, the gendered discourse of hygiene and concealment that surrounds menstruation and participates in the disciplining of the orifices according to the regulation of proper times and spaces characteristic of the civilizing process of modernity. We need, rather, to grasp the significance of the gender asymmetry that blood so flagrantly marked within the context of the derangement of gender norms that was already ongoing in the prisons. There is little doubt that the Blanketmen found themselves positionally feminized within the regime of the H-Blocks, both in relation to the unaccustomed vulnerability and visibility of their bodies and in relation to the discovery of the 'body full of holes' that marked the transformative dimension of their experience. Ellmann describes the latter aspect of their feminization in graphically ironic terms: in the Blocks, 'the male body was more prized for its interiorities than for its much vaunted protuberances. Depth rather than length became the measure of genital superiority'.[111] For the male prisoners, however, the experience of their vulnerability, including their transformation into objects of derision and sexual commentary, was one of a humiliation that had to be survived and countered:

I had to walk naked to the wing I was allocated to. All the way down the cell I was burning with humiliation as I had to walk past other prisoners and, worse, more screws, who stood glaring at me. For me, that was the worst experience of the whole time I spent on the Blanket protest.

Every time we left the cell naked, it was to a tirade of every kind of abuse you could think of … If I was embarrassed by the screws or the other prisoners seeing me naked, I made sure they weren't aware of it because it would have given them a moral victory over me. Not once did I try to cover my nakedness with my hands.[112]

The common term for the warders, the screws, succinctly condenses the language of sexual penetration with the reminiscence of torture, the infamous thumbscrew, underlining the prisoners' perception of them as agents of a brutality expressed most powerfully in the form of sexual abuse. That humiliating sexual subjection was correspondingly contested by deliberate inversion in the idiom of the jails. The ruses of the prisoners' collective that subverted the prison regime were generally expressed in sexual terms that responded to the experience of being 'fucked' or 'fucked about' by the authorities. 'We fucked the screws' is the recurrent idiom of successful resistance and more often than not refers to the Blanketmen's use of their orifices to 'bangle' contraband or to the use of Gaelic as a means to evade surveillance.[113] In such acts, the orifice that has been the site of abuse and ridicule is reclaimed and transvalued as the means to forging an alternative community even within the violent space of the jail.

In part, the feminization of the male Republican prisoners is continuous with an older set of stereotypes of the Irish, consolidated and given pseudo-scientific standing by ethnographers, linguists and cultural critics in the nineteenth century. At that moment, femininity connoted an undisciplined emotional turbulence, pathological impulsiveness and ungovernability, signifying a sensibility that required to be disciplined into domesticity and docility rather than naturally embodying it.[114] We have seen already the ways in which Irish nationalism in the late nineteenth and early twentieth centuries sought to overcome such stereotypes precisely by adopting the gendered languages and disciplines of the modern state. But the Blanketmen experienced their feminization not as an attributed ethnic essence but as an effect of the prison regime. In their discovery of the pathological body, they underwent a corporeal feminization that had to do both with their resistance and with their vulnerability, and a contradictory set of responses emerged that in a different way awkwardly condensed femininity and ungovernability. If the pathological 'body full of holes', with its labile and disseminative orifices, was the means to resistance in the culture it sustained as in the functions it performed, it was simultaneously the site of maximum vulnerability and – especially in the case of the cavity searches – of a penetrability that was explicitly gendered. After one especially violent wing search that involved intrusive body searches, a shaken Sands writes in a com to Adams: 'Comrade, this was sexual assault'.[115] The tone of Sands's outrage differs from that recorded by the women prisoners in Armagh when subjected to violent and intrusive searches, frequently by male warders or in the presence of warders in full riot gear. While no less violent and – given especially the small numbers of women prisoners – more profoundly traumatizing than the men's experience, that of the women was continuous with other dimensions of the regime in women's prisons and recognized as such. Corcoran notes the much higher degree of pathologization and sexualization of female prisoners, criminal or political, and the regularity of interventions like strip-searching in women's prisons generally. At least since Mary Carpenter's time, the sexuality and the bodies of women have been direct objects of surveillance and discipline in the penal system.[116] This sexualized and gendered discipline, by which women are regularly reduced to pathologized cases and subjected to social and sexual control, is continuous with the norms of patriarchal society beyond the prison walls.

What Sands's disbelief registers, however, is something more akin to the shocking literalization of a metaphor. The concept-metaphor 'rape' is among the most prevalent figures for colonial violence and expropriation, no less in Irish culture, both high and popular, than in other colonized societies. In its currency as a metaphor, the specificity of rape as a means of social and political control wears thin and both its violence and its gendered meanings are derealized. The H-Block prisoners' sudden realization that the anal searches to which they were routinely subjected were in actual practice deliberate forms of sexual humiliation and control was equally the recognition that their feminization was at once a literal effect and no more than a politicized figure of speech. Literal, in the sense that what they underwent did indeed open them to a transformative experience of the body and to an intuition of a differently grounded sociality; a mere figure insofar as the very possibility of reading their experience as 'feminization' was constitutively unavailable to the women prisoners in Armagh, for whom the prison experience was an intensification rather than a transformation of the oppressive gender norms in the society at large. If the pathologization of the male prisoners was tantamount to their feminization, that accorded with the historically consistent logic of the penal system for which female prisoners were always already pathologized. Faced with pathologization as the very condition of their incarceration and treatment by the prison regime, the women could only experience the brutality they faced – strip-searching that always amounted to actual rape – as an intensification of their subjection without the potential for its negation or inversion. Protest of the conditions of Armagh virtually always took the form of direct confrontation and invoked the alternative image of the woman as embodiment of vulnerability and purity. Accordingly, the presence of menstrual blood became, within that very oppositional logic, the mark of shame rather than subversion. As the signifier of an irreducible gendered difference, menstrual blood thus marked the limit to the imagination of an alternative community grounded in the indifferent bare life of the pathological body. Even as a certain experience of 'feminization' furnished the possibility of reconstituting the forms of an oral community in and through the conditions of the modern penal apparatus, the asymmetry of the gendered experience of that apparatus signalled the impossibility of translating that experience as a utopian model.[117] It could, in a very real sense, 'go nowhere'.

It is generally accepted that the experience of political imprisonment in Northern Ireland was a continual crucible for the ideological and practical transformation of the Republican movement. If the cages of Long

Kesh became the school for a younger and more revolutionary generation of activists who learnt to see their struggle in relation to anti-colonial movements globally, the hunger strikes on the blocks led to the re-entry of Sinn Féin into the democratic political process as a left-wing party and paved the way towards the peace process. The *ranganna* of the blocks also furthered the political self-education and conscientization of the prisoners both during the blanket protest and after the hunger strikes had won them most of the advantages of Special Category status and a more flexible prison regime. Not only could the H-Blocks be seen as being 'at the vanguard of republicanism' but many of those formed politically in the prisons also entered into leadership roles in the Republican movement on their release.[118] Aretxaga shows in depth how both the experience of activism on behalf of prisoners in the Relatives Action Committees and the experience, even the very impasse, of the Armagh protests led to a politicization of Republican women and to a considerable degree of feminist transformation of Republican ideology.[119] It is tempting in light of such developments and their unanticipated emergence from the unpromising conditions of imprisonment to reinscribe the blanket and no-wash protests into a teleological narrative that would redeem them from their stasis and transform them into exemplary moments in the curve of a political evolution. Thus, for Feldman, the fundamentally fragmented experience of the blanket protest is contained within the horizon of a *future* totality:

> The body fragment and the absent totality formed a novel dialectic. Fragmentation of the body became a political technique that enabled the signification, the evocation, of absent wholes: the eventual unification of the prisoners with their political organizations and support communities, with a United Ireland and a postcolonial and separatist Gaelic speech community ... Hunger striking was posited as the last act because in its consumption of flesh it was the ultimate fragmentation technique that finally invoked the body whole in a shimmering moment of historical clarity.[120]

This account is not alone in finding the political significance of the prison experience in its movement from fragmentation to totality, from stasis to development, from darkness to light and clarity, or, as Aretxaga puts it, in the gaining of 'recognition and voice' against 'the possibility of historical erasure'.[121]

This teleological form of narrative, however, enacts another mode of erasure. It renders of no account the intuitions of alternative forms of life that are constitutively antagonistic to representation in and by the public spheres of state and civil society. And yet the utopian promise of such intuitions lies precisely in the incoherence of the shapes and relations that they limn with the common sense of modernity. Preserved not in remote and alien spaces, but at the heart of the modern institutions that aim at their annihilation or subsumption, they suggest the contours of modes of living that might have issued from a different conception of life in common. Partial, momentary, fragmented and certainly damaged by the violence of the domination they oppose, the value of the insights they tender into other possibilities, the possibility of living otherwise, cannot be entered into the balance sheets of representation. Precisely their invisibility, their occlusion in the 'underworld' of unspeakable things, shelters the alternative forms that they gesture incompletely towards. Their fate is not to participate in the totality that redeems only what coheres with its own unilateral declaration of universality, but to persist in a partial and damaged apprehension of what might have been and yet might be in a world where the unrestrained potentials of human life were not reduced by domination and shattered into the functional units of a larger whole.

Imperfect as they are, and deformed by the violence in which they are forged, such momentary formations of utopian possibility have their value precisely in their suspension outside developmental time. What they offer opens out onto a different future than can be thought in the terms of the modern state or realized in the spaces it offers for representation. These are different openings in the fabric of historical time, scarcely audible echoes that speak forward to us on unfamiliar frequencies, conjoining discontinuous times in momentary and often dissonant configurations, shaping possibility out of violence and privation. If, as Benjamin imagines, 'every second of time was the strait gate through which the Messiah might enter',[122] these fleeting and imperfect openings in a world that seems sunk in irredeemable damage still hold out the promise of that world's transformation, even as they vanish in its shadow.

CHAPTER 5

*The breaker's yard: from forensic to
interrogation modernity*

> In the sealed hotel men are handled
> as if they were furniture, and passion
> exhausts itself at the mouth.
> Medbh McGuckian[1]

I

The Northern Irish prison struggles, which to a large extent anticipated and set a pattern for political prison struggles that are ongoing in the era of the war on terror, were in every respect a phenomenon of modernity, though of a modernity whose forms have shifted and modified in the faltering era of neo-liberalism. As a philosophy which, like nineteenth-century political economy, was at once economic and political and envisaged a particular form of state, neo-liberalism rose to dominance coincidentally with the Troubles in Northern Ireland, in the wake of the fiscal crisis of the early 1970s.[2] If its economic prescriptions face crisis in our own moment, it has not failed to bequeath to the present its political and security apparatus, shaped as these were around the passage from a hegemonic welfare state to a state of privatization and forced expropriation. The previous chapter explored the contrapuntal emergence in the course of Irish anti-colonial struggles of a modern penal system with its disciplinary architectures and of the strategies and tactics of resistance conditioned by its various architectural forms, from the prison camp to the cellular jail. But the story of Irish political imprisonment and resistance is also part of the larger story of the emergence of the modern state and, in and through the recent Troubles, of the emergence of the new British and, increasingly, of the global 'strong state'.[3]

The H-Block prisoners consistently transformed the terms of their imprisonment, inverting the confined interior of the jail into a metaphor for the condition of Northern Ireland as a whole and the jail itself into a space of regained freedom. The ghettoes of Derry or Belfast were, for them, spaces analogous to those they inhabited within the larger colonial apparatus of surveillance and regulation of movement.[4] This was not a merely rhetorical claim, but one that recognized the ways in which modernity replicates the disposition of space across diverse architectural domains. Prisons may be seen, as they are in Foucault's *Discipline and Punish*, to represent the quintessential form of the modern disciplinary apparatus. But it is important to recognize that the prison, for all its appearance of specialization of function and spatial hermeticism, is in most respects continuous with other forms and terrains of discipline that emerge within the capitalist state. It aligns not only with factories and barracks and schools, as Foucault so thoroughly demonstrates, but with the modern city itself, as a site of biopolitical organizing of the population under conditions of regulated movement, surveillance and architectural rationality. The cellular seriality of the prison block, after all, intimately resembles in miniature form the serial array of urban housing along straightened boulevards or the terraced dwellings of new industrial cities. What I will suggest in this chapter is that the primary icon of modernity, the city, with its crowds, its streets, its movements and its *flâneurs* or detectives, has been displaced within our later modernity by the site that was always its shadowy counterpart, the prison, with its inmates, its corridors, its cells and its interrogators. The segmented, regular spaces of the 'lettered city'[5] that represent the ideal order set against the through-otherness of the *clachan*'s oral space, give way here to the numbered enclosures of coerced speech and pained bodies.

We can best focus this shift by bringing together two moments whose constellation effectively suggests the rewriting of an iconic encounter of urban modernity within the framework of the late-modern prison, the political prison in the colonial sphere of Northern Ireland. One is the Paris of Charles Baudelaire as analysed by Walter Benjamin in his essays on the poet and in the *Arcades Project* from which they largely derive. The other is the interrogation centre as rendered in Bobby Sands's political ballad, 'The Crime of Castlereagh'. The unexpected echoes that link these two moments calibrate both the distance and the continuity between the streets of mid-nineteenth-century Paris as it underwent the processes of Haussmannization, oriented towards control and surveillance of the population, and the corridors and cells of a counter-insurgency interrogation centre in the late twentieth century. Taken together, these two symbolic moments bear witness to a shift in the formation of subjectivity across modernity, from the urban mode understood as the field of forensic desire to a state of surveillance and interrogation that increasingly penetrates the biopolitical life of the individual. The two passages I will bring into conjunction may stand as dialectical and diagnostic figures for this shift, marking by their structural similarities as by the differences in their subject positioning the passage from one mode of modernity to another. It may be that this shift is less epochal or historical than geographical, referrable to a change in location rather than a temporal transition, a change, that is, from the metropolitan to the colonial sphere. But my larger claim is that it involves both: increasingly, and with accelerating force in our own moment, the models of policing and of the biopolitical state that developed in colonial spheres have gained global applicability, collapsing some of the distinctions that might have been pertinent between the colonial and the democratic, industrial state. With that global transformation, the prisoner and the interrogator, rather than the urban crowd and the *flâneur* or the detective, become the iconic figures of late modernity.

Benjamin's method in his *Arcades Project* was to compose an archeology of 'high capitalism' through a painstaking analysis of its debris, of the superannuated forms of its manufacture and commerce, of its already obsolescent commodities, of its abandoned and derelict subjects. He traces capitalism's contours through the cast-offs of its progress and development rather than in its most dynamic and advanced forms. Nonetheless, his chosen terrain for this archeological project remains 'the capital of the nineteenth century', Paris, the centre rather than the periphery. In keeping with the larger claim of this book, which is that the processes of modernity cannot be fully grasped without attending to the apparently marginal sites that were in fact its laboratories, my own approach to the late modernity of neo-liberal capital proceeds by attending to its often overlooked but nonetheless experimental spaces and, in particular, to the anomalous terrain of Ireland, Britain's 'doorstep colony'.[6] In such spaces we can trace the emergent figures of a new formation, in their resistance as in their subjectification, whose outlines foreshadowed the elements of a global present.

I take, then, as the two poles of this transformation, Charles Baudelaire's famous sonnet, 'A Une Passante', as read by Benjamin in his no less celebrated essay, 'The Paris of the Second Empire in Baudelaire'; and a passage from Sands's lesser-known prison ballad, 'The Crime of Castlereagh', in his 'trilogy'.[7]

La rue assourdissante autour de moi hurlait.
Longue, mince, en grand deuil, douleur majestueuse,
Une femme passa, d'une main fastueuse
Soulevant, balançant le feston et l'ourlet;

Agile et noble, avec sa jambe de statue.
Moi, je buvais, crispé comme un extravagant,
Dans son oeil, ciel livide où germe l'ouragan,
La douceur qui fascine et le plaisir qui tue.

Un éclair ... puis la nuit! – Fugitive beauté
Dont le regard m'a fait soudainement renaître,
Ne te verrai-je plus que dans l'éternité?

Ailleurs, bien loin d'ici! trop tard! jamais peut-être!
Car j'ignore où tu fuis, tu ne sais où je vais,
Ô toi que j'eusse aimée, ô toi qui le savais!

['To a Passer-By'

The street about me roared with a deafening sound.
Tall, slender, in heavy mourning, majestic grief,
A woman passed, with a glittering hand
Raising, swinging the hem and flounces of her skirt;

Agile and graceful, her leg was like a statue's.
Tense as in a delirium, I drank
From her eyes, pale sky where tempests germinate,
The sweetness that enthralls and the pleasure that kills.

A lightning flash ... then night! Fleeting beauty
By whose glance I was suddenly reborn,
Will I see you no more before eternity?

Elsewhere, far, far from here! too late! *never* perhaps!
For I know not where you fled, you know not where I go,
O you whom I would have loved, O you who knew it!]

'A Une Passante', Charles Baudelaire

>
> They walked me through an avenue
> Where devils lay in wait.
> The very air was charged with care
> For there lay evil fate.
> A man could feel the agony steal
> Quietly o'er his skin,
> They looked at me expectantly
> And each bore his own grin.

> We came to halt for some default
> Caused two groups to collide.
> They looked perplexed stopped in their tracks
> For passage wasn't wide.
> They shuffled back, then made attack
> Then shuffled back in shame,
> For no one knew quite what to do
> So all just tried again.
>
> They led her by, her head held high
> Their faces hanging low.
> It seemed to me quite obviously
> That they had come to woe.
> She looked at me determinedly
> Across that gap of doom,
> And smiled did she so pitifully
> Like rose in winter bloom
>
> And in her wake she left an ache
> That gripped my very heart.
> If men but knew what she went through
> They'd tear their souls apart.
> 'In here,' he said, with nod of head,
> The door closed like a cave.
> I stood like one in face of gun
> With one foot in the grave.
>
> from 'The Crime of Castlereagh',
Bobby Sands

Baudelaire's poem is a familiar and exemplary high-modernist poem, complex in its own diagnosis of urban movements and desires, and formally exacting. Sands's ballad, produced fragmentarily and under extreme duress, probably at night on toilet- and cigarette paper, and smuggled out of the prison in coms, bears the marks of its subaltern conditions of production: the poem of a twenty-three-year-old prisoner with only high school education, it is episodic and fragmentary, often rhythmically uncertain, and moves somewhat vertiginously from evocations of literary cliché to moments of startling vernacular expressiveness.[8] It is, moreover, marked by the trauma of what it relates: internment and torture in the infamous British interrogation centre at Castlereagh Barracks. Its very form is that of what Susan Stewart has dubbed a 'distressed genre', adopting and adapting a ballad form already long characteristic of both popular and literary Irish prison and rebel ballads and refunctioning it for oral performance in the prison cells. Its rhythmic structure and metre forcefully recall Oscar Wilde's famous 'The Ballad of Reading Gaol', itself perhaps a penitential metrical echo of his mother Lady Wilde's nationalist ballad poetry, written under the pen-name 'Speranza'. Both in turn echo Romantic ballads like Coleridge's 'Ancient Mariner' or Shelley's 'Mask of Anarchy', the latter made peculiarly apposite by its references to Lord Castlereagh.

Stewart defines the 'distressed genre', by analogy with 'distressed furniture', as a contemporary creation that recurs to a bygone genre without ever being able to shake the aura of inauthenticity that hangs about it:

> *To distress*: in common usage (although, curiously, not in dictionaries), 'to make old, to antique,' particularly in reproducing material goods from previous times. Simultaneously, the dictionary definition: 'to afflict, to place in a state of danger and trouble, bad straits.' In law, *to distrain* is 'to force by seizure of goods,' coming from the Latin root *dis* (apart) + *stringere* (to draw tight or stretch): 'to seize and hold property as security or indemnity for a debt.' In such usage, 'to distress' involves a process of appropriation by reproduction, or manipulation through affliction. All these meanings bear upon the distressing of genres – in particular on the literary imitation of folklore forms. Like the distressing of objects, the distressing of forms involves a process of separation and manipulation serving certain ideological functions.[9]

But in thus signalling this genealogy of appropriations of a perhaps passé form by reference to Stewart's work on 'distressed genres' and ballad poetry, I am suggesting also the need to give a further turn to the notion of distress in that phrase. The distressed form of the poem is not only the consequence of the literal distress and distraint of the prisoner, distrained by law and physical pain, but the sign of a counter-modern reactivation of oral forms that had always worked to recall and transmit resistance, and of a reactivation of those forms within the context of the reconstituted oral community of dispossessed prisoners. In that context, the poem bears traces of the stress and strains of the writing, the scars of its own condition, and is scarified by the traces of previous works that sought in their own way to come to terms with the trauma of imprisonment: its rendering of the real is mediated through the deliberate generic and rhythmic recall of other, no less generically mediated, reals. As we shall see further, the poem performs the re-vernacularization of a once-vernacular form that has been mediated institutionally through modern schooling and informally through the recycling of literary ballads as exemplary models for a dissident popular canon. It deploys its very literariness to reconstitute a folkloric mnemonic device that is refunctioned for oral circulation in the prison.

The distressed poem thus bears an intimate relation to resistance, not only as its expression but in its refusal of a certain conception of the subject formed through aesthetic distance: given the recurrence of negative aesthetic judgement as a means to delegitimate the cultural work of prisoners, 'taste' is precisely what is in question materially and thematically. The brutal and unhygienic conditions under which the Blanketmen lived in the H-Blocks involved, as we have seen, nothing less than a systematic undoing of all the lessons of the 'civilizing process' that culminate in good taste, a dismantling of bodily disciplines that ground the formation of the subject, and a transvaluation of the very stereotype of Irish barbarity that opposes English civility. Prison resistance operates as a transformation of disciplinary deprivation into a means of refusal of discipline in the largest sense. We might see the poem, then, like the protest itself, as a response to what Elaine Scarry has seen as the systematic inversion of civilization and its protective relation to the body in torture and imprisonment, achieved through the transformation of everyday objects – rooms, beds, cigarettes, tools – into the means of deprivation or pain.[10] Sands's own ironic lines thus resonate beyond the context of the desperate daily search for a smoke:

> If one had luck a lousy butt
> Could calm the nerves no end.
> For cultured taste takes second place
> When you're in hell, my friend! (112)

We will return to Sands's capacity for the vernacular rendition of literary forms and the vernacular critique of both cultural and disciplinary institutions momentarily.

II

As Walter Benjamin's analysis of Baudelaire's 'A Une Passante' shows, it too was bound up with a vernacular figuration of the modern. Benjamin's commentary on the poem arises with a certain abruptness in the midst of his discussion of the figure of the detective and of the emergence of the detective story genre in the nineteenth century. Abruptly, because the thematics of the poem concern less the forensic gaze of the detective or even of the *flâneur* who reads the 'types' that make up a crowd than the erotic desire of the *flâneur* caught in the trammels of the scopic drive. What occluded logic links the detective's desire to identify the criminal who shelters in the crowd or to gain a masterful overview of the labyrinth of the city with the erotic gaze of the man in the crowd that bears his object to him for a moment only to carry it away the next? Benjamin's argument concerning the emergence of the detective as an urban figure with whom the ordinary denizen of the city identifies is familiar. The density of the population massed in the city and the difficulty of knowing and of penetrating its streets and slums require the specialized knowledge of the detective:

> Here the masses appear as the asylum that shields an asocial person from his persecutors. Of all the menacing aspects of the masses, this one became apparent first. It is at the origin of the detective story.
>
> In times of terror, when everyone is something of a conspirator, everybody will be in a situation where he has to play detective. Strolling gives him the best prospects of doing so.[11]

The idleness of the *flâneur* thus becomes in fact a mode of specialized knowledge, observation. Observation penetrates beneath the flows and shocks of city life, descrying in the crowd the possible miscreant, the peculiar in the undifferentiated mass. The irruption of Benjamin's brief discussion of 'A Une Passante' into this account of the function of the detective in the city seems to take us from the sphere of the forensic to that of the erotic: 'This sonnet presents the crowd not as the refuge of a criminal but as that of love which eludes the poet. One may say that it deals with the function of the crowd not in the life of the citizen but in the life of the erotic person.'[12] The sheer contingency of the encounter, which is also that of the individual in the urban crowd, is cured by the scopic drive in its connection with the drive to know.[13]

In the first instance, the apparition of the woman in the crowd, already with the démarche of an aesthetic object, *'avec sa jambe de statue'*, overpowers and paralyses the poet, *'crispé comme un extravagant'*. It is, however, the shock or flash, *éclair*, of this apparition that fixes it in turn and causes the rebirth of the subject. The moving on of the person is counterpointed exactly by the fixing of the image in its place. This image, the object that reconstitutes the subject who was at first undone by desire, outlives the relation with the other. Its fixation guarantees the repetition of the singular moment – its transformation into a *type* for the poet, and, no less, for the critic: it is precisely thus that Benjamin reads the figure of *la Passante*. In the tercets, a subtle shift carries them from the domain of mutual ignorance to that of an apparently shared and co-implicating knowledge:

> *Ne te verrai-je plus que dans l'éternité?*
> *Ailleurs, bien loin d'ici! trop tard! jamais peut-être!*
> *Car j'ignore où tu fuis, tu ne sais où je vais,*
> *Ô toi que j'eusse aimée, ô toi qui le savais!*

And yet, for all the chiasmus of the penultimate line, which seems to assert a perfectly equilibrated reciprocity in ignorance, things are not quite so balanced. In the final line, the poet saves his subjectivity precisely by transforming his desire into the object of his object's knowledge, like a mask that saves the subject from the other's gaze.[14] What she knows is not the poet, but his perpetually suspended, subjunctive desire: *Ô **toi** que j'eusse aimée, ô toi qui **le** savais!* ['O **you whom** I might have loved, o you who knew **it**!']. The image of his desire is the recuperable object that secures the subject in his place after the disappearance of the woman herself. In this respect, we can recognize in this 'primal scene' of modernity the echo of another primal scene in which the woman who passes away in the crowd recapitulates the mother who, to the infant, seems to come and go, approach and disappear, and must be fixed in the controlling play of the *fort-da*. 'Anything', as Benjamin remarks somewhat later, 'about which one knows that soon one will not have it around becomes an image'.[15] Between the erotic desire that fixes [on] the image, and the scopic drive to know, a constant relay circulates.

No accident then, that when Benjamin returns to the motif of the detective, after a brief detour through the history of domiciliary policing, another mode of fixing the mobile subject to which we will return, he arrives at the photograph as forensic means of identification:

Photography made it possible for the first time to preserve permanent and unmistakeable traces of a human being. The detective story came into being when this most decisive of *all conquests of a person's incognito* had been accomplished. Since then the end of efforts to capture a man in his speech and actions has not been in sight.[16]

In both photography and the poetic image, the presence of the subject is displaced and preserved in the form of an object for eternally repeatable identifications in a process that is inseparable from the mourning of a lost object.[17] But that mourning is no less bound up with the law of identification that sutures the subject through its desires into the logic of policing that is the logic of the state. The transformation of the transient, anonymous other in the crowd into an object of identification with its two-step process, from identifying *with* to identifying *as*, shapes modern erotic desire into line with the desire to police. Thus the state succeeds in transforming its autonomous subjects back into subjects bound to the law by their own desire. Baudelaire, who, in discovering the law of urban, modern desire, launches it with a *nouveau frisson*, no less anticipates exactly how what appears as the loose, wandering erotic desire of the urban scene will be refunctioned for discipline. More than just a type of the modern urban encounter, what Benjamin identifies in 'A Une Passante' may well be the primal scene of the modern subject's erotic investment in the law.

Benjamin's analysis of 'A Une Passante' in relation to the detective motif serves to throw into relief the structural similarity and the critical differences that shape the scenario of Bobby Sands's prison ballad – which will, in turn, throw 'A Une Passante' into yet another relief. The similarities between one passage in Sands's long ballad and Baudelaire's sonnet are striking, and would be more uncanny were it not for the fact that the erotic encounter in the latter has, in the course of subsequent poetry both popular and elite, become the very type of 'sex in the city'. The passage records an encounter between the poet and an unknown female passer-by who share a reciprocal exchange of glances. This encounter takes place, however, not in a street but in a prison corridor that is characterized as an 'avenue', a term which deftly serves to mark both the structural similarities and the coeval genealogy of the prison corridor and the modern city street, both laid out serially in numbered units. We know that the cellular system emerged to prominence in Britain and Ireland between about 1850 and 1870. It was during the same moment, in the effort to better survey and regulate the movement and dwelling of the population, that the numbering of houses and the establishment of individuals' places of residence became an increasingly systematic practice of urban domiciliary policing. Benjamin's account of the 'numbering of houses in big cities' sees it as part of 'an extensive network of controls [that] had brought bourgeois life ever more tightly into its meshes' and as an index of 'progressive standardization'.[18] Such controls were inseparable from the process of Haussmannization in Paris that had its counterparts in modern cities everywhere, both in its function – to ameliorate surveillance and allow access to policing and military interventions into neighbourhoods formerly impenetrable by virtue of their warren-like complexity – and in its appearance: 'long perspectives down broad straight thoroughfares.'[19] The 'avenue', lined with serially arrayed and numbered houses, offers to surveillance a uniform surface, unlike the narrow and twisting streets of working-class slums or medieval settlements. Designed ultimately to facilitate the policing goals of a perpetual 'emergency regime', the Haussmannian avenue precludes the barricades that would hamper military manoeuvre but also makes of surveillance and regulation an everyday matter, habitual and unconscious for the individual citizen.[20] In this respect, Sands's comparison of the cellular corridor with an avenue is a precise diagnosis of a psychic as well as a visual analogy. The corridors of the interrogation centre seem, in the memory of one former interrogatee, like a nightmarish projection of the 'long perspective' of the avenue: 'two sealed parallel walls running down forever with no end to them.'[21]

The cell and the private house also share the quality of inversion. The cell, as we have seen, is a peculiar interior space that folds out into public view: in the principle of cellular imprisonment, the space designed for withdrawal, seclusion and meditation by the individual subject is also utterly exposed to surveillance. The greatest interiority corresponds to the maximum of exposure. Benjamin notes a similar reversibility of urban spaces in which 'Parisians make the street an interior' and inhabit an 'intoxicated interpenetration of street and residence'.[22] Of course, even as their interiors are captured in the architecture of surveillance and regulation, the urban dwellers – like prisoners in their blocks – transform the street once more into a space of defiance, that of the unruly crowd of individuals each with his or her own anonymous interiority that the *flâneur*/detective will seek to penetrate: 'Streets are the dwelling place of the collective. The collective is an eternally unquiet, eternally agitated being that – in the space between the building fronts – experiences, learns, understands, and invents as much as individuals do within the privacy of their own four walls.'[23] This collective, both produced by and resistant to a disciplinary architecture, forms the background against which the movements and the encounters of the individual are cast into relief: it is the very type of the paradox of simultaneous individuation and massification that is the fate of the modern subject. Its peculiar counterpart is the prisoner in the cell: at once utterly individuated and yet subjected to the homogenization and mass control that can be inverted into a reconstitution of resistant community.

The movement of the *flâneur*/detective in this urban crowd, stimulated by but wary of the shocks it constantly subjects him to, finds its metaphor in the motions of the fencer. The staccato rhythm of shuffling, sidestepping, advance and withdrawal that marks Baudelaire's '*fantasque escrime*' with the crowd through which it is 'designed to open a path' is figured in the approach of *la passante* towards the poet.[24] '*Agile et noble, avec sa jambe de statue*', her pose of classical *contrapposto* is equally that of a fencer stepping forward with her weight balanced on one leg.[25] The poet's response can thus be seen as an elaborate rhetorical parrying of the desire he imputes to her, just as their approach and avoidance in the crowd is understood by Benjamin as a form of fencing. Such movements of evasion comically hinder Sands's progress along the corridor that is suddenly crowded with the warders and their charges:

> We came to halt for some default
> Caused two groups to collide.
> They looked perplexed stopped in their tracks
> For passage wasn't wide.
> They shuffled back, then made attack
> Then shuffled back in shame,
> For no one knew quite what to do
> So all just tried again.

Compressed into the narrow space of the prison, the motions of the 'press' or throng and of the police, of resistance and discipline, play themselves out in a kind of baffled feint and parry.

Sands and the unknown *passante* are dragged past one another in the corridor, expressing defiance in an exchange of glances that cuts across the gaze of surveillance and refuses the downcast eyes and gait of the conforming prisoner. The 'shaming' of the interrogators who 'have come to woe' is crucial here: resistant subjects of interrogation knew that their ability to control the terms and rhythm of their interrogation, even by eliciting beatings, could frustrate the efforts of the interrogator. Hence it is the warders, rather than the prisoners, whose eyes are downcast.[26] Such tactics, however, require the subject actively to assume pain, which is perhaps the gift that this anonymous woman offers to Sands in passing. Like Baudelaire, Sands carries away a memory of the encounter, or, one should perhaps say, a *remainder* of the encounter. For it survives not as an image, but as an ache: 'And in her wake she left an ache / That gripped my very heart.' The ache of loss is also an ache of anticipation as the balladeer not only mourns her passing on, but also identifies with the pain she has felt and that he will momentarily undergo. This identification at the level of bodily pain rather than in the register of knowledge fortifies the prisoner for his coming ordeal and is aurally marked as a kind of *pharmakon* inoculating him against the suffering that will ensue. The word *ache* both evokes and echoes the word *break*, anticipating what the interrogatee will undergo in the prison that Sands famously dubbed 'the breaker's yard', while affirming that he will not break under torture.[27]

A consistent pattern of significant differences counterpoints the similarities between 'A Une Passante' and 'The Crime of Castlereagh'. In the first place, both Sands and the unknown woman are the objects of interrogation rather than subjects of knowledge. They are, furthermore, subject to an at times quite literal, and not merely figurative, penetration of their bodies by the agents of the state in their pursuit of forensic knowledge. The interrogatee 'becomes a political orifice, a dual passageway into the state and its Others'.[28] There, gender difference operates not around the structures of desire but instrumentally in the different pains and forms of humiliation that each will undergo, as Sands seems to mark in the rhythmically underscored phrase 'If *men* but knew what *she* went through'. And while the relation of the subject to the forensic gaze is reversed, so also the relation to the erotic is complicated: the gaze of erotic longing between them stands against the erotics of interrogation which Sands will later narrate as a kind of dance or ritual of seduction: 'They try to coax, they try to hoax / They murder you with charm' (117). We will return to Sands's understanding of this dynamic later with regard to the split identifications that constitute the scene of interrogation in general.

What is recorded here, then, is not so much a relation between subjects differentially positioned as subject and object by gender difference, as a relation among persons reduced to equivalence as *things* or objects of interrogation. We may recall once again that the prisoners are in the condition of *distraint*, reduced by the fiat of an emergency law to mere things that lack the rights that attach to persons, held over for security at the administration's pleasure. This condition is intrinsically related to the form of the ballad itself, and not only on account of its 'distressed' literary status. Particularly in the Irish tradition, prison ballads are legion, from the anonymous 'The Night before Larry Was Stretched' to Behan's 'The Auld Triangle'. Peter Linebaugh suggests, indeed, that the Irish may even have invented the hanging ballad.[29] In Sands's case, we can be even more specific. It is known – as well as audible – that Sands took the inspiration and rhythms as well as thematic material for his trilogy from Oscar Wilde's 'The Ballad of Reading Gaol', a poem itself closely related to Irish nationalist experience of British prisons.[30] In drawing on the traditions of the Romantic literary ballad, both 'The Ballad of Reading Gaol' and 'The Crime of Castlereagh' obey formal logics that are antithetical to the sonnet form and its historical relation both to individuating inwardness and, metaphorically, to the enclosed space of the cell.[31] Just as the performance of the ballad is an instance of the reconstitution of the oral community, so the form, in its deliberate linking together of multiple experiences and multiple communicating spaces, seeks to assert the communal identity of prisoners against the isolating effect of the cellular prison system. Wilde, indeed, powerfully dramatizes that shift from the collectivity of the prisoners, even under the serial conditions of hard labour, to the deadly isolation of the cell in the third section of his ballad:

> We tore the tarry rope to shreds
> With blunt and bleeding nails;
> We rubbed the doors and scrubbed the floors,
> And cleaned the shining rails:
> And, rank by rank, we soaped the plank,
> And clattered with the pails.
> ...
> The hangman, with his little bag,
> Went shuffling through the gloom
> And I trembled as I groped my way
> Into my numbered tomb.[32]

In 'The Crime of Castlereagh', Sands's trajectory reverses that of Wilde's ballad even as it imitates its form. Unlike Wilde's ballad, published anonymously under the signature of his prison number, it opens with Sands writing his name on the cell wall in a vigorous assertion of his presence against the fear that he will be annihilated by the prison system. It then moves through the pain of isolation, deprivation and interrogation to envision the community of the Blanketmen that is predicated on that shared experience of absolute bodily vulnerability, the death-in-life of being reduced to bare life together. Within the context of the prison, it reproduces the kind of 'counter-collectivization' or inversion of the practice of mass internment and interrogation that the community as a whole performed.[33] Sands's prophetic vision of the Blanketmen transforms Wilde's description of the rounds of the prisoners exercising in the yard or trampling the treadmill into a hallucinatory *danse macabre* that results from his torture and isolation:

> They moved around and moved around
> Just staring at the bed.
> They marched in pairs with tortured stares
> For they were marching dead. (122)

If, as I have suggested, the prison experience became for Republican prisoners a kind of reconstitution of destroyed Irish oral community, Sands's transformation of Wilde's ballad is at the same time a re-vernacularization of a literary ballad, forged under the conditions of distraint and distress out of which the collective re-emerges against cellular isolation. It partakes of a necessary orality and accordingly bears the scars of damage on its aesthetically very uneven surface – a surface that is an unashamed offence to 'cultured taste'.

In its orality, it also brings together in the passage we have been analysing a moment that echoes the primal scene of erotic-forensic modernity with another distressed genre drawn from the ruined repertoire of Gaelic poetry. For Sands's encounter with the unknown woman also draws self-consciously on the Gaelic and Jacobite *aisling* or vision poem in which the male poet meets with an allegorical female figure who enjoins the young poet to struggle for Ireland's sovereignty. At the same time, Sands 'democratizes' that tradition, reducing the female goddess or *Sidhe* to a companion in interrogation. The ballad as a whole 'remembers' formally, deploying, in a way Wilde only intermittently does and as Irish popular ballads generally do, on patterns of internal rhyme and assonance that entered English-language poetry through translations or renderings of Gaelic poetry in the nineteenth century.[34] In the *aisling*, Laura O'Connor observes, 'the bardic device of the revenant creates the literary illusion of coevalness between "the unthought known" and cultural consciousness and the return, however partially and obliquely, of the Gaelic world to the realm of the English-only'.[35] Sands's 'revenant', the revenant that is at once the ghostly *passante* he encounters *and* the two-fold ghosts of re-vernacularized and distressed literary forms, enacts a regressive movement that is in the service of anticipation, descrying emergent forms of offence and defence in the inchoate moment of their emergence.

III

What Sands anticipates in his ballad is not only his own physical pain under torture and interrogation, nor just the blanket protest that the end of the ballad 'prophecies', but, I would argue, a new apparatus of biopolitical power that was – like so many colonial apparatuses – gradually moving from the colonial 'periphery' to the metropolitan core of the state. In that shift, Northern Ireland furnished one crucial laboratory and conduit, 'the first major testing ground for the technology of political control'.[36] In order to apprehend what it is that Sands and the anonymous female prisoner might have anticipated undergoing, and to comprehend the significance of the countermovement that regression and identification entail, we need to elaborate the longer history of the torture and interrogation practices that were applied and experimented with in Northern Ireland. To anyone familiar with the conditions of imprisonment and practices of interrogation in British political prisons in Northern Ireland, the more recent photos and reports of Abu Ghraib and Guantanamo were drearily familiar, from the hooded figures to the rituals of humiliation and exposure that were designed to 'soften up' the prisoners before interrogation. In the wake of the introduction of internment in late 1971, some 1,500 suspected Republicans were interrogated, a handful of them being subjected to 'depth interrogation', a practice that turns on the technique of 'sensory deprivation' – and, one should add, over-stimulation. This small number of 'guinea pigs', who must have been selected randomly given that none of them had any real connections with the IRA, were subjected to what appears to have been an experimental procedure that synthesized techniques of interrogation that had been developed and used in various combinations in previous British counter-insurgency campaigns in other colonial theatres.[37]

Tim Pat Coogan gives a succinct description of the abuse, brutal enough in itself, that internees in general underwent in the course of attempts to rapidly accumulate information on Republican neighbourhoods that were traditionally impenetrable to British military or police intelligence: 'Internees were beaten with batons, kicked and forced to run the gauntlet between lines of club wielding soldiers. Some, like Michael Farrell, were forced to stand on a tea-chest and sing "God Save the Queen" in circumstances which added a new definition to the term "conductor's baton".'[38] Liz Curtis cites the treatment of another former internee who later sued the British government, treatment that was aimed at humiliation, exhaustion and fear:

Bernard O'Connor told how for three to four hours '[he] was made to stand on [his] toes with [his] knees in a bent position and [his] hands out in front of [him]'. If he moved, he was slapped. He was kicked, punched and hurled across the room. The interrogators made him run on the spot, and do press-ups and sit-ups, and then repeat these activities naked. They made him stand with his slightly soiled underpants over his head, and pick up cigarette butts from the floor with his mouth. They tied a tracksuit top over his head and blocked his nose and mouth so that he fainted. All the while they were trying to get him to sign a confession.[39]

Such treatment, already tantamount to torture, was supplemented by the application of the 'five techniques' that we now recognize as being those of sensory deprivation. Each on its own would have been merely a form of ill-treatment, thus allowing them to be disregarded as instances of excessive zeal or occasional brutality when made known to the public. In their combination, however, and when applied over many hours and even days, they were known to produce serious bodily pain, severe disorientation, states of terror and even psychosis. Alfred McCoy in his study of 'sensory disorientation' remarks on this peculiar effect of the combination of 'simple, even banal procedures' into 'a systematic attack on all human senses' which 'creates a synergy of physical and psychological trauma whose sum is a hammer-blow to the fundamentals of personal identity'.[40]

Coogan summarizes the techniques and their effects as they were used in Northern Ireland:

The five techniques consisted of hooding, sleep deprivation, white noise, a starvation diet, and standing for hours spreadeagled against a wall, '... leaning on their fingertips like the hypotenuse of a right-angled triangle. The only sound that filled the room was a high-pitched throb, which the detainees usually liken to an air compressor. The noise literally drove them out of their minds.' These techniques were accompanied by continual harrassment, blows, insults, questioning. This treatment usually went on for six or seven days. It produced acute anxiety states, personality changes, depression, and, sometimes, an early death.[41]

There was nothing casual about the treatment meted out to the 'guinea pigs'. The techniques had, as Coogan, John McGuffin and others have shown, been developed systematically 'in theatres such as Aden, Cyprus, Kenya, and in the brainwashing techniques employed against British and American servicemen in Korea'.[42] Tim Shallice, in one of the first psychological studies of torture in Northern Ireland, recognized that what was most significant about the procedures was their 'conscious application of scientific information'. Methods that been developed in colonial counter-insurgency campaigns and been taught to the Royal Ulster Constabulary at the English Intelligence Centre four months before internment advanced from 'a "craft" type handed down from one interrogator to his successor' to ones based on scientific investigation and systematized in the process.[43] Shallice's observation that modern torture involves a scientized practice is underscored by Darius Rejali, who argues that 'Modern torture is clinical, not ritual, torture. The torturer operates on his patient. His methods and instruments are drawn from medicine, engineering, psychology, and physiology'.[44] It is this shift from casual or 'craft' brutality to scientific procedure based on psychological research that marks Northern Ireland not only as a laboratory for torture but as a significant threshold in the emergence of the strong or security state that has emerged globally in the last three or so decades, together with a related shift in the forms of domination and subjection.

The technique of sensory deprivation was not an isolated British discovery but resulted, rather, from the research and practice of what we might call an international torture network that links the intelligence services and military of the former colonial powers, Britain and France, with the United States and its client states, including Israel. Both the nature and effects of the practice, and the reasons for its deployment, are succinctly expressed in the now-notorious CIA manual on interrogation, a fact that concretizes the links between British practice in Northern Ireland and the 'softening-up' techniques made public by way of Abu Ghraib. If, as Elaine Scarry argues, 'intense pain is world-destroying', the effects of torture can be achieved without resort to an evidently brutal *external* infliction of pain, which had the occasional disadvantage of strengthening the resistant prisoner's resolve as well as proving difficult for a democratic state to defend whenever it was exposed to public scrutiny. The new methods, developed through extensive psychological and practical research, relied more on the destroying of the victim's psychic world than on the externally inflicted pain that had seemed necessary to effect it. The CIA's KUBARK Manual on interrogation explains:

> All coercive techniques are designed to induce regression. As [L.E.] Hinkle notes in 'The Physiological State of the Interrogation Subject as it Affects Brain Function', the result of external pressures of sufficient intensity is the loss of those defenses most recently acquired by civilized man: '… the capacity to carry out the highest creative activities, to meet new, challenging, and complex situations, to deal with trying interpersonal relations, and to cope with repeated frustrations. Relatively small degrees of homeostatic derangement, fatigue, pain, sleep loss, or anxiety may impair these functions.' As a result, 'most people who are exposed to coercive procedures will talk and usually reveal some information that they might not have revealed otherwise.'[45]

In the course of the application of sensory-deprivation techniques, fatigue and the 'stress positions' the interrogatee is forced to assume and maintain over long periods induce a sense of self-inflicted pain, through which the body appears to betray itself. Sensory-deprivation techniques thus replicate the effects of traditional forms of physical brutality in which, as Scarry puts it, 'The prisoner's body … is, like the prisoner's voice, made to betray him on behalf of the enemy, made to be the enemy'.[46] Sensory deprivation, however, achieves this end even more effectively precisely because stress positions and fatigue induce a sense of pain that emanates from within the body itself as the prisoner's body becomes 'an active agent, and actual cause of pain'. The resistance that, as we have already noted, externally inflicted violence tends to elicit, is thus undermined by the subject's own feeling that his body hurts him.[47]

This sense not only of utter disorientation but also of self-betrayal leads rapidly to what the KUBARK Manual, relying on psychological research, describes as *regression*:

The deprivation of stimuli induces regression by depriving the subject's mind of contact with an outer world and thus forcing it in upon itself. At the same time, the calculated provision of stimuli during interrogation tends to make the regressed subject view the interrogator as a father-figure. The result, normally, is a strengthening of the subject's tendencies toward compliance.[48]

Interrogation through sensory deprivation thus seeks to break the subject by inducing the combined effects of regression and dependence through the abject prisoner's identification with the 'father-figure' of the torturing interrogator. As Rejali puts it, 'Modern torture works by transforming individuals into asocial, apolitical, and dependent individuals if it does not deliver a personality in shreds':

It is now possible to understand the pastoral character of the torture interrogation. No longer at home in his being, the prisoner lived in a condition of dread, self-mortification, and helplessness. In this context, the interrogator sought to assume a position of confidence and trust ...

In essence, the interrogator said, 'I am not torturing you; you are torturing yourself. I can, however, intervene on your behalf and liberate you from this unfortunate condition. But our success depends on your cooperation.' The procedure was shaped by psychological and medical practice.[49]

Torture in the Northern Irish interrogation centres, with its peculiar combination of sheer brutality, designed to produce dread and radical uncertainty, and highly medicalized procedures, designed to produce psychic disintegration, regression and dependence, was ultimately directed beyond the body and to 'a finer, more diffuse object, a human life'.[50]

Torture and interrogation in Northern Ireland had certain immediate goals. In the first place, the Army and police sought to penetrate the IRA's organization by locating in the course of internment a number of suspects who had what is now called 'actionable intelligence'. But the mass arrests during the period of internment had further goals, as was signalled by the virtually indiscriminate incarceration of enormous numbers of mostly Catholic young men. Nearly 75,000 homes, one-fifth of all houses in Northern Ireland, were raided in 1973 alone; within six months of the internment order, nearly 2,400 people had been interned, mostly from nationalist communities. In 1977–1978, nearly 3,000 people were detained under the Emergency Provisions and Prevention of Terrorism Acts.[51] Figures like these indicate that the principal purpose of the interrogations was the accumulation of data. As Robin Evelegh, former CO of the Royal Green Jackets, admits with some candour: 'The vast majority of those arrested were arrested without being suspected of anything except in the most general sense, because there was no other way whereby the

Army could find out who were the people living in the terrorist-affected areas, what they looked like or where they lived.'[52] Given the long history of segregation and 'ghettoization' of Northern Ireland, and in particular its urban areas, nationalist or Republican communities were especially difficult for the security forces to operate in. The nationalist ghettoes in particular, shaped by state-enforced discrimination and the hostility of the Royal Ulster Constabulary, functioned as oral spaces akin to those that Hugh Dorian described in Chapter 2: spaces difficult to penetrate and bound by informal modes of communication and recognition. In order to subdue them, it was essential to break open those spaces and to get their inhabitants to 'open their mouths', if necessary by force. Such practices have become known, somewhat anaesthetically, as *surveillance*, a term that connotes what its etymology suggests, a process of remote visual monitoring and observation whose model may be the sterile space of the Panopticon. What is not sufficiently recognized is the degree to which surveillance, especially in the sphere of colonial counter-insurgency, deploys not only visual media but also, and more importantly, intrusions into oral space that range from eavesdropping and the ubiquitous military 'listening posts' to the coercion of speech through interrogation. The aim of internment and interrogation was, once again, to break the paradoxically silent recalcitrance of oral space, and to make its subjects 'sing' or 'squeal'. The subject's speech, exacted by the infliction of corporeal pain, was the path to the psychic and physical control of the population.

Internment was thus the first, rather blunt instrument applied in the attempt to conduct massive, even total *oral* surveillance of a dissident population. It conformed to the logic of 'low-intensity conflict' developed in the course of British colonial counter-insurgency campaigns, which demanded mass interrogation as the basis for building a reliable data bank on potentially rebellious communities. But the widespread and highly visible practices of search and arrest and the regular use of torture in interrogation were also intended to intimidate, to signal to potential insurgents and to the population as a whole that they would be met with the violence of the state. The very generalization that made it seem indiscriminate was also a means to the normalization of state violence and of the intrusive practices of surveillance that it required.

This rapid normalization of state violence in Northern Ireland was made possible – as it was required – by its contradictory status as at once an integral political part of the United Kingdom and an entity that was administratively and militarily treated as a colony. Though the latter status could never officially be acknowledged, because it would have contradicted the government's attempt to cast the Troubles as a 'law and order problem' and thus to criminalize Republicans, it was evident both in British attitudes to Ireland and in the anomalous legal and police procedures in force there. Responding to the revelations of torture, *The Sunday Times* made the discrepancy all too clear: 'The notorious problem is how a civilised country can overpower uncivilised people without becoming less civilised in the process.'[53] As an 'uncivilized' colonial space that was also within the United Kingdom, Northern Ireland became in turn the cusp through which colonial practices – internment, coercive interrogation, suspension of habeas corpus, imprisonment without trial or term – could be 'domesticated' into the so-called 'mainland'. Northern Ireland became the point of emergence of what Tim Shallice and others came to term the 'strong state' and the conduit for its importation into Britain itself.[54] The counter-insurgency campaign enabled the province to become a laboratory for new forms of biopolitical and legal intervention that targeted the most intimate domains of the life of its citizens and of which the intrusive modes of interrogation and incarceration were but the most dramatic and violent instances. The question of torture in the context of counter-insurgency in Northern Ireland becomes, then, not merely a matter of historical interest but an important index of the transformation of state power and its relation to its populations that is ongoing in the present.

The logic of counter-insurgency in Northern Ireland was enabled by several factors, consequent on its semi-colonial condition, principal of which was the virtually permanent Special Powers Act that transformed the province into an effective state of emergency at will, one justified by 'reason of state' rather than mere security.[55] Anomalous in the United Kingdom, this measure ironically signalled the settler–colonial nature of the polity and the permanent sense of the Unionist majority that they existed in a state of siege. Its regulations included a clause so broad in its potential application that even Evelegh comments that it would be 'possible to think that merely to be a Roman Catholic in Northern Ireland would have been an offence under that section'.[56] Compounding the readiness to hand of this act, Unionist Prime Minister of Northern Ireland Brian Faulkner declared immediately before the introduction of internment that the society was 'at war with the terrorists'[57] thus effectively converting, in ways all too familiar to us now, a civil strife into a war on terror. The 'exceptional' use of torture was thus legitimated by the extension of a generalized state of exception whose effects gradually 'seeped their way into Great Britain'.[58] Understood within the matrix of colonial insurgency, and seen as one more in a series of insurrections against British colonialism in the post-war period, Northern Ireland also became the port of entry of colonial counter-insurgency methods into the practice and the imaginary of the metropolitan state itself. In this way, it provides a peculiarly prescient model for the generalized form of the security state that has emerged subsequently in consequence of the declaration of a global war on terror. Emanating from within that context, Sands's writings, and the practices of incarceration and interrogation that they track, offer clues as to a still-emerging transformation of subjectivity and are as iconic for the late-modern relation of subject to state as Baudelaire's poem was for the 'era of high capitalism'.

We live in a historical moment when the practices of counter-insurgency and the legal and political structures that enable and legitimate them have become globalized in highly visible ways. It is not, as we have seen, that practices of incarceration and torture were not already internationalized, but, rather, that their deployment has become dramatically public in ways that have almost imperceptibly shifted the ethical relation of the citizen to violence as a means of state power. We can summarize the shift that has taken place for liberal democracies by saying that we currently confront in more or less explicit ways the permanence and generalization of an effective state of emergency, the systematic erosion of habeas corpus, and the public and quite shameless espousal of torture which demands the recruitment of citizens to the attitude of the torturer as one of its strategies of legitimation. What appears as a *response* to acts of terrorism, most obviously to the events of 11 September 2001 or to Britain's 7 July 2005, and is legitimated by appeal to an ongoing terrorist threat, has in fact a far longer history. Indeed, in Britain the Prevention of Terrorism Acts that were supposedly framed as temporary emergency measures to deal with the Irish Troubles were based on a continuous tradition of Coercion Acts dating back to the nineteenth century and have continually been extended to deal with international terrorism.[59]

The Acts turn to a large degree around extensive powers of detention and interrogation and the figure of the interrogatee must be seen as the product of colonial relations imported into the modern strong state in the metropolis. But the interrogatee does not function only as an object that has been contained and subjected by the violence of incarceration, relegated to the threshold of permanent outsiderliness even as it is trapped in the paradoxical interior exteriority of the cell. It is also a figure that affects the imaginary of the non-incarcerated just as the posture of the detective once shaped the erotic-forensic identifications of the high-modern subject. Where the detective was among the erotically charged vernacular icons of modernity, the victim of torture has begun to occupy the imaginary identifications of the contemporary subject. In this respect, it is significant that the *physical* coercion that torture generally connotes has been extended in contemporary methods of torture to focus on the *mental* breakdown of the subject, in line with their genealogy in colonial domains where the psychic subjection of the colonized was essential for the security of the settler or occupier. As the practice of interrogation under torture seeks to penetrate the psychic interior space of the captive, the discourse on torture comes correspondingly to life in the intimate fantasies of the modern subject.

This shift in subjectivity that has taken place in the relation to the *imagination of torture* is played out with heightened acuity in recent discussions of the ethics and practices of torture. In order to comprehend the significance of this new imaginary of torture as an index of the normalization of new modes of state power and of subjection, we will need to analyse carefully the terms in which the discussion of torture and its legitimacy have themselves been disseminated and routinized. For a clear rupture has taken place in the discourse on torture in the very fact that it has become a matter of public debate rather than being maintained in the discursive extra-territoriality of secretive or disavowed practices. In the long history of the application of torture and of a whole spectrum of brutal punishments and sanctions in colonial and slave regimes, what we confront is the normal usage of legally non-normative modes, generally justified by the assumption of a more or less permanent state of siege.[60] Practices that are believed to be 'exceptional' in modern liberal democracies are routinized in the state of emergency that is, as Benjamin remarked, the rule for the oppressed, not least for the colonized and other racial minorities.[61] We need only recall the virtually permanent state of exception that defined the 'rule of law' in colonial Ireland throughout the nineteenth century and Northern Ireland from the moment of its inception. Nonetheless, contemporary discussions of torture extend that myth of the unusual nature of state violence, relying consistently on the invocation of the 'exceptional' moment while denying both the normality of the state of exception and the historical normality of the use of torture. What they seek to do, however, is to generalize and make permanent the state of exception that legitimates the use of torture as a normal practice of the state. In doing so, they presume an unspoken transformation of both the idea and the psychic formation of the subject that is becoming the norm for late modernity.

To recall and document the long history of the use of torture by liberal Western democracies both domestically and in the colonial sphere is a crucial historical corrective to the customary expressions of moral disgust at what have recently been presented as aberrant practices in the 'global war against terror'.[62] It equally serves as the foundation of any critique of the nonsensical proposition, more and more frequently advocated, that torture might be resorted to as an exceptional or emergency procedure without undermining the foundations of liberal ethics and law. As Elaine Scarry has succinctly put it, 'Introducing an "imaginable" occasion for torture that has no correspondence with the thousands of cases that actually occur has the effect of seeming to change torture to a sanctionable act'.[63] A critical historicization is, however, only partially what I wish to contribute to here. What is no less important to explore is the covert structure of recent discussions of torture and the pattern of split identifications that sustain it. Even as we acknowledge the long history of the normality or regularity of torture, we need to locate the shift that has begun to take place in the imagination of the subject's relation to the state and to torture as the intimate expression of its coercive power.

Philosophical and legal justifications of torture 'in exceptional cases', or in what Alan Dershowitz, promulgator of the 'torture warrant' doctrine, refers to as 'the extraordinarily rare situation', consistently invoke 'the ticking bomb' scenario: if we knew we had in our custody the terrorist who had planted a bomb and could prevent its imminent explosion by extracting the information by torture, would we not do so?[64] Such arguments self-evidently ignore the explicit condemnation of torture under *any* circumstances mandated by the Convention against Torture, Article 2.2: 'No exceptional circumstances whatsoever, whether a state of war or a threat of war, internal political instability or any other public emergency, may be invoked as a justification of torture.'[65] They also tend deliberately to dissociate the complex of techniques that we have seen to constitute the sensory-deprivation procedure into discrete applications of force that can then be labelled as something short of torture. Dershowitz's account of what he calls 'very rough interrogation' practised by Israel, the United States and Britain is typical of such fudging, as is Richard Posner's sanitary hair-splitting with its obscenely temporizing colloquialism: 'When … there is no touching, though there may be sleep deprivation, close confinement in chilly or dirty cells, bright lights (the old "third degree"), shouting, threats, truth serums, and lies, I think it becomes an option whether to call the interrogation torture or merely coercive.'[66] Such sophistry aside, however, what is of more peculiar interest in contemporary philosophical and legal justification of torture is what seems its rhetorical requirement: the identification of the interlocutor with the fictional police officer faced with the supposed moral dilemma – 'What would *you* do were you in a position to discover the bomb's location by torturing the terrorist?'[67] In such questions, the citizen is asked, through the invocation of an emergency, to identify with the potential torturer, in a rhetorical move that not only assumes the citizen's assent, but further transforms the unthinkable from being the act of torture to the act of refusing to torture. Anyone, according to such parables, who would *not* torture under such exceptional circumstances becomes guilty of the unethical decision to sacrifice thousands of fellow citizens to his misplaced moral scruples. Through dramatic identification, the torturer thus becomes the representative ethical citizen.

The invocation of this identificatory position is not confined to rarefied philosophical debate. It permeates popular culture. As analysis of the scenario by the Association for the Prevention of Torture has it:

The ticking bomb scenario operates by manipulating the emotional reactions of the audience. It creates a context of fear and anger. It artificially tilts the circumstances to evoke sympathy or even admiration for the torturer, and hatred or indifference towards the torture victim. Its dramatic nature has made it a favourite plotline for popular television programs and action movies. It creates a powerful mental image that has to some extent captured the imagination of a portion of the global public, meaning that discussion of the scenario has taken on a momentum of its own, beyond its original explicitly legal/political context.[68]

Crucial here is not so much the familiar dehumanization of the victim as the humanization of the torturer, which operates as a crucial vehicle of normalization. It has long been regarded as one of the monstrous aberrations of societies in which torture has become routine that the torturer could be a family man living next door to the unaware citizen. The new discourse on torture proclaims that the good citizen, defender of society and civilization, is and should be one of us, with whom we can ethically identify. More than your neighbour, the torturer is you.

Identification with the position of the torturer, however abhorrent it may seem, follows the simple logic of the defence of liberty in a state of exception, once its simple if preposterous postulates are assumed. But another more paradoxical identificatory position is simultaneously invoked and with a regularity that suggests that it has become intrinsic to the framing of the discussion of the ethics of torture. That is the identification of the interlocutor with the position of the *tortured*. Increasingly, the judgement as to what constitutes torture has been given over to individuated assessments of thresholds of pain and endurance. As Fionnuala Ní Aoláin has pointed out, even the European Court of Human Rights has shown an insidious tendency to lay 'extensive emphasis on the subjective experience and characteristics of the individuals alleging violations under article 3 [of the European Convention on Human Rights]'.[69] Ariel Dorfman's critical appeal to imaginative identification deploys the same logic to an antithetical end when he asks of the assessment of what constitutes torture: 'If it were done to you and those you love, one by one, wouldn't you want that practice abolished?'[70] In addition to employing in most cases the familiar technique of dissociating a complex of practices into individual components in order to minimize the appearance of brutality, such queries and comparisons assume that the threshold of pain is whatever each individual can *imagine* tolerating. Exponents of the new brutality in public affairs always overestimate their own capacity for endurance; those who oppose torture tend probably to underestimate it.

What is at stake in these arguments is hardly the extraordinary capacity of human beings both to endure and to inflict pain, but the problem of the inter-subjectivity of pain in defining what it means to be a human subject at all. Such imaginary assessments fly in the face of the aporia that Elaine Scarry elaborates regarding the sensation of pain and its communicability, that 'Though indisputably real to the sufferer, it is ... unreal to others'.[71] Where such recognition of the incommunicability of pain underwrites the necessity for categorical standards for determining what constitutes torture, the subjective measures of pain posited in the *imagination* of being tortured not only allow for a considerable degree of blurring of the definition of torture, they also cast the threshold of torture onto what one might imagine surviving. It is not only that this tendency 'can significantly skew the identification and application of abstract standards per se' that presents a problem both legally and ethically. It is moreover that, in Ní Aoláin's words, 'The [European] Court's willingness to focus on the experienced nature of the incident(s) for the victim moves us some ways away from a fully objective set of criteria that might easily be transferrable from one case to another'.[72] A comparable legal problem emerges, though the resolution is more consistently one-sided, when acts of prison brutality or torture are adjudicated on the basis of intentionality.[73] At issue is not that the definition or even description of torture has become more difficult than in the past, but that the foundational ethical tenets on which a categorical ban on torture or cruelty could be articulated have broken down. In the normalization and routinization of torture, or of 'rough' or *enhanced* interrogation (to use the brilliantly vicious euphemism of late coinage), the ethical injunction against torture that had been maintained from an effectively Kantian categorical position is abolished.

Kant's formulation of the categorical imperative that prohibits any use of any human person as if they were not ends in themselves, not subjects, is telling:

> Man is indeed unholy enough; but he must regard *humanity* in his own person as holy. In all creation everything one chooses, and over which one has any power, may be used *merely as means*; man alone, and with him every rational creature, is an *end in himself*. By virtue of the autonomy of his freedom he is the subject of the moral law, which is holy. Just for this reason, every will, even every person's own individual will, in relation to itself, is restricted to the condition of agreement with the *autonomy* of the rational being, that is to say, that it is not to be subject to any purpose which cannot accord with a law which might arise from the passive subject himself; the latter is, therefore, never to be employed merely as a means, but as itself also, concurrently, an end.[74]

Kant's maxim, which assumes that any infringement on the autonomy that not only belongs to but actually defines the human subject is an infringement on the autonomy of humanity in general, furnishes the grounds for a categorical condemnation not only of torture, but also of any such infringement as, for example, slavery. It expresses most clearly the philosophical foundation for an ethical, legal and ultimately political condemnation and sanction of torture and its agents that is based not on subjective feeling but on the very category of the human as such. It is, immediately or remotely, the ground of virtually all conventions against torture.[75] Precisely as Kant would have predicted, respect for the categorical imperative gives way in a state of terror, where subjects abandon the dictates of reason for what he describes throughout the *Second Critique* as the 'pathological' condition of being driven by impulse or sensation, fear or desire. The immediacy of identification takes the place of deliberation while the manipulation of sensations like fear and rage displaces rational and ethical procedures and the supposed indifference of the law. What this signals is a breakdown of the subject position of modernity that has been underwritten throughout its history by both an ethical and an aesthetic commitment to *disinterest* on the part of the spectator.

For Kant, aesthetic disinterest is, just as much as his ethical principle, necessarily abstracted from the suffering and enjoying human body. It cannot be derived from what he refers to as the 'physiological' grounds of prior thinkers like Edmund Burke, for whom the foundations of aesthetic taste lay in physical sensation: the actual pleasures and pains of the body, its senses of taste and smell, and even the muscular sensations of attraction and repulsion, tension and relaxation, furnished the model for all other judgements of pleasure and pain. Just as the aesthetic *sensus communis*, the universality of subjective but disinterested judgement, provided Kant with the condition of possibility for imagining the political community of non-coercive subjects, so the refusal of the pathological assessment of ethical human conduct towards others offers a universal principle for condemning torture that is absolutely opposed to subjective or experiential assessments.[76] The categorical imperative would lead one to repudiate any judgement on torture, whether positive or negative, Dershowitz or Dorfman, predicated on physical sensation or on emotional impulse, including fear. It is intimately bound up with a liberal idea of the political community of autonomous subjects who are ends in themselves, not means for others, or even means to intelligence.

IV

The Kantian imperative furnishes such forceful grounds for the categorical condemnation of torture under any circumstances that one might be drawn to conclude with a lament for the passing of its sway and to demand its reinstatement as the foundation of just law and practice. For in its passing, what passes is not only the prohibition on torture, but the principle on which the autonomy of the human subject and the entire concept of human rights have been established. What takes their place is the subject of what one might call 'interrogation modernity', who abandons disinterest to identification, and to an identification always potentially split between the position of the torturer and the position of the tortured. In this reading of what the torture debates reveal, we have abandoned autonomy to the biopolitical inroads of the sovereign state, as both its objects and its agents, in a new version of Benjamin's permanent state of exception: a permanent state of terror that spills from the torture chamber into the public sphere, transforming the relation of the subject to the state.[77] As Henry Shue puts it:

The extraction of information from the victim, which perhaps – whatever the deepest motivation of torturers may have been – has historically been a dominant explicit purpose of torture is now, in world practice, overshadowed by the goal of the intimidation of people other than the victim…

… Terroristic torture is a pure case – the purest possible case – of the violation of the Kantian principle that no person may be used *only* as a means.[78]

In the long shadow of the torture chamber, whose procedures are now virtually as public as the capital punishments once inflicted by the autocratic state in order to affirm the sovereignty of the monarch, the relation of the subject to the state ceases to be founded on the ideal of the autonomous subject's willing self-subjection to the law. In a less dramatic manner than in the torture chamber with its notorious theatricality, this late-modern subject is one that *embraces* dependence on the state and a certain psychological regression that enables that dependence. Even as the apparatus of biometrical surveillance employed by the state is increasingly directed at the interior of the biological individual, investing its orifices and interior spaces, it is supplemented by a practice and an imagination of interrogation that seeks to invest and destroy the psychic interiority of the subject, transforming the paradoxically exterior inner space of the cell into the utterly exposed theatre of the torture chamber. In this painful loss of interiority, we can envisage the waning of the 'private space' of the liberal subject, with its roots in the concept of property and enclosure and its articulation through notions of interiority, of the proper divisions of social and psychic space, and of the individual's sovereignty over its inner and outer spaces. That sovereignty has long been under assault by the inroads of both corporate and state power. The enclave of private space has succumbed to the penetration of new modes of biopower that unfold the subject in its desires and fantasies out into what was once a distinct public realm. Increasingly the subject becomes familiar with inhabiting a realm of routinized torture that makes of the citizen not the autonomous subject but one whose identifications are split between being the one who might torture and the one who might be subjected to torture.

Yet appeal to the categorical imperative can no longer reverse the rupture that has taken place, which is effectively the collapse of the always porous boundary between the colonial and the metropolitan spheres, or the coming home of the permanent state of emergency that is colonial and racial law. Nor can it extricate the Kantian ethic from its profound co-implication with the regime of torture itself. For if torture operates by the reduction of the subject to its sheer objecthood, by transforming a person's world into what Scarry calls a 'totality of pain',[79] it equally legitimates itself by doing so. It does so by declaring the subject under torture to have already been an object or, in the luminous terms elaborated by Denise da Silva, 'a subject of affectability'.[80] Framed as it is within the logic of development or the 'civilizing process' in which certain humans remain bound to their tutelage, the categorical imperative and its predication on the autonomy of the fully human subject relegates a whole fraction of potential human subjects to the status of 'pathological subjects'. For them, torture, or the regime of perpetual corporal punishment that is slavery and colonialism, is the norm. It is only 'by virtue of the autonomy of his freedom' that the person is 'the subject of the moral law'. For all other categories of human beings, existence as a *means* is not merely routine, it is justified by their not-yet-human status. The categorical imperative, in its very own terms, cannot dispel the violent regime of torture. Rather, it offers a covert justification of it that is entirely complicit in the logic of colonialism. We will unfold this contradiction further in the following chapter.

The dominant logic of civilization has always allowed for the practice of violence against those whom it regards as the uncivilized or the enemies of civilization. In the logic of contemporary capitalism, the transformation of the autonomous subject into the subject of desire and sensation that Kant would have recognized as the pathological antithesis of the autonomous subject is a virtually realized end. In the present moment, the hegemonic relation of the liberal state to that autonomous subject is being displaced by a convergence of the logic of capital with that of the colonial state: all subjects become the pathological subjects of the strong or security state. And yet neither the negative valence of the so-called pathological subject nor the predication of the idea of human rights on the abstract equivalence of the autonomous subject have ever been either necessary or inevitable. There have always been alternative possibilities. At almost the same moment as Kant was critiquing the Burkean 'physiological aesthetic' and its implicit embrace of the tyranny of sensation and the political sensationalism of tyranny, the anarchist political philosopher William Godwin insisted on finding in the same physiological attributes of human beings, in their capacity for feeling pleasure and pain, an alternative foundation for inalienable human rights:

> Justice has relation to beings endowed with perception, and capable of pleasure and pain. Now it immediately results from the nature of such beings, independently of any arbitrary constitution, that pleasure is agreeable and pain odious, pleasure to be desired and pain to be disapproved. It is therefore just and reasonable that such beings should contribute, so far as it lies in their power, to the pleasure and benefit of each other. Among pleasures, some are more exquisite, more unalloyed and less precarious than others. It is just that these should be preferred.
>
> From these simple principles we may deduce the moral equality of mankind.[81]

Godwin's derivation of 'the moral equality' of human beings from their physical sensations differs from Kant's categorical imperative not only in its embrace of corporeal 'affectability', but also in its refusal of the logic of equivalence that subtends the abstract or formal universality of the subject. A conception of moral equality grounded in the capacity for pleasure and pain neither prescribes a hierarchy of acceptable pleasures nor insists on the commensurability of pleasures. It leaves open the possibility of non-equivalence within the framework of a life in common that affirms the obdurate recalcitrance of corporeal existence to abstraction and identity. Unrealized as that tradition may have been, and overshadowed by a liberal conception of rights based primarily on the right to property, it furnishes nonetheless a robust subaltern alternative to the negation and subjection of the 'pathological subject'.

Godwin's optimistic late-eighteenth-century discourse of rights is predicated upon a notion of human *capacity*. A conception of human potential that has to account critically for the condition of the pathological subject in the wake of a liberal democratic regime of torture begins perforce from the perspective of the *vulnerability* of the embodied human being. What I have sought to explore in these last chapters are the ways in which, for the prisoners of Northern Ireland, the extreme experience of interrogation and torture, and their corollary, the abusive deprivation of the prison block, could be converted through their deliberate assumption of 'the body in pain' into a means, temporary and resistant, of life in common, a way of living that even from the most extreme conditions could shape an alternative collective ethic. What they articulated, both in their resistance and their writings, was not merely opposition to an ongoing form of colonial domination, but also the anticipation of a new condition of domination that was in the process of being generalized. Their reinvention or raising of the oral community against the deprivations of the prison regime and the violent coercion of speech under interrogation did not stop at the expression of defiance, but bore the conviction that even in the most extreme assumption of the body's vulnerability the contours of another possible life live on. The vision of the Blanketmen and their suffering that ends the first part of Sands's trilogy implies that it was in the interrogation chambers of Castlereagh that the strategies of the prison protests were first descried and there that the possibility of inverting the 'ache' of objectification into a life in common first emerged.

Benjamin descried in the erotic longing of Baudelaire's sonnet an anticipation of a forensic stance of the modern subject that was to become normative. In turn, Sands's poem represents the vernacularization of anticipatory insights into the transformation of political possibility that, paradoxically, could open even out of the widespread use of torture, in colonies and post-colonies, and increasingly in the so-called democratic states. Buried in the brutality of Castlereagh was the utopian possibility of another life in common. But that possibility could only come to light by undergoing and transforming the conditions that were emerging in and through their subjection to a new form of state. Reversion to a liberal model of protest or of representation that had already failed in its own terms to circumvent a permanent state of colonial exception was an already bankrupt option. Unexpectedly, the resources of the 'pathological' subject whose claims had been erased in the modernization project of the nineteenth century may find their place again at the threshold of a new regime of modernity.

CHAPTER 6

On extorted speech: back to How It Is

The first stirrings of a general transformation of late-twentieth-century subjectivity, which Sands limned in his vernacular refunctioning of a generic script of modernity, were registered with singular force by an earlier Irish writer, Samuel Beckett. Few critics have engaged with the prominent place assumed by scenarios of interrogation, incarceration and even of torture, both psychological and physical, in Beckett's later work. Yet from *Godot*'s Lucky to the unnamed personages of *What Where*, his plays resonate with the voices of those subjected to the coercion of their speech, as if the figures in these works both literalized and generalized the predicament of the artist that Beckett famously defined, in the aftermath of the Second World War, as the 'obligation to express', even where there is 'nothing to express, nothing with which to express, nothing from which to express, no power to express, no desire to express'.[1] In the wake of *The Unnamable*, too, Beckett's prose work seems overtaken by another scenario, counterpart to interrogation, that of the trial, a scene apparently first sketched in the rather Kafkaesque parable 'As the Story was Told'.[2] The monological quartet of self-recorders, Molloy, Moran, Malone and the Unnamable, give way to the couple of *Texts for Nothing* – court clerk or scribe and accused.

At the threshold between the *Texts* and the late plays stands Beckett's last long prose work, disintegrative and extreme in its form as in its matter, *How It Is* (*Comment C'est*, as it was first published in French in 1961). This work integrates both the scenario of interrogation and that of the scribe-accused in an endless inferno where the tortured become the torturers and the scribe – Krim or Kram – records the 'extorted voices' of those who themselves seem to do no more than cite a voice that envelops and enters them where they crawl in the mud. Probably Beckett's most desolate, unrelievedly abysmal text, one which, unlike the later plays, offers little of the breath-taking formal beauty that counterpoints the misery of their situations, *How It Is* pushes to the limit his exploration of the condition of what Kant would describe as the *pathological* subject: the subject that *undergoes* rather than the subject that is sovereign. It is for that reason that I turn to this text to continue to elaborate the 'new thing that has happened, or the old thing that has happened again' in our own time, the emergence of a subject pathologically determined through the imaginary relation to torture.[3]

Beckett's sustained concern with the subject that suffers the violence of interrogation, even as it suffers the physical disintegration of ageing and decay, should scarcely be surprising, were it not for the determination of critics to free him from history as from politics. But torture is the historical image of the catastrophe that has overtaken the subject, even as age and decay are the register of the 'havoc' of its ruins.[4] *How It Is* was first published in France at the height of the Algerian war of decolonization, a conflict whose counter-insurgency practices had produced, from 1957 on, 'a virtual explosion of information on torture' that had forced the issue of 'extorted speech' into public consciousness.[5] It coincides almost exactly with Frantz Fanon's *The Wretched of the Earth* (1961), whose final chapter gives a vivid analysis of the split subjectivities of both the tortured and the torturer, and more generally with the campaigns and writings of public intellectuals like Simone de Beauvoir, Albert Memmi and Pierre-Henri Simon. Through his publisher, Jérôme Lindon of *Editions de Minuit*, who published the documentation of French practices of torture, Beckett was closely connected with these debates and with the writers and intellectuals who signed Lindon's '*Manifeste des 121*'.[6] Like these intellectuals, Beckett was no stranger to military occupation and its techniques: he had been a member of a French Resistance cell before fleeing into Vichy France when the cell was broken by the Gestapo.[7] Given the formation of the Resistance around a cellular logic that goes back to the secret societies of the nineteenth century, it is impossible that Beckett was not aware of the reasons for such formations – to minimize the knowledge that any arrested member would have of the movement as a whole – or of the ways in which the arrested would be treated. It is hard to imagine that he and his fellow cell members, for whom he operated as a kind of scribe, did not discuss in some detail what was likely to happen to them and how they would confront the inevitable torture. And he would not have been unaware, like other intellectuals in Paris at the time, of how the Front de Libération Nationale replicated such cellular structures and the French Army the tactics of the Gestapo in order to break them.

Nor was Beckett's involvement in the French Resistance likely to have been his first encounter with such issues. Born in 1906, he was a teenager during the Anglo-Irish and Civil Wars, when the violent interrogation of prisoners was both commonplace and highly publicized. In the later 1920s and through the 1930s, he was an associate of many former Republicans who frequented Dublin's bohemian circles, including Thomas MacGreevy, Francis Stuart, Liam O'Flaherty, Charlie Gilmore and Joseph Campbell, and he was an acquaintance of Ernie O'Malley, the Republican veteran and intellectual, who describes his own experience of torture and interrogation at British hands in his memoir *On Another Man's Wound*.[8] That Beckett was close to many of these figures, artists and intellectuals with Republican leanings or commitments certainly does not define his personal political views, but it is suggestive of the lifelong context within which the scenario of imprisonment and torture resonates, from the call of his post-war art criticism for 'an art of incarceration' to the brief late play *Catastrophe*, dedicated to the Czech political prisoner and playwright, Vaclav Havel.[9] Nothing in the continual concern Beckett shows for the condition of the incarcerated suggests that the latter work was a singular protest against totalitarian censorship in solidarity with a fellow writer. Rather, the image of the cell and of interrogation, of 'the man alone, thinking (thinking!) in his box',[10] resonates throughout his work, and not only as a figure for the 'existential condition' or as an image of skull-bound solipsism. This often acoustic image is the index of a historical shift in the modalities of human subjecthood where the technical instrumentality of the production process has entered into that most intimate dimension of human being, the subject's relation to its voice.[11]

The multiple contexts for Beckett's sustained interest in such images of the pathological subject suggest that his awareness of the shifts in the forms of modern subjecthood derived not only from his observation of European fascism, but from the colonial contexts to which his Irish experience was a significant point of entry, as well as from the general forms of modern capitalism. Saturated as it is with allusions to the Irish landscape and memories of Beckett's own youth in Ireland, *How It Is* also brings another, precisely *subterranean* dimension of Irish culture into relation with tendencies that converge with it from elsewhere. As so often in his works, Beckett draws elements that are evidently or surmisably of Irish provenance into constellation with materials that come from elsewhere. In such constellations, specificity is not in the materials themselves, but in the exacting elaboration of the formal structures that bring them into assemblage. It is in its formal processes rather than in any referential framework that *How It Is* brings its Irish hauntings into conjunction with other catastrophic scenarios and shapes the space where the pathological subject comes into its own.

Since *How It Is* would appear to be the least discussed, possibly the least read, of any of Beckett's works, it is worth commencing with some description of the text and its dynamics.[12] A minimal description is not difficult, given that the text opens with a precise abstract of its unfolding from start to finish: 'how it was I quote before Pim with Pim after Pim how it is three parts I say it as I hear it.'[13] Following this 'invocation' (7), Part 1 presents an anonymous narrator crawling through the mud in the dark and reciting his conditions as he travels towards Pim.[14] Recitation it is, since it appears through most of the text that the discourse of the narrator is all quotation of a voice whose source is uncertain – 'once without quaqua on all sides then in me' (7) – and is itself improperly transmitted: 'ill-said ill-heard ill-recaptured ill-murmured' (7). This narrator drags himself forward through the mud, 'right leg right arm push pull ten yards fifteen yards', equipped only with a sack of tins of tunny and sardines, a tin opener and a cord, which are all described in exhaustive detail despite their redundancy to a creature that seems to lack appetite, hunger or thirst. This painstaking account is interrupted on and off by flashes of the life above that appear in the form of images: 'a few images on and off in the mud earth sky a few creatures in the light some still standing' (8). These images, no matter that they evoke material that can be and has been identified with moments in Beckett's own life – and that appear in more apparently autobiographical works such as *Company* – are explicitly not subjective memories. The same images, or ones akin to them – 'that family' as the text has it of its various sets of resemblances – the narrator will elicit from Pim as part of his 'extorted speech', meaning that precisely where they do recur, they recur as those of another, not as the subject's own memories. Otherwise, in this 'warmth of primeval mud impenetrable dark' (12) the narrator proceeds on an evidently preordained trajectory towards Pim, speculating on occasion on the state of things here below and sifting the fragments of what remains of a life that may or may not be his, hoping always for the silence that will put an end to 'all the doing suffering bungling achieving' (25). We are, thus far, in a universe familiar from Beckett's *Trilogy* and from the *Texts for Nothing*, with their perpetually frustrated desire for the word or act that would put an end to self-consciousness and inaugurate the silence.

Part 2, 'with Pim', opens another territory, however, one that occupies in unusually violent ways the no less familiar terrain of the Beckettian couple. It recounts the period of the narrator's life with Pim, 'our life in common' (61, 62, 63, etc.) that involves the 'problem of training and concurrently little by little solution and application of same and concurrently moral plane bud and bloom of relations proper' (63). This 'training' – a dark parody of the 'civilizing process', perhaps – involves the extortion of speech from Pim through successive tortures, painful stimuli that are intended to exact a specific response. Fingernails stabbing the armpit comes to mean 'sing!'; a thump on the skull, burying Pim's face in the mud, 'silence!'; the blade of the tin opener jabbed in Pim's arse signifies 'speak!', and so it continues:

> ... the day comes we come to the day when stabbed in the arse now an open wound instead of the cry a brief murmur done it at last
> with the handle of the opener as with a pestle bang on the right kidney handier than the other from where I lie cry thump on skull silence brief rest jab in arse unintelligible murmur bang on kidney signifying louder once and for all cry thump on skull silence brief rest (75)

This 'training' continues until eventually a 'table of basic stimuli' is composed:

> ... one sing nails in armpit two speak blade in arse three stop thump on skull four louder pestle on kidney
> five softer index in anus six bravo clap athwart arse seven lousy same as three eight encore same as one or two as may be (76)

This basic catalogue of torments becomes more sophisticated as Part 2 progresses and the narrator develops the technique of carving Roman capitals in Pim's back with his fingernails, forming words and sentences to whose questions Pim must respond in an extended interrogation session. The responses, however, fail to resolve matters: the images of life above, which in most cases seem versions of the narrator's own images in Part 1, are no more reliable than the narrator's speculations:

> the proportion of invention vast assuredly vast proportion a thing you don't know the threat the bleeding arse the cracking nerves you invent but real or imaginary no knowing it's impossible it's not said it doesn't matter it does it did that's superb a thing that matters (80)

Of life above or below, Pim can neither affirm nor deny anything:

> they are not memories no he has no memories no nothing to prove he was ever above no in the places he sees no but he may have been yes skulking somewhere yes hugging the walls yes by night yes he can't affirm no deny anything no so one can't speak of memories no but at the same time one can speak of them yes (106)

Shortly after this acknowledgement of the futility of the torments that extort Pim's speech, Pim departs as anticipated, leaving the narrator alone in the mud.

The final section of *How It Is* finds the narrator static and alone, awaiting the approach of a creature he names Bom or Bem, who in turn will torment him: 'and instead of Pim's cries his song and extorted voice be heard indistinguishable similar mine' (142).[15] This imagined scenario generates his mathematical speculations on the possibility of an endless series of creatures and on all the impossible permutations of such a series:

a million then if a million strong a million Pims now motionless agglutinated two by two in the interests of torment too strong five hundred thousand little heaps colour of mud and now a thousand thousand nameless solitaries half abandoned half abandoning (125)

These endless speculations – strictly endless since each is abandoned without final resolution – on the cosmology of this inferno, on the possibility of a scribe, Krim or Kram, who witness and notes all, on the possibility of a god who observes all, elaborately play out the antinomies of pure reason with all the earnest ingeniousness of J.W. Dunne's doubtless forgotten *A Serial Universe*.[16] But the section concludes with an extended scene of what amounts to either self-interrogation or the interrogation of the narrator by the sourceless voice that surrounds him, or perhaps the interrogation of that voice by the narrator: greater certainty is not forthcoming (158). And yet the actual conclusion seems only to lead back again to the commencement of the text: 'good good end at last of part three and last that's how it was end of quotation after Pim how it is' (160). The final sentence is the virtual mirror image of the opening sentence; in French, the final phrase, *comment c'est*, the title of the work, is a homophone of the imperative or infinitive form *commencer*, infamously suggesting not only that in the text's end is its beginning but also that the resigned affirmation of a state of being is equally its inauguration: 'how it is' is no less than the performative 'let it be' of the beginning itself.

The insistent circularity of *How It Is* is not the symbol of life's self-replenishing fullness that it is for *Ulysses* or *Finnegans Wake*, master's voices that the conclusion of Beckett's text no doubt dryly echoes. It is rather, as in *Waiting for Godot* or *Endgame*, the formal complement of the exhaustion and entrapment that the text stages and the mark of the failure of any concept of moral progress towards enlightenment that has sustained the literary project of some two centuries at least. In this tripartite malign comedy without ascent or salvation, the inferno repeats itself at every level of the text and according to a rigorously serial logic. Within the carapace of its formal unity, the narrative correlative of Beckett's strict adherence to the Aristotelian unities of time, place and action in his plays, a process of dissolution and fragmentation is sustained that belies the customary symbolic import of a formal perfection that is otherwise almost classical in its self-containment. That process is instantly evident to the reader from the first lines of the text. Gone are the extended, breathless but grammatically impeccable sentences that typified the monologue of the Unnamable or of the nameless narrators of *Texts for Nothing*. In their place are bursts of unpunctuated, elliptical prose, almost entirely deprived of the grammatical marks of subordination or relation that establish the hierarchical regime of sense and perspective in 'good writing'. These bursts of prose of differing length, separated by white spaces of silence or blankness, approximate the breathless, panting, interrupted speech of the narrator as he transmits what the voice around him or in him dictates. They perform, in other words, an eternal present, the present of a speaking voice for which nothing that is in the utterance seems to survive the moment of utterance itself.[17] This is a writing that undoes from within the forms of interiority and historical consciousness that literacy supposedly inaugurated. Accordingly, the text lacks any of the markers of the subject that anchored the traditional realist novel and that even survived into Beckett's previous prose works – temporal continuity, location in space or time, relation to a world or to others. Even the sets of images of the world above in the light flash on and off in fragments that yield no information that might account for the narrator's present condition: as the text lacks a sense of progress, so it lacks any sense of its own development, of some genealogical logic that would connect the glimpses of the child at his mother's knees, of the man at a table with a woman looking on, of the boy and girl walking across the racecourse to the mountains, even to the past of the narrator, let alone to any chain of causality that might make sense of the present. It is as if the distinct components of the text, 'bits and scraps' like the narrator's own utterances, occupy discrete and disconnected realms, resisting totalization even within the rigorous totality of the work's formal circularity. Not even the three major divisions of the text and the events that take place within them seem to have any *transformative* effect on one another. Despite the entirely predicted sequence that leads from one to the other, and the material that repeats within each, the episodes are virtually self-contained and will repeat interminably, we suppose, in the same form and order ad infinitum.

What then is the formal principle of *How It Is* and what does that principle signify? We may define the dominant logic of the text as repetition, although it does not operate on the algorhythmic principles of later texts from *Ping* to *Worstward Ho* or of late plays like *What Where* or *Quad*, in which phrases or movements are repeated until virtually all available permutations have been exhausted. In *How It Is*, it is not so much that the textual materials are repeated, although certain key utterances are recycled and taken up again and again throughout in a pattern of self-conscious self-citation, rather that a number of series of elements repeat each other's formal logics on different levels and in different registers.[18] In Parts 1 and 2, there are two dominant series, that of life down below whose medium is the voice and that of life above in the light whose medium is the image. The flashing on and off of the images corresponds, with a different rhythm, to the oscillation between silence or panting and speaking on the part of the voice. Although the images are necessarily represented by the speaking voice, they remain, as we have seen, entirely discrete from the world below, appearing and disappearing autonomously of the narrator's will and affecting the unfolding of that world as little as it affects them. They represent not the depth of the narrator's subjective world, whether as unconscious traces of traumatic incidents or as the accumulated body of personal experience, but 'bits and scraps' of an interrupted series that intersects 'on and off' with the series of the narrator's world below through the relay of his utterances. In Part 3, the series of images virtually disappears, to be replaced by an extended meditation on the serial form of the world below: its series of creatures, Pim and Pom, Bem and Bom, extended into a mathematical progression towards infinity. This series is doubled by the narrator's speculation that there may exist a correlative series of scribes, the series Krim–Kram – 'it's preferable more logical for Kram to note and if we are innumerable then Krams innumerable if you like or one alone my Kram mine alone' (146).

The formal logic or model for these complementary series is given briefly, early on in Part 1: 'sudden series subject object subject object quick succession and away' (12). Each of the series designated is a set of objects for the subject who appears as the narrator of *How It Is*; but it is no less apparent that he is an object for them, certainly for Pim and, in a hypothetical future, for Bom or Bem, and for the scribes Krim and Kram; it is uncertain whether in fact he is not the object of the man in the images of Part 1 who sits at the table observing himself observed by a woman and who may represent the figure of the writer. To say this is already to exaggerate the degree of relation that the text proposes, captured as we may be by the 'neatness of identifications';[19] the essential point is, first, that the narrator himself moves from the position of subject to that of object 'on and off' with an insistent binary logic, and, second, that he does so throughout the text, in several adjacent series, in relation to the things that become his objects while constituting his interiority.

One such series circulates, especially in Parts 1 and 3, around the sack that the creatures are each inexplicably supplied with. The sack seems to operate as some primal object, although its function and that of the objects it contains is unclear, given their redundancy to the narrator in his virtually absolute lack of biological needs. This redundancy, however, suggests that rather than functioning as a residue of realism within the text, the sack is an emblem for object relation itself. It not only inaugurates a series within the series that is 'life below', a series that involves descriptions of the narrator's provisions and, later, those of the whole chain of creatures in the mud, but also acts as a relay or node between that series and another that has to do with the constitutive elements of language.[20] In this respect it opens up a means of modelling the operations of the text as a whole.

In the first instance, the sack appears on its own as an element of the description of life below:

the sack sole good sole possession coal-sack to the feel small or medium five stone six stone wet jute I clutch it drips in the present but long past long gone vast stretch of time the beginning this life first sign very first of life (8)

But as *sign* as well as object, primal object and primal sign, the sack connects with an alternate series that has to do with more than a mere descriptive catalogue. It becomes an element of what the narrator ironically describes as 'all my great categories of being' (15). For it soon appears not simply as a thing in use, but as a *word*: 'the sack when it's empty my sack a possession this word faintly hissing brief void and finally apposition' (19). Thus it enters a series of primal words that begins with the fundamental exhalation of breath or hiss: 'escape hiss it's air of the little that's left of the little whereby man continues standing laughing weeping and speaking his mind nothing physical the health is not in jeopardy a word from me and I am again' (29). Thus physical needs, for which the sack may be a figure, enter into an alternate register as symbolic functions, betokening not mere existence but being as a question of meaning. The fundamental breath, *as*, becomes the mark of *spirit*, and is in turn reflected in the primal possession, *sa*-ck.[21]

Such words, composed of basic syllables and designating the infant's primary objects, perhaps even the act of designation itself, recur throughout *How It Is*, drawing the sack, as it were, from one series into another that then connects back through it with the series we might entitle 'possessions'. It is not, therefore, that one cluster of objects for the subject functions as a metaphor for another. The sack is not 'like' words, nor words 'like' possessions. It is rather that the sack functions both as a thing in the world of the subject's material objects *and* as a word among others in his reduced vocabulary. Words, similarly, function as possessions as well as signifiers, both 'at the disposal' of the subject and constitutive of him – 'a word from me and I am again' – in a chain of alienable signifiers that at once designate his objects and establish an endless set of substitutions. These objects, like the primal object that is the mother, continually escape:

it comes the word we're talking of words I have some still it would seem at my disposal at this period one is enough aha signifying mamma impossible with open mouth it comes I let it at once or in extremis or between the two there is room to spare aha signifying mamma or some other thing some other sound barely audible signifying some other thing no matter the first to come and restore me to my dignity (29)

If every word is generated from a single articulation of breath, *aha*, that is no more than the designation of any percept indifferently – a kind of infinitely convertible *aha-Erlebnis*[22] – then language becomes subject to an irredeemable seriality that repeats over and again the same relation while unmooring the subject into an interminable quest to find that final word that will 'restore the silence'.[23] 'Aha' is not an original word that will serve to anchor the philological investigations of the subject in its primal identity, but a differentiating utterance that, in designating for the subject any object – 'no matter' – inaugurates simultaneously the subject's displacement into chains of objects and signifiers.

But nor for this text is 'aha' a mere signifier. It is also a material sound, an escape of air, which the narrator unmistakably associates with other emanations from the body: 'a word from me and I am again I strain with open mouth so as not to lose a second a fart fraught with meaning issuing through the mouth no sound in the mud' (29). If indeed it seems that 'we're talking of words', it is no less true that we are simultaneously talking of farts, in farts, and the 'open mouth' conjoins the series of words with another series that has to do with the body's multiple orifices and their function as sites of entry and of issue for the body. This is the no less 'expressive' series of bodily functions, secretions and excretions, that range throughout the text from weeping and howling to eating, sucking, shitting, pissing and passing gas in various forms. These primordial yet nonetheless highly symbolic bodily functions, it must be noted, are themselves supplemented or displaced by the function of most of the orifices as organs of perception – seeing, hearing, tasting, smelling – and of communication – speaking, murmuring, singing. Beckett's creatures are utterly at home with the insistent lability of the orifices, not least that of the mouth, and they seem in no way subject to the disciplines that the 'civilizing process' has imposed on their social uses. But they are no less at home with the fungibility of orifices: it is as indifferent whether speech issues from the anus or farts from the mouth as whether the mouth functions to take in food or expel words. For child development and Freudian analysis alike, the discipline (the stoppage, one might say) and the reterritorialization of orifices follows a graduated series that plots the subject's moral and ethical development, from mouth to anus to eye and ear. Beckett's creatures – like the H-Block prisoners – inhabit, rather, a world in which the series of orifices relays with those of words, and of objects, and of images in a continuous switching that establishes their simultaneity on the same fundamental plane.[24]

Two related observations follow from this analysis of the serial form of *How It Is*. The first concerns the notion of interiority, the second the fate of the ethical subject. Clearly, Beckett's creatures throughout the text no longer inhabit the interior of a skull, though that image may offer a momentary hypothesis to the narrator in Part 3 – 'little vault empty closed eight planes bone-white' (140) – as if in an echo of earlier prose texts. But already the skull, image of the absolute fortress of interiority, has become here indistinguishable from the *cell*, that peculiar space in which absolute seclusion and withdrawal from the public becomes the condition for perpetual surveillance and the loss of privacy, interiority or free contemplation. It is, as it were, the spatial equivalent of language itself: the medium of an interiority that can never be the unique possession of the subject. 'I'm in words, made of words, others' words.'[25] The cell, one of the locutions for seriality to which the narrator recurs in order to imagine his condition, is equally imagined as an interior space that folds outwards:

quick the head in the sack where saving your reverence I have all the suffering of the ages I don't give a curse for it and howls of laughter in every cell tins rattle like castanets and under me convulsed the mud goes guggle-guggle I fart and piss in the same breath (42)

The turning outward of the space of concealment here as elsewhere not only leaves the subject exposed, in this case to the imaginary laughter of other inmates in adjacent cells, but articulates the spatial relations of the subject with those of language and, almost indistinguishably, with those of the body and its orifices. The condition of the subject that emerges is that of being suspended in relation to its objects, objects that include the sack and its contents, Pim's body and utterances, its own body and its excretions, its possibly hallucinated images, the mud and the dark below and, in ways whose significance we shall explore further, the voice that is both its own and not its own. The very refinement of the narrator's dispossession throws into relief the extent to which interiority is object-relation, a condition imagined within an inner space but constituted by relation to things, including speech, that are 'outside'.[26] It is the condition that Benjamin so strikingly captures in a 'dialectical image' from the *Arcades Project*:

Brief description of misery; probably under the bridges of the Seine: 'A bohemian woman sleeps, her head tilted forward, her empty purse between her legs. Her blouse is covered with pins that that glitter in the sun, and the few appurtenances of her household toilette – two brushes, an open knife, a closed tin – are so well arranged that this semblance of order creates almost an air of intimacy, the shadow of an *intérieur*, around her.'[27]

Interiority is not a thing *in* itself, but is folded outwards, exteriorized, as a phenomenon, just as the subject's relation *to* objects parallels the subject's own status *as* an object.

It is precisely this condition that constitutes for Kant the ethical insufficiency of the empirical or, as he has it throughout the *Critique of Practical Reason*, the *pathological* subject. Subjected to and attached or aversive to pleasures and pains that are subjective, not objective, and therefore not universally communicable, this subject's maxims can never rise to the level of a moral law for all. That subject, being thus subjected to impulses and desires that are governed by the laws of natural causality, is not only not free in the domain of its physical pains and pleasures, it is in effect an object even as it is suspended in its relation to objects whose noumenal reality always escapes it. It is, moreover, not merely an object of nature and an object among objects, it is an object for itself: *'the thinking subject is to itself in internal intuition only a phenomenon'*.[28] As Jacques Lacan notes in 'Kant avec Sade', this condition of the pathological subject 'would submit the subject to the same phenomenal seriality as determines its objects'.[29] Kant's solution is to establish the subject of reason in its freedom over and above the empirical subject, thus apparently saving the subject only by splitting it between a subject tied to its objects and a subject that I have elsewhere described as the 'subject without properties'.[30] For Lacan, this split is equivalent to his own distinction between the subject of the enunciation and the subject of the enounced,[31] a designation that captures nicely the predicament of the narrator of *How It Is*, suspended in a speech that is at once his utterance and a voice that speaks through him: 'voice once without quaqua on all sides then in me' (7). But what is this external voice that appears to constitute the subject in his interiority, that appears as at once an utterance and as an object: 'I say it as I hear it'?

As Lacan points out, in establishing the subject of reason or freedom as the subject of the moral law, Kant not only splits the subject but unwittingly makes that subject without objects dependent upon a never-acknowledged object, the voice.[32] The 'categorical imperative' is just that: an apparently inner voice that commands, assuming the subject's consent (*Einstimmigkeit*) to the universal law it pronounces. That assent can be assured when, and only when, the reason is free of the contingencies that afflict the pathological individual body. The sourceless interior voice that commands becomes another inaccessible or supersensible thing-in-itself, even as its pronouncements, its utterances, become an object for the inner ear of the subject. If the phenomenal subject, suspended among its objects, splits off from the subject of reason, ostensibly not subject to objects, the latter finds itself generating a second pair of series, that of the voice as empty transcendental *form* and that of voice-as-object in the shape of its utterances. The pathological thus restores itself in the very site where the integrity of the subject was to be established in the unity of its voice with that of the Law. Literalizing a *voice* whose objecthood was concealed even from itself in the guise of a metaphor, *How It Is* accords with Lacan's reading of Kant with Sade in finding in that voice an agency of torment:

For we will see revealed this third term that, according to Kant, is lacking in moral experience. That is to say the object which, in order to secure his willing accomplishment of the Law, he is constrained to dismiss to the unthinkable realm of the Thing-in-itself. Is that object not there, descended from its inaccessibility, in the Sadean experience, unveiled as the Being-there, the *Dasein*, of the agent of torture?[33]

For the narrator of *How It Is*, it is the voice itself, long before any actual instrument of torture comes into play on Pim's body, that already extorts speech, the alienated and alienating stream of utterance that issues from the unwilling subject's orifices: it is the 'oakum of old words' that the narrator in his 'little chamber all bone-white' (146) is obliged so painfully to pick.

How It Is thus generalizes as its condition of possibility the terrifying world that, according to Elaine Scarry, the victim of torture inhabits, where 'the prisoner's voice … is made to betray him',[34] issuing as an alien thing from the pained body that has no less become estranged. Yet in its very generalization of that alien voice as the condition of possibility for its world, *How It Is* generates the logic of a universe in which Kant's categorical imperative has neither empirical sway over the domain of law, punishment and interrogation, nor analytical truth for the subject. We may read it as a dark parody of the *Second Critique*, one which transforms the inner voice of the moral law into an agonizing injunction to speak and which refuses to depart from the 'pathological' world of the feeling subject who appears as an object for himself and an object for others whom he takes as his objects in an endless series of substitutions, 'tormentor always of the same and victim always of the same' (124). In this respect, it registers the conditions of a world in which the determination that every subject is an end in himself and not a means for others is systematically traduced – and in the voice of one whose hypotheses and postulates constantly interrogate 'all my great categories of being' (15). Yet that parodic rewriting of what is surely the dominant ethical paradigm of modernity is not solely contingent upon a historically given 'time-honoured conception of humanity in ruins',[35] not a mere petulant 'so there' in the face of ethical idealism or the doctrine of progress. On the contrary, as I have suggested in relation to its Irish materials, Beckett's work operates on whatever material it may seize from the world of historical experience in order to find the forms that can investigate the discrete dynamics that determine it. *How It Is* is not a representation of the world as it appears to be, but a demonstration of its inner logic. That process, and its formally parodic relation to Kant's *Critique*, become evident in two ways in particular, ones that open back out onto what we might call the 'deep structure' of historical conditions.

Kant's splitting of the human subject into 'the subject of freedom' and the empirical, pathological subject, captured in its 'phenomenal seriality', answers to the need to predicate on the multitude of contingent individuals a single and universal form for the moral law, without which ethics would be mired in the particularities of singular pleasures and pains: 'rules are objectively and universally valid only when they hold without any contingent subjective conditions, which distinguish one rational being from another'.³⁶ The critique furnishes, accordingly, 'the mere *form* of a universal legislation', since the law must be abstracted 'from all matter' that might determine a subject in its particularity.³⁷ The formal subject of freedom corresponds to this formal law: it is the point at which, abstracted from the contingent differences that determine the pathological subject in its particularity, all subjects are alike. It is structured thus as a metaphor, bringing disparate subjects together in terms of their identity and laying their differences in abeyance. The very possibility of the 'subject of freedom' is then grounded in the moment of the *indifference* of subjects, any one of whom can take the others' place. It is this logic of substitution that, in fact, shapes the legal and political imaginary of modernity, whether in the form of the nation state, composed of a citizenry that shares a common political and cultural identity, or in the related form of formal equality before the law. In this system of representation, a single figure, the formal subject whose institutional expression is the state, can stand for the moment of universality in every particular subject.³⁸

In *How It Is*, however, the refusal of metaphorical sublimation and of any ascent from particularity to representation leads, as we have seen, to a formal principle of intersecting seriality in which every subject, every object, can supplant every other in an endless succession of relations. Where, as Lacan formulates it, the object escapes or is lacking (*cet objet se dérobe*³⁹), the place of the symbolic instance, of the formal subject that represents humanity, is empty. Beckett's formulation of this dissolution of the species into the 'so on' cannily echoes Freud's '*wo Es war, soll Ich werden*' by inverting its therapeutic sense:⁴⁰

... present formulation seeking that which I have lost there where I have never been
   dear figures when all fails a few figures to wind up with part one before Pim the golden age the good moments the losses of species I was young I clung on on to the species we're talking of the species the human saying to myself brief movements no sound two and two twice two and so on (52)⁴¹

The mathematical sublime subsists here only under the condition of its evacuation: the endless possible series of additions and multiplications appears throughout the text with no point of anchorage and with no assurance to the subject of its practical mastery of the infinite extension of the series of substitutions it inaugurates. In Part 3, the 'present formulation' echoes again with that frustrated need:

thus need for the billionth time part three and last present formulation at the end before the silence the panting without pause if we are to be possible our couplings journeys and abandons need of one not one of us an intelligence somewhere a love who all along the track at the right places according as we need them deposits our sacks (150)

The endless series of 'brotherly likes' (41 etc.) furnishes a 'horizontal comradeship' but without the instance of nation or state, moral law or divine intelligence, that would transform the multitude of individuals into a common identity.[42]

Its model is in fact that of commodity exchange, Marx's infinitely extensible series CMC, whose vertiginous substitutions can only be governed by the metaphorical instance of 'the sublime money form' in whose abstraction as the commodity of commodities all other values are symbolized. Money represents the moment of identity of all commodities as commodities, as exchange values rather than particular use values. But, as the instance which represents the relations among commodities as value, it takes the place of human social relations: the human individual, abstracted in the form of labour power, becomes – as money also is – one among other commodities, part of a set of intersecting series of things and objects, persons and commodities. The spare and desolate image of this subordination of the individual, unleashed by the promise of formal freedom and equality, to the inferno of domination and equivalence, is *How It Is*. Its creatures take one another's place successively, in endless substitution: 'from the next mortal to the next leading nowhere and saving correction no other goal than the next mortal' (69). The necessary indifference of the subject of the moral law becomes the nightmare of an utterly reductive justice, the justice of universal equivalence rather than universal equality:

… what the fuck I quote does it matter who suffers faint waver here faint tremor
   the fuck who suffers who makes to suffer who cries to who to be left in peace in the dark the mud gibbers ten seconds fifteen seconds of sun clouds earth sea patches of blue clear nights and of a creature if not standing still still capable of standing always the same imagination spent looking for a hole that he may be seen no more in the middle of this faery who drinks that drop of piss of being and who with his last gasp pisses it to drink the moment it's someone each in his turn as our justice wills and never any end it wills that too dead or none (144)

In this scenario of relentless exchange, where each substitutes for the other, each becomes equally an instrument for the other, in a sense literalized by the narrator's violent playing with Pim until he sings, a term hardly innocent of its connotations of torture and interrogation. The victim of the 'agent of torment' is not merely the torturer's object, he is ultimately a *means* employed in the interests of domination, and his speech, or song, the product to be elicited rather than the expression of his autonomy.

Hence in *How It Is* this 'extorted voice' that is an object for the subject rather than the imperative pronouncement of the law as representative of the universal human species never can give rise to a figure for univocality, of the *sensus communis* in which the representative individual conjoins with 'the voice of all'. That 'voice of us all' (116) is no expression of commonality but the interminable repetition of what passes from one to the next, 'quaqua the voice of us all who all those here before me and to come alone in this wallow or glued together all the Pims tormentors promoted victims past if it ever passes and to come' (116). Voice refuses to become a figure for the subject abstracted into autonomy or identity, *vox populi* or *vox dei*. Instead, Beckett's text everywhere insists on its materiality, on its physical presence and texture as breath, on its peculiar spatiality that allows it to produce effects of interiority and of externality, on its rhythms and interruptions, on the orifices through which it issues and the tormented body which is its organ or instrument. This effect of the materiality of the voice derives from the formal features of the text in a way that obliges one to term *How It Is* – at the risk of a paradoxical tautology – an oral text. Its 'midget grammar', that dispenses very visibly with the aids to sense-making of punctuation, subordination, logical conjunction and relation, forces attention to the syntagmatic axis of language, the endless paratactic flow of words aligned by contiguity, emphasizing the production of the utterance rather than the symbolic dimension in which one or other privileged figure might arrest the slippage of meaning from chain to chain or series to series. It equally obliges enunciation in order to retrieve momentarily some sense from the insubordinate flow of words. The reader needs to voice the text in order to decide upon an order of words that will in every instance be shadowed by provisionality, inducing a hesitation that mimes the narrator's 'ill-said ill-heard ill-recaptured ill-murmured' (7) transmission of what is for him already an exercise in dictation: 'I say it as I hear it.' Voicing is thus not the echo of an inner singularity, but the repetition of an imperative that leaves the subject subjected to the dictation of another and suspended in a desire that is always at least in part the desire for homeostasis, the desire for the torment of utterance to end. *How It Is*, one might say, is the speaking writing of the death drive. The terror of the work, that makes it so difficult to return to, surely lies in part in its capacity to effect a possession of the reader, captured by this voice that demands not only to be read or heard but to be spoken. If this is the voice of a humanity ruined by its own instrumentality – and indeed, no one is exonerated from its fundamental condition – then it is also a voice that refuses to die, to be silenced. In its very insubordination, in its insistent questioning of how things are, in its ungoverned blather, it obeys the last injunction, to live on.

Riven from its first page by speech that comes to it unbidden and imperative, Beckett's text is haunted by voices that recall destruction of which it may not even be aware. Yet its form, destined as it is to the dismantling of the logics of such destruction, is ready and adequate to receive them. It is as if Beckett constructs a cell tuned in to transmissions that reverberate on the air across the devastation. As the oral community speaks again through the prisoners' unwitting recomposition of its forms, so Beckett's oeuvre makes spaces through which the suffering human subject, reduced by modernity to the not-yet-human status of the pathological, can find its voice. This is why critical reception of Beckett that reads in it the humanist script of the subject's courageous survival in the face of disaster seems so inadequate to the 'conception of humanity in ruins' that his work approaches. It wants to carry on as if the enormity of the destruction that the instrumentality of domination has turned into a universal norm under the euphemistic rubrics of 'progress and development', 'freedom and democracy', 'human and material resources', 'collateral damage', were no more than things as they are, things as they always have been, a 'human condition' in the face of which ironic resignation is enough. Beckett takes these moral positivists at their word. *How It Is* subjects the human subject to the extreme of deprivation: dispossessed of almost every thing, of memory, of all but 'bits and scraps', of the human relations that still endured in *Godot* and *Endgame*, of even the grammar that secures it in relation to its predicates, the subject lives on, crawling through the mud. But there, everything changes. What the optimistic humanist wants to preserve, the common identity of the universal, dissolves with the structures that *How It Is* so painstakingly ruins. The logic of instrumentality, whose precepts are so uncomfortably secreted in the *Second Critique* in the very name of freedom and the moral law, appears as the constitutive principle of things as they are: where we begin is how it is. The relentless ugliness of *How It Is* is its proper response to the brutal regime of ugliness that instrumentality imposes on the world. In it, the voices of those whom progress consigned to the ash heaps of history find room to resound in ways that do not diminish the brutality of their fate.

How It Is is a text framed around questions, a relentless interrogation of the conditions of a certain form of being, being deprived of the conditions of universality, offering no ground for the 'subject without properties' that guarantees the categorical imperative and the common identity of humanity. It dismantles the fundamental tenet of modern political society and culture, the assumption of the formal identity of subjects. It refuses all the connotations of *voice* that organize that system: its univocity, its consistency, its autonomy, its representativeness, its status, in other words, as the mark of the subject's *Mundigkeit*. It does so in part by rematerializing a voice which – as both the representative of moral law and as the mark of autonomy – had been alienated into metaphor, into the correlative of the general equivalence that subtends the claim to equality. Accordingly, this bleakest of Beckett's works anticipates and mimes what increasingly appears as the real 'condition of humanity', promised autonomy as the reward for playing along, but, as the condition of that autonomy, reduced to the heteronomy of exchange and, finally, become the always potential object of coerced speech. Already under perpetual surveillance and obliged to imagine oneself subject to the violence of interrogation and torture that has always secretly been the prerogative of the state that claims the monopoly of violence, we confront at last the material form of the universal moral law that demands our free consent.

But if this is what the text suggests to be the fate of the subject, what questions does it demand that we pose back to it? Should we not interrogate in turn this scenario of perpetual interrogation, this vision of a collectivity of suffering and alienation, as to what its dystopian contours may secrete? Is there any utopian potential in this pathological world that might make another sense of the 'life in common' that its creatures are said over and again to enjoy together? In the living on of this voice in the darkness, in the ruptures and silences of its discontinuous breathing, is there anything that – beyond the destruction of the subject – persists in suggesting the conditions of another possible life? Or is it no more than the enraged negation of a negation, a cry of pain at the ruination of human life that was the price of the erection of humanity as a universal value? What lies on the far side of this savage dismantling of the categories of domination if not the commonality of the needing, desiring, enjoying and suffering human life that the split subject and its complementary couple, torturer–tortured, subject–object, have subordinated under the category of the 'pathological'? This spectacle of life reduced to its bare minimum – 'poor, bare, forked animal' – finally betrays not so much its savagery as its *good*: the good that even out of the condition of the utmost damage, the demand persists that things be otherwise, not in some transcendent imaginary, but *within* the horizon of mortal being:

so things may change no answer end no answer I may choke no answer sink no answer sully the mud no more no answer the dark no answer trouble the peace no more no answer the silence no answer DIE screams I MAY DIE screams I SHALL DIE screams good (160)

Its final refusal of consolation is the stake the text places on another 'life in common' that does not shirk the pathological, which is to say, the fully *aesthetic* dimension of human being.

Why, it will and must be asked, should such an aesthetic dwell on the spectacle of human wretchedness, on the reduced forms of what is scarcely even 'bare life'? The new biopolitical state has increasingly targeted the *vulnerable* body as the object of both care and violence, and has steadily intruded ever further into the intimate life of its pleasures and its pains. The rearticulation of an aesthetic that embraces its foundation in the pathological subject necessarily passes then by way of the body's vulnerability rather than, as Godwin hoped in declaring the grounds of human equality to lie in our equivalent capacity to feel pleasure and pain, in its potentialities. But that is also to say that both the hope and the fragility of life in common lie in the recognition of that shared and ineluctable but always singular vulnerability. Pain and pleasure, as Kant acknowledged, offer intuitions of commonality but never a basis for identity or universality. The promise that Herbert Marcuse once expressed may yet be realized, that only when contingent sources of pain have been abolished, when the perpetual production of artificial scarcity and anxiety is not the rule, will human beings be able to confront and know the inevitable sorrow of mortality and finitude:

Such a Utopia would not be a state of perennial happiness. The 'natural' individuality of man is also the source of his natural sorrow. If human relations are nothing but human, if they are freed from all foreign standards, they will be permeated with the sadness of their singular content. They are transitory and irreplaceable, and their transitory character will be accentuated when concern for the human being is no longer mingled with fear for his material existence and overshadowed by the threat of poverty, hunger and ostracism.[43]

Until that point, which is already realizable materially however hard it may be to render imaginable, we continue to project our utopias from within the limited horizons of damage. But only a utopia conceived in the knowledge of human suffering escapes the lure of utopianism. Only a utopian imagination that does not shirk the historical charge of violence and domination can do justice to the hope that another world is possible.

Our current moment offers little prospect of any diminution in the rule of violence or of any relief from domination. As the regime of neo-liberal capital faces its global crisis, within which the recent and entirely predictable collapse of the 'Celtic Tiger' made scarcely a ripple, the promise of an abundant life in common is all the more brutally subjected to the instrumental logic of rationalization. The second commons – those institutions of welfare and education that were the parsimonious compensation wrested from the state in place of the expropriated commons – is slated for privatization and commodification. Austerity measures are the universal rule. The welfare state gives way to the maximum security state and the expectation of care and well-being shrinks to the acceptance of an imposed protection. The citizen gradually reverts to the status of mere subject. Far from offering freedom from fear, the state secures the monopoly on property at the cost of the endless anxiety of the majority: fear of want, fear of illness, fear of failure; these become once more the primitive disciplinary tools of domination. In an era of unbounded, even reckless surplus, artificial scarcity is the norm: the old adage that Ireland starved in the midst of plenty now offers insight into the general condition of humanity.

Never has Fanon's critical insight, that there has been a unilateral declaration of universality, resonated with such force. Margaret Thatcher famously ushered in the era of neo-liberalism with the lugubrious slogan, 'There is no alternative'; George W. Bush recently echoed the sentiment, proclaiming that the United States represented 'a single sustainable model for national success'.[44] Slouching towards bankruptcy in its effort to maintain the vice-grip of a unipolar world, the United States – like any failing empire – resorts to sheer military force in order to assert its will and secure its strategic dominance over the world's resources. In this, the agenda of Obama is and can be little different from that of his predecessor. But the issue is not the success or failure of a single imperial power in the competition for global hegemony. It is rather, the terrifying prospect of a world subjected to a single economic and political model, the triumph of the empty homogeneous time of progress that Walter Benjamin so feared. The drive to rationalize and homogenize space and the superordination of the ethical subject of reason are face and obverse of the same developmental project. Time and again, however, the realization of economic reason requires, as we have seen, means that ethical reason decries as anathema to its ends. The instrumentality of rationalization defies the autonomy that reason makes a supreme value. And yet the universal claims of ethical reason themselves demand the rationalization of the world of reflection just as relentlessly as instrumental reason requires the uniformity of the material realm. Subject and object alike are flattened in a like insistence on identity.[45] Just this impasse of liberal ethics in the face of the violence of the neo-liberal state *How It Is*, in all its ugliness and wretchedness, now seems to anticipate.

This book has been devoted to the history of what escapes rationalization. By that, clearly, I mean to signal not merely the incompletion of every drive to homogeneity or domination, but more importantly the process by which social forms and cultural practices that are slated for destruction at one moment live on to become the recalcitrant or resistant potentialities of another. This is not, as we have seen, usually a process of conscious revival or reactivation. On the contrary, it is more often than not the disciplinary formations of modernity that preserve, impersonally and materially, the memory of what they were designed to suppress. Oral spaces, and the pathological subjects for whose pleasures and pains, needs and desires they make abundant or restricted room, furnish instances of survival that are specific to Irish culture but not necessarily peculiar to it. Doubtless examples of comparable but differently articulated processes of living on could be identified in every colonial culture. That they are comparable, however, does not at all make them identical. On the contrary, where domination aims at the uniform and the unipolar, the single successful model, the name of the alternative is legion. It is the very condition of what lives on that it cannot be reduced to identity. For this very reason, indeed, the spaces and practices on which this book has dwelt proved no less incompatible with a modernizing nationalist discipline than with the aims of colonial modernization.

For this same reason, the social and cultural formations of oral space do not easily lend themselves to political programmes or to even the riskiest predictions. They defy prescriptive conclusions. The resources for hope that they nonetheless secrete lie precisely in their manifold and unsubsumable irregularity. Their promise is that they persist, on some dissonant frequency barely perceptible to historical sense. The claim of this book is that they do and that they remain effective unpredictably, discontinuously, and in forms that constantly refract the past and project futures that are out of kilter with every developmental goal. What they cleave to, for all the indigence that is too often their condition, is the abundance of the present, in defiance of the logic of artificial scarcity and the dismal laws of accumulation. Improvident of the future, they agree in their practice with Adorno's insight that 'the goal of the revolution is the elimination of anxiety'.[46] The paradox that in their wretchedness the Irish peasantry could experience a certain contentment, or that the Blanketmen discovered the inarticulable good of life in common under conditions of radical deprivation, holds open the space from which to pose the impossible demand: that we imagine a world in which that abundance of the present is realized in the freedom of all from any contingent want and from the coercive force of fear.

Notes

INTRODUCTION: A HISTORY OF THE IRISH ORIFICE

1 John Wilkinson, 'Time Enough', in *Contrivances* (Cambridge: Salt, 2003), p. 79.
2 Seamus Deane has written eloquently of what issues from the Irish mouth:

> Verbose, inaccurate, melodramatic, unreliable, in sad need of some form of sobriety, Irish speech and the Irish political condition required a rational articulation that was beyond the capacity of the Irish national character to produce. Irish eloquence became the index of Irish inarticulacy, speech removed from fact – blarney ... The sounds that issue from the mouths of the Irish – as speech, song, or wail – pose a challenge for those who wish to represent them in print. Similarly, what is taken in by those mouths – food and drink – poses a problem of another sort. Food is problematic, especially during the Famine, because there is so little of it; and drink is problematic because there is so much of it. A starving or a drunken people obviously lack articulacy.

See Seamus Deane, *Strange Country: Modernity and Nationhood in Irish Writing since 1790* (Oxford: Clarendon Press, 1997), p. 55.
3 Ibid., p. 55.
4 Kingsley cited in L.P. Curtis, *Anglo-Saxons and Celts: A Study of Anti-Irish Prejudice in Victorian England* (University of Bridgeport Press, 1968), p. 84.
5 The articulation of racial or ethnic distinctions in Northern Ireland around the practice of 'telling' perfectly encapsulates the peculiar convergence of oral interpretive strategies with the desire for visual immediacy. See David Lloyd, 'Ruination: Partition and the Expectation of Violence (On Allan deSouza's Irish Photography)', in *Irish Times: Temporalities of Modernity* (Dublin: Field Day, 2008), pp. 141–3.
6 Hiram Perez, 'You Can Have My Brown Body and Eat It Too!', *Social Text* 23.3–4 (Fall–Winter 2005), pp. 183–5.
7 Judith Butler, *Gender Trouble: Feminism and the Subversion of Identity* (New York: Routledge, 1990), p. 7 and passim.
8 On the recalcitrance of the oral tradition – 'various, uncentralized, polysemic, and often contradictory' – to the standardization required by nationalism and the state, see Angela Bourke, 'Irish Stories of Weather, Time, and Gender: Saint Brigid', in Marilyn Cohen and Nancy J. Curtin, eds., *Reclaiming*

Gender: Transgressive Identities in Modern Ireland (New York: St. Martin's Press, 1999), p. 14.

9 On the relation between written and oral culture in Irish, see Dáithí O hOgáin, 'Folklore and Literature: 1700–1850', in Mary Daly and David Dickson, eds., *The Origins of Popular Literacy in Ireland: Language Change and Educational Development 1700–1920* (Department of Modern History, Trinity College Dublin and Department of Modern Irish History, University College Dublin, 1990), pp. 1–13; on the transcription and transmission of Gaelic manuscripts as a means of preserving literacy in the language in the eighteenth century, see L.M. Cullen, 'Patrons, Teachers and Literacy in Irish: 1700–1850', in Daly and Dickson, eds., *The Origins of Popular Literacy*, pp. 15–44; on hedge schools and their role in preserving and disseminating literacy in both Irish and English, see J.R.R. Adams, 'Swine-Tax and Eat-Him-All-Magee: The Hedge Schools and Popular Education in Ireland', in J.S. Donnelly, Jr and Kerby A. Miller, eds., *Irish Popular Culture, 1650–1850* (Dublin: Irish Academic Press, 1998), pp. 97–117, and Antonia McManus, *The Irish Hedge School and Its Books, 1695–1831* (Dublin: Four Courts Press, 2002).

10 See E. Estyn Evans, *Irish Folk Ways* (London: Routledge & Kegan Paul, 1957), p. 24, on the state of 'decay' in which rundale existed by the nineteenth century. On the 'non-modern' and the dynamic interface between it and the modern state, see David Lloyd, *Ireland after History* (Cork University Press, 1999), pp. 2 and 45–6.

11 See David Lloyd and Paul Thomas, *Culture and the State* (London: Routledge, 1998), pp. 81–9, on the resistance of radical working-class circles to the division of spheres between politics, labour and education.

12 Henri Lefebvre, *The Production of Space*, trans. Donald Nicholson-Smith (Oxford: Blackwell, 1991), p. 63.

13 Richard Stivers, *Hair of the Dog: Irish Drinking and Its American Stereotype*, rev. edn (London: Continuum, 2000), chs. 4 and 5.

14 Mike Tomlinson, 'Imprisoned Ireland', in Vincenzo Ruggiero et al., eds., *Western European Penal Systems: A Critical Anatomy* (London: Sage, 1995), p. 196, cites Michael Farrell's estimate that 'Between 1800 and 1921 the British Government brought in 105 separate Coercion Acts dealing with Ireland'. According to Joe Lee, the British by the end of the nineteenth century normally stationed between 25,000 and 30,000 troops and 10,000 armed police in Ireland: see 'The Background: Anglo-Irish Relations, 1898–1921', in Cormac K.H. O'Malley and Anne Dolan, eds., *'No Surrender Here!' The Civil War Papers of Ernie O'Malley, 1922–1924* (Dublin: Lilliput, 2007), p. xi.

15 Lefebvre, *The Production of Space*, p. 382.

16 Ibid., p. 384.

17 On the institutions of governmentality in nineteenth-century Ireland, see Patrick Carroll, *Science, Culture and Modern State Formation* (Berkeley: University of California Press, 2006), chs. 5–6. On the influence of Indian education and curricula on the emergence of British literary education, see Gauri Viswanathan, *Masks of Conquest: Literary Study and British Rule in*

India (New York: Columbia University Press, 1989); for an overview of the history of colonial and metropolitan policing, see Randall Williams, 'A Permanent State of Exception: The Birth of Modern Policing in Colonial Capitalism', *Interventions: International Journal of Postcolonial Studies* 5.3 (2003), pp. 322–44.
18 Carroll, *Science, Culture and Modern State Formation*, p. 164.
19 See Karl Marx, *Capital: A Critique of Political Economy*, ed. Frederick Engels, trans. Samuel Moore and Edward Aveling, 3 vols. (London: Lawrence and Wishart, 1954), vol. 1, pp. 664–5; and Rosa Luxemburg, *The Accumulation of Capital*, trans. Agnes Schwarzwild (London and New York: Routledge, 2003), p. 350.
20 Lefebvre, *The Production of Space*, pp. 57, 358 and 63.
21 Ibid., p. 52.
22 On the emergence and long history of that measurable space in Ireland, one that William Petty described somewhat hopefully in 1662 as a 'white paper' or tabula rasa, see Carroll, *Science, Culture and Modern State Formation*, ch. 4.
23 David Harvey, *The Condition of Postmodernity: An Enquiry into the Origins of Cultural Change* (Oxford: Blackwell, 1990), pp. 284–307.
24 Homi Bhabha, 'DissemiNation: Time, Narrative and the Margins of the Modern Nation', in *The Location of Culture* (New York: Routledge, 1994), p. 142; Harvey, *The Condition of Postmodernity*, pp. 141–72.
25 Neferti X.M. Tadiar, *Things Fall Away: Philippine Historical Experience and the Makings of Globalization* (Durham, NC: Duke University Press, 2009), p. 10.
26 David Harvey, *The New Imperialism* (Oxford University Press, 2003), pp. 137–82.
27 Lefebvre, *The Production of Space*, p. 384.
28 Tadiar, *Things Fall Away*, p. 21.
29 Frantz Fanon, 'Racism and Culture', in *Toward the African Revolution: Political Essays*, trans. Haakon Chevalier (New York: Grove Press, 1988), p. 31: 'The unilaterally decreed normative value of certain cultures deserves our careful attention.'

1 IRISH HUNGER: THE POLITICAL ECONOMY OF THE POTATO

1 J.E. Cairnes, *Political Essays* (London: Macmillan, 1873), pp. 134–5.
2 Kevin Whelan, 'Pre- and Post-Famine Landscape Change', in Cathal Póirtéir, ed., *The Great Irish Famine* (Cork: Mercier, 1995), pp. 19–33, is a valuable summary essay on both the historical emergence of the cottier system and on its ecological and agricultural adaptations and innovations.
3 On the pervasiveness of the discourse of 'improvement' in nineteenth-century Ireland, see Helen O'Connell's *Ireland and the Fiction of Improvement* (Oxford University Press, 2006).
4 The previous two paragraphs have been adapted from my essay 'The Indigent Sublime: Spectres of Irish Hunger', in *Irish Times: Temporalities of Modernity*

(Dublin: Field Day, 2008), pp. 40–1. For an extended description of the *clachan*, its distribution and the role of the potato in subsistence, see Kevin Whelan, 'The Modern Landscape: From Plantation to Present', in F.H.A. Aalen *et al.*, eds., *Atlas of the Irish Rural Landscape* (Cork University Press, 1997), pp. 79–89.

5 See Thomas A. Boylan and Timothy P. Foley, *Political Economy and Colonial Ireland: The Propagation and Ideological Function of Economic Discourse in the Nineteenth Century* (London: Routledge, 1992). The most extensive demonstration of the policy-making role of British political economists with regard to Ireland is R.D. Collison Black, *Economic Thought and the Irish Question, 1817–1870* (Cambridge University Press, 1960).

6 Denis Meuret, 'A Political Genealogy of Political Economy', trans. Graham Burchell, in *Economy and Society* 17.2 (May 1988), pp. 231 and 227.

7 Black, *Economic Thought and the Irish Question*, p. 18. The causes of the Famine and the responsibility of British administration for its enormous mortality have been more thoroughly explored in the last fifteen years than at any previous time. Both adherence to political economic orthodoxy and the considerably less scientific belief in 'providential' workings played a considerable role in shaping relief policy. See especially Christine Kinealy, *This Great Calamity: The Irish Famine, 1845–52* (Boulder, CO: Roberts Rinehart, 1995), pp. 295 and 349–59; Peter Gray, *Famine, Land and Politics: British Government and Irish Society, 1830–1850* (Dublin: Irish Academic Press, 1999), pp. 331–3. The findings of such studies to some extent contradict the orthodoxy of so-called 'revisionist history' in Ireland, which has generally sought to diminish administrative responsibility and attributed harsher assessments of the ideological and religious discourses that contributed to policy, as well as of the policies themselves, to nationalist propagandizing. For a useful summary of the revisionist position (initially written before the upsurge of research in the 1990s), see James S. Donnelly, Jr, *The Great Irish Potato Famine* (Stroud: Sutton Publishing, 2001), ch. 9: 'Constructing the Memory of the Irish Famine'.

8 Cairnes, *Political Essays*, pp. 151–2.

9 Ibid., pp. 153–4.

10 Ibid., pp. 154–5. Cairnes is here citing Henry J.S. Maine's *Ancient Law* (1861).

11 On the genealogy of the discourse of development economics, see Arturo Escobar, *Encountering Development: The Making and Unmaking of the Third World* (Princeton University Press, 1995), ch. 1. My argument would, however, date the emergence of that discourse to a much earlier date than Escobar does.

12 David Scott, *Refashioning Futures: Criticism after Postcoloniality* (Princeton University Press, 1999), p. 41 (Scott's emphasis). On the emergence of the modern state and its governmental technologies in nineteenth-century Ireland, see Patrick Carroll, *Science, Culture and Modern State Formation* (Berkeley: University of California Press, 2006), chs. 5 and 6.

13 In a pioneering essay on economic debates about Irish land-holding in the nineteenth century, Clive Dewey establishes a distinction between the 'assimilationist' view of classical political economy, which would have imposed English norms on Ireland, and the 'historicist' view that displaced it. See Clive Dewey, 'Celtic Agrarian Legislation and the Celtic Revival: Historicist Implications of Gladstone's Irish and Scottish Land Acts, 1870–1886', *Past and Present* 64 (August 1974), pp. 30–70.
14 See further David Lloyd, 'Colonial Trauma/Postcolonial Recovery? Mourning the Irish Famine', in *Irish Times*, pp. 22–38.
15 On the remarkable degree to which Irish conditions appeared anomalous to British economists, see Boylan and Foley, *Political Economy and Colonial Ireland*, pp. 134–9.
16 For an extended critique of the tendency to view the Famine from the perspective of hindsight, see Stuart McLean, *The Event and Its Terrors: Ireland, Famine, Modernity* (Stanford University Press, 2004), pp. 1–9.
17 See Cormac Ó Gráda, *Black '47 and Beyond: The Great Irish Famine in History, Economy and Memory* (Princeton University Press, 1999), pp. 25–6. Ó Gráda elsewhere discusses at length Joel Mokyr's celebrated critique in *Why Ireland Starved* of Malthusian accounts of the Famine and emphasizes the extent to which more recent scholarship confirms that the Famine was more unpredictable than inevitable. See Cormac Ó Gráda, *Ireland: A New Economic History, 1780–1939* (Oxford: Clarendon Press, 1994), pp. 188–9.
18 Thomas Robert Malthus, 'Newenham and Others on the State of Ireland', *Edinburgh Review* 24 (July 1808), p. 345 (Malthus's emphases). The essay is a review of Thomas Newenham's *Inquiry into the Population of Ireland* (1808). Though Malthus's prognosis regarding demographic tendencies has been borne out by more recent demographers, Newenham's projection for the population of Ireland in 1837 seems remarkably close to actual figures, given the figure of 8.1 million given in the British census of 1841.
19 Malthus, 'Newenham and Others on the State of Ireland', p. 343 (Malthus's emphasis). As Catherine Gallagher and Stephen Greenblatt comment, 'the potato is the root of misery *because* it is the root of plenty'. See Catherine Gallagher and Stephen Greenblatt, 'The Potato in the Materialist Imagination', in *Practicing the New Historicism* (University of Chicago Press, 2000), p. 128.
20 On Malthus's 'quite benign prognosis' on Irish population adjustment and on his lack of any prediction of a major famine in this review, see Cormac Ó Gráda, 'Malthus and the Pre-Famine Economy', in Antoin E. Murphy, ed., *Economists and the Irish Economy from the Eighteenth Century to the Present Day* (Blackrock: Irish Academic Press, 1984), pp. 79–80.
21 Adam Smith, *An Inquiry into the Nature and Causes of the Wealth of Nations*, general eds., R.H. Campbell and A.S. Skinner, textual editor W.B. Todd, 2 vols. (Oxford: Clarendon Press, 1976), vol. i, p. 177.
22 Ibid., pp. 176–7. Smith's allusion to rice is interesting here. As we shall see, the potato becomes blamed for Ireland's prodigious rate of reproduction, for

the excess of labour that therefore undercuts English wage rates, and for sustaining a servile culture anathematic to Anglo-Saxon virtues. Virtually the same stereotypes will circulate around rice as the staple of 'Asiatic' labour in late-nineteenth-century North America. See, for example, Ronald T. Takaki, *Iron Cages: Race and Culture in 19th-Century America* (Seattle: University of Washington Press, 1985), ch. 10, 'The "Heathen Chinee" and American Technology'.

23 Arthur Young, *A Tour in Ireland; with General Observations on the Present State of that Kingdom* [1780], ed. Arthur Wollaston Hutton, 2 vols. (London: George Bell and Sons, 1892), vol. II, pp. 41–2. Young's comment on the 'regularity' of the potato underscores how unanticipated the disaster of the Famine actually was. See Ó Gráda, *Black '47 and Beyond*, pp. 20–1, for a discussion of the rarity of crop failures prior to the Famine. On Young, see also Gallagher and Greenblatt, 'The Potato in the Materialist Imagination', pp. 119–22.

24 Charles Trevelyan, 'The Irish Crisis', *Edinburgh Review* 175 (January 1848), p. 230. Trevelyan, in his zeal, goes so far as to deny what most contemporaries accepted, the nutritional benefits of the potato for all its occasional failures, and attributes the Irish incapacity to 'endure continuous labour' to this diet: 'Irish Crisis', pp. 318–19n. The shift in the economic analysis of the grounds and the dangerous potentialities of Irish conditions could be said to follow the track of what Keith Tribe suggests is the gradual emancipation of political economy from its embeddedness, through Smith, Malthus and even Ricardo, in what is still a fundamentally *agrarian* model for capital. See Keith Tribe, *Land, Labour and Economic Discourse* (London: Routledge & Kegan Paul, 1978), pp. 102–3 and 132–3.

25 Malthus, 'Newenham on Ireland', pp. 343–4.
26 Ibid., pp. 352–3.
27 See especially Ó Gráda, Kinealy and Gray, cited above.
28 J.R. McCulloch, *The Principles of Political Economy* (4th edn, Edinburgh: Adam and Charles Black, 1849), p. 397.
29 Ibid., p. 406.
30 Ibid., p. 411.
31 Tribe points out how fundamentally bound political economy is to a specific anthropology, one that desires to pose itself as universal:

> Only where Man is conceived as the constitutive element of the economy – where it is the economic action of this Man on external objects for the purpose of his preservation – can the terms 'land' and 'labour' be treated as such essential constituents of economic thought. The treatment of economics as universal and eternal thus relies on a humanism which obliterates and naturalises the specific conditions of existence of social forms.

Tribe, *Land, Labour and Economic Discourse*, p. 160.

32 Malthus, 'Newenham on Ireland', p. 353.
33 Nassau Senior, 'Ireland', *Edinburgh Review* 79.159 (January 1844), p. 192.
34 Ibid., 196–8.
35 Ibid., p. 200.

36 Ibid., p. 209.
37 McCulloch, *Principles of Political Economy*, pp. 422 and 421. McCulloch's phrase, *officina pauperum* ('workshop of paupers'), echoes Malthus's *officina militum* ('workshop of soldiers') ('Newenham on Ireland', p. 342), while marking an interesting index of the decline in the image of the Irish in the intervening decades.
38 James Kay, *The Moral and Physical Conditions of the Working Classes ... in Manchester* (1832), cited in Mary Poovey, *Making A Social Body: British Cultural Formation, 1830–1864* (University of Chicago Press, 1995), pp. 63–4.
39 Thomas Carlyle, 'Chartism', in *Critical and Miscellaneous Essays*, 5 vols., in *The Works of Thomas Carlyle*, 30 vols. (New York: Charles Scribner, 1904), vol. 29, pp. 138–9. On Carlyle's anti-Irish racism and its context in Victorian Britain, see Amy E. Martin, 'Blood Transfusions: Constructions of Irish Racial Difference, the English Working Class, and Revolutionary Possibility in the Work of Carlyle and Engels', *Victorian Literature and Culture* 32 (2004), pp. 83–102.
40 Poovey, *Making a Social Body*, p. 71.
41 For a discussion of Carlyle's infamous essay, 'On the Nigger Question', and of John Stuart Mill's response to it, see Thomas C. Holt, *The Problem of Freedom: Race, Labour, and Politics in Jamaica and Britain, 1832–1938* (Baltimore, MD: Johns Hopkins University Press, 1992), and David Lloyd, 'Black Irish, Irish Whiteness and Atlantic State Formation: Some Reflections', in Peter D. O'Neill and David Lloyd, eds., *The Black and Green Atlantic: Crosscurrents of the African and Irish Diasporas* (London: Palgrave, 2009), pp. 9–12.
42 Homi Bhabha, 'Of Mimicry and Man: The Ambivalence of Colonial Discourse', in *The Location of Culture* (New York: Routledge, 1994), pp. 89–90. The importance of metonymy, the trope of contiguity, is of course crucial to the ambiguous place of the Irish in nineteenth-century social commentary.
43 McCulloch, *Principles of Political Economy*, p. 421.
44 I have elaborated the theoretical concept of the interface between the modern and the non-modern in *Ireland after History* (Cork University Press, 1999), pp. 45–6; on the distinction between non-modern formations and capitalism's 'pre-history', see Dipesh Chakrabarty, 'Two Histories of Capital', in *Provincializing Europe: Postcolonial Thought and Historical Difference* (Princeton University Press, 2000), pp. 63–71.
45 Carlyle, 'Chartism', p. 137.
46 Richard Whately, *Introductory Lectures on Political Economy*, 3rd edn (London: John W. Parker, 1847), p. 93.
47 Ibid.
48 Alexander Somerville, *Letters from Ireland during the Famine of 1847*, ed. K.D.M. Snead, (Blackrock: Irish Academic Press, 1994), pp. 174–6.
49 Whately, *Introductory Lectures*, p. 112, argues that corn is at once the vehicle and the metaphor for the transformation of the savage and his wastes into the fertile ground of civilization:

As the soil itself and the climate of New-Holland [Australia] are excellently adapted to the growth of corn, and yet (as corn is not indigenous there) could never have borne any, to the end of the world, if it had not been brought thither from another country, and sown; so, the savage himself, though he may be, as it were, a soil capable of receiving the seeds of civilization, can never, in the first instance, produce it, as of spontaneous growth; and unless those seeds be introduced from some other quarter, must remain forever in the sterility of barbarism.

50 E.P. Thompson, 'The Moral Economy of the English Crowd in the Eighteenth Century', *Past and Present* 50 (February 1971), pp. 76–136.
51 Trevelyan, 'The Irish Crisis', p. 233.
52 Ibid., p. 234.
53 Ibid., p. 233.
54 Ibid., pp. 232–3.
55 Ibid., pp. 231–2.
56 Whelan, 'Pre- and Post-Famine Landscape Change', pp. 19–33. Whelan, 'The Modern Landscape', p. 82, cites the Irish proverb 'If we had potatoes and turf, we could take life easy'. Ó Gráda, *Black '47 and Beyond*, pp. 217–21, cites several laments in Irish for the passing of the potato, including the comment that 'The potato was good and generous, leaving plenty to share among God's poor; and every stranger who passed the way had a week's lodging and shelter from the elements...', suggesting the intimate relation between the abundance of the potato and the moral economy that prevailed among the pre-Famine Irish poor.
57 Trevelyan, 'The Irish Crisis', p. 240.
58 Cited in, respectively, Laurence M. Geary, '"The Late Disastrous Epidemic": Medical Relief and the Great Famine', and James S. Donnelly, Jr, '"Irish Property Must Pay for Irish Poverty": British Public Opinion and the Great Irish Famine', both in Chris Morash and Richard Hayes, eds., *'Fearful Realities': New Perspectives on the Famine* (Blackrock: Irish Academic Press, 1996), pp. 56 and 61.
59 As Robert Scally has put it, in *The End of Hidden Ireland: Rebellion, Famine and Emigration* (Oxford University Press, 1995), p. 35: 'The absence of the material goods to articulate social distinctions and pretensions also tended to confirm impressions that had taken root long before both in Ireland and Britain: that the rural poor of Ireland were a more or less uniform mass whose individuality was hardly discernible, except perhaps by gender or age.'
60 Karl Marx, *The Eighteenth Brumaire of Louis Bonaparte* (Moscow: Progress Publishers, 1954), p. 106.
61 Far from marking 'the virtual end of culture', as Stephen Greenblatt and Catherine Gallagher argue, the potato marks a dangerously different culture to that sustained by English wheat. See their essay, 'The Potato in the Materialist Imagination', p. 112.
62 Joseph Robins, *The Miasma: Epidemic and Panic in Nineteenth Century Ireland* (Dublin: Institute of Public Administration, 1995), pp. 64–8.
63 Friedrich Engels, *The Condition of the Working Class in England*, ed. with foreword by Victor Kiernan (Harmondsworth: Penguin, 1987), p. 124.

On Engels' views of the Irish and his relation to Carlyle, see Martin, 'Blood Transfusions', pp. 94–9. It should be noted that such renderings of the Irish propensity to living in filth is strongly countered by no less an authority on the poor than Henry Mayhew, whose section on 'The Street Irish' in his voluminous compendium of research on the conditions of the poor in London emphasizes the unexpected cleanliness of the Irish homes he visits and the attempts made at furnishing them. See Henry Mayhew, *London Labour and the London Poor: A Cyclopaedia of the Conditions and Earnings of Those That Will Work, Those That Cannot Work, and Those That Will Not Work*, 4 vols. (1851) (New York: August M. Kelley, 1967), vol. I, p. 110.

64 Carlyle, 'Chartism', p. 137.
65 On the science of 'contagion' and its relation to social regulation, see Andrew Aisenberg, *Contagion: Disease, Government, and the 'Social Question' in Nineteenth-Century France* (Stanford University Press, 1999), which is, at the least, suggestive for the Irish and British contexts.
66 McCulloch, *Principles of Political Economy*, p. 421.
67 See Alain Corbin, *The Foul and the Fragrant: Odor and the French Social Imagination* (Cambridge, MA: Harvard University Press, 1986) and Dominique Laporte, *History of Shit*, trans. Nadia Benabid and Rodolphe El-Khoury (Cambridge, MA: MIT Press, 2000).
68 Handbill, to the Officers of Health in the City of Cork, produced by Samuel R. Wily, reproduced in Robins, *The Miasma*, p. 83.
69 Whelan, 'The Modern Landscape', p. 81. On the importance of proximity to the dunghill for peasant society in general, see Corbin, *Foul and Fragrant*, pp. 156 and 213.
70 Somerville, *Letters from Ireland*, p. 136.
71 For recorded oral comments on this belief, see Cathal Póirtéir, *Famine Echoes* (Dublin: Gill and Macmillan, 1995), pp. 37–40.
72 Quoted in Black, *Economic Thought and the Irish Question*, p. 22.
73 Quoted in Robins, *The Miasma*, p. 113.
74 For a fuller account of this model, see David Lloyd and Paul Thomas, *Culture and the State* (London: Routledge, 1998), pp. 66–70.
75 Carlyle, 'Chartism', pp. 139, 137.
76 That said, it is important to note that, although recalcitrant to the political forms being instituted in Britain, those of a disciplined and contained 'representative democracy', the Irish contribution to 'modern' mass politics was signal, from the mass mobilizations for Emancipation and Repeal in Ireland to the emergence of the Irish as a political force in the United States as well as in British Chartism. The forms of Irish political movement seem to draw on precisely the features that made them seem threateningly effective to successive British administrations – their decentralized and contagious mobility in particular. These forms of mass mobilization are the antagonistic counterpart to modern representative democracy and in striking dialectic relation to them.

77 On the transformation of 'living labour' into 'labour-power', see Karl Marx, *Capital: A Critique of Political Economy*, ed. Frederick Engels, trans. Samuel Moore and Edward Aveling, 3 vols. (London: Lawrence and Wishart, 1954), vol. I, pp. 178–80.
78 James Fintan Lalor, 'A New Nation: Proposal for an Agricultural Association between Landowners and Occupiers' (1847), in L. Fogarty, ed., *James Fintan Lalor: Patriot and Political Essayist (1807–1849)* (Dublin: Talbot Press, 1918), pp. 8–10.
79 Sir William Robert Wills Wilde, *Irish Popular Superstitions* (1852) (Shannon: Irish University Press, 1973), p. 24.
80 Marx, 'The Metamorphosis of Commodities', *Capital*, vol. I, pp. 106–15.
81 That labour-power is '*a source not only of value, but of more value than it has itself*' is of course the burden of *Capital*: see Marx, *Capital*, vol. I, p. 188 and passim.
82 Whelan, in 'Pre- and Post-Famine Landscape Change', p. 22, points out that the 'lazy bed' was in fact an ingenious solution to the problems of maximizing the crop of the potato under the environmental conditions of western Ireland.

2 CLOSING THE MOUTH: DISCIPLINING ORAL SPACE

1 Sinéad O'Connor, 'Famine', on *Universal Mother* (New York: Ensign Records, 1994).
2 John Waters, 'Sinéad the Keener', *Irish Times*, 28 January 1995.
3 On the relation between verisimilitude and *doxa*, or common sense and opinion, see Tzvetan Todorov, 'An Introduction to Verisimilitude', in *The Poetics of Prose*, trans. Richard Howard, foreword Jonathan Culler (Ithaca, NY: Cornell University Press, 1977), pp. 80–8. On the spectres of the Famine that haunt contemporary and later writers, see David Lloyd, 'The Indigent Sublime: Spectres of Irish Hunger', in *Irish Times: Temporalities of Modernity* (Dublin: Field Day, 2008), pp. 39–72.
4 George Petrie, *The Ancient Music of Ireland* (1855), cited in Seamus Deane, *A Short History of Irish Literature* (South Bend, IL: University of Notre Dame Press, 1994), p. 79.
5 Hugh Dorian, *The Outer Edge of Ulster: A Memoir of Social Life in Nineteenth-Century Donegal*, ed. Breandán Mac Suibhne and David Dickson (Dublin: Lilliput Press, 2001), p. 215.
6 Liam O'Flaherty, *Famine* (1937) (Dublin: Wolfhound, 1984), pp. 302, 304.
7 Thomas Gallagher, *Paddy's Lament: Ireland 1846–1847 – Prelude to Hatred* (New York: Harcourt Brace Jovanovich, 1982), pp. 5–6.
8 William Carleton, *The Black Prophet: A Tale of Irish Famine* (London: Simms and McIntyre, 1847), pp. 178–9.
9 For a different reading of Carleton's novel, which sees the writer as somewhat opportunistic in exploiting the Famine, see Melissa Fegan, *Literature and the Irish Famine, 1845–1919* (Oxford: Clarendon Press, 2002), pp. 151–7. For

interesting local reports of food riots and appropriations during the Famine, see the documents collected in Liam Swords, *In Their Own Words: The Famine in North Connacht, 1845–1849* (Blackrock: The Columba Press, 1999), pp. 112 and 119. Such unfiltered reports are an index of the dailiness of such events, counterpointing the usual reports of Irish passivity.

10 Mr and Mrs S.C. Hall, *Ireland: Its Scenery, Character, and History*, 2 vols. (1841) (Boston: Nicholls and Co., 1911), vol. I, p. 294n. Strictly speaking, of course, the kind of informal expressions of grief or anxiety implied here are not identical with the highly artful practice of keening as it is now understood. See Angela Bourke, 'Performing, not Writing', *Graph* 11 (Winter 1991–1992), pp. 28–31, for an account of the formal complexities and traditions of keening.

11 Hall, *Ireland*, vol. II, p. 86.

12 See Angela Bourke, 'Performing, not Writing', p. 30: 'Lamenting the dead was a central and essential part of funeral rituals in Ireland until modern times. The woman who led the *caoineadh* was both poet and performer: she took charge of the community's grief and expressed it in all its complexity thorough her appearance, her behaviour, her voice and her poetry.'

13 Hall, *Ireland*, vol. II, p. 90.

14 T. Crofton Croker, *Researches in the South of Ireland, Illustrative of the Scenery, Architectural Remains, and the Manners and Superstitions of the Peasantry* (London: John Murray, 1824), pp. 172–3.

15 Croker, *Researches*, pp. 181–2. That the keen was often used as a means to articulate political anger is borne out by Mrs S.C. Hall's more extensive account, in *Ireland*, II, pp. 90–2. The keen's articulation of political or social criticism was, however, by no means confined to comment on British colonialism. As Angela Bourke remarks: 'The texts that survive howl in protest and anger at death and at injustice in the world of the living, and the oral tradition offers many examples of women engaging in verbal battles with priests.' See Bourke, 'Performing, not Writing', p. 31. Ó Crualaoich argues that 'the merry wake was in fact a central social mechanism for the articulation of resistance': see Gearóid Ó Crualaoich, 'The "Merry Wake"', in J.S. Donnelly, Jr and Kerby A. Miller, eds., *Irish Popular Culture, 1650–1850* (Dublin: Irish Academic Press, 1998), p. 173.

16 For a discussion of Arnold's *On the Study of Celtic Literature*, see my *Nationalism and Minor Literature: James Clarence Mangan and the Emergence of Irish Cultural Nationalism* (Berkeley: University of California Press, 1987), pp. 6–13. On ethnic stereotypes of the Irish, which have force down to the present, and on the ethnographic writings that gave them scientific legitimacy in the nineteenth century, see L.P. Curtis, *Anglo-Saxons and Celts: A Study of Anti-Irish Prejudice in Victorian England* (Conference on British Studies at the University of Bridgeport, 1968) and *Apes and Angels: The Irishman in Victorian Caricature* (Washington, DC: Smithsonian Institution Press, 1971). For a more recent, and rather more sympathetic account of Arnold on the Celts, see Robert J.C. Young, *The Idea of English Ethnicity* (Oxford: Blackwell, 2008), ch. 5.

17 For important reflections on allegories of loss as a function of ethnographic writings, see James Clifford, 'On Ethnographic Allegory', in James Clifford and George E. Marcus, eds., *Writing Culture: The Poetics and Politics of Ethnography* (Berkeley and Los Angeles: University of California Press, 1986), pp. 98–121.
18 Norbert Elias, *Power and Civility*, vol. II of *The Civilizing Process*, 2 vols. (New York: Pantheon, 1982), p. 238.
19 Hall, *Ireland*, vol. II, p. 87. Ó Crualaoich's accounts of the customs of the wake, 'The "Merry Wake"', pp. 173–200, markedly confirm Mrs Hall's sense of the inappropriate 'merriment' that took place at such events.
20 Croker, *Researches*, p. 2.
21 John Stuart Mill's *Considerations on Representative Government* (1861) in *Essays on Politics and Society*, vol. II, ed. J.M. Robson, intro. Alexander Brady (University of Toronto Press, 1977), pp. 371–577, is one of the classic statements of the distinction between English readiness for government and the necessity for a government of 'leading strings' in the case of subject peoples like those of India.
22 Croker, *Researches*, pp. 12–13. For a full discussion of notions of Irish national character in the nineteenth century, see Seamus Deane, *Strange Country: Modernity and Nationhood in Irish Writing since 1790* (Oxford: Clarendon Press, 1997), ch. 2.
23 On the ways in which this notion of the project of a liberal cultural Unionism, that sought to compete with an emerging cultural nationalism, was articulated around a sense of the malleability of Irish affections, see Lloyd, *Nationalism and Minor Literature*, pp. 83–5.
24 Deane, *Strange Country*, p. 55.
25 Elsewhere I have discussed this hierarchy of the senses, from Kant's and Schiller's aesthetic theory to Freudian analysis, in relation to the imbrication of race and culture. See 'Race under Representation', *Oxford Literary Review* 13.1–2 (1991), pp. 62–94 and 'The Narrative of Representation: Culture, the State and the Canon', in Robert Bledsoe, ed., *Rethinking Germanistik: Canon and Culture* (New York: Peter Lang, 1991), pp. 125–38.
26 Seán de Fréine, 'The Cultural Consequences of the Great Famine', in Breandán Ó Conaire, ed., *The Famine Lectures/Léachtaí an Ghorta* (Boyle: Comhdhail an Chraoibhín, 1995–1997), pp. 144–5. See also Neil Buttimer, 'A Stone on the Cairn: The Great Famine in Later Gaelic Manuscripts', in Chris Morash and Richard Hayes, eds., *'Fearful Realities': New Perspectives on the Famine* (Dublin: Irish Academic Press, 1996), pp. 101–2, on the ways in which 'the Famine brought the language's very survival as a widespread vernacular seriously into question'.
27 See Peter Gray, 'Ideology and the Famine', in Cathal Póirtéir, ed., *The Great Irish Famine* (Cork: Mercier, 1995), pp. 86–103, for a discussion of religious attitudes to the Famine. Christine Kinealy, *This Great Calamity: The Irish Famine, 1845–52* (Boulder, CO: Roberts Rinehart, 1995), p. 357, makes explicit the connection between the popular belief in the Famine

as 'divine punishment' and the 'punitive relief measures' of the colonial administration.
28 On clerical antagonism to the wake and its rituals, see Ó Crualaoich, 'The "Merry Wake"', pp. 173–6 and 193–4.
29 On this conjunction of unworked-through grief and melancholia in the wake of the Famine, see my essays 'Colonial Trauma/Postcolonial Recovery? Mourning the Irish Famine' and 'The Indigent Sublime: Spectres of Irish Hunger', in *Irish Times*, pp. 22–38 and 39–72.
30 Walter J. Ong, *Orality and Literacy: The Technologizing of the Word* (London: Routledge, 1982), p. 178.
31 Ibid., pp. 178–9.
32 Jack Goody, *The Power of the Written Tradition* (Washington, DC: Smithsonian Institute Press, 2000), p. 79.
33 Ibid., p. 78.
34 Brian V. Street, *Literacy in Theory and Practice* (Cambridge University Press, 1984), p. 2.
35 Ibid., pp. 5 and 46. See also Donald Lowe, *History of Bourgeois Perception* (University of Chicago Press, 1982), pp. 2–8.
36 Ong, *Orality and Literacy*, p. 135.
37 Street, *Literacy in Theory and Practice*, pp. 20–1.
38 On this notion of the history of private property and its relation to the moral personality that largely stems from Locke, see Alan Ryan, *Property* (Minneapolis: University of Minnesota Press, 1987), pp. 70–1.
39 Sigmund Freud, 'The "Uncanny"' (1919), in *An Infantile Neurosis and Other Works*, vol. 17 of *The Standard Edition of the Complete Psychological Works*, 24 vols. trans. James Strachey (London: The Hogarth Press, 1955), pp. 220–1.
40 E. Estyn Evans, *Irish Heritage: The Landscape, the People and Their Work* (Dundalk: Dundalgan Press, 1945), p. 48.
41 E. Estyn Evans, *Irish Folk Ways* (London: Routledge & Kegan Paul, 1957), p. 30.
42 Dorian, *The Outer Edge of Ulster*, pp. 121–2.
43 Ibid., p. 130.
44 Ibid., p. 136 and 138.
45 Ibid., p. 177.
46 Ibid., p. 178.
47 Frantz Fanon, *The Wretched of the Earth*, trans. Constance Farrington (New York: Grove Press, 1968), pp. 37–8.
48 Ibid., p. 227: 'this zone of occult instability where the people dwell.'
49 Dorian, *The Outer Edge of Ulster*, p. 157.
50 Robert Scally, *The End of Hidden Ireland: Rebellion, Famine and Emigration* (Oxford University Press, 1995), p. 16. Redcliffe N. Salaman comments usefully on the 'vertical social cleavage in Irish society, as opposed to the horizontal social layering of English society' that is instantiated in the dichotomy of domestic architecture between landowners and tenants of all classes. See

The History and Social Influence of the Potato (Cambridge University Press, 1985), pp. 336–7.
51 Estyn Evans, *Irish Folk Ways*, p. 30.
52 Scally, *End of Hidden Ireland*, p. 35.
53 Dorian, *The Outer Edge of Ulster*, p. 69. José Carlos Mariátegui describes a similar survival and expropriation of indigenous communal labour by the hacienda system in colonial Peru in *Seven Interpretive Essays on Peruvian Reality*, trans. Marjory Urquidi (Austin: University of Texas Press, 1971), pp. 55–8. Salaman interestingly comments on the commonalities between Peruvian and Irish indigenous methods of cultivation and shared labour, based in both cases on the potato as staple, in *History and Social Influence of the Potato*, p. 234.
54 On rumour and the lateral or metonymic forms of communication characteristic of peasant societies and their organizational forms and mobilizations, see Ranajit Guha, *Elementary Aspects of Peasant Insurgency in Colonial India* (Durham, NC: Duke University Press, 1999), pp. 233–68.
55 Asenath Nicholson, *Annals of the Famine in Ireland*, ed. Maureen Murphy (Dublin: Lilliput Press, 1998), p. 165.
56 Ibid., p. 70. Nicholson's emphasis. On Nicholson's 'new domestic economy', see Gordon Bigelow, *Fiction, Famine, and the Rise of Economics in Victorian Britain and Ireland* (Cambridge University Press, 2003), pp. 134–41. Neither Bigelow nor Nicholson's other recent commentator, Margaret Kelleher in her *The Feminization of Famine: Expressions of the Inexpressible* (Durham, NC: Duke University Press, 1997), makes mention of this episode in her narrative, though it clearly presents a moment where political and domestic economy intersect in their prescriptions for famine and poverty. For a scathing account of Lord Hill's 'improvements', which suggests that Hill in fact merely enclosed land that the tenants had themselves already improved, consigning them to hovels on more marginal land, see Denis Holland, *The Landlord in Donegal* (Belfast: The Ulsterman, 1856–1863), pp. 60–70. My thanks to Breandán Mac Suibhne for this reference.
57 Matthew Stout, 'The Geography and Implications of Post-famine Population Decline in Baltyboys, Co. Wicklow', in Morash and Hayes, *'Fearful Realities'*, pp. 15–34.
58 Scally, *End of Hidden Ireland*, p. 63.
59 Estyn Evans, *Irish Folk Ways*, p. 32.
60 Mac Suibhne and Dickson, 'Introduction to Dorian', *The Outer Edge of Ulster*, p. 20.
61 Scally, *End of Hidden Ireland*, gives a wonderfully detailed account of one small townland's efforts to resist its destruction. On efforts at 'improvement' in Donegal and local resistance to them in Dorian's Doaghbeg, see Mac Suibhne and Dickson, 'Introduction to Dorian', *The Outer Edge of Ulster*, pp. 13–14. They also discuss the post-Famine destruction of rundale on Lord Leitrim's estate in Donegal and the resurgence of Ribbonism in conjunction with the new Fenianism that confronted it, pp. 23–5. On the

popular forms of struggle associated with the Land League in particular, and their derivation from both ideas of the commons and from the customs of the oral community, see Heather Laird, *Subversive Law in Ireland, 1879–1920: From 'Unwritten Law' to the Dail Courts* (Dublin: Four Courts Press, 2005).

62 On the recent vintage of the apparently traditional Irish landscape, and its emergence across the Famine in the course of the Irish 'agricultural revolution', see Estyn Evans, *Irish Folk Ways*, pp. xiv and 20. On the predominance of grazing in post-Famine Irish agricultural practice, see Kevin Whelan, 'The Modern Landscape: From Plantation to Present', in F.H.A. Aalen *et al.*, eds., *Atlas of the Irish Rural Landscape* (Cork University Press, 1997), pp. 90–2.

63 Kevin Whelan, 'Pre- and Post-Famine Landscape Change', in Póirtéir, *The Great Irish Famine*, p. 32.

64 Sir William Robert Wills Wilde, *Irish Popular Superstitions* (1852) (Shannon: Irish University Press, 1973), pp. 9–11. This essay was originally published in the *Dublin University Magazine* in May 1849. The lines cited are from Shakespeare's *Midsummer Night's Dream*, iv.i. Ironically, the reference there is not to keening or any other popular practice, but to the cry of the hounds in the hunt. Anglo-Irish hunting would soon become a widely protested-against activity in the Irish countryside in acts of creative disruption that drew heavily on popular traditions whose demise Wilde here laments. See Laird, *Subversive Law in Ireland*, pp. 77–102.

65 On Wilde's elegiac tone and its recapitulation of 'the very inaugurating gesture of modern historiography', the silencing of the dead, see Stuart McLean, *The Event and Its Terrors: Ireland, Famine, Modernity* (Stanford University Press, 2004), p. 11.

66 On the elegiac quality of what he calls 'allegories of salvage' in ethnographic texts, see Clifford, 'On Ethnographic Allegory', pp. 112–16.

67 Cited in L.A. Clarkson and E. Margaret Crawford, *Feast and Famine: Food and Nutrition in Ireland, 1500–1920* (Oxford University Press, 2001), p. 69.

68 G.D.H. Cole, *Chartist Portraits* (1941), intro. Asa Briggs (New York: Macmillan, 1965), p. 7.

69 Ibid.

70 E.J. Hobsbawm, *Industry and Empire: An Economic History of Britain since 1750* (London: Weidenfeld & Nicholson, 1968), pp. 266–7.

71 Mill, *Morning Chronicle*, 10 October 1846, in *John Stuart Mill on Ireland*, ed. Richard Ned Lebow (Philadelphia: Institute for the Study of Human Issues, 1979), p. 6.

72 On these aspects of Feargus O'Connor's biography, see Cole, *Chartist Portraits*, pp. 307–9; David Jones, *Chartism and the Chartists* (New York: St. Martin's Press, 1975), p. 129; John Saville, 'Introduction to R.G. Gammage', *History of the Chartist Movement, 1837–1854* (2nd edn, 1894) (New York: Augustus M. Kelley, 1969), p. 54; and Dorothy Thompson, *The Chartists: Popular Politics in the Industrial Revolution* (London: Temple Smith; New York: Pantheon, 1984), p. 301.

73 See Feargus O'Connor, *A Practical Work on the Management of Small Farms* (London: John Cleave, 1843). The deeply hostile Cole makes this connection briefly, *Chartist Portraits*, p. 325. Saville, in Gammage, *History of the Chartist Movement*, p. 59, cites a largely overlooked report in the *Newcastle Daily Chronicle* of 1875 that affirmed that a four-acre farm constituted 'a viable economic unit'.
74 O'Connor, *Management of Small Farms*, p. 67.
75 Ibid., p. 47. On O'Connor's own experiments with spade-husbandry, see his remarks to the 1848 Select Committee of Parliament inquiring into the Land Plan (and which eventually pronounced the company illegal) in F.C. Mather, ed., *Chartism and Society: An Anthology of Documents* (London: Bell and Hyman, 1980), p. 112.
76 O'Connor, *Management of Small Farms*, p. 61.
77 He suggests a ratio of one acre of potatoes to one of wheat, the other two acres being given over to grazing and market gardening; ibid., p. 151.
78 Ibid., p. 100.
79 See, for example, William Conner, *A Letter to the Right Honourable the Earl of Devon, Chairman of the Land Commission on the Rackrent System of Ireland: Showing Its Cause, Its Evils and Its Remedy* (Dublin: Samuel L. Machen, 1843); William Conner, *A Letter to the Tenantry of Ireland, Containing an Exposition of the Rackrent System; and Pointing Out a Valuation and Perpetuity as Its Only Effectual Remedy* (Dublin: James B. Gilpin, 1850); and Isaac Butt, *Land Tenure in Ireland: A Plea for the Celtic Race*, 3rd edn (Dublin: John Falconer, 1866). For a discussion of these and other such proposals in Ireland – based often on Ulster's 'customary tenure' right – in opposition to the view 'that Ireland could only prosper through the introduction of medium- and large-scale farming carried on by capitalist tenants, and the conversion of the cottier population into hired labourers', see R.D. Collison Black, *Economic Thought and the Irish Question, 1817–1870* (Cambridge University Press, 1960), pp. 24–30.
80 Joseph Epstein, *The Lion of Freedom: Feargus O'Connor and the Chartist Movement, 1832–1842* (London: Croom Helm, 1982), p. 253.
81 On the Land Plan as alternative to capital, see Dorothy Thompson, *The Chartists*, p. 302.
82 See Saville, in Gammage, *History of the Chartist Movement*, p. 49.
83 O'Connor, *Management of Small Farms*, pp. 142–3 and 149.
84 On the Irish models for the proposed clay houses, see ibid., pp. 176–9.
85 Ibid., p. 97.
86 Ibid., pp. 155 and 114. For more on the principle of co-operative labour and individual possession, see O'Connor's remarks to the Select Committee, in Mather, *Chartism and Society*, p. 113.
87 Eileen Yeo, 'Some Practices and Problems of Chartist Democracy', in J. Epstein and D. Thompson, eds., *The Chartist Experience: Studies in Working Class Radicalism and Culture, 1830–60* (London: Macmillan, 1982) pp. 348–9.

88 On the history of Irish syndicalism and the labour movement, see Emmet O'Connor, *Syndicalism in Ireland, 1917–1923* (Cork University Press, 1988) and *A Labour History of Ireland, 1824–1960* (Dublin: Gill and Macmillan, 1992). On the problems for a Marxist understanding of Irish radicalism, see David Lloyd, 'Rethinking National Marxism: James Connolly and "Celtic Communism"', in *Irish Times*, pp. 101–26.

89 John Stuart Mill, *Principles of Political Economy, Books III–V and Appendices*, in *Collected Works*, ed. J.M. Robson, intro. V.W. Bladen, 21 vols. (University of Toronto Press, 1965), vol. III, p. 1001.

90 Somerville, 'On the Value of Small Farms', in *Letters from Ireland*, pp. 165–71; Thompson, *The Chartists*, p. 305, for his suspicion of land nationalization programmes and his anti-Corn Law League connection, p. 305.

91 Yeo, 'Some Practices and Problems of Chartist Democracy', p. 372.

92 Cole, *Chartist Portraits*, pp. 304–5.

93 Ibid., p. 303 and 324–5; Thompson, *The Chartists*, p. 302, is clearest on the practical intent of the Plan.

94 Ibid., pp. 3–5.

95 Nicholson, *Annals*, p. 70.

3 COUNTERPARTS: THE PUBLIC HOUSE, MASCULINITY AND TEMPERANCE NATIONALISM

1 See John A. O'Brien, ed., *The Vanishing Irish: The Enigma of the Modern World* (New York: McGraw Hill, 1953), an alarmed and alarmist collection by a remarkable range of Irish writers, whose editor portrays a nation 'teetering perilously on the brink of extinction', p. 3. For a scholarly assessment of Irish migrations and depopulation, see Timothy W. Guinnane, *The Vanishing Irish: Households, Migration, and the Rural Economy in Ireland, 1850–1914* (Princeton University Press, 1997). I have drawn here on his summary of recent demographic and economic studies of post-Famine Ireland in ch. 2, 'The Rural Economy in the Nineteenth Century', pp. 34–58.

2 Patrick Kavanagh, 'The Great Hunger', in *Collected Poems* (London: Martin O'Brian and O'Keeffe, 1972), pp. 34–5.

3 Ibid., p. 45.

4 Richard Stivers, *Hair of the Dog: Irish Drinking and Its American Stereotype*, rev. edn (New York: Continuum, 2000), p. 9.

5 On the gradual regulation of the pub and of beer houses and other drinking establishments like 'spirit grocers' in nineteenth-century Britain and Ireland, see Stivers, *Hair of the Dog*, pp. 18–27; and Kevin C. Kearns, *Dublin Pub Life and Lore: An Oral History* (Dublin: Gill and Macmillan, 1996), pp. 15–24.

6 Stivers, *Hair of the Dog*, p. 78.

7 Ibid., p. 94.

8 Paul Gilroy, *The Black Atlantic: Modernity and Double Consciousness* (Cambridge, MA: Harvard University Press, 1993), pp. 36 and 37–8.

9 Stivers, *Hair of the Dog*, p. 104, citing Max Horkheimer and T.W. Adorno, *Dialectic of Enlightenment*, trans. John Cumming (New York: Continuum, 1972), p. 33.
10 See Kearns, *Dublin Pub Life*, p. 6, on this 'woefully ignored topic of study'. Unfortunately, his own study, being an oral history, offers only a brief, if useful, survey of the history of the pub and of drinking practices in the Britain and Ireland. Stivers, *Hair of the Dog*, pp. 10–30, offers another helpful overview of the history of drinking, focusing in particular on 'occupational drinking'.
11 Cheryl Herr, *Joyce's Anatomy of Culture* (Urbana: University of Illinois Press, 1986). Though it deals extensively with the press, the stage and the Church, this book – perhaps surprisingly – has little to say of the public house in Joyce's work.
12 James Joyce, 'After the Race', in *Dubliners* (New York: Penguin, 1992), p. 35. On *Dubliners* in the context of colonialism, and on this story in particular, see Vincent J. Cheng, *Joyce, Race and Empire* (Cambridge University Press, 1995), pp. 103–10.
13 Joyce, 'Counterparts', in *Dubliners*, p. 86.
14 On the discreteness of culture's work of interpellation in nineteenth-century Britain, see David Lloyd and Paul Thomas, *Culture and the State* (London: Routledge, 1998).
15 Since the literature on nationalism from which I have drawn here is so voluminous, let me cite those from which I have drawn most closely here: Frantz Fanon, *The Wretched of the Earth*, trans. Constance Farrington (New York: Grove Press, 1968), esp. pp. 223–4; Partha Chatterjee, *Nationalism and the Colonial World: A Derivative Discourse?* (London: Zed Books, 1986); Luke Gibbons, 'Identity without a Centre: Allegory, History and Irish Nationalism', and, indeed, the whole book in which this essay is collected, *Transformations in Irish Culture* (Cork University Press, 1996), pp. 134–7.
16 Chatterjee, *Nationalism and the Colonial World*, p. 42.
17 Frantz Fanon, *Black Skin White Masks*, trans. Charles Lam Markmann (London: Pluto, 1986), p. 130. The chapter, translated as 'The Fact of Blackness', is Fanon's reckoning with the subjective implications of the stereotype and its inversion.
18 Joyce, 'Counterparts', in *Dubliners*, p. 90.
19 Matthew Arnold, 'On the Study of Celtic Literature', in *Lectures and Essays in Criticism*, ed. R.H. Super, *The Complete Prose Works of Matthew Arnold*, 7 vols. (Ann Arbor: University of Michigan Press, 1962), vol. III, p. 347.
20 Ibid., p. 85.
21 On the Victorian representation of the Celt, see L.P. Curtis, *Anglo-Saxons and Celts: A Study of Anti-Irish Prejudice in Victorian England* (Conference on British Studies at the University of Bridgeport, 1968) and *Apes and Angels: The Irishman in Victorian Caricature* (Washington, DC: Smithsonian Press, 1971). On Fenian 'terrorism' and the consolidation of British domestic ideology, see Amy E. Martin, *Alter-Nations: Nationalisms, Terror and the State in*

Nineteenth-Century Britain and Ireland (Columbus: Ohio State University Press, forthcoming).

22 Arnold, 'On the Study of Celtic Literature', p. 347. Arnold's aesthetic appreciation of the sentimentality of the Celt, which finds expression in the propensity to elegiac poetry, lamenting their perpetual defeats, finds a precise correlative in John Ruskin's highly popular text on male and female dispositions, *Sesame and Lilies*, where one of woman's principal functions is to mourn: 'she is to extend the limits of her sympathy ... to the contemporary calamity, which, were it but rightly mourned by her, would recur no more hereafter.' See John Ruskin, *Sesame and Lilies*, in *Sesame and Lilies, The Two Paths and The King of the Golden River* (London: J.M. Dent, 1907), p. 63.

23 See again Martin, *Alter-Nations*, for discussion of the use of caricatures of the Fenians to consolidate a sense of virtuous working-class domestic ideology in Britain.

24 I use the term also by analogy with Kumkum Sangari and Sudesh Vaid's conception of the 'reconstitution of patriarchies' that takes place continually both under the British Raj and in the context of Indian nationalism. See their Introduction to *Recasting Women: Essays in Colonial History* (New Delhi: Kali for Women, 1989), pp. 1, 25 and passim.

25 Thomas Osborne Davis, 'The Young Men of Ireland', *The Nation*, 15 July 1843, p. 32.

26 Partha Chatterjee, 'The Nationalist Resolution of the Woman Question', in Sangari and Vaid, *Recasting Women*, pp. 232–53.

27 See W.B. Yeats, 'Gods and Fighting Men', in *Explorations* (New York: Macmillan, 1962), pp. 24–6. Marjorie Howes has explored in detail the ways in which Yeats responded to the Arnoldian stereotype by setting his own masculinity against the femininity of folk culture. See her *Yeats's Nations: Gender, Class and Irishness* (Cambridge University Press, 1996), pp. 18–43.

28 On the gender politics of the Irish Literary Theatre, see Susan Cannon Harris, *Gender and Modern Irish Drama* (Bloomington: Indiana University Press, 2002).

29 Thomas A. Boylan and Timothy P. Foley, *Political Economy and Colonial Ireland: The Propagation and Ideological Function of Economic Discourse in the Nineteenth Century* (London: Routledge, 1992), pp. 150–5, contains a fascinating account of the debates on domestic ideology, the role of women in the home and the workplace, and the relation of Irish family and 'clan' systems to economic under-development that took place among Irish political economists in the mid nineteenth century. These show the drive, common among nationalists, Catholic clergy and most political economists, to 'normalize' Irish gender relations, an ideological project that only gradually affected institutional and material relations.

30 Stivers, *Hair of the Dog*, p. 4, prefers terms like 'hard drinking' or the less colloquial 'habitual social drinking' to the more loaded term 'alcoholism'.

31 Ibid., p. 31: 'That industrialism missed Ireland helps explain why the Irish variant of middle-class morality encouraged hard drinking.' Stivers,

pp. 10–30, also indicates how Ireland retained longer than England and Scotland popular drinking customs that were once common to all those cultures.

32 Elizabeth Malcolm, 'The Rise of the Pub: A Study in the Disciplining of Popular Culture', in J.S. Donnelly, Jr and Kerby A. Miller, eds., *Irish Popular Culture, 1650–1850* (Dublin: Irish Academic Press, 1998), p. 57. See also John F. Quinn, *Father Mathew's Crusade: Intemperance in Nineteenth-Century Ireland and Irish America* (Amherst and Boston: University of Massachusetts Press, 2002), pp. 47–51.

33 Malcolm, 'The Rise of the Pub', p. 65.

34 See Stivers, *Hair of the Dog*, pp. 22–30; Colm Kerrigan, *Father Mathew and the Irish Temperance Movement, 1838–1849* (Cork University Press, 1992), p. 20; and Quinn, *Father Mathew's Crusade*, pp. 44–5.

35 See E. Estyn Evans' citation of Wilde in Chapter 2, above, p. 71 (n59).

36 On Father Mathew's antagonism to secret societies and other manifestations of social unrest, see Kerrigan, *Father Mathew and the Irish Temperance Movement*, pp. 103–4 and Stivers, *Hair of the Dog*, p. 42.

37 Kerrigan, *Father Mathew and the Irish Temperance Movement*, pp. 131 and 122.

38 Elizabeth Malcolm, *'Ireland Sober, Ireland Free': Drink and Temperance in Nineteenth Century Ireland* (Dublin: Gill and Macmillan, 1986), p. 147. For a briefer overview of temperance work in the period, see Malcolm's 'Temperance and Irish Nationalism', in F.S.L. Lyons and R.A.J. Hawkins, eds., *Ireland under the Union: Varieties of Tension* (Oxford: Clarendon Press, 1980), pp. 69–114.

39 Fr C.J. Herlihy, *The Celt above the Saxon* (1904), cited in Luke Gibbons, 'Race against Time: Racial Discourse and Irish History', *Oxford Literary Review* 13 (1991), p. 103. On the emergence and spread of such views in temperance nationalism, see Malcolm, 'Temperance and Irish Nationalism', pp. 101–8.

40 Douglas Hyde, 'The Necessity for Deanglicising Ireland', in Breandán O Conaire, ed., *Language, Lore and Lyrics: Essays and Lectures* (Blackrock: Irish Academic Press, 1986), pp. 153–70.

41 Revd J. Halpin, P.P., *The Father Mathew Reader on Temperance and Hygiene* (Dublin: M.H. Gill, 1907), p. 7.

42 Ibid., pp. 14–15.

43 Ibid., pp. 20–1.

44 Ibid., pp. 22–3.

45 Malcolm, 'The Rise of the Pub', p. 51. See also Quinn, *Father Mathew's Crusade*, p. 45; Stivers, *Hair of the Dog*, p. 19, and Kearns, *Dublin Pub Life*, p. 3.

46 Ibid., pp. 15–19. He discusses the effect of the Liquor Licensing Law of 1872 on the promotion of the 'good character' of the publican – and on the economic value of pubs themselves, p. 18. Davy Byrne's was not the only 'moral pub' to be found in Dublin.

47 Surprisingly, as both Malcolm and Kearns note (Malcolm, 'The Rise of the Pub', p. 73, n13; Kearns, *Dublin Pub Life*, p. 6), there has been as little anthropological as historical work done on the Irish pub or on Irish drinking practices. I have drawn extensively on their pioneering work for this chapter. For a very suggestive analysis of the cultural significance of the pub, or saloon, which has considerable insight to offer on Irish practices despite examining the context of Massachusetts, see Roy Rosenzweig, 'The Rise of the Saloon', in Chandra Mukerji and Michael Schudson, eds., *Rethinking Popular Culture: Contemporary Perspectives in Cultural Studies* (Berkeley: University of California Press, 1991), pp. 121–56.
48 Quoted in Kevin Rockett, 'Disguising Dependency: Separatism and Foreign Mass Culture', *Circa* 49 (January/February 1990), p. 22. On nationalist censure of the vulgarity and anglicizing effects of the music hall, see Herr, *Joyce's Anatomy of Culture*, pp. 199–204.
49 Malcolm alludes to all these elements in the late-nineteenth-century pub: it was a site of politics and of gambling, music, singing and athletics, and of 'family and community functions' as well as of more public concerns: 'trade unions, young men's societies, and Fenian circles all held meetings in pubs.' See Malcolm, 'The Rise of the Pub', pp. 51–2.
50 Walter Benjamin, *The Origin of German Tragic Drama*, trans. John Osborne (London: Verso, 1985), p. 45.
51 It is equally far from the anthropological notion of 'Survival in Culture' coined by E.B. Tylor at the very moment that Irish oral space was undergoing its destructive transformation. The notion of survival in play here bears no relation to Tylor's 'primaeval monuments of barbaric thought' or remnants 'fossilized in superstition', though it is interesting that anthropology should have coined the term at this precise moment. Tylor's 'survivals' are stranded and give rise to nothing new. See Edward Burnett Tylor, *The Origins of Culture* (New York: Harper, 1958), pp. 21–2.
52 See Rosenzweig, 'Rise of the Saloon', pp. 121–6. See also Stivers, *Hair of the Dog*, p. 31, on the survival of hard drinking in Ireland as a consequence of low levels of industrialization.
53 Malcolm, 'The Rise of the Pub', p. 51.
54 On the imbrication at any historical moment, and especially in modernity, of past and emergent modes of cultural transmission and practice, see Donald Lowe, *History of Bourgeois Perception* (University of Chicago Press, 1982), pp. 14–16.
55 On the ways in which, 'well into the first half of the nineteenth century, the publican straddled the worlds of both government-sanctioned, indoor drinking and outdoor, unregulated popular festivals', in close proximity 'with both the illicit distiller and the shebeen keeper', see Malcolm, 'The Rise of the Pub', p. 72. Malcolm's observations are borne out by Dorian's account of the duty-day festivities and the presence of both the licensed drink-seller and the half-concealed shebeen, quoted in the previous chapter.
56 Joyce, 'Counterparts', in *Dubliners*, pp. 87, 88 and 90.

57 Malcolm, 'The Rise of the Pub', p. 51.
58 Ibid., p. 72.
59 On the theatre and gender roles, in particular transvestism, see ch. 2: 'The Stage: Transvestism and Transformation', in Herr, *Joyce's Anatomy of Culture*.
60 Stivers, *Hair of the Dog*, pp. 28 and 90–1.
61 In one of his most suggestive analyses of drinking culture, Stivers points out that within what he terms 'avunculate' society, the home becomes closely identified with the mother and with the father's rivalry with the son who becomes the object of her affection. See ibid., pp. 72–7.
62 See, for example, Maria Luddy, *Women and Philanthropy in Nineteenth-Century Ireland* (Cambridge University Press, 1995); Caitriona Clear, 'The Limits of Female Autonomy: Nuns in Nineteenth-Century Ireland', in Maria Luddy and Cliona Murphy, eds., *Women Surviving: Studies in Irish Women's History in the 19th and 20th Centuries* (Dublin: Poolbeg Press, 1990), pp. 15–50; and Margaret MacCurtain, 'Godly Burden: Catholic Sisterhoods in 20th-Century Ireland', in Anthony Bradley and MaryAnn Gialanella Valiulis, eds., *Gender and Sexuality in Modern Ireland* (Amherst: University of Massachusetts Press, 1997), pp. 245–56.
63 This is perhaps also allegorized in the fate of Jimmy in the story 'After the Race', whose attempt to emulate the representatives of more powerful modern nations – England, France and the United States – leads him into drunkenness and enormous gambling debts.
64 See Mark Shell, *The Economy of Literature* (Baltimore, MD: Johns Hopkins University Pess, 1978), pp. 32–3. Internal citation from H.G. Liddell and Robert Scott, *A Greek–English Lexicon* (Oxford: Clarendon Press, 1940).
65 See W.B. Yeats, *Autobiography* (New York: Macmillan, 1953), p. 119. I have discussed Yeats and the politics of nationalist symbolism more fully in 'The Poetics of Politics: Yeats and the Founding of the State', in *Anomalous States: Irish Writing and the Post-Colonial Moment* (Durham, NC: Duke University Press, 1993), pp. 70–4.
66 James Joyce, *Stephen Hero*, ed. Theodore Spencer (New York: Granada, 1977), p. 188.
67 See Joyce, 'The Dead', in *Dubliners*, p. 211: 'There was grace and mystery in her attitude as if she were a symbol of something. He asked himself what is a woman standing on the stairs in the shadow, listening to distant music, a symbol of?' 'The Dead', of course, is set at the Feast of the Epiphany, and this passage represents, as it were, Joyce's metacommentary on the relationship between the secular epiphany and the urge to symbolization, an urge which is directly associated with the formation of male heterosexual desire that Gretta seems to elude. For further commentary on this story and its understanding of male desire, see Luke Gibbons, 'Identity without a Centre', pp. 134–47. See also Terence Brown's introduction to *Dubliners*, pp. xxxiv–xxxv, and his citation of C.H. Peake: 'there could hardly be a more emphatic

assertion that an epiphany was an apprehension of the thing's unique particularity, and not a symbol of something else' (p. xxxv).
68 James Joyce, *Letters*, ed. Stuart Gilbert (New York: Viking Press, 1966), pp. 63–4.

4 'GOING NOWHERE': ORAL SPACE IN THE CELL BLOCK

1 Colin Crawford, 'The Compound System: An Alternative Penal Strategy', *The Howard Journal* 21 (1982), pp. 155–8.
2 On the language of 'gangsterism' deployed in reporting on the IRA, see Liz Curtis, *Ireland: The Propaganda War – The British Media and the 'Battle for Hearts and Minds'* (London: Pluto, 1984), pp. 128–30.
3 Richard Kearney, 'Myth and Terror', *The Crane Bag* 2.1–2 (Dublin, 1977), pp. 125–39.
4 Ibid., p. 125.
5 Ibid., p. 130.
6 Ibid., p. 131.
7 Ibid., p. 132.
8 Padraig O'Malley, *Biting at the Grave: The Irish Hunger Strikes and the Politics of Despair* (Boston, MA: Beacon Press, 1990), p. 6.
9 Ibid., p. 7.
10 Allen Feldman, *Formations of Violence: The Narrative of the Body and Political Terror in Northern Ireland* (University of Chicago Press, 1991), p. 5.
11 Ibid., p. 265.
12 Begoña Aretxaga, *Shattering Silence: Women, Nationalism and Political Subjectivity in Northern Ireland* (Princeton University Press, 1997), p. 103.
13 Aretxaga, *Shattering Silence*, pp. 137–42.
14 This is the overall argument of Mary S. Corcoran, *Out of Order: The Political Imprisonment of Women in Northern Ireland, 1972–98* (Portland, OR: Willan Publishing, 2006). See also Jude McCulloch and Amanda George, 'Naked Power: Strip-Searching in Women's Prisons', in Phil Scraton and Jude McCulloch, eds., *The Violence of Incarceration* (London: Routledge, 2009), pp. 107–23.
15 Max Horkheimer and T.W. Adorno, *Dialectic of Enlightenment*, trans. John Cumming (New York: Continuum, 1972), p. 111.
16 Corcoran, *Out of Order*, p. 89. Kieran McEvoy, *Paramilitary Imprisonment in Northern Ireland: Resistance, Management, and Release* (Oxford University Press, 2001), p. 74, also critiques O'Malley's account of the hunger strikes in relation to 'Catholic notions of self-sacrifice' and the legacy of Brehon laws, arguing that 'such accounts may become reductive or deterministic unless they are accompanied by a real understanding of the social and political context in which they occur'. His emphasis is rather on hunger striking as 'a rational, pragmatic and strategic tactic to employ' than on 'the fact that the prisoners came from a Catholic background'.

17 Louise Purbrick, 'The Architecture of Containment', in Donovan Wylie, *The Maze* (London: Granta Books, 2004), p. 92.
18 Michel Foucault, *Discipline and Punish: The Birth of the Prison*, 2nd edn, trans. Alan Sheridan (New York: Vintage, 1995), part 1. See also Norman Johnston, *Forms of Constraint: A History of Prison Architecture* (Urbana and Chicago: University of Illinois Press, 2000). For an account of the potential anarchy of 'congregate' prisons at a relatively late date, see Noel Ignatiev's description of Walnut Street Jail in Philadelphia in the 1820s, in *How the Irish Became White* (New York: Routledge, 1995), pp. 42–51.
19 See Randall McGowen, 'The Well-Ordered Prison: England 1780–1865', in Norval Morris and David J. Rothman, eds., *The Oxford History of the Prison: The Practice of Punishment in Western Society* (Oxford University Press, 1995), p. 91.
20 Sean Grass, *The Self in the Cell: Narrating the Victorian Prisoner* (New York: Routledge, 2003), p. 23.
21 Revd John Burt, assistant chaplain to Pentonville Prison, cited in Seán McConville, 'The Victorian Prison: England, 1865–1965', in Morris and Rothman, *The Oxford History of the Prison*, p. 136.
22 McGowen, 'The Well-Ordered Prison', p. 86.
23 Ibid., p. 89.
24 Patrick Carroll-Burke, *Colonial Discipline: The Making of the Irish Convict System* (Dublin: Four Courts Press, 2000), p. 51.
25 Ibid., p. 91. See also Stanley Cohen, 'Prisons and the Future of Control Systems: From Concentration to Dispersal', in Mike Fitzgerald *et al.*, *Welfare in Action* (London: Routledge & Kegan Paul, 1977), p. 220.
26 I follow here Benedict Anderson's highly suggestive analysis of the forms of colonial state governmentality in *Imagined Communities: Reflections on the Origin and Spread of Nationalism*, rev. edn (London: Verso, 2006), pp. 169 and 184.
27 Sir Robert Peel, 1826, cited by McGowen, 'The Well-Ordered Prison', p. 99.
28 See McGowen, 'The Well-Ordered Prison', pp. 101–2 and 103–4, and McConville, 'The Victorian Prison', p. 147.
29 Mr Merry, Chairman of Berkshire Magistrates, cited by William Tallack, *Defects in the Criminal Administration and Penal Legislation of Great Britain and Ireland, with Remedial Suggestions* (London: Kitto, 1872), p. 62.
30 William Tallack, *The Cellular (But not Rigidly Solitary) System of Imprisonment, as Carried out at the Prisons of Louvain, Amsterdam, etc.* (London: Kitto, 1872), p. 6. This paper was delivered by Tallack to the English Social Science Association's Annual Congress, Leeds, 1871, and printed for circulation at the International Penal and Prison Congress, London, July 1872.
31 Mary Carpenter, *Reformatory Prison Discipline, As Developed by the Rt. Hon. Sir William Crofton, in the Irish Convict Prisons* (London: Longmans, Green, Reader and Dyer, 1872). According to the preface, this work was prepared 'at the request of the United States Commissioner, Dr. [Enoch Cobb] Wines, to whom is due the original conception of this congress'. Wines responded

favourably at this conference to Tallack's proposals for a cellular system. See Tallack, *The Cellular System*, pp. 27–8.
32 Carpenter, *Reformatory Prison Discipline*, pp. vi and ix.
33 Ibid., pp. 9 and xi.
34 Ibid., p. 3.
35 Ibid., p. 16.
36 Ibid., p. 6.
37 Ibid., pp. 6–7. On the practice of 'ranking' through serial steps or grades in the disciplinary institution, see Foucault, *Discipline and Punish*, pp. 146–9 and 160–2.
38 Carpenter, *Reformatory Prison Discipline*, p. 7.
39 Ibid., p. 124.
40 Ibid., p. 10.
41 Mike Tomlinson, 'Imprisoned Ireland', in Vincenzo Ruggiero *et al.*, eds., *Western European Penal Systems: A Critical Anatomy* (London: Sage, 1995), p. 196.
42 Carpenter, *Reformatory Prison Discipline*, pp. 107–8. Carroll-Burke emphasizes this 'Irish system of police surveillance which linked the centralized convict system with the centralized police system', *Colonial Discipline*, p. 20.
43 Ibid., p. 85.
44 Mike Tomlinson, 'Imprisoned Ireland', p. 197.
45 Carpenter, *Reformatory Prison Discipline*, pp. ix–x.
46 Ibid., pp. 93–4.
47 Asenath Nicholson, *Annals of the Famine in Ireland*, ed. Maureen Murphy (Dublin: Lilliput Press, 1998), p. 59.
48 On the origins and development of the Irish national school system, see Donald H. Akenson, *The Irish Education Experiment: The National System of Education in the Nineteenth Century* (London: Routledge & Kegan Paul, 1970).
49 Breandán Mac Suibhne and Amy Martin, 'Fenians in the Frame: Photographing Irish Political Prisoners, 1865–68', *Field Day Review* 1 (2005), pp. 101–20.
50 Jeremiah O'Donovan Rossa, *Irish Rebels in English Prisons*, ed. Thomas J. Cox (Dingle: Brandon Books, 1991), p. 159. McGowen corroborates O'Donovan Rossa's observations on the prisoners' capacity to subvert the prison regime: 'Prisoners were inventive in discovering ways to subvert penal discipline … They developed a form of ventriloquism, the art of talking without moving one's lips. The prison at night was filled with the sounds of tapping as pipes became a medium for telegraphic communication. Some prisoners created chat holes through which they could speak to one another' ('The Well-Ordered Prison', p. 106).
51 O'Donovan Rossa, *Irish Rebels*, pp. 91–2.
52 Ibid., p. 161.
53 Ibid., pp. 83–4, 161. Writing of a slightly later Fenian prisoner, Thomas J. Clarke, who endured fifteen years of solitary confinement from 1883 to 1898,

mostly under a regime of total silence, Sean O'Brien remarks: 'because the prison sustains itself as an entirely self-contained unit, the primary means with which to survive it are found within the structure itself' (*Irish Prison Writing and the Victorian Penitentiary*, PhD dissertation, University of Notre Dame, 2008, p. 102). He goes on to argue that, 'Once the cell and the prison have been imaginatively dismantled and reconfigured, all of the elements of his imprisonment become potential sources of resistance and consequently of survival' (p. 109). This suggests that O'Donovan Rossa's experience and tactics were by no means unique to him, but part of a set of Fenian responses to imprisonment dictated by the very form of the prison in their historical moment.
54 O'Donovan Rossa, *Irish Rebels*, p. 152.
55 Ibid., p. 158.
56 On the distinction between *zoe*, or mere biological life, and *bios*, or life as political or cultural, see Giorgio Agamben, *Homo Sacer: Sovereign Power and Bare Life*, trans. Daniel Heller-Roazen (Stanford University Press, 1998), pp. 1–3.
57 W.J. Brennan-Whitmore, *With the Irish in Frongoch* (Dublin: Talbot Press, 1917), pp. 30–1.
58 Sean O Mahony, *Frongoch: University of Revolution* (Killiney: FDR Teoranta, 1987), p. 58. Tim Healy, the Irish nationalist MP at the time, described it as 'a Sinn Fein University' (ibid.). The overlap between the barracks, the camp and the educational institution is underlined by the fact that Darrell Figgis could see Richmond Barracks in Inchicore, where 1916 rebels were first interned, as 'the clearing house for rebels … the university in which the doctrines, methods and hopes of the men of Easter Week were folded into the life of men from every part of Ireland' (ibid., p. 19).
59 On the nation state as an imagined community within a limited space, see Anderson, *Imagined Communities*, pp. 6–7.
60 O Mahony, *Frongoch*, p. 58.
61 Ibid.
62 Brennan-Whitmore, *With the Irish in Frongoch*, pp. 91 and 197–8.
63 Dorothy MacArdle, *The Irish Republic*, quoted in O Mahony, *Frongoch*, p. 60.
64 See, for example, Ronan Bennett's brief account of time in Long Kesh, 'What the Kid Knows Now', in Danny Morrison, ed., *Hunger Strike: Reflections on the 1981 Hunger Strike* (Dingle: Brandon, 2006), pp. 42–7.
65 See Gerry Adams, *Cage Eleven: Writings from Prison* (Boulder, CO: Roberts Rinehart, 1997), p. 9; Denis O'Hearn, *Nothing But an Unfinished Song: Bobby Sands, The Irish Hunger Striker Who Ignited a Generation* (New York: Nation Books, 2006), pp. 51–2 and 55–6.
66 Feldman, *Formations of Violence*, p. 152.
67 See Brian Campbell *et al.*, eds., *Nor Meekly Serve My Time: The H Block Struggle, 1976–1981* (Belfast: Beyond the Pale, 1998), p. 2.
68 Jackie McMullan, in ibid., p. 2.

69 Sean Lennon, in ibid., p. 24.
70 Feldman, *Formations of Violence*, p. 164. Feldman emphasizes here the *discontinuity* of the H-Block struggles with past Republican campaigns, despite its being 'camouflaged' in the rhetoric of the Republican tradition. See pp. 163–4.
71 Lawrence McKeown, *Out of Time: Irish Republican Prisoners, Long Kesh 1972–2000* (Belfast: Beyond the Pale, 2001), p. 56; Campbell *et al.*, *Nor Meekly Serve My Time*, pp. 20 and 107.
72 Feldman, *Formations of Violence*, pp. 201–2.
73 Ned Flynn, cited in Campbell *et al.*, *Nor Meekly Serve My Time*, p. 21.
74 Ned Flynn, cited in ibid., p. 22. Though reinvented in the H-Blocks, 'shooting the line' resembled a practice also used by the Fenian Thomas J. Clarke in Portland Jail. See O'Brien, *Irish Prison Writing*, p. 110. This is an interesting instance of the way in which the constraints and openings of prison construction lend themselves to what might look like a continuous 'tradition' of resistance techniques, but is actually determined by the cell's own 'memory' of strategies of containment.
75 Joe McQuillan, cited in Campbell *et al.*, *Nor Meekly Serve My Time*, p. 45. On the prefabricated construction of the H-Blocks, based on a Louisiana State prison design adapted in England, see Purbrick, 'Architecture of Containment', pp. 99–100.
76 Cited in Feldman, *Formations of Violence*, p. 188. This is what led Bobby Sands to dub the prison 'The Breaker's Yard': cf. Feldman, *Formations of Violence*, pp. 161–2.
77 Former PIRA prisoner cited in ibid., p. 201.
78 See Jacques Lacan, 'The Mirror Stage as Formative of the *I* Function, as Revealed in Psychoanalytic Experience', in *Ecrits: A Selection*, trans. Bruce Fink (New York: Norton, 2004), pp. 6–7.
79 This sense of the reduction of the Blanketmen to the degree zero of human existence is vividly captured in Cardinal Ó Fiaich's shocked report of his visit to the H-Blocks in July 1978: 'One would hardly allow an animal to remain in such conditions, let alone a human being. The nearest approach to it I have seen was the spectacle of hundreds of homeless people living in sewer pipes in the slums of Calcutta.' Cited in Campbell *et al.*, *Nor Meekly Serve My Time*, p. 46. On the condition of 'civil death', a legal fiction that descends from slavery to modern forms of incarceration, see Joan Dayan, 'Poe, Persons and Property', in J. Gerald Kennedy and Liliane Weisberg, eds., *Romancing the Shadow: Poe and Race* (Oxford University Press, 2001), pp. 115–20.
80 Maud Ellmann, *The Hunger Artists: Starving, Writing and Imprisonment* (Cambridge, MA: Harvard University Press, 1993), p. 100.
81 Feldman, *Formations of Violence*, p. 181.
82 Ciaran McGillicuddy, cited in Campbell *et al.*, *Nor Meekly Serve My Time*, p. 57. For an account by one prison social worker of the impact of the saturation of the warders' clothing and bodies with the contaminating odour

of the Blocks, including high rates of marital breakdown, see Feldman, *Formations of Violence*, p. 193.
83 Ranajit Guha, *Elementary Aspects of Peasant Insurgency in Colonial India* (Durham, NC: Duke University Press, 1999), pp. 260–1. On the signification of the chapati, see ibid., pp. 238–46, and Homi Bhabha, 'By Bread Alone: Signs of Violence in the Mid-Nineteenth Century', in *The Location of Culture* (London: Routledge, 1994), pp. 198–208; on Irish agrarian 'metonymic' movements, see David Lloyd, 'Violence and the Constitution of the Novel', in *Anomalous States: Irish Writing and the Postcolonial Moment* (Durham, NC: Duke University Press, 1993), pp. 138–50.
84 Corcoran, *Out of Order*, p. 126.
85 McKeown, *Out of Time*, p. 67. For other prisoners' comments on the pragmatic use of Irish in the H-Blocks, and on its idiosyncracies, see Feldman, *Formations of Violence*, pp. 211–14.
86 McKeown, *Out of Time*, p. 68.
87 Former INLA prisoner cited in Feldman, *Formations of Violence*, p. 214.
88 Seamus Deane, 'Civilians and Barbarians', in Field Day Theatre Company, eds., *Ireland's Field Day* (South Bend, IL: University of Notre Dame Press, 1986), pp. 41–2 and passim.
89 On the learning of Irish in this fashion, see McKeown, *Out of Time*, p. 68:

> Pacing up and down the cell for hours on end he [his cellmate] would repeat the irregular verbs; Ar chuala tú – Did you hear?; Chuala mé – I heard; Níor chuala mé – I did not hear. Despite efforts on my part to resist it I soon found myself mentally repeating, Ar chuala tú, chuala mé, níor chuala mé, and that was how I began to learn the Irish language.

Irish also contaminated the warders who sought to pick up some of the prisoners' language: see Feldman, *Formations of Violence*, pp. 212 and 214. On the ethos of collective self-education, see McKeown, *Out of Time*, pp. 65–71 and 129–48. On the prisoners' transformation of Republican ideology and strategy see, for example, Feldman, *Formations of Violence*, pp. 161–4, and O'Hearn, *Nothing But an Unfinished Song*, pp. 381–3.
90 See McEvoy, *Paramilitary Imprisonment*, p. 89 and n89.
91 Ellmann, *The Hunger Artists*, p. 105.
92 For this transition from 'pregenital' to 'genital organization' in infantile sexuality, see Sigmund Freud, 'On Transformations of Instinct as Implied in Anal Erotism' (1917) and 'The Infantile Genital Organization (An Interpolation into the Theory of Sexuality)' (1923), in *The Standard Edition of the Complete Psychological Works*, trans. James Strachey, 24 vols. (London: The Hogarth Press, 1955), vol. 17, pp. 125–33 and vol. 19, pp. 139–45, respectively.
93 Feldman, *Formations of Violence*, p. 204.
94 See Campbell et al., *Nor Meekly Serve My Time*, 'Craic and Camaraderie', pp. 71–83; see also Feldman, *Formations of Violence*, pp. 182–4. Feldman also cites the testimony of a prison welfare officer on the close bonding of the prisoners, pp. 193–4. On the utopian ways in which 'the seeds of a more humane and dignified way of organizing society' were laid by the Blanketmen in the 'bare

prison regime of the H-Blocks', see Denis O'Hearn, 'Embodied Perception and Prefigurative Movements: Connections across the Atlantic', in Peter D. O'Neill and David Lloyd, eds., *The Black and Green Atlantic: Crosscurrents of the African and Irish Diasporas* (London: Palgrave, 2009), p. 235.
95 Feldman, *Formations of Violence*, pp. 164–5.
96 Ellmann, *The Hunger Artists*, p. 100.
97 See also prisoners' comments on their lack of a sense of time during the no-wash protest, Feldman, *Formations of Violence*, p. 228.
98 See especially ibid., ch. 6, 'Eschatology', for the most detailed account of this kind. The thematic of sacrifice and martyrdom is also evident in O'Malley, *Biting at the Grave* and Elmann, *The Hunger Artists*.
99 Aretxaga, *Shattering Silence*, p. 101.
100 Ibid., p. 102.
101 Steve McQueen, dir., *Hunger* (Blast! Films, 2008).
102 See McKeown, *Out of Time*, p. 231 on the 'cold, rational, clinical analysis' that informed Sands's decision to embark on the hunger strike and for an assessment of the various ideological strategies that informed the prisoners' relation to the Republican movement and its history. David Beresford, *Ten Men Dead: The Story of the 1981 Irish Hunger Strike* (New York: Atlantic Monthly Press, 1987), pp. 64, 67, 125, 189–90, cites coms sent out during the hunger strike that detail the weight and blood pressure of the strikers, indicating the consistent medicalization of their action.
103 See Campbell *et al.*, *Nor Meekly Serve My Time*, pp. 148–51, for various accounts of this transition.
104 G.W.F. Hegel, *Philosophy of Right*, trans. T.M. Knox (Oxford University Press, 1967), p. 115.
105 Perhaps the emblematic instance of this erasure is Allen Feldman's literally parenthetical acknowledgement of the 1980 Armagh no-wash protest: '(In February 1980 thirty-two IRA women went on dirt protest in Armagh prison.)' Feldman, *Formations of Violence*, p. 174.
106 Nell McCafferty, 'It is my belief that Armagh is a feminist issue', *Irish Times*, 17 June 1980. McCafferty comments on 'the uproar within and without the paper' that greeted the article and on the 'personal and financial price' she and others paid for their engagement with the North in her essay, 'When All Thought Fails', in Morrison, *Hunger Strike*, p. 78. On the Northern Ireland Women's Rights Movement's antagonism to Republicanism and to the women in Armagh, see also Aretxaga, *Shattering Silence*, p. 162.
107 Tim Pat Coogan, *On the Blanket: The Inside Story of the IRA Prisoners' 'Dirty' Protest* (Boulder, CO: Roberts Rinehart, 1997), pp. 230–1. In introducing ch. 10, 'Women on the Dirty Protest', Coogan comments that: 'The "dirty protest" is bad enough to contemplate when men are on it, but it becomes even worse when it is embarked on by women, who apart from the psychological and hygienic pressures which this type of protest generates, also have the effects of the menstrual cycle to contend with' (p. 129).

108 Aretxaga, *Shattering Silence*, pp. 137, 144 and 142. Corcoran discusses the ways in which the Armagh protest 'was subject different interpretations about the character and meaning of the *women's* strategy of degradation'. See *Out of Order*, pp. 179–81.
109 Aretxaga, *Shattering Silence*, p. 135; cf. Corcoran, *Out of Order*, p. 179.
110 Aretxaga, *Shattering Silence*, p. 139.
111 Ellmann, *The Hunger Artists*, p. 84. She also suggests that 'the prisoners in Northern Ireland were feminized by their starvation in that their bodies were transformed into the images of meanings rather than the instruments of acts' (pp. 71–2). Lochlan Whalen also remarks on the gender reversal implicit in the transfer of the com from female visitor to male Blanketman, describing it as a form of insemination. See Lochlan Whalen, *Contemporary Irish Republican Prison Writing: Writing and Resistance* (New York: Palgrave Macmillan, 2007), p. 61.
112 Jackie McMullan and Ned Flynn, cited in Campbell *et al.*, *Nor Meekly Serve My Time*, pp. 9 and 11–12.
113 Feldman, *Formations of Violence*, pp. 167, 214.
114 See the discussion of this aspect of the racial gendering of the Irish in Chapter 3.
115 Beresford, *Ten Men Dead*, p. 36.
116 See Corcoran, *Out of Order*, p. 48 and ch. 3, 'Paradoxes of Women's Political Imprisonment'. See also Jude McCulloch and Amanda George, 'Naked Power', p. 108: 'The routine use of strip searches against prisoners, particularly female prisoners, means that "[s]exual abuse is surreptitiously incorporated into the most habitual aspect of women's imprisonment".' They cite Angela Davis, *Are Prisons Obsolete?* (New York: Free Press, 2003). For Mary Carpenter's views on the 'very strong development of the passions and of the lower nature' in female convicts and on their 'extreme excitability' and 'frequent outbursts of passion', see *Reformatory Prison Discipline*, p. 68.
117 See Corcoran, *Out of Order*, p. 181:

> The women's no-wash protest was constantly beset with the problem of being overshadowed by the Blanket protest at the Maze. In part, this was because the symbolic and instrumental effects of the Blanket protest were not immediately transferable to the no-wash protest, and in part because of gender-specific and culturally embedded prohibitions that surrounded the acceptable use by women of their bodies and sexualities both publicly and politically. Yet, these social prohibitions were also catalysts for articulating underlying doubts about the *political* legitimacy of the women's protest.

118 McKeown, *Out of Time*, pp. 227, 223–5 and 230.
119 Aretxaga, *Shattering Silence*, pp. 151–69.
120 Feldman, *Formations of Violence*, p. 204.
121 Aretxaga, *Shattering Silence*, p. 174.
122 Walter Benjamin, 'Theses on the Philosophy of History', in *Illuminations: Essays and Reflections*, ed. Hannah Arendt, trans. Harry Zohn (New York: Schocken, 1985), p. 264.

5 THE BREAKER'S YARD: FROM FORENSIC TO INTERROGATION MODERNITY

1 Medbh McGuckian, 'The Over Mother', in *Captain Lavender* (Winston-Salem, NC: Wake Forest University Press, 1995), p. 64.
2 For a summary of the rise of 'neo-liberal hegemony', see David Harvey, *The New Imperialism* (Oxford University Press, 2003), pp. 62–74.
3 For the term 'strong state', see Carol Ackroyd et al., *The Technology of Political Control*, 2nd rev. edn (London: Pluto, 1980).
4 See, for example, Allen Feldman, *Formations of Violence: The Narrative of the Body and Political Terror in Northern Ireland* (University of Chicago Press, 1991), p. 227, on such continuities and inversions. See also Lochlan Whalen's careful analysis of the ways in which Sands's writings were deliberately disseminated in forms that sought 'to obliterate the binary of *taoibh amuigh* and *faoi glas* [between those outside and the inmates]' in *Contemporary Irish Republican Prison Writing: Writing and Resistance* (New York: Palgrave Macmillan, 2007), p. 97.
5 I take this resonant phrase from Angel Rama's study of the colonial city in Latin America, *The Lettered City*, ed. and trans. John Charles Chasteen (Durham, NC: Duke University Press, 1996).
6 See Patrick Carroll, *Science, Culture and Modern State Formation* (Berkeley: University of California Press, 2006), p. 164. Joseph Ruane and Jennifer Todd, *The Dynamics of Conflict in Northern Ireland: Power, Conflict and Emancipation* (Cambridge University Press, 1996), p. 208, similarly refer to Ireland as an 'intermediary' between Britain and its colonies.
7 See Charles Baudelaire, 'A Une Passante', in *Les Fleurs du Mal* (Paris: Editions Gallimard, 1972), p. 126; translation by William Aggeler, *The Flowers of Evil* (Fresno, CA: Academy Library Guild, 1954), p. 311; Bobby Sands, 'Trilogy: The Crime of Castlereagh', in *Writings from Prison* (Boulder, CO: Roberts Rinehart, 1997), pp. 114–15; Walter Benjamin's writings on Baudelaire are collected in *Charles Baudelaire: A Lyric Poet in the Era of High Capitalism*, trans. Harry Zohn (London: Verso, 1983).
8 On the difficult conditions of production of Sands's writings, including 'The Trilogy', see Whalen, *Irish Republican Prison Writing*, pp. 60–8.
9 Susan Stewart, 'Notes on Distressed Genres', in *Crimes of Writing: Problems in the Containment of Representation* (Durham, NC: Duke University Press, 1994), pp. 67–8.
10 Elaine Scarry, *The Body in Pain: The Making and Unmaking of the World* (Oxford University Press, 1985), p. 45.
11 Benjamin, *Charles Baudelaire*, p. 40.
12 Ibid., p. 45.
13 On the 'scopic drive' and the city, see Michel de Certeau, 'Walking in the City', in *The Practice of Everyday Life*, trans. Steven Rendall (Berkeley: University of California Press, 1988), p. 92.
14 It is this tendency of Baudelaire to act as if he were masked that Sartre emphasizes in his critical (in every sense) biography. See Jean-Paul Sartre, *Baudelaire*, trans. Martin Turnell (London: Horizon, 1949), pp. 141–7.

15 Benjamin, *Charles Baudelaire*, p. 87. For the *fort-da*, see Freud, 'Beyond the Pleasure Principle' (1920) in *The Standard Edition of the Complete Psychological Works*, 24 vols., trans. James Strachey (London: The Hogarth Press, 1955), vol. 18, pp. 14–16.
16 Benjamin, *Charles Baudelaire*, p. 49; my emphasis.
17 On the rich connections between mourning and photography itself, see Eduardo Cadava, *Words of Light: Theses on the Photography of History* (Princeton University Press, 1997), pp. 7–26. Elissa Marder, *Dead Time: Temporal Disorders in the Wake of Modernity (Baudelaire and Flaubert)* (Stanford University Press, 2001), pp. 77–87, discusses Benjamin's reading of 'A Une Passante' and specifically its relation to the photograph. Her discussion of the final tercet unaccountably stops short of the final line.
18 Benjamin, *Charles Baudelaire*, p. 47. His notes on 'the new system of sequential numbering of houses' and other innovations in urban planning and surveillance can be found in Walter Benjamin, 'Convolute P: "The Streets of Paris"', in *The Arcades Project*, ed. Rolf Tiedemann, trans. Howard Eiland and Kevin McLaughlin (Cambridge, MA: Belknap Press, 1999), pp. 520 and 516–26.
19 Benjamin, *Arcades Project*, p. 11.
20 On Haussmannization and its establishment of an emergency regime, see Benjamin, *Arcades Project*, p. 12.
21 Quoted in Feldman, *Formations of Violence*, p. 124. The same former prisoner also emphasizes here the serial arrangement of the holding cells.
22 Benjamin, *Arcades Project*, M.3,1 and M.3a5, pp. 421 and 423.
23 Ibid., M.3a4, p. 423.
24 On the metaphor of the fencer, see Benjamin, *Charles Baudelaire*, pp. 68–9 and 117–20.
25 My thanks to Talia Pauwels Lloyd for helping me clarify this insight.
26 Feldman, *Formations of Violence*, pp. 138–45, for an account of such 'inversions of violence'. Frantz Fanon, *The Wretched of the Earth*, trans. Constance Farrington (New York: Grove Press, 1968), pp. 268–89, provides striking case history on the frustration and even exhaustion of the torturer.
27 The rhyme pattern that is left implicit in this stanza is played out in full in the third section of the ballad where the breaker's yard has become that of the H-Blocks themselves:

> So sleep we 'pon each day of pain
> That screams within its w**ake**,
> And screeches at each shattered mind
> How much dare you to t**ake**?
> How much, how much, for pain is such
> That even heroes qu**ake**?

28 Feldman, *Formations of Violence*, p. 115.
29 See Anonymous, 'The Night before Larry Was Stretched', in Brendan Kennelly, ed., *The Penguin Book of Irish Verse* (Harmondsworth: Penguin, 1970), pp. 181–3; Dominic Behan, 'The Auld Triangle', sung in Brendan Behan,

The Quare Fellow (1954), in Terence Brown, 'The Counter-Revival, 1930–60: Drama', in Seamus Deane, ed., *The Field Day Anthology of Irish Writing* (Derry: Field Day, 1991), p. 201; Peter Linebaugh, *The London Hanged: Crime and Civil Society in the Eighteenth Century* (London: Penguin, 1993), p. 324.

30 Denis O'Hearn, *Nothing But an Unfinished Song: Bobby Sands, The Irish Hunger Striker Who Ignited a Generation* (New York: Nation Books, 2006), p. 265. Sean O'Brien, *Irish Prison Writing and the Victorian Penitentiary*, PhD dissertation, University of Notre Dame, 2008, pp. 71–3, discusses Wilde's close relation to Michael Davitt, whom he asked to write an introduction to the ballad on account of the common experience of the poet and the Land League activist with the British penal system.

31 O'Brien comments on the availability of the metaphor of the sonnet as prison in William Wordsworth, 'Nuns Fret Not at Their Convent's Narrow Room': O'Brien, *Irish Prison Writing*, p. 72. He also mentions Wilde's knowledge of William Scawen Blount's sonnet cycle, *In Vinculis*, written on his own experience in jail for Land League activity (p. 73). On the individuating function of the sonnet that is bound up with the very history of the form, see Paul Oppenheimer, *The Birth of the Modern Mind: Self, Consciousness, and the Invention of the Sonnet* (Oxford University Press, 1989), p. 3.

32 Oscar Wilde, 'The Ballad of Reading Gaol', pt. 3, in *The Works of Oscar Wilde* (Leicester: Blitz Editions, 1990), pp. 826–7.

33 Feldman, *Formations of Violence*, pp. 89 and 94.

34 On the forms of the *aisling* and its English versions, see Laura O'Connor, *Haunted English: The Celtic Fringe, the British Empire, and Deanglicization* (Baltimore, MD: Johns Hopkins University Press, 2006), p. 23.

35 Ibid., p. 18.

36 Ackroyd *et al.*, *The Technology of Political Control*, p. 46.

37 The fullest account of the treatment of these internees and of its colonial genealogy is given by John McGuffin, *The Guinea Pigs* (Harmondsworth: Penguin, 1974).

38 Tim Pat Coogan, *The Troubles: Ireland's Ordeal 1966–1996 and the Search for Peace* (Boulder, CO: Roberts Rinehart, 1996), p. 126. For a similar account, see J. Bowyer Bell, *The Irish Troubles: A Generation of Violence, 1967–1992* (New York: St. Martin's Press, 1993), p. 226.

39 Liz Curtis, *Ireland: The Propaganda War – The Media and the 'Battle for Hearts and Minds'* (London: Pluto Press, 1984), pp. 52–3. Sands relates a version of these treatments in 'The Crime of Castlereagh', though he was never consistently subjected to the full application that we might call 'sensory deprivation/over-stimulation'. He was in time responsible for debriefing interrogatees in jail, building a considerable intimacy with depth-interrogation procedures and their physical and mental effects on the victims. O'Hearn, *Nothing But an Unfinished Song*, p. 146.

40 Alfred W. McCoy, *A Question of Torture: CIA Interrogation, from the Cold War to the War on Terror* (New York: Henry Holt, 2006), p. 8. The disaggregation of these combined techniques into separate forms of 'rough' treatment

remains a principal means by which the systematic use of torture in the present era has been 'hidden in plain sight'.
41 Coogan, *The Troubles*, pp. 126–7. Coogan cites *The Sunday Times* special report, reprinted as The London Sunday Times Insight Team, *Northern Ireland: A Report on the Conflict* (New York: Random House, 1972), p. 291. For a more technical account of the effects of the treatment on these men, see T. Shallice, 'The Ulster Depth Interrogation Techniques and Their Relation to Sensory Deprivation Research', *Cognition* 1.4 (1972), p. 398.
42 Coogan, *The Troubles*, p. 125. See also McGuffin, *The Guinea Pigs*, pp. 23–35.
43 Shallice, 'The Ulster Depth Interrogation Techniques', pp. 386–7.
44 Darius M. Rejali, *Torture and Modernity: Self, Society, and State in Modern Iran* (Boulder, CO: Westview Press, 1994), p. 13.
45 Cited from *KUBARK Counterintelligence Interrogation* (1963), p. 83, posted at www2.gwu.edu/~nsarchiv/NSAEBB/NSAEBB27/01-01.htm, 21 March 2009. A highly edited version of this manual can be found at www2.gwu.edu/~nsarchiv/NSAEBB/NSAEBB27/02-11.htm. The document was declassified in January 1997 in response to a 1994 Freedom of Information Act request by the *Baltimore Sun*, and the *Sun*'s threat of a lawsuit under FOIA. Corrections are done in handwriting on typescript. See Gary Cohn *et al.*, 'Torture Was Taught by CIA; Declassified Manual Details the Methods Used in Honduras; Agency Denials Refuted', *Baltimore Sun*, 27 January 1997. For L.E. Hinkle's role in furnishing information on sensory deprivation through US government-sponsored psychological research, see McCoy, *A Question of Torture*, pp. 41–2, and on the KUBARK manual, pp. 50–3. McCoy also regards the British methods used in Northern Ireland as 'a textbook example' of the methods extended in Abu Ghraib and Baghram (pp. 58–9).
46 Scarry, *The Body in Pain*, p. 48.
47 Ibid., p. 47.
48 *KUBARK Counterintelligence Interrogation*, p. 90.
49 Rejali, *Torture and Modernity*, pp. 75–6.
50 Ibid., p. 14.
51 Feldman, *Formations of Violence*, pp. 87–8. Both the numbers and the effects of such raids on domestic space, producing both fear and resistance, uncannily recall those of the mid- to late-nineteenth-century evictions. Tim P. O'Neill estimates that some '19,660 houses or 983 per year were levelled between 1849 and 1868', in 'Famine Evictions', in Carla King, ed., *Famine, Land and Culture in Ireland* (University College Dublin Press, 2000), p. 56.
52 Robin Evelegh, *Peace Keeping in a Democratic Society: The Lessons of Northern Ireland* (London: C. Hurst, 1978), p. 120.
53 Cited in Curtis, *Propaganda War*, p. 55.
54 Ackroyd *et al.*, *The Technology of Political Control*. The literature on the 'strong' or 'coercive' state and on the role of Northern Ireland in its emergence is not extensive, but it is remarkably consistent. In addition to Ackroyd

et al., similar formulations can be found in Paddy Hillyard and Janie Percy-Smith, *The Coercive State* (London and New York: Pinter Publishers, 1988) and in Ruane and Todd, *The Dynamics of Conflict*, ch. 8. Evelegh's prescriptions in *Peace Keeping in a Democratic Society* for massive surveillance and data collection, including finger-printing, photographing, the issue of identity cards and the mining of private data by the security forces, are forceful reminders of the ways in which the experience of 'peace keeping' in Northern Ireland laid out the security agenda that is still being implemented. Laura K. Donoghue's invaluable *Counter-terrorist Law and Emergency Powers in the United Kingdom, 1922–2000* (Dublin and Portland, OR: Irish Academic Press, 2001) gives a detailed account of the transfer of Emergency Powers between Ireland and Britain, going back to the Defence of the Realm Act (DORA) and continuing down to the Prevention of Terrorism Acts of the last few decades.
55 Donoghue, *Counter-terrorist Law*, pp. 307–8.
56 Evelegh, *Peace Keeping in a Democratic Society*, p. 117. He refers to Section 2(4): 'If any person does an act of such a nature as to be calculated to be prejudicial to the preservation of the peace or maintenance of order in Northern Ireland and not specially provided for in the regulations, he shall be deemed guilty of an offence against the regulations.'
57 Bowyer Bell, *The Irish Troubles*, p. 220.
58 Donoghue, *Counter-terrorist Law*, p. xxii.
59 Ibid., pp. 321–2.
60 On the colonial state of exception, see Nasser Hussain, *The Jurisprudence of Emergency: Colonialism and the Rule of Law* (Ann Arbor: University of Michigan Press, 2003). His argument regarding the transfer of colonial emergency powers to the metropolis is interestingly borne out by Donoghue's *Counter-terrorist Law*. C.L.R. James offers one of the most harrowing accounts of the routine nature of torture and punishment in the slave colony in *The Black Jacobins: Toussaint L'Ouverture and the San Domingo Revolution*, 2nd rev. edn (New York: Vintage, 1989), pp. 11–14.
61 Walter Benjamin, 'Theses on the Philosophy of History', in *Illuminations: Essays and Reflections*, ed. Hannah Arendt, trans. Harry Zohn (New York: Schocken Books, 1969), p. 257.
62 The most comprehensive work on the history of the use of torture by liberal democracies is Darius M. Rejali, *Torture and Democracy* (Princeton University Press, 2007).
63 Elaine Scarry, 'Five Errors in the Reasoning of Alan Dershowitz', in Sanford Levinson, ed., *Torture: A Collection* (Oxford University Press, 2004), p. 282.
64 Alan Dershowitz, 'Tortured Reasoning', in Levinson, *Torture*, p. 259.
65 Cited in Sanford Levinson, 'Contemplating Torture: An Introduction', in Levinson, *Torture*, p. 24.
66 Richard A. Posner, 'Torture, Terrorism, and Interrogation', in Levinson, *Torture*, p. 292.

67 Michael Levin, 'Torture and Other Extreme Measures Taken for the General Good: Further Reflections on a Philosophical Problem', in Peter Suedfeld, ed., *Psychology and Torture* (New York: Hemisphere, 1990), p. 290.
68 Association for the Prevention of Torture, *Defusing the Ticking Bomb Scenario: Why We Must Say No to Torture, Always* (Geneva: Association for the Prevention of Torture, 2007), p. 2. For a full philosophical dismantling of the 'sheer fantasy' of the 'ticking bomb scenario', see Bob Brecher's thorough *Torture and the Ticking Bomb* (Oxford: Blackwell, 2007).
69 Fionnuala Ní Aoláin, 'The European Convention on Human Rights and Its Prohibition on Torture', in Levinson, *Torture*, p. 215.
70 Ariel Dorfman, 'Foreword: The Tyranny of Terror – Is Torture Inevitable in Our Century and Beyond?', in Levinson, *Torture*, p. 8.
71 Scarry, *The Body in Pain*, p. 56.
72 Ní Aoláin, 'The European Convention on Human Rights', p. 215.
73 Colin Dayan, *The Story of Cruel and Unusual* (Cambridge, MA: MIT Press, 2007), pp. 27–33.
74 Immanuel Kant, *Critique of Practical Reason*, trans. T.K. Abbott (Amherst, NY: Prometheus Books, 1996), p. 109.
75 See Brecher, *Torture and the Ticking Bomb*, p. 13, and Levin, 'Torture and Other Extreme Measures', pp. 93–8, for the Kantian basis of the categorical prohibition on torture.
76 On the contrary claims of the Kantian and the Burkean 'physiological' aesthetic, see my essay 'The Pathological Sublime: Pleasure and Pain in the Colonial Context', in Daniel Carey and Lynn Festa, eds., *The Postcolonial Enlightenment* (Oxford University Press, 2009), pp. 71–102.
77 Naomi Klein, *The Shock Doctrine: The Rise of Disaster Capitalism* (New York: Picador, 2007), offers a way of understanding the relation between the infliction of trauma through torture and the economic effects of shock in the interests of accumulation, a connection which powerfully generalizes the scenario of torture we are concerned with here.
78 Henry Shue, 'Torture', in Levinson, *Torture*, p. 53.
79 Scarry, *The Body in Pain*, p. 55.
80 Denise Ferreira da Silva, *Toward a Global Idea of Race* (Minneapolis: University of Minnesota Press, 2007), p. xxxix.
81 William Godwin, *Enquiry Concerning Political Justice*, ed. Isaac Kramnick (Harmondsworth: Penguin, 1976), p. 183.

6 ON EXTORTED SPEECH: BACK TO *HOW IT IS*

1 See Samuel Beckett, 'Three Dialogues' with Georges Duthuit, in *Disjecta: Miscellaneous Writings and a Dramatic Fragment*, ed. Ruby Cohn (New York: Grove Press, 1984), p. 139. A rare exception to the silence on Beckett's preoccupation with torture and interrogation is Tyrus Miller, 'Beckett's Political Technology: Expression, Confession, and Torture in the Later Drama', *Samuel Beckett Today/Aujourd'hui* 9 (2000), pp. 255–78.

2 Samuel Beckett, 'As the Story Was Told', in *As the Story Was Told: Uncollected and Late Prose* (London: Calder, 1990), pp. 103–7.
3 Beckett, 'Recent Irish Poetry', in *Disjecta*, p. 70.
4 Beckett, 'Saint-Lô' (1946), *Collected Poems in English and French* (New York: Grove Press, 1977), p. 32. On the evacuation of political concerns from evaluations of Beckett's work, see Peter Boxall, 'Introduction to "Beckett/Aesthetics/Politics"', special issue of *Samuel Beckett Today/Aujourd'hui* 9 (2000), p. 208. Miller, 'Beckett's Political Technology', p. 258, notes how critics have tended to 'make the political implications of the work all but disappear under the guise of artistic or existential concerns'.
5 Rita Maran, *Torture: The Role of Ideology in the French–Algerian War* (New York: Praeger, 1989), p. 145. The summary of the French intellectual debates on torture that follows is derived from ch. 4 of this work. One cannot help being struck by how monotonously repetitive is the discourse on the 'exceptional' use of torture, here in the context of the *'mission civilatrice'*. See also Marnia Lazreg, *Torture and the Twilight of Empire: From Algiers to Baghdad* (Princeton University Press, 2008), chs. 9 and 10, especially.
6 See James Knowlson, *Damned to Fame: A Life of Samuel Beckett* (New York: Simon & Schuster, 1996), pp. 440–2.
7 For a detailed account of Beckett's role in the French Resistance, see ibid., pp. 278–87.
8 Anthony Cronin, *Samuel Beckett: The Last Modernist* (New York: HarperCollins, 1997), pp. 252–3, 261, mentions several of these relationships, but does not engage with their possible significance beyond the tenor of Dublin bohemian life of the time. Ernie O'Malley's *Letters and Papers (1924–1957)*, ed. Cormac K.H. O'Malley and Nicholas Allen (Dublin: Lilliput Press, forthcoming), contains materials from the mid 1950s describing a visit to Beckett in Paris. Beckett and O'Malley would have shared a bond in their common friendships with MacGreevy and Jack B. Yeats. Nicholas Allen's *Modernism, Ireland and Civil War* (Cambridge University Press, 2009) is a pioneering study of the central place of Republicanism and its relation to Irish experimental modernism in the post-colonial decades that is very suggestive for rethinking Beckett's relation to the political and cultural milieu of the time. Miller, 'Beckett's Political Technology', p. 257, mentions almost all of these 'referential horizon[s] for his work', and I follow his lead in asking 'what does this figural system suggest about the political significance of Beckett's later work?'
9 See Beckett's description of the Van Veldes' work in 'Peintres de l'Empêchement', in *Disjecta*, pp. 136–7: 'cell painted on the stone of the cell, art of incarceration.' My translation.
10 Beckett, 'MacGreevy on Yeats', in *Disjecta*, p. 97.
11 It is important to stress that the convergence of repressive technologies that shape the strong or coercive state are not, as Ackroyd *et al.* point out, identical with a revival of fascism, even if that state draws from elements of fascist states' technologies. They constitute something new. Just as in aesthetic

terms, Beckett seems to offer a bridge between high modernism and postmodernism, so we might say that the forms of subjectivity he tracks map the psychic transition from the subject of fascism, as a state form of political modernism, to that of the new mode of strong state. See Carol Ackroyd et al., *The Technology of Political Control*, 2nd rev. edn (London: Pluto, 1980), ch. 9.

12 Even Pascale Casanova, who argues in her book, *Samuel Beckett: Anatomy of a Literary Revolution* (London: Verso, 2006), that Beckett inaugurates an 'abstract literature', denouncing 'the taken-for-granted realist assumptions on which the whole literary edifice is based' and heading 'towards a working drawing of abstraction or darkness' (p. 26), fails to engage with *How It Is*, even if it is surely a principal threshold at which such an inauguration might be seen to take place. For valuable attempts to describe the 'organizing principles' and the linguistic systems of the text respectively, see Leslie Hill, *Beckett's Fiction: In Different Words* (Cambridge University Press, 1990), pp. 134–40; Eyal Amiran, *Wandering and Home: Beckett's Metaphysical Narrative* (University Park: Pennsylvania State University, 2006), pp. 162–8, especially; and Ann Banfield, 'Beckett's Tattered Syntax', *Representations* 84 (Autumn 2003), pp. 6–29.

13 Samuel Beckett, *How It Is* (London: Calder and Boyars, 1964), p. 7. Page numbers given in the text hereafter.

14 I say 'he' and 'his' only because the narrator, who shares the name of Pim to whom he refers as 'he', occasionally refers to a 'life above' in which he appears to play a conventional male role. No gender markers, anatomical or conventional, other than the pronoun are evident for any of the personae in the text.

15 These names – and the serial form of their appearance – recur in *What Where* in the forms Bam, Bem, Bim and Bom. Samuel Beckett, *The Collected Shorter Plays* (New York: Grove Weidenfeld, 1984), pp. 307–16. Evelyne Grossman, *La Défiguration: Artaud – Beckett – Michaux* (Paris: Editions de Minuit, 2004), p. 59, claims that the play was inspired by the fate of prisoners tortured in Turkey. I am indebted to Ann Banfield for this reference.

16 I have in mind in particular the discussion of the problem of the 'unconditioned' and of 'infinite regress and series' in Section One of 'The Antinomy of Pure Reason' and the 'Fourth Conflict of the Transcendental Ideas', whose thesis is that 'There belongs to this world, either as its part or as its cause, a being that it absolutely necessary'. Kant is seeking to resolve the old theological conundrum of seeking to prove the existence of God through infinite regress: Immanuel Kant, *Critique of Pure Reason*, trans. Norman Kemp Smith (London: Macmillan, 1978), pp. 391–2 and 415–35. The Irishman J.W. Dunne's *The Serial Universe* (London: Faber & Faber, 1934), like his earlier *An Experiment with Time* (New York: Macmillan, 1927), is a popular attempt to prove the existence of God from the impossibility of an infinite series of observers. His work was well-known in the 1930s and an influence on Aldous Huxley and J.B. Priestley, among others.

17 Hill, *Beckett's Fiction*, pp. 83–5, discusses the suspension of time in Beckett's work and invokes the eponymous Molloy of the first novel of his *Trilogy*, who refers to what he calls '*le présent mythologique*'. Thanks to Eyal Amiran for pointing me to this discussion.
18 Ibid., p. 136.
19 Beckett, 'Dante ... Bruno . Vico .. Joyce', in *Disjecta*, p. 19.
20 The seriality of *How It Is*, which embraces both chains of objects and chains of beings, strikingly resembles the 'social series', defined by Iris Marion Young, after Jean-Paul Sartre, as a unity that 'derives from the way individuals pursue their own individual ends in respect to the same objects conditioned by a continuous material environment'. See Iris Marion Young, 'Gender as Seriality', in *Intersecting Voices: Dilemmas of Gender, Political Philosophy, and Policy* (Princeton University Press, 1997), pp. 24–5.
21 In this respect, 'sack' belongs with those primal words in *Molloy*, 'ma' and 'da', which are each negated by the addition of a single final consonant: Ma-g and Da-n. See Banfield's discussion of this operation in 'Beckett's Tattered Syntax', pp. 9–10. As with them, in the sack, breath, speech, 'is reduced to an excrement'.
22 On the 'illuminative mimicry of the *Aha-Erlebnis*', see Jacques Lacan, 'The Mirror Stage as Formative of the *I* Function as Revealed in Psychoanalytic Experience', in *Écrits: A Selection*, trans. Bruce Fink (New York: Norton, 2004), p. 3.
23 'To restore silence is the role of objects': Samuel Beckett, *Molloy*, in *Molloy, Malone Dies, The Unnamable* (London: Calder and Boyars, 1973), pp. 13–14.
24 It may be evident that my emphasis on the seriality of the text is informed by, though not identical with, that developed by Gilles Deleuze in *Logique du Sens*, where the series he explores in sophistic logic are the series of events and the series of meanings, and, in Lewis Carroll – more germane to the present context – those of eating and speaking. See Gilles Deleuze, *Logique du Sens* (Paris: Editions de Minuit, 1977), throughout, but especially the chapters 'Sixième série sur la mise en séries' and 'Septième série des mots ésotériques'. The separation of the subject into distinct zones and functions – hearing/speaking, words/things, image/voice/thing, etc. – seems to anticipate the disintegration of the 'character' into distinct functions in the later plays, or, as Miller puts it, 'Beckett's Political Technology', p. 262, 'his disaggregation of organically linked, coordinated elements such as voice and body, gesture and discourse, words and music, and so on, into separate, dramatically embodied agencies'.
25 Beckett, 'The Unnamable', in *Molloy, Malone Dies, The Unnamable*, p. 390.
26 I am not here attempting to reduce the universe of *How It Is* to an exemplum of object-relations theory in the technical psychoanalytic sense. Despite his brief period of analysis with Wilfred Bion (which in any case pre-dated the latter's full engagement with object-relations psychoanalysis), Beckett's play with the subject–object series seems more driven by philosophical than psychoanalytical motives.

27 Walter Benjamin, *The Arcades Project*, ed. Rolf Tiedemann, trans. Howard Eiland and Kevin McLaughlin (Cambridge, MA: Belknap Press, 1999), p. 426. Benjamin is citing Marcel Jouhandeau, *Images de Paris* (1934). The relation of this image to Beckett's contemporaneous play, *Happy Days* (1961), is remarkable.
28 Immanuel Kant, *Critique of Practical Reason*, trans. T.K. Abbott (Amherst, NY: Prometheus Books, 1996), p. 16. Cited in the text hereafter as *CPR*.
29 Jacques Lacan, 'Kant avec Sade', in *Ecrits II* (Paris: Editions du Seuil, 1971), p. 120: 'Dans la pratique, il soumettrait le sujet au même enchaînement phénoménal qui détermine ses objets' (my translation).
30 See David Lloyd, 'Race under Representation', *Oxford Literary Review* 13.1–2 (1991), p. 70.
31 Lacan, 'Kant avec Sade', p. 125.
32 Ibid., p. 127.
33 Ibid. (my translation). Lacan is not alone in posing Sade as the 'truth' of Kant. He was anticipated by Max Horkheimer and T.W. Adorno in their essay 'Juliette or Enlightenment and Morality', in *Dialectic of Enlightenment*, trans. John Cumming (New York: Continuum, 1972), pp. 81–119. For commentary on both essays, see Rebecca Comay, 'Adorno Avec Sade', *differences* 17.1 (2006), pp. 6–19.
34 Elaine Scarry, *The Body in Pain: The Making and Unmaking of the World* (Oxford University Press, 1985), p. 48.
35 Samuel Beckett, 'The Capital of the Ruins', in *As the Story Was Told*, p. 28. This brief essay was intended as a broadcast on Irish radio, Radio Éireann, in 1946, following Beckett's return from work as an orderly at the Irish hospital in war-shattered St-Lô. It is another instance of the ways in which his own historical experience entered into his artistic work, stimulating 'the terms in which our condition is to be thought again' (ibid.).
36 Kant, *Critique of Practical Reason*, p. 33.
37 Ibid., p. 41; cf. pp. 83–4.
38 For some elaboration of this system of representation, see my essay 'Representation's Coup' (forthcoming) and David Lloyd and Paul Thomas, *Culture and the State* (London: Routledge, 1998). See also Young, 'Gender as Seriality', p. 24: 'Individuals in the series are fungible; while not identical, from the point of view of the social practices and objects that generate the series, the individuals could be in one another's place.'
39 Lacan, 'Kant avec Sade', p. 122.
40 For this formula of the end of therapy, see Sigmund Freud, 'Analysis Terminable and Interminable' (1937) in *The Standard Edition of the Complete Psychological Works*, trans. James Strachey, 24 vols. (London: The Hogarth Press, 1955), vol. 23, pp. 211–54.
41 The 'few figures to wind up' may bring to mind Kant's dismissive reference to the moral conduct of the empirical subject, motivated by fear or desire, as 'mere mechanism, in which, as in a puppet show, everything would *gesticulate* well, but there would be no *life* in the figures' (*CPR*, p. 176). As he puts

it elsewhere, 'Man would be a marionette or an automaton … prepared and wound up by the Supreme Artist' (*CPR*, pp. 123–4).
42 'Horizontal comradeship' is Benedict Anderson's phrase for the national fraternity or community in *Imagined Communities: Reflections on the Origin and Spread of Nationalism*, rev. edn (London: Verso, 2006), p. 7.
43 Herbert Marcuse, 'Some Social Implications of Modern Technology', in Andrew Arato and Eike Gebhardt, eds., *The Essential Frankfurt School Reader* (New York: Urizen Books, 1978), pp. 161–2.
44 George W. Bush, 'Introduction' to US National Security Council, *The National Security Strategy of the United States of America*, September 2002, cited in Stephen Zunes, 'The United States: Belligerent Hegemon', in Rick Fawn and Raymond Hinnebusch, eds., *The Iraq War: Causes and Consequences* (Boulder, CO: Lynne Rienner, 2006), p. 26.
45 See Max Horkheimer, 'The End of Reason', in Arato and Gebhardt, *The Essential Frankfurt School Reader*, pp. 26–48, for an all too prescient analysis of the post-enlightenment convergence of critical and instrumental reason.
46 Theodor W. Adorno, 'Letter to Walter Benjamin, 18 March 1936', in Theodor W. Adorno and Walter Benjamin, *The Complete Correspondence, 1928–1940*, ed. Henri Lonitz, trans. Nicholas Walker (Cambridge, MA: Harvard University Press, 1999), p. 131.

Bibliography

Aalen, F.H.A., Kevin Whelan and Matthew Stout, eds., *Atlas of the Irish Rural Landscape*, (Cork University Press, 1997).
Ackroyd, Carol, Karen Margolis, Jonathan Rosenhead and Tim Shallice. *The Technology of Political Control*, 2nd rev. edn (London: Pluto, 1980).
Adams, Gerry. *Cage Eleven: Writings from Prison* (Boulder, CO: Roberts Rinehart, 1997).
Adams, J.R.R. 'Swine-Tax and Eat-Him-All-Magee: The Hedge Schools and Popular Education in Ireland', in J.S. Donnelly, Jr and Kerby A. Miller, eds., *Irish Popular Culture, 1650–1850* (Dublin: Irish Academic Press, 1998), pp. 97–117.
Adorno, Theodor W. and Walter Benjamin. *The Complete Correspondence, 1928–1940*, ed. Henri Lonitz, trans. Nicholas Walker (Cambridge, MA: Harvard University Press, 1999).
Agamben, Giorgio. *Homo Sacer: Sovereign Power and Bare Life*, trans. Daniel Heller-Roazen (Stanford University Press, 1998).
 State of Exception, trans. Kevin Attell (University of Chicago Press, 2005).
Aggeler, William. *Charles Baudelaire's The Flowers of Evil* (Fresno, CA: Academy Library Guild, 1954).
Aisenberg, Andrew. *Contagion: Disease, Government, and the 'Social Question' in Nineteenth-Century France* (Stanford University Press, 1999).
Akenson, Donald H. *The Irish Education Experiment: The National System of Education in the Nineteenth Century* (London: Routledge & Kegan Paul, 1970).
Allen, Nicholas. *Modernism, Ireland and Civil War* (Cambridge University Press, 2009).
Althusser, Louis. 'Ideology and Ideological State Apparatuses', in *Lenin and Philosophy and Other Essays*, trans. Ben Brewster (New York: Monthly Review Press, 1971), pp. 127–86.
Amiran, Eyal. *Wandering and Home: Beckett's Metaphysical Narrative* (University Park, PA: Pennsylvania State University, 2006).
Anderson, Benedict. *Imagined Communities: Reflections on the Origin and Spread of Nationalism*, rev. edn (London: Verso, 2006).

Aoláin, Fionnuala Ní. 'The European Convention on Human Rights and its Prohibition on Torture', in Sanford Levinson, ed., *Torture: A Collection* (Oxford University Press, 2004), pp. 213–28.
Arato, Andrew and Eike Gebhardt, eds., *The Essential Frankfurt School Reader* (New York: Urizen Books, 1978).
Aretxaga, Begoña. *Shattering Silence: Women, Nationalism and Political Subjectivity in Northern Ireland* (Princeton University Press, 1997).
Arnold, Matthew. 'On the Study of Celtic Literature', in *Lectures and Essays in Criticism*, ed. R.H. Super, vol. III of *The Complete Prose Works of Matthew Arnold*, 7 vols. (Ann Arbor, MI: University of Michigan Press, 1962), pp. 291–395.
Association for the Prevention of Torture. *Defusing the Ticking Bomb Scenario: Why We Must Say No to Torture, Always* (Geneva: Association for the Prevention of Torture, 2007).
Banfield, Ann. 'Beckett's Tattered Syntax', *Representations* 84 (Autumn 2003), pp. 6–29.
Baudelaire, Charles. 'A Une Passante', in *Les Fleurs du Mal* (Paris: Editions Gallimard, 1972).
Beckett, Samuel. *As the Story Was Told: Uncollected and Late Prose* (London: Calder, 1990).
  The Collected Shorter Plays (New York: Grove Weidenfeld, 1984).
  Disjecta: Miscellaneous Writings and a Dramatic Fragment, ed. Ruby Cohn (New York: Grove Press, 1984).
  Collected Poems in English and French (New York: Grove Press, 1977).
  Molloy, Malone Dies, The Unnamable (London: Calder and Boyars, 1973).
  How It Is (London: Calder and Boyars, 1964).
Bell, J. Bowyer. *The Irish Troubles: A Generation of Violence, 1967–1992* (New York: St. Martin's Press, 1993).
Benjamin, Walter. *The Arcades Project*, ed. Rolf Tiedemann, trans. Howard Eiland and Kevin McLaughlin (Cambridge, MA: Belknap Press, 1999).
  The Origin of German Tragic Drama, trans. John Osborne, intro. George Steiner (London: Verso, 1985).
  Charles Baudelaire: A Lyric Poet in the Era of High Capitalism, trans. Harry Zohn (London: Verso, 1983).
  'Theses on the Philosophy of History', in *Illuminations: Essays and Reflections*, ed. Hannah Arendt, trans. Harry Zohn (New York: Schocken, 1969), pp. 253–64.
Bennett, Ronan. 'What the Kid Knows Now', in Danny Morrison, ed., *Hunger Strike: Reflections on the 1981 Hunger Strike* (Dingle: Brandon, 2006), pp. 42–7.
Bentham, Jeremy. *Panopticon: Or, The Inspection House – The Panopticon Writings*, ed. Miran Bozovic (London: Verso, 1995).
Beresford, David. *Ten Men Dead: The Story of the 1981 Irish Hunger Strike* (New York: Atlantic Monthly Press, 1987).

Bhabha, Homi. *The Location of Culture* (New York: Routledge, 1994).
Bigelow, Gordon. *Fiction, Famine, and the Rise of Economics in Victorian Britain and Ireland* (Cambridge University Press, 2003).
Black, R.D. Collison. *Economic Thought and the Irish Question, 1817–1870* (Cambridge University Press, 1960).
Bourke, Angela. 'Irish Stories of Weather, Time, and Gender: Saint Brigid', in Marilyn Cohen and Nancy J. Curtin, eds., *Reclaiming Gender: Transgressive Identities in Modern Ireland* (New York: St. Martin's Press, 1999), pp. 13–31.
'Performing not Writing', *Graph* 11 (Winter 1991–1992), pp. 28–31.
Boxall, Peter. 'Introduction to "Beckett/Aesthetics/Politics"', special issue of *Samuel Beckett Today/Aujourd'hui* 9 (2000), pp. 207–14.
Boylan, Thomas A. and Timothy P. Foley. *Political Economy and Colonial Ireland: The Propagation and Ideological Function of Economic Discourse in the Nineteenth Century* (London: Routledge, 1992).
Bradley, Anthony and MaryAnn Gialanella Valiulis, eds., *Gender and Sexuality in Modern Ireland* (Amherst: University of Massachusetts Press, 1997).
Brecher, Bob. *Torture and the Ticking Bomb* (Oxford: Blackwell, 2007).
Brennan-Whitmore, W.J. *With the Irish in Frongoch* (Dublin: Talbot Press, 1917).
Butler, Judith. *Gender Trouble: Feminism and the Subversion of Identity* (New York: Routledge, 1990).
Butt, Isaac. *Land Tenure in Ireland: A Plea for the Celtic Race*, 3rd edn (Dublin: John Falconer, 1866).
Buttimer, Neil. 'A Stone on the Cairn: The Great Famine in Later Gaelic Manuscripts', in Chris Morash and Richard Hayes, eds., *'Fearful Realities': New Perspectives on the Famine* (Dublin: Irish Academic Press, 1996), pp. 93–109.
Cadava, Eduardo. *Words of Light: Theses on the Photography of History* (Princeton University Press, 1997).
Cairnes, John Elliott. *Essays in Political Economy* (1873) (New York: August M. Kelley, 1965).
Political Essays (London: Macmillan, 1873).
Campbell, Brian, Laurence McKeown and Felim O'Hagan, eds., *Nor Meekly Serve My Time: The H Block Struggle, 1976–1981* (Belfast: Beyond the Pale, 1998).
Carleton, William. *The Black Prophet: A Tale of Irish Famine* (London: Simms and McIntyre, 1847).
Carlyle, Thomas. 'Chartism', in *Critical and Miscellaneous Essays*, 5 vols., in *The Works of Thomas Carlyle*, 30 vols. (New York: Charles Scribner, 1904), vol. 29, pp. 118–204.
Carpenter, Mary. *Reformatory Prison Discipline, As Developed by the Rt. Hon. Sir William Crofton, in the Irish Convict Prisons* (London: Longmans, Green, Reader and Dyer, 1872).
Carroll, Patrick. *Science, Culture and Modern State Formation* (Berkeley: University of California Press, 2006).

Carroll-Burke, Patrick. *Colonial Discipline: The Making of the Irish Convict System* (Dublin: Four Courts Press, 2000).
Casanova, Pascale. *Samuel Beckett: Anatomy of a Literary Revolution* (London: Verso, 2006).
Central Intelligence Agency. 'Human Resource Exploitation Training Manual', *CIA Training Manual* (1983), in Tom Blanton, 'The CIA in Latin America', *The National Security Archive: Electronic Briefing Books*, 14 March 2000, The George Washington University, 21 March 2009: www2.gwu.edu/~nsarchiv/NSAEBB/NSAEBB27/02-11.htm.
'KUBARK Counterintelligence Interrogation', *CIA Training Manual* (1963), in Tom Blanton, 'The CIA in Latin America', *The National Security Archive: Electronic Briefing Books*, 14 March 2000, The George Washington University, 21 March 2009: www2.gwu.edu/~nsarchiv/NSAEBB/NSAEBB27/01-01.htm.
Certeau, Michel de. *The Practice of Everyday Life*, trans. Steven Rendall (Berkeley: University of California Press, 1988).
Chakrabarty, Dipesh. *Provincializing Europe: Postcolonial Thought and Historical Difference* (Princeton University Press, 2000).
Chatterjee, Partha. 'The Nationalist Resolution of the Woman Question', in Kumkum Sangari and Sudesh Vaid, eds., *Recasting Women: Essays in Colonial History* (New Delhi: Kali for Women, 1989), pp. 232–53.
Nationalism and the Colonial World: A Derivative Discourse? (London: Zed Books, 1986).
Cheng, Vincent J. *Joyce, Race and Empire* (Cambridge University Press, 1995).
Clarkson, L.A. and E. Margaret Crawford. *Feast and Famine: Food and Nutrition in Ireland, 1500–1920* (Oxford University Press, 2001).
Clear, Caitriona. 'The Limits of Female Autonomy: Nuns in Nineteenth-Century Ireland', in Maria Luddy and Cliona Murphy, eds., *Women Surviving: Studies in Irish Women's History in the 19th and 20th Centuries* (Dublin: Poolbeg Press, 1990), pp. 15–50.
Clifford, James. 'On Ethnographic Allegory', in James Clifford and George E. Marcus, eds., *Writing Culture: The Poetics and Politics of Ethnography* (Berkeley and Los Angeles: University of California Press, 1986), pp. 98–121.
Cohen, Marilyn and Nancy J. Curtin, eds., *Reclaiming Gender: Transgressive Identities in Modern Ireland* (New York: St. Martin's Press), 1999.
Cohen, Stanley. 'Prisons and the Future of Control Systems: From Concentration to Dispersal', in Mike Fitzgerald, Paul Halmos, John Muncie and David Zeldin, eds., *Welfare in Action* (London: Routledge & Kegan Paul, 1977), pp. 217–28.
Cohn, Gary, Ginger Thompson and Mark Matthews. 'Torture was Taught by CIA; Declassified Manual Details the Methods Used in Honduras; Agency Denials Refuted', *Baltimore Sun*, 27 January 1997, final edn.
Cole, G.D.H. *Chartist Portraits* (New York: Macmillan, 1965).

Comay, Rebecca. 'Adorno Avec Sade', *differences* 17.1 (2006), pp. 6–19.
Conner, William. *A Letter to the Tenantry of Ireland, Containing an Exposition of the Rackrent System; and Pointing out a Valuation and Perpetuity as Its Only Effectual Remedy* (Dublin: James B. Gilpin, 1850).
— *A Letter to the Right Honourable the Earl of Devon, Chairman of the Land Commission on the Rackrent System of Ireland: Showing Its Cause, Its Evils and Its Remedy* (Dublin: Samuel L. Machen, 1843).
Coogan, Tim Pat. *On the Blanket: The Inside Story of the IRA Prisoners' 'Dirty' Protest* (Boulder, CO: Roberts Rinehart, 1997).
— *The Troubles: Ireland's Ordeal 1966–1996 and the Search for Peace* (Boulder, CO: Roberts Rinehart, 1996).
Corbin, Alain. *The Foul and the Fragrant: Odor and the French Social Imagination* (Cambridge, MA: Harvard University Press, 1986).
Corcoran, Mary S. *Out of Order: The Political Imprisonment of Women in Northern Ireland, 1972–98* (Portland, OR: Willan Publishing, 2006).
Crawford, Colin. 'The Compound System: An Alternative Penal Strategy', *The Howard Journal* 21 (1982), pp. 155–8.
Croker, T. Crofton. *Researches in the South of Ireland, Illustrative of the Scenery, Architectural Remains, and the Manners and Superstitions of the Peasantry* (London: John Murray, 1824).
Cronin, Anthony. *Samuel Beckett: The Last Modernist* (New York: HarperCollins, 1997).
Cullen, L.M. 'Patrons, Teachers and Literacy in Irish: 1700–1850', in Mary Daly and David Dickson, eds., *The Origins of Popular Literacy in Ireland: Language Change and Educational Development 1700–1920* (Department of Modern History, Trinity College Dublin and Department of Modern Irish History, University College Dublin, 1990), pp. 15–44.
Curtis, L.P. *Apes and Angels: The Irishman in Victorian Caricature* (Washington, DC: Smithsonian Institution Press, 1971).
— *Anglo-Saxons and Celts: A Study of Anti-Irish Prejudice in Victorian England* (Conference on British Studies at the University of Bridgeport, 1968).
Curtis, Liz. *Ireland: The Propaganda War – The Media and the 'Battle for Hearts and Minds'* (London: Pluto Press, 1984).
Daly, Mary and David Dickson, eds., *The Origins of Popular Literacy in Ireland: Language Change and Educational Development 1700–1920* (Department of Modern History, Trinity College Dublin and Department of Modern Irish History, University College Dublin, 1990).
da Silva, Denise Ferreira. *Toward a Global Idea of Race* (Minneapolis: University of Minnesota Press, 2007).
Davis, Angela. *Are Prisons Obsolete?* (New York: Free Press, 2003).
Davis, Thomas Osborne. 'The Young Men of Ireland', *The Nation* 15 July (1843), pp. 32.
Dayan, Colin. *The Story of Cruel and Unusual* (Cambridge, MA: MIT Press, 2007).

Dayan, Joan. 'Poe, Persons and Property', in J. Gerald Kennedy and Liliane Weisberg, eds., *Romancing the Shadow: Poe and Race* (Oxford University Press, 2001), pp. 107–26.
Deane, Seamus. *Strange Country: Modernity and Nationhood in Irish Writing since 1790* (Oxford: Clarendon Press, 1997).
  A Short History of Irish Literature (South Bend: University of Notre Dame Press, 1994).
  The Field Day Anthology of Irish Writing (Derry: Field Day, 1991).
  'Civilians and Barbarians', in Field Day Theatre Company, eds., *Ireland's Field Day* (South Bend: University of Notre Dame Press, 1986), pp. 33–42.
de Fréine, Seán. 'The Cultural Consequences of the Great Famine', in Breandán Ó Conaire, ed., *The Famine Lectures/Léachtaí an Ghorta* (Boyle: Comhdhail an Chraoibhín, 1995–1997), pp. 130–52.
Deleuze, Gilles. *Logique du Sens* (Paris: Editions de Minuit, 1977).
Dershowitz, Alan. 'Tortured Reasoning', in Sanford Levinson, ed., *Torture: A Collection* (Oxford University Press, 2004), pp. 257–80.
Dewey, Clive. 'Celtic Agrarian Legislation and the Celtic Revival: Historicist Implications of Gladstone's Irish and Scottish Land Acts, 1870–1886', *Past and Present* 64 (August 1974), pp. 30–70.
Donnelly, James S., Jr. *The Great Irish Potato Famine* (Stroud: Sutton Publishing, 2001).
  '"Irish Property Must Pay for Irish Poverty": British Public Opinion and the Great Irish Famine', in Chris Morash and Richard Hayes, eds., *'Fearful Realities': New Perspectives on the Famine* (Blackrock: Irish Academic Press, 1996), pp. 60–76.
Donnelly, James S., Jr and Kerby A. Miller, eds., *Irish Popular Culture, 1650–1850* (Dublin: Irish Academic Press, 1998).
Donoghue, Laura K. *Counter-Terrorist Law and Emergency Powers in the United Kingdom, 1922–2000* (Dublin and Portland, OR: Irish Academic Press, 2001).
Dorfman, Ariel. 'Foreword: The Tyranny of Terror – Is Torture Inevitable in Our Century and Beyond?', in Sanford Levinson, ed., *Torture: A Collection* (Oxford University Press, 2004), pp. 3–22.
Dorian, Hugh. *The Outer Edge of Ulster: A Memoir of Social Life in Nineteenth-Century Donegal*, ed. Breandán Mac Suibhne and David Dickson (Dublin: Lilliput, 2001).
Dunne, J.W. *The Serial Universe* (London: Faber & Faber, 1934).
  An Experiment with Time (New York: Macmillan, 1927).
Elias, Norbert. *Power and Civility*, vol. II of *The Civilizing Process*, 2 vols. (New York: Pantheon, 1982).
Ellmann, Maud. *The Hunger Artists: Starving, Writing and Imprisonment* (Cambridge, MA: Harvard University Press, 1993).
Engels, Friedrich. *The Condition of the Working Class in England*, ed. Victor Kiernan (Harmondsworth: Penguin, 1987).

Epstein, Joseph. *The Lion of Freedom: Feargus O'Connor and the Chartist Movement, 1832–1842* (London: Croom Helm, 1982).

Escobar, Arturo. *Encountering Development: The Making and Unmaking of the Third World* (Princeton University Press, 1995).

Evans, E. Estyn. *Irish Folk Ways* (London: Routledge & Kegan Paul, 1957).

Irish Heritage: The Landscape, the People and Their Work (Dundalk: Dundalgan Press, 1945).

Evelegh, Robin. *Peace Keeping in a Democratic Society: The Lessons of Northern Ireland* (London: C. Hurst, 1978).

Fanon, Frantz. 'Racism and Culture', in *Toward the African Revolution: Political Essays*, trans. Haakon Chevalier (New York: Grove Press, 1988), pp. 29–44.

Black Skin White Masks, trans. Charles Lam Markmann (London: Pluto, 1986).

The Wretched of the Earth, trans. Constance Farrington (New York: Grove Press, 1968).

Fegan, Melissa. *Literature and the Irish Famine, 1845–1919* (Oxford: Clarendon Press, 2002).

Feldman, Allen. *Formations of Violence: The Narrative of the Body and Political Terror in Northern Ireland* (University of Chicago Press, 1991).

Foucault, Michel. *Discipline and Punish: The Birth of the Prison*, trans. Alan Sheridan, 2nd edn (New York: Vintage, 1995).

Freud, Sigmund. 'Analysis Terminable and Interminable' (1937), in *The Standard Edition of the Complete Psychological Works*, 24 vols., trans. James Strachey (London: The Hogarth Press, 1955), vol. 23, pp. 211–54.

'The Infantile Genital Organization (An Interpolation into the Theory of Sexuality)' (1923), in *The Standard Edition of the Complete Psychological Works*, vol. 19, pp. 139–45.

'Beyond the Pleasure Principle' (1920), in *The Standard Edition of the Complete Psychological Works*, vol. 18, pp. 1–64.

'The "Uncanny"' (1919), in *The Standard Edition of the Complete Psychological Works*, vol. 17, pp. 217–56.

'On Transformations of Instinct as Implied in Anal Erotism' (1917), in *The Standard Edition of the Complete Psychological Works*, vol. 17, pp. 125–33.

Gallagher, Catherine and Stephen Greenblatt. *Practicing the New Historicism* (University of Chicago Press, 2000).

Gallagher, Thomas. *Paddy's Lament: Ireland 1846–1847 – Prelude to Hatred* (New York: Harcourt Brace Jovanovich, 1982).

Geary, Laurence M. '"The Late Disastrous Epidemic": Medical Relief and the Great Famine', in Chris Morash and Richard Hayes, eds., *'Fearful Realities': New Perspectives on the Famine* (Blackrock: Irish Academic Press, 1996), pp. 49–59.

Gibbons, Luke. 'Identity without a Centre: Allegory, History and Irish Nationalism', in *Transformations in Irish Culture* (Cork University Press, 1996), pp. 134–47.

Transformations in Irish Culture (Cork University Press, 1996).
'Race against Time: Racial Discourse and Irish History', *Oxford Literary Review* 13 (1991), pp. 95–117.
Gilroy, Paul. *The Black Atlantic: Modernity and Double Consciousness* (Cambridge, MA: Harvard University Press, 1993).
Godwin, William. *Enquiry Concerning Political Justice*, ed. Isaac Kramnick (Harmondsworth: Penguin, 1976).
Goody, Jack. *The Power of the Written Tradition* (Washington, DC: Smithsonian Institute Press).
Grass, Sean. *The Self in the Cell: Narrating the Victorian Prisoner* (New York: Routledge, 2003).
Gray, Peter. *Famine, Land and Politics: British Government and Irish Society, 1830–1850* (Dublin: Irish Academic Press, 1999).
'Ideology and the Famine', in Cathal Póirtéir, ed., *The Great Irish Famine* (Cork: Mercier, 1995), pp. 86–103.
Grossman, Evelyne. *La Défiguration: Artaud – Becket – Michaux* (Paris: Editions de Minuit, 2004).
Guha, Ranajit. *Elementary Aspects of Peasant Insurgency in Colonial India*, foreword James Scott (Durham, NC: Duke University Press, 1999).
Guinnane, Timothy W. *The Vanishing Irish: Households, Migration, and the Rural Economy in Ireland, 1850–1914* (Princeton University Press, 1997).
Hall, S.C. *Ireland: Its Scenery, Character, and History*, 2 vols. (1841) (Boston: Nicholls and Co., 1911).
Halpin, J., Revd P.P. *The Father Mathew Reader on Temperance and Hygiene* (Dublin: M.H. Gill, 1907).
Harris, Susan Cannon. *Gender and Modern Irish Drama* (Bloomington, IN: Indiana University Press, 2002).
Harvey, David. *The New Imperialism* (Oxford University Press, 2003).
The Condition of Postmodernity: An Enquiry into the Origins of Cultural Change (Oxford: Blackwell, 1990).
Hegel, G.W.F. *Aesthetics: Lectures on Fine Art*, 2 vols., trans. T.M. Knox (Oxford: Clarendon Press, 1975).
Philosophy of Right, trans. T.M. Knox (Oxford University Press, 1967).
Herr, Cheryl. *Joyce's Anatomy of Culture* (Urbana, IL: University of Illinois Press, 1986).
Hill, Leslie. *Beckett's Fiction: In Different Words* (Cambridge University Press, 1990).
Hillyard, Paddy and Janie Percy-Smith. *The Coercive State* (London and New York: Pinter Publishers, 1988).
Hobsbawm, E.J. *Industry and Empire: An Economic History of Britain Since 1750* (London: Weidenfeld & Nicholson, 1968).
Holland, Denis. *The Landlord in Donegal* (Belfast: The Ulsterman, 1856–1863).
Holt, Thomas C. *The Problem of Freedom: Race, Labour, and Politics in Jamaica and Britain, 1832–1938* (Baltimore, MD: Johns Hopkins University Press, 1992).

Horkheimer, Max. 'The End of Reason', in Andrew Arato and Eike Gebhardt, eds., *The Essential Frankfurt School Reader* (New York: Urizen Books, 1978), pp. 26–48.

Horkheimer, Max and T.W. Adorno. *Dialectic of Enlightenment*, trans. John Cumming (New York: Continuum, 1972).

Howes, Marjorie. *Yeats's Nations: Gender, Class and Irishness* (Cambridge University Press, 1996).

Hussain, Nasser. *The Jurisprudence of Emergency: Colonialism and the Rule of Law* (Ann Arbor: University of Michigan Press, 2003).

Hyde, Douglas. 'The Necessity for Deanglicising Ireland', in *Language, Lore and Lyrics: Essays and Lectures*, ed. Breandán O Conaire (Blackrock: Irish Academic Press, 1986), pp. 153–70.

Ignatiev, Noel. *How the Irish Became White* (New York: Routledge, 1995).

James, C.L.R. *The Black Jacobins: Toussaint L'Ouverture and the San Domingo Revolution*, 2nd rev. edn (New York: Vintage, 1989).

Johnston, Norman. *Forms of Constraint: A History of Prison Architecture* (Urbana and Chicago: University of Illinois Press, 2000).

Jones, David. *Chartism and the Chartists* (New York: St. Martin's Press, 1975).

Joyce, James. *Dubliners*, intro. Terence Brown (New York: Penguin, 1992).

Stephen Hero, ed. Theodore Spencer (New York: Granada, 1977).

Letters, ed. Stuart Gilbert (New York: Viking Press, 1966).

Kant, Immanuel. *Critique of Practical Reason*, trans. T.K. Abbott (Amherst, NY: Prometheus Books, 1996).

Critique of Pure Reason, trans. Norman Kemp Smith (London: Macmillan, 1978).

Kavanagh, Patrick. *Collected Poems* (London: Martin O'Brian and O'Keeffe, 1972).

Kearney, Richard. 'Myth and Terror', *The Crane Bag* 2.1–2 (1977), pp. 125–39.

Kearns, Kevin C. *Dublin Pub Life and Lore: An Oral History* (Dublin: Gill and Macmillan, 1996).

Kelleher, Margaret. *The Feminization of Famine: Expressions of the Inexpressible* (Durham, NC: Duke University Press, 1997).

Kennelly, Brendan, ed. *The Penguin Book of Irish Verse* (Harmondsworth: Penguin, 1970).

Kerrigan, Colm. *Father Mathew and the Irish Temperance Movement, 1838–1849* (Cork University Press, 1992).

Kinealy, Christine. *This Great Calamity: The Irish Famine, 1845–52* (Boulder, CO: Roberts Rinehart, 1995).

Klein, Naomi. *The Shock Doctrine: The Rise of Disaster Capitalism* (New York: Picador, 2007).

Knowlson, James. *Damned to Fame: A Life of Samuel Beckett* (New York: Simon & Schuster, 1996).

Lacan, Jacques. 'The Mirror Stage as Formative of the *I* Function, as Revealed in Psychoanalytic Experience', in *Écrits: A Selection*, trans. Bruce Fink (New York: Norton, 2004), pp. 3–9.

'Kant avec Sade', in *Écrits II* (Paris: Editions du Seuil, 1971), pp. 119–48.
Laird, Heather. *Subversive Law in Ireland, 1879–1920: From 'Unwritten Law' to the Dail Courts* (Dublin: Four Courts Press, 2005).
Lalor, James Fintan. 'A New Nation: Proposal for an Agricultural Association between Landowners and Occupiers' (1847), in L. Fogarty, ed., *James Fintan Lalor: Patriot and Political Essayist (1807–1849)* (Dublin: Talbot Press, 1918), pp. 8–10.
Laporte, Dominique. *History of Shit*, trans. Nadia Benabid and Rodolphe El-Khoury (Cambridge, MA: MIT Press, 2000).
Lazreg, Marnia. *Torture and the Twilight of Empire: From Algiers to Baghdad* (Princeton University Press, 2008).
Lee, Joe. 'The Background: Anglo-Irish Relations, 1898–1921', in Cormac K.H. O'Malley and Anne Dolan, eds., *'No Surrender Here!' The Civil War Papers of Ernie O'Malley, 1922–1924* (Dublin: Lilliput, 2007), pp. xi–xxxii.
Lefebvre, Henri. *The Production of Space*, trans. Donald Nicholson-Smith (Oxford: Blackwell, 1991).
Levin, Michael. 'Torture and Other Extreme Measures Taken for the General Good: Further Reflections on a Philosophical Problem', in Peter Suedfeld, ed., *Psychology and Torture* (New York: Hemisphere, 1990), pp. 89–98.
Levinson, Sanford. 'Contemplating Torture: An Introduction', in Sanford Levinson, ed., *Torture: A Collection* (Oxford University Press, 2004), pp. 23–46.
Liddell, H.G. and Robert Scott. *A Greek–English Lexicon* (Oxford: Clarendon Press, 1940).
Linebaugh, Peter. *The London Hanged: Crime and Civil Society in the Eighteenth Century* (London: Penguin, 1993).
Lloyd, David. 'Black Irish, Irish Whiteness and Atlantic State Formation: Some Reflections', in Peter D. O'Neill and David Lloyd, eds., *The Black and Green Atlantic: Crosscurrents of the African and Irish Diasporas* (London and New York: Palgrave, 2009), pp. 3–19.
  'The Pathological Sublime: Pleasure and Pain in the Colonial Context', in Daniel Carey and Lynn Festa, eds., *The Postcolonial Enlightenment* (Oxford University Press, 2009), pp. 71–102.
  Irish Times: Temporalities of Modernity (Dublin: Field Day, 2008).
  Ireland after History (Cork University Press, 1999).
  'The Memory of Hunger', in Tom Hayden, ed., *Irish Hunger* (Boulder, CO: Roberts Rinehart, 1997), pp. 32–47.
  'The Narrative of Representation: Culture, the State and the Canon', in Robert Bledsoe, ed. *Rethinking Germanistik: Canon and Culture* (New York: Peter Lang, 1991), pp. 125–38.
  'Race under Representation', *Oxford Literary Review* 13.1–2 (1991), pp. 62–94.
  Anomalous States: Irish Writing and the Post-Colonial Moment (Durham, NC: Duke University Press, 1993).

Nationalism and Minor Literature: James Clarence Mangan and the Emergence of Irish Cultural Nationalism (Berkeley: University of California Press, 1987).
'Representation's Coup' (forthcoming).
Lloyd, David and Paul Thomas. *Culture and the State* (London: Routledge, 1998).
The London Sunday Times Insight Team. *Northern Ireland: A Report on the Conflict* (New York: Random House, 1972).
Lowe, Donald. *History of Bourgeois Perception* (University of Chicago Press, 1982).
Luddy, Maria. *Women and Philanthropy in Nineteenth-Century Ireland* (Cambridge University Press, 1995).
Luddy, Maria and Cliona Murphy, eds., *Women Surviving: Studies in Irish Women's History in the 19th and 20th Centuries* (Dublin: Poolbeg Press, 1990).
Luxemburg, Rosa. *The Accumulation of Capital*, trans. Agnes Schwarzwild (London and New York: Routledge, 2003).
McCafferty, Nell. 'When all Thought Fails', in Danny Morrison, ed., *Hunger Strike: Reflections on the 1981 Hunger Strike* (Dingle: Brandon, 2006), pp. 77–82.
'It Is My Belief That Armagh Is a Feminist Issue', *Irish Times* 17 June (1980).
McConville, Seán. 'The Victorian Prison: England, 1865–1965', in Norval Morris and David J. Rothman, eds., *The Oxford History of the Prison: The Practice of Punishment in Western Society* (Oxford University Press, 1995), pp. 117–50.
McCoy, Alfred W. *A Question of Torture: CIA Interrogation, from the Cold War to the War on Terror* (New York: Henry Holt, 2006).
McCulloch, J.R. *The Principles of Political Economy*, 4th edn (Edinburgh: Adam and Charles Black, 1849).
McCulloch, Jude and Amanda George. 'Naked Power: Strip-Searching in Women's Prisons', in Phil Scraton and Jude McCulloch, eds., *The Violence of Incarceration* (London: Routledge, 2009), pp. 107–23.
MacCurtain, Margaret. 'Godly Burden: Catholic Sisterhoods in 20th-Century Ireland', in Anthony Bradley and MaryAnn Gialanella Valiulis, eds., *Gender and Sexuality in Modern Ireland* (Amherst: University of Massachusetts Press, 1997), pp. 245–56.
McEvoy, Kieran. *Paramilitary Imprisonment in Northern Ireland: Resistance, Management, and Release* (Oxford University Press, 2001).
McGowen, Randall. 'The Well-Ordered Prison: England 1780–1865', in Norval Morris and David J. Rothman, eds., *The Oxford History of the Prison: The Practice of Punishment in Western Society* (Oxford University Press, 1995), pp. 71–99.
McGuckian, Medbh. *Captain Lavender* (Winston-Salem, NC: Wake Forest University Press, 1995).
McGuffin, John. *The Guinea Pigs* (Harmondsworth: Penguin Books, 1974).

McKeown, Laurence. *Out of Time: Irish Republican Prisoners, Long Kesh, 1972–2000* (Belfast: Beyond the Pale, 2001).
McLean, Stuart. *The Event and Its Terrors: Ireland, Famine, Modernity* (Stanford University Press, 2004).
McManus, Antonia. *The Irish Hedge School and its Books, 1695–1831* (Dublin: Four Courts Press, 2002).
McQueen, Steve, dir. *Hunger* (Blast! Films, 2008).
Mac Suibhne, Breandán and David Dickson. 'Introduction', in Breandán Mac Suibhne and David Dickson, eds., *The Outer Edge of Ulster: A Memoir of Social Life in Nineteenth-Century Donegal* (Dublin: Lilliput, 2001), pp. 1–56.
Mac Suibhne, Breandán and Amy Martin, 'Fenians in the Frame: Photographing Irish Political Prisoners, 1865–68', *Field Day Review* 1 (2005), pp. 101–20.
Malcolm, Elizabeth. 'The Rise of the Pub: A Study in the Disciplining of Popular Culture'. In J.S. Donnelly, Jr and Kerby A. Miller, eds., *Irish Popular Culture, 1650–1850* (Dublin: Irish Academic Press, 1998), pp. 50–77.
  'Ireland Sober, Ireland Free': Drink and Temperance in Nineteenth Century Ireland (Dublin: Gill and Macmillan, 1986).
  'Temperance and Irish Nationalism', in F.S.L. Lyons and R.A.J. Hawkins, eds., *Ireland under the Union: Varieties of Tension* (Oxford: Clarendon Press, 1980), pp. 69–114.
Malthus, Thomas Robert. 'Newenham and Others on the State of Ireland', *Edinburgh Review* 24 (July 1808), pp. 336–55.
Maran, Rita. *Torture: The Role of Ideology in the French–Algerian War* (New York: Praeger, 1989).
Marcuse, Herbert. 'Some Social Implications of Modern Technology', in Andrew Arato and Eike Gebhardt, eds., *The Essential Frankfurt School Reader* (New York: Urizen Books, 1978), pp. 138–62.
Marder, Elissa. *Dead Time: Temporal Disorders in the Wake of Modernity (Baudelaire and Flaubert)* (Stanford University Press, 2001).
Mariátegui, José Carlos. *Seven Interpretive Essays on Peruvian Reality*, trans. Marjory Urquidi (Austin: Texas University Press, 1971).
Martin, Amy E. *Alter-Nations: Nationalisms, Terror and the State in Nineteenth-Century Britain and Ireland* (Columbus: Ohio State University Press, forthcoming).
  'Blood Transfusions: Constructions of Irish Racial Difference, the English Working Class, and Revolutionary Possibility in the Work of Carlyle and Engels', *Victorian Literature and Culture* 32 (2004), pp. 83–102.
Marx, Karl. *Capital: A Critique of Political Economy*, ed. Frederick Engels, trans. Samuel Moore and Edward Aveling, 3 vols. (London: Lawrence and Wishart, 1954).
  The Eighteenth Brumaire of Louis Bonaparte (Moscow: Progress Publishers, 1954).
Mather, F.C., ed. *Chartism and Society: An Anthology of Documents* (London: Bell and Hyman, 1980).

Mayhew, Henry. *London Labour and the London Poor: A Cyclopaedia of the Conditions and Earnings of Those that Will Work, Those that Cannot Work, and Those that Will Not Work*, 4 vols., vol. i: *The London Street-Folk* (1851) (New York: August M. Kelley, 1967).

Meuret, Denis. 'A Political Genealogy of Political Economy', trans. Graham Burchell, *Economy and Society* 17.2 (1988), pp. 225–50.

Mill, John Stuart. *John Stuart Mill on Ireland*, ed. Richard Ned Lebow (Philadelphia: Institute for the Study of Human Issues, 1979).

  Considerations on Representative Government (1861), in *Collected Works*, 21 vols., vol. 19: *Essays on Politics and Society*, 2 vols., ed. J.M. Robson (University of Toronto Press, 1977), vol. 2, pp. 371–577.

  Principles of Political Economy, With Some of Their Applications to Social Philosophy, Books I–II, in *Collected Works*, vol. 2, ed. J.M. Robson (University of Toronto Press, 1965).

  Principles of Political Economy, Books III–V and Appendices, in *Collected Works*, vol. III, ed. J.M. Robson, Intro. V.W. Bladen (University of Toronto Press, 1965).

Miller, Tyrus. 'Beckett's Political Technology: Expression, Confession, and Torture in the Later Drama', *Samuel Beckett Today/Aujourd'hui* 9 (2000), pp. 255–78.

Mokyr, Joel. *Why Ireland Starved: A Quantitative and Analytical History of the Irish Economy, 1800–1850* (London: Allen & Unwin, 1983).

Morris, Norval and David J. Rothman, eds., *The Oxford History of the Prison: The Practice of Punishment in Western Society* (Oxford University Press, 1995).

Morrison, Danny, ed. *Hunger Strike: Reflections on the 1981 Hunger Strike* (Dingle: Brandon, 2006).

Nicholson, Asenath. *Annals of the Famine in Ireland*, ed. Maureen Murphy (Dublin: Lilliput Press, 1998).

O'Brien, John A., ed. *The Vanishing Irish: The Enigma of the Modern World* (New York: McGraw Hill, 1953).

O'Brien, Sean. *Irish Prison Writing and the Victorian Penitentiary*, PhD dissertation, (University of Notre Dame, 2008).

O'Connell, Helen. *Ireland and the Fiction of Improvement* (Oxford University Press, 2006).

O'Connor, Emmet. *A Labour History of Ireland, 1824–1960* (Dublin: Gill and Macmillan, 1992).

  Syndicalism in Ireland, 1917–1923 (Cork University Press, 1988).

O'Connor, Feargus. *A Practical Work on the Management of Small Farms* (London: John Cleave, 1843).

O'Connor, Laura. *Haunted English: The Celtic Fringe, the British Empire, and Deanglicization* (Baltimore: Johns Hopkins University Press, 2006).

O'Connor, Sinéad. 'Famine', on *Universal Mother* (New York: Ensign Records, 1994).

Ó Crualaoich, Gearóid 'The "Merry Wake"', in J.S. Donnelly, Jr and Kerby A. Miller, eds., *Irish Popular Culture, 1650–1850* (Dublin: Irish Academic Press, 1998), pp. 173–200.

O'Donovan Rossa, Jeremiah. *Irish Rebels in English Prisons*, ed. Thomas J. Cox (Dingle: Brandon Books, 1991).
O'Flaherty, Liam. *Famine* (Dublin: Wolfhound, 1984).
Ó Gráda, Cormac. *Black '47 and Beyond: The Great Irish Famine in History, Economy and Memory* (Princeton University Press, 1999).
  Ireland: A New Economic History, 1780–1939 (Oxford: Clarendon Press, 1994).
  'Malthus and the pre-Famine Economy', in Antoin E. Murphy, ed., *Economists and the Irish Economy from the Eighteenth Century to the Present Day* (Blackrock: Irish Academic Press, 1984), pp. 75–95.
O'Hearn, Denis. 'Embodied Perception and Prefigurative Movements: Connections across the Atlantic', in Peter D. O'Neill and David Lloyd, eds., *The Black and Green Atlantic: Crosscurrents of the African and Irish Diasporas* (London and New York: Palgrave, 2009), pp. 228–243.
  Nothing But an Unfinished Song: Bobby Sands, The Irish Hunger Striker Who Ignited a Generation (New York: Nation Books, 2006).
O hOgáin, Dáithí. 'Folklore and Literature: 1700–1850', in Mary Daly and David Dickson, eds., *The Origins of Popular Literacy in Ireland: Language Change and Educational Development 1700–1920* (Department of Modern History, Trinity College Dublin and Department of Modern Irish History, University College Dublin, 1990), pp. 1–13.
O Mahony, Sean. *Frongoch: University of Revolution* (Killiney: FDR Teoranta, 1987).
O'Malley, Ernie. *Letters and Papers (1924–1957)*, ed. Cormac K.H. O'Malley and Nicholas Allen (Dublin: Lilliput Press, forthcoming).
  'No Surrender Here!' The Civil War Papers of Ernie O'Malley, 1922–1924, ed. Cormac K.H. O'Malley and Anne Dolan (Dublin: Lilliput, 2007).
O'Malley, Padraig. *Biting at the Grave: The Irish Hunger Strikes and the Politics of Despair* (Boston, MA: Beacon Press, 1990).
O'Neill, Peter D. and David Lloyd, eds., *The Black and Green Atlantic: Crosscurrents of the African and Irish Diasporas* (London: Palgrave, 2009).
O'Neill, Tim P. 'Famine Evictions', in Carla King, ed., *Famine, Land and Culture in Ireland* (University College Dublin Press, 2000), pp. 29–70.
Ong, Walter J. *Orality and Literacy: The Technologizing of the Word* (London: Routledge, 1982).
Oppenheimer, Paul. *The Birth of the Modern Mind: Self, Consciousness, and the Invention of the Sonnet* (Oxford University Press, 1989).
Perez, Hiram. 'You Can Have My Brown Body and Eat It Too!', *Social Text* 23.3–4 (Fall–Winter 2005), pp. 171–91.
Póirtéir, Cathal. *Famine Echoes* (Dublin: Gill and Macmillan, 1995).
Poovey, Mary. *Making A Social Body: British Cultural Formation, 1830–1864* (University of Chicago Press, 1995).
Posner, Richard A. 'Torture, Terrorism, and Interrogation', in Sanford Levinson, ed., *Torture: A Collection* (Oxford University Press, 2004), pp. 291–8.
Purbrick, Louise. 'The Architecture of Containment', in Donovan Wylie, *The Maze* (London: Granta Books, 2004), pp. 91–110.

Quinn, John F. *Father Mathew's Crusade: Intemperance in Nineteenth-Century Ireland and Irish America* (Amherst and Boston, MA: University of Massachusetts Press, 2002).
Rama, Angel. *The Lettered City*, ed. and trans. John Charles Chasteen (Durham, NC: Duke University Press, 1996).
Rejali, Darius M. *Torture and Democracy* (Princeton University Press, 2007).
  Torture and Modernity: Self, Society, and State in Modern Iran (Boulder, CO: Westview Press, 1994).
Robins, Joseph. *The Miasma: Epidemic and Panic in Nineteenth-Century Ireland* (Dublin: Institute of Public Administration, 1995).
Rockett, Kevin. 'Disguising Dependency: Separatism and Foreign Mass Culture', *Circa* 49 (January–February 1990), pp. 20–5.
Rosenzweig, Roy. 'The Rise of the Saloon', in Chandra Mukerji and Michael Schudson, eds., *Rethinking Popular Culture: Contemporary Perspectives in Cultural Studies* (Berkeley: University of California Press, 1991), pp. 121–56.
Ruane, Joseph and Jennifer Todd. *The Dynamics of Conflict in Northern Ireland: Power, Conflict and Emancipation* (Cambridge University Press, 1996).
Ruggiero, Vincenzo, Mick Ryan and Joe Sim, eds., *Western European Penal Systems: A Critical Anatomy* (London: Sage, 1995).
Ruskin, John. *Sesame and Lilies*, in *Sesame and Lilies, The Two Paths and The King of the Golden River* (London: J.M. Dent, 1907), pp. 1–79.
Ryan, Alan. *Property* (Minneapolis: University of Minnesota Press, 1987).
Salaman, Redcliffe N. *The History and Social Influence of the Potato* (Cambridge University Press, 1985).
Sands, Bobby. 'Trilogy: The Crime of Castlereagh', in *Writings from Prison*, foreword Gerry Adams, Intro. Sean McBride (Boulder, CO: Roberts Rinehart, 1997), pp. 114–15.
Sangari, Kumkum and Sudesh Vaid. 'Introduction', in *Recasting Women: Essays in Colonial History* (New Delhi: Kali for Women, 1989), pp. 1–26.
Sartre, Jean-Paul. *Baudelaire*, trans. Martin Turnell (London: Horizon, 1949).
Saville, John. 'Introduction', in R.G. Gammage, ed., *History of the Chartist Movement, 1837–1854* (2nd edn 1894) (New York: Augustus M. Kelley, 1969).
Scally, Robert. *The End of Hidden Ireland: Rebellion, Famine and Emigration* (Oxford University Press, 1995).
Scarry, Elaine. 'Five Errors in the Reasoning of Alan Dershowitz', in Sanford Levinson, ed., *Torture: A Collection* (Oxford University Press, 2004), pp. 281–90.
  The Body in Pain: The Making and Unmaking of the World (Oxford University Press, 1985).
Scott, David. *Refashioning Futures: Criticism after Postcoloniality* (Princeton University Press, 1999).
Senior, Nassau. 'Ireland', *Edinburgh Review* 79.159 (January 1844), pp. 189–266.
Shakespeare, William. *Midsummer Night's Dream*, in *Works* (Oxford: The Shakespeare Head Press, 1944), pp. 279–301.

Shallice, T. 'The Ulster Depth Interrogation Techniques and their Relation to Sensory Deprivation Research', *Cognition* 1.4 (1972), pp. 385–405.
Shell, Mark. *The Economy of Literature* (Baltimore: Johns Hopkins University Press, 1978).
Shue, Henry. 'Torture', in Sanford Levinson, ed., *Torture: A Collection* (Oxford University Press, 2004), pp. 47–60.
Smith, Adam. *An Inquiry into the Nature and Causes of the Wealth of Nations*, general eds., R.H. Campbell and A.S. Skinner, textual editor, W.B. Todd, 2 vols. (Oxford: Clarendon Press, 1976).
Somerville, Alexander. *Letters from Ireland during the Famine of 1847*, ed. K.D.M. Snead (Blackrock: Irish Academic Press, 1994).
Stewart, Susan. *Crimes of Writing: Problems in the Containment of Representation* (Durham, NC: Duke University Press, 1994).
Stivers, Richard. *Hair of the Dog: Irish Drinking and Its American Stereotype*, rev. edn (London: Continuuum, 2000).
Stout, Matthew. 'The Geography and Implications of Post-Famine Population Decline in Baltyboys, Co. Wicklow', in Chris Morash and Richard Hayes, eds., *'Fearful Realities': New Perspectives on the Famine* (Dublin: Irish Academic Press, 1996), pp. 15–34.
Street, Brian V. *Literacy in Theory and Practice* (Cambridge University Press, 1984).
Swords, Liam. *In Their Own Words: The Famine in North Connacht, 1845–1849* (Blackrock: The Columba Press, 1999).
Tadiar, Neferti X.M. *Things Fall Away: Philippine Historical Experience and the Makings of Globalization* (Durham, NC: Duke University Press, 2009).
Takaki, Ronald T. *Iron Cages: Race and Culture in 19th-Century America* (Seattle: University of Washington Press, 1985).
Tallack, William. *The Cellular (But nor Rigidly Solitary) System of Imprisonment, as Carried out at the Prisons of Louvain, Amsterdam, etc.* (London: Kitto, 1872).
Defects in the Criminal Administration and Penal Legislation of Great Britain and Ireland, with Remedial Suggestions (London: Kitto, 1872).
Thompson, Dorothy. *The Chartists: Popular Politics in the Industrial Revolution* (London: Temple Smith and New York: Pantheon, 1984).
Thompson, E.P. 'The Moral Economy of the English Crowd in the Eighteenth Century', *Past and Present* 50 (1971), pp. 76–136.
Todorov, Tzvetan. *The Poetics of Prose*, trans. Richard Howard, foreword Jonathan Culler (Ithaca, NY: Cornell University Press, 1977).
Tomlinson, Mike. 'Imprisoned Ireland', in Vincenzo Ruggiero, Mick Ryan and Joe Sim, eds., *Western European Penal Systems: A Critical Anatomy* (London: Sage, 1995), pp. 194–227.
Trevelyan, Charles. 'The Irish Crisis', *Edinburgh Review* 175 (January 1848), pp. 229–320.
Tribe, Keith. *Land, Labour and Economic Discourse* (London: Routledge & Kegan Paul, 1978).

Tylor, Edward Burnett. *The Origins of Culture*, intro. Paul Radin (New York: Harper, 1958).
Viswanathan, Gauri. *Masks of Conquest: Literary Study and British Rule in India* (New York: Columbia University Press, 1989).
Waters, John. 'Sinéad the Keener', *Irish Times*, 28 January (1995).
Whalen, Lochlan. *Contemporary Irish Republican Prison Writing: Writing and Resistance* (New York: Palgrave Macmillan, 2007).
Whately, Richard. *Introductory Lectures on Political Economy*, 3rd edn (London: John W. Parker, 1847).
Whelan, Kevin. 'The Modern Landscape: From Plantation to Present', In F.H.A. Aalen, Kevin Whelan and Matthew Stout, eds., *Atlas of the Irish Rural Landscape* (Cork University Press, 1997), pp. 79–89.
'Pre- and Post-Famine Landscape Change', in Cathal Póirtéir, ed., *The Great Irish Famine* (Cork: Mercier, 1995), pp. 19–33.
Wilde, Oscar. *The Works of Oscar Wilde* (Leicester: Blitz Editions, 1990).
Wilde, Sir William Robert Wills. *Irish Popular Superstitions*, facsimile reproduction of Dublin 1852 edition (Shannon: Irish University Press, 1973).
Wilkinson, John. *Contrivances* (Cambridge: Salt, 2003).
Williams, Randall. 'A Permanent State of Exception: The Birth of Modern Policing in Colonial Capitalism', *Interventions: International Journal of Postcolonial Studies* 5.3 (2003), pp. 322–44.
Yeats, W.B. *Explorations* (New York: Macmillan, 1962).
The Collected Poems (London: Macmillan, 1961).
Autobiography (New York: Macmillan, 1953).
Yeo, Eileen. 'Some Practices and Problems of Chartist Democracy', in J. Epstein and D. Thompson, eds., *The Chartist Experience: Studies in Working Class Radicalism and Culture, 1830–60* (London: Macmillan, 1982), pp. 345–80.
Young, Arthur. *A Tour in Ireland; With General Observations on the Present State of That Kingdom* (1780), 2 vols., ed. Arthur Wollaston Hutton (London: George Bell and Sons, 1892).
Young, Iris Marion. *Intersecting Voices: Dilemmas of Gender, Political Philosophy, and Policy* (Princeton University Press, 1997).
Young, Robert J.C. *The Idea of English Ethnicity* (Oxford: Blackwell, 2008).
Zunes, Stephen. 'The United States: Belligerent Hegemon', in Rick Fawn and Raymond Hinnebusch, eds., *The Iraq War: Causes and Consequences* (Boulder, CO: Lynne Rienner, 2006), pp. 21–36.

Index

Abu Ghraib, 180, 183
accumulation, 47
accumulation by dispossession, 17,
    see also primitive accumulation
Adams, Gerry, 156, 162
Aden, 13, 182
Adorno, Theodor, 89, 124, 220
aesthetics, 112
Africa, 13
    Algeria, 15, 199
    Kenya, 13, 116, 182
Agamben, Giorgio, 139
agrarian movement, 39
aisling, 180
alcohol, 57, 102, 103, 110
Anderson, Benedict, 158
anglicization, 55
Aretxaga, Begoña, 123, 124, 155, 160, 164
Armagh Gaol, 12, 117, 118, 119, 124, 159–61, 162
Arnold, Matthew, 10, 55, 96
    On the Study of Celtic Literature, 55, 96
Association for the Prevention of Torture, 190

ballad, 1, 167, 168, 170, 171, 175, 178, 179, 180
Baltiboys, Co. Wicklow, 70
Bandon, Co. Cork, 53
bare life, 139, 146, 163, 179, 217
Baudelaire, Charles, 14, 167, 168, 174, 187, 196
    'A Une Passante', 168–9, 172, 173, 175, 177
Beckett, Samuel, 14, 198–219
    Catastrophe, 200
    Company, 201
    Endgame, 203, 215
    How It Is, 15, 198, 199, 200–9, 210, 211, 212, 213, 214, 215, 216, 219
    Ping, 205
    Quad, 205
    Texts for Nothing, 198, 201, 204
    The Unnamable, 198
    Waiting for Godot, 198, 203, 215
    What Where, 198, 205
    Worstward Ho, 205
Behan, Brendan, 178
Belfast, 101, 167
Bengal, 98, 104
Benjamin, Walter, 14, 107, 158, 165, 168, 188, 193, 196, 209, 218
    Arcades Project, 167, 168
    on Baudelaire, 172–6
Bentham, Jeremy, 129
Bhabha, Homi, 16
biopolitical power, 180, 186
biopolitics, 14
Blackburn, William, 128
Blanketmen, 144, 146, 148, 153, 156, 161, 162, 172, 179, 196, 220
Bloody Sunday, 141
Boylan, Thomas, 21
Brecht, Bertolt, 114
Bristol, 133
British Raj, 98
Burke, Edmund, 192, 195
Butt, Isaac, 79

Cabral, Amílcar, 141
Cairnes, J.E., 22, 33, 134
Campbell, Joseph, 200
capital, 9, 15, 16, 20, 26, 29, 30, 31, 32, 33, 35, 37, 41, 45, 46, 76, 77, 195, 218, 226, 236
capitalism, 23, 25, 28, 31, 36, 47, 168, 200
    agricultural, 7, 20, 21, 30, 36, 38, 79, 85
    British, 35, 46, 47, 98
    colonial, 16, 18, 43
    discipline, 46, 87, 102
    financial, 16
    industrial, 8, 34, 79, 82, 83
    labour, 9
    modernity, 9, 16, 111
    modernization, 81, 88, 101
    print, 3
    rationalization, 6, 8, 22, 44, 72, 108

279

Carleton, William, 37, 52–3
Carlyle, Thomas, 32–3, 35, 40, 44, 47
Carpenter, Mary, 131, 132, 133, 162
Carroll, Patrick, 13
Castlereagh Interrogation Center, 170, 196, 197
categorical imperative, 192, 193, 194, 196, 210, 211, 216, *see also* Kant, Immanuel
Catholic Church, 30, 103, 108
Catholicism, 86, 120
ceilidh, 108
census, 13, 19
Central Intelligence Agency (CIA), 183, *see also* Kubark Manual
Chartists, 8, 40, 77, 78, 80, 81, 82, *see* O'Connor, Feargus; O'Brien, Bronterre
Chatterjee, Partha, 93, 96, 98, 104
Citizen Army, 140
civility, 119
civilizing mission, 134
civilizing process, 11, 12, 56, 57, 63, 70, 89, 127, 132, 151, 153, 161, 172, 194, 202, 208, *see* Elias, Norbert; modernization
clachan, 6, 8, 10, 20, 67, 68, 69, 70, 71, 72, 79, 80, 83, 85, 88, 103, 134, 150, 151, 167, *see also* rundale
clearance, 7, 70
Coercion Acts, 11, 132, 187
Colditz, 126, 141
Cole, G.D.H., 77, 82
Coleridge, Samuel Taylor, 171
colonialism, 4, 15, 18, 22, 23, 69, 83, 92, 93, 95, 98, 100, 104, 123, 187, 195
combinations, 30, 102
commodification, 36, 44, 46, 110, 218
commodity, 36, 37, 44, 45, 46, 213
commodity exchange, 15, 17, 45, 46, 88, 110, 213
Connaught, 35
Conner, William, 79
Connolly, James, 141
contagion, 158
Irish as, 39, 40, 43, 44, 47, 77, 150, 151
Convention against Torture, 189
Coogan, Tim Pat, 160, 181, 182
Corbin, Alain, 41
Corcoran, Mary, 124, 125, 160, 162
corn, 7, 35, 36–7, 45, 46, *see also* wheat
Corn Laws, the, 7
repeal of, 82
cottierism, 20, 32, 35, 77, 83
counter-insurgency, 13, 14, 100, 116, 117, 119, 126, 127, 142, 150, 159, 167, 181, 182, 185, 186, 187, 199, *see also* internment; interrogation; sensory deprivation; torture
counter-modern spaces, 9, 107
counter-space of modernity, 12, 15, 64
Crane Bag, The, 120
criminalization, 11, 117, 119, 120, 123, 126, 137, 142, 157, 159
Crofton, Sir Walter, 54, 58, 97, 131, 132, 244
Croke, Archbishop, 106
Croker, Thomas Crofton, 54, 58, 97
Cruise O'Brien, Conor, 119
culture
  colonial, 4, 92, 219
  Irish, 9, 39, 43, 49, 53, 55, 56, 60, 71, 77, 87, 89, 90, 91, 97, 98, 99, 163, 200, 219
  oral, 3, 4, 5, 8, 9, 10, 14, 35, 36, 57, 59, 60, 61, 64, 65, 69, 84, 86, 87, 88, 90, 93, 99, 102, 103, 111
  print, 3, 99, 108
Curtis, Liz, 181
Cyprus, 116, 182

da Silva, Denise, 194
Davis, Thomas, 97, 98
de Beauvoir, Simone, 199
De Valera, Eamonn, 139
Deane, Seamus, 59, 150, 221
decolonization, 71, 199
Derry, 160, 167
Dershowitz, Alan, 189, 193
development, 17, 22, 27, 30, 34, 59, 86, 95, 126, 133, 134, 135
Dickson, David, 71
diet, 27, 131, 182
differential space, 12, 15, 16
Diplock courts, 117
dirty protest, 117, 154, 155, 160, 249
domestic ideology, 96, 97, 98, 104, 111, *see also* gender; masculinity
Donegal, 50, 66
  Doaghbeg, 65
  Gweedore, 69, 84, 134
Dorfman, Ariel, 191, 193
Dorian, Hugh, 14, 50, 65–9, 185
Douglas, Mary, 160
drinking, 57, 95, 101–2, 108, 111
Dublin, 10, 90, 91, 101, 109, 114, 200, 228, 230, 234
dung, 35, 41–3, 47
Dunne, J.W., 203

Easter Rising, 119, 139
economy
  capitalist, 23, 28, 31, 43, 47
  colonial, 95
  Irish, 23

Elias, Norbert, 56, 151
Ellmann, Maud, 147, 152, 154, 161
Emergency Provisions Act, 184
emigration, 19, 31, 73, 73, 85
  assisted, 70
enclosure, 8, 12, 14, 20, 36, 44, 62, 73, 85, 86, 144, 145, 194
Engels, Friedrich, 40, 47
English Intelligence Centre, 182
epiphany, 113–14
eschatology, 123
Estyn Evans, E., 64, 68, 71
ethnography, 55, 76, 94, 123
European Court of Human Rights, 191
Evelegh, Robin, 184, 186
eviction, 20, 57, 70, 83
excrement, 43, 147

Famine
  administration, 21, 28, 52, 133
  and trauma, 8, 60, 64, 75, 86
  consequences of, 50, 61, 70, 73, 85, 134
  memory of, 49
  representation of, 50
Famine, the (1845–52), 1, 3, 6, 7, 8, 10, 11, 19, 21, 22, 23, 24, 25, 27, 28, 35, 36, 38, 40, 42, 49–53, 59, 60, 64, 69, 71, 75, 76, 81, 82, 83, 85, 97, 133, 134
Fanon, Frantz, 18, 67, 94, 115, 141, 199, 218
  The Wretched of the Earth, 93, 199
Farrell, Michael, 181
Faulkner, Brian, 186
Feldman, Allen, 123, 142, 143, 147, 153, 155, 164
feminine space, 97, 98, 99
feminization, 96–7, 98, 99, 161, 162, 163
Fenianism, 81, 83
Fenians, 77, 96, 100, 120, 135, 136, 137, 139, 141, 144
flâneur, 14, 167, 168, 172, 173, 176
Foley, Timothy, 21
folklore, 5, 99, 108, 158, 171
Foucault, Michel, 125, 129
  Discipline and Punish, 62, 127, 167
Foucaultian, 125
France, 14, 27, 182, 199
  French Resistance, 199
  Vichy France, 199
Freud, Sigmund, 212
Frongoch prison camp, 139, 140
Front de Liberation Nationale (FLN), 199

Gaelic Athletic Association (GAA), 106
Gaelic League, 99, 106
Gaelic poetry, 180

Gallagher, Thomas, 51
Gammage, Robert, 79
gender, 3, 10, 57, 88, 91, 108, 123, 134, 160, 161, 163, 178
gendered space, 10, 91, 109, 124
Gilmore, Charlie, 200
Gilroy, Paul, 88
Gladstone, William, 21, 79
Gladstone's Land Acts, 21
global war on terror, 13, 187
Godwin, William, 195, 196
Goody, Jack, 61
Guantanamo Bay Prison, 180
Guevara, Che, 141
Guha, Ranajit, 148

Hall, Mrs. S.C., 53, 57
Halpin, Revd. J., 104, 105
Harvey, David, 15, 16, 17
Haussmannization, 167, 175
Havel, Vaclav, 200
H-Blocks, 12, 17, 118, 122, 123, 124, 126, 142–58, 159, 163, 164, 166, 172, 208, *see also* Long Kesh; The Maze
Hegel, G.W.F., 61, 121, 159
hegemony, 11, 28, 218
Herr, Cheryl, 90
Hill, Lord George, 69, 70, 71, 134
historicism, 4, 24, 33, 34, 48, 59, 61, 82–3, 89
historicist logic, 94, 115
Hobsbawm, Eric, 77
homosociality, 10, 91, 95, 108, 109, 111
Horkheimer, Max, 89, 124
Howard Society, 130
Howard, John, 128
hunger strike, 116, 118, 119, 123, 144, 154, 155, 156, 157
Hyde, Douglas, 94, 104

ideology, 39, 40, 83
imagined community, 140, 150
improvement, 11, 20, 21, 29, 30, 31, 33, 72, 84, 85, 97, 103, 130, 132
India, 13, 22, 98, 148
intemperance, 95, 101, 102, 103, 104
internment, 13, 116, 140, 141, 180, 185, 186
interrogation, 13, 14, 15, 66, 67, 168, 177, 178, 179, 180, 183, 184, 185, 186, 187, 189, 194, 196, 198, 199, 200, 202, 211, 213, 216
  center, 167, 170, 176, 184, 196
  depth or enhanced, 116, 141, 181, 192
  techniques, 180, 181, 184, 188
invented tradition, 149
Irish Convict System, 131, 132, 132

Irish language, 60, 148, 164
Irish Literary movement, 106
Irish literature, 14
Irish National Liberation Army (INLA), 157
Irish National Theatre, 106
Irish Republican Army (IRA), 124, 139, 141, 181, 184, *see also* Provisional IRA
Irish Republican Brotherhood (IRB), 120
Irish Volunteers, 140
Israel, 182, 189

Joyce, James, 10, 90, 114, 115
  Dubliners, 10, 90–2, 111, 113, 114
    Counterparts, 90, 91, 95, 109, 111, 112
  Finnegans Wake, 203
  Stephen Hero, 113
  Ulysses, 10, 14, 106, 203

Kant, Immanuel, 5, 96, 192–3, 195, 196, 199, 209, 210, 211, 217
Kavanagh, Patrick, 86
Kay, James, 32, 33, 40, 47
Kearney, Richard, 120, 121–2
keening, 7, 49, 51, 53–6, 63, 73, 108
Kerry, 53
Kingsley, Charles, 2
Korea, 182
Kubark Manual, 183, *see also* Central Intelligence Agency (CIA)

labour, 6, 11, 15, 26, 29, 30, 35, 39, 41, 43, 46, 58, 59, 63, 68, 69, 75, 79, 80, 85, 89, 90, 95, 104, 105, 108, 109, 111, 133, 133, 135, 136
  abstract, 41, 44, 45, 46, 114, 213
  agricultural, 20, 36, 101
  discipline, 9, 76, 87, 88, 102, 132
  division of, 5, 7, 36, 48, 68, 69, 78
  hard, 130, 131, 135, 139, 178
  history, 76, 77
  industrial, 8
  movement, 77, 81, 83, 101
  power, 16, 44
  surplus, 27, 47, 79
Lacan, Jacques, 209, 210, 212
Lalor, James Fintan, 44, 141
Land League, 71
Land Plan, 77–84, *see also* Chartists; O'Connor, Feargus
landlord, 6, 7, 14, 20, 26, 67, 71, 85
Laporte, Dominique, 41
lazy bed, 46
Lefebvre, Henri, 9, 12, 15, 16, 18
Lindon, Jérôme, 199
Linebaugh, Peter, 178

literacy, 5, 61–4
Liverpool, 133
Locke, John, 62
Long Kesh, 117, 126, 140, 141, 142, 147, 160, 164, *see also* H-Blocks; Maze Prison
Luxemburg, Rosa, 14

Mac Suibhne, Breandan, 71
MacDonagh, Thomas, 120
MacGreevy, Thomas, 200
Malaya, 13
Malcolm, Elizabeth, 102, 105
Malthus, Thomas, 27–8, 29, 30, 36, 47, 77
Manchester, 35
Marcuse, Herbert, 217
Markievicz, Countess, 139
Martin, Henri, 55
Marx, Karl, 14, 16, 38, 39, 41, 44, 45, 46, 47, 121, 213
  Capital, 46
Marx, Karl and Friedrich Engels
  Communist Manifesto, 46
Marxism, 81
masculinity, 3, 10, 95, 96, 97, 100, 110
Mathew, Father, 102, 103
Maze Prison, 142, *see also* H-Blocks; Long Kesh
McCafferty, Nell, 160
McCoy, Alfred, 181
McCulloch, J.R., 29, 31, 32, 33, 36, 40, 47
McGuckian, Medbh, 166
McGuffin, John, 182
McKeown, Lawrence, 149
Mellowes, Liam, 141
Memmi, Albert, 199
menstrual blood, 124, 159, 160
metaphor, 35, 40, 43, 44, 45, 47, 155, 158, 163, 166, 176, 210, 212
metonymy, 3, 4, 7, 12, 35, 39, 43, 45, 46, 47, 87, 95, 155, 158
miasma, 35, 40, 147
migration, 3, 34, 39, 43, 44, 76, 85
Mill, John Stuart, 21, 22, 33, 77, 79, 81, 134
Millbank Prison, 11, 129
mimesis, 114
Mitchel, John, 14
modern
  subject of, 175
modernity, 5, 6, 15, 23, 48, 50, 59, 63, 84, 85, 86, 87, 88, 89, 92, 93, 94, 99, 101, 110, 111, 119, 123, 126, 158, 161, 165, 166, 168, 174, 179, 188, 197, 198, 211, 215, 219
  capitalist, 9, 81, 88, 101
  colonial, 4, 91, 92, 107, 134

institutions of, 1, 2, 4, 9, 11, 16, 34, 73, 75, 84, 87, 88, 125, 149
interrogation, 193
Irish, 13, 44, 61, 99, 109, 110
nationalist, 92, 94, 107
political, 58, 59, 93, 212
spaces of, 3, 9, 16, 61, 63, 64, 86, 106, 110, 111, 113, 115, 167
subject of, 44, 70, 75, 86, 87, 168, 176, 192, 196, 200
urban, 11, 14, 167, 175
modernization, 4, 88, 94, 197
capitalist, 16
colonial, 91, 101, 135, 219
nationalist, 92, 93, 95, 97, 99, 100, 219
of Ireland, 8, 9, 23, 47, 68, 75, 87, 88, 105
More, Thomas, 17
Morning Chronicle, 21
mouth, 1, 2, 3, 4, 7, 47, 49, 57, 60, 64, 73, 86, 87, 108, 109, 146, 152, 166, 181, 207
myth, 119, 120, 123, 124
mythologization, 119–22

Napoleonic wars, 27
National H-Block–Armagh Committee, 118
national police force, 30
national school system, 30
national schools, 13, 134
nationalism, 100, 101, 107, 111
nationalist discourse, 98–101
nationalist ideology, 106, 125
necessary wage, 29, 30, 31
Negritude, 94
neo-liberalism, 14, 16, 18, 166, 168, 218, 219, 251
Newgate Prison, 127
Ni Aolain, Fionnuala, 191
Nicholls, George, 43
Nicholson, Asenath, 69, 70, 84, 103, 133, 134
nomadism, 32, 34, 114
Northern Star, 78
no-wash protests, 117, 124, 143, 144, 150, 151, 153, 154, 157, 159, 164, *see also* Blanketmen; dirty protest; H-Blocks
Nugent, Kieran, 143

O'Brien, Bronterre, 77, 79
O'Connor, Feargus, 77, 82
O'Connor, Laura, 180
O'Connor, Sinéad, 49, 52
O'Donovan Rossa, Jeremiah, 14, 135–9, 142
O'Flaherty, Liam, 51, 53, 200
O'Malley, Ernie, 200
O'Malley, Padraig, 122–3
odour, 40, 114–15, 147, 229

Ong, Walter, 61, 62
oral space, 1, 2, 3, 4, 6, 8, 9, 11, 12, 15, 16, 17, 18, 33, 34, 48, 61, 64, 86, 87, 91, 93, 95, 99, 102, 103, 108, 111, 167, 185, 219
orality, 5, 12, 47, 61–4, 69, 76, 86, 87, 90, 106, 108, 111, 150, 151, 179
Ordinary Decent Criminals (ODCs), 118, 126, 142, 144
ordnance survey, 13
orifice, 1, 15, 146, 152

Panopticon, 129, 185
pathological subject, 9, 15, 17, 87, 96, 121, 195, 196, 199, 200, 201, 209, 211, 217, 219
pathologization, 124, 126, 162, 163
pauperism, 32, 79
Pearse, Patrick, 100, 120
peasant, 14, 20, 21, 22, 37, 38, 39, 41, 51, 52, 55, 58, 65, 66, 72, 74, 77, 79, 81, 82, 83, 99, 133, 134, 220
Penal Laws, 3
Pentonville Prison, 11, 129
Perez, Hiram, 3
photography, 174, *see also* surveillance
Polanyi, Karl, 16
police, 11, 13, 14, 30, 67, 116, 132, 168, 174, 175, 177, 181, 184, 186, 190, 245
political economy, 7, 8, 21, 22, 23, 25, 26, 28, 30, 31, 33, 34, 36, 37, 38, 45, 46, 51, 58, 59, 60, 83, 103, 133, 166
Poor Laws, 28, 42, 43
Poovey, Mary, 33
population, 21, 26, 29, 31, 86,
see also reproduction (biological)
Posner, Richard, 189
postcolonialism, 16, 164
post-Kantian ethics, 15
potato, 7, 10, 27, 32, 35, 39, 43, 47, 103
consumption, 26
cultivation, 20, 78
Prevention of Terrorism Act, 184, 187
primitive accumulation, 26, 44, 47,
see also accumulation
primogeniture, 85, 109, 134
prison, 11, 116–63, 168, 171, 172, 177
architecture, 11, 12, 125, 127, 129–130, 144, 159
cellular system, 11, 126, 127, 130, 131, 134–5, 136, 137, 139, 140, 142, 148, 149, 175
Prison Act (1865), 130
Provisional IRA, 120, 141, 157
psychoanalysis, 2, 5
pub, 1, 10, 89, 91, 105, 106, 108, 109, 110, 111, *see* public house; sheebeen

public house, 10, 12, 87, 88, 89, 90, 91, 105, 106, 108, 109, 110, 115, *see also* pub; sheebeen
public sphere, 63, 89, 97, 99, 100, 105, 106, 193

racial difference, 2, 3, 56
racialization, 3, 137
rackrenting, 20, 26
rationalization, 6, 8, 15, 20, 48, 84, 99, 158, 218, 219
Rejali, Darius, 182, 184
Relatives Action Committees, 164
Renan, Ernest, 55
rent, 20, 26, 30, 38, 47, 66, 70
Repealers, 77
reproduction (biological), 10, 20, 24–5, 28, 29, 30, 32, 86, 100, 124
reproduction (cultural), 24, 27, 28, 29, 41, 71
reproduction (economic), 29, 36
Republican ideology, 123, 143, 164
Republicanism, 119, 120, 121, 122, 126, 141
revisionism, Irish historical, 119, 123
Rosenzweig, Roy, 108
Royal Ulster Constabulary (RUC), 182, 185
rundale, 6, 20, 39, 64, 71, 77, 84

Sands, Bobby, 14, 118, 141, 155, 156, 157, 162, 163, 170, 172, 175, 176–8, 179, 180, 187, 196, 197
  The Crime of Castlereagh, 167, 168, 170, 177, 178, 179
Scally, Robert, 67
Scarry, Elaine, 172, 183, 189, 191, 194, 211
scopic drive, 172, 173, 174
Scott, David, 22
Scrope, George Poulett, 42
Senior, Nassau, 29, 30, 31, 36, 102
sensory deprivation, 13, 67, 131, 181, 182, 183, 184, 189
seriality, 130, 144, 155, 167, 207, 208, 209, 211, 212
settler colonialism, 19, *see also* colonialism; decolonialism; postcolonialism
Shallice, Tim, 182, 186
sheebeen, 89, 105, 108, *see also* pub; public house
Shelley, Percy Bysshe, 171
Shue, Henry, 193
Simon, Pierre-Henri, 199
Sinn Fein, 118, 158, 164
Smith, Adam, 26, 29, 35
Smith, Mrs. Elizabeth, 70
Social Democratic and Labour Party (SDLP), 118
Somerville, Alexander, 37, 42, 81
sonnet, 168, 175, 178, 196

space, 86, 89, 91
space-time compression, 15
Special Category status prisoners, 116
Special Powers Act, 13, 186
Spivak, Gayatri Chakravorty, 160
state
  apparatuses, 125
  biopolitical, 13, 14, 168, 217
  British, 11, 103
  capitalist, 48, 167
  colonial, 2, 4, 8, 9, 11, 13, 33, 93, 106, 132, 136, 151, 153, 157, 159, 195
  of emergency, 13, 186, 187, 188, 194
  of exception, 139, 186, 188, 190, 193
  state formation, 9, 28, 93, 97
stereotype, 33, 87, 94, 95, 96, 97, 99, 172, 238
Stewart, Susan, 170, 171
Stivers, Richard, 10, 87, 89, 109
Street, Brian, 62
strip-searching, 118, 137, 138, 147, 162, 163
Strokestown House, Co. Roscommon, 66
Stuart, Francis, 200
subsistence, 8, 19, 26, 29, 31, 32, 34, 37, 38, 43, 68, 73, 76, 80, 133
Sunday Times, The, 186
surveillance, 13, 67, 129, 130, 132, 138, 146, 147, 149, 151, 161, 162, 167, 175, 176, 177, 185, 194, 208, 216
Swift, Jonathan, 17
symbol, 7, 42, 112, 113, 160, 203
symbolism, 2, 38, 90, 112, 113, 114, 120, 121, 135, 140, 143, 149, 154, 157, 158, 168, 204, 206, 208, 212, 214
symbolon, 112
syndicalism, 81, 83, 101

Tadiar, Neferti, 16, 18
Tallack, William, 130
temperance, 102–5, *see also* alcohol; drinking; intemperance
terror, 121
terrorism, 120, 121, 135, 187
Thompson, Dorothy, 82
Thompson, E.P., 37
through-otherness, 7, 68, 72, 79, 134, 150, 154, 158, 167
Tomlinson, Mike, 132, 133
torture, 14, 15, 161, 177, 179, 180, 182, 184, 186, 187–97, 198, 199, 200, 202, 210, 211, 213, 216
  definition of, 191
  history of, 188, 189
  in Algeria, 15, 199

in Northern Ireland, 13, 170, 180, 182, 184, 185, 186
techniques of, 13, 172, 180, 181, 182, 183, 184, 185, 188
Trevelyan, Charles, 27, 36, 37, 38–9, 46, 85, 105
Tyrone, 118

uncanny, the, 63
Union (1800), 55
United States of America (USA), 98, 118, 127, 182, 218
utopia, 17, 18, 34, 217
utopian, 101
utopianism, 10, 17, 71, 80, 81, 88, 154, 163, 164, 165, 217

vernacular, 74, 170, 171, 172, 188, 198, 232

wages, 8, 20, 29, 31, 32, 36, 38, 46, 77, 79, 80, 134
wake, 7, 51, 57, 69, 87, 108
waking, 73
West Indies, 33
Whately, Archbishop Richard, 36
wheat, 7, 26, 27, 36, 78, *see also* corn
Whelan, Kevin, 38, 41, 73
Whiteboys, 77
Wilde, Lady (Speranza), 171
Wilde, Oscar, 179
    "The Ballad of Reading Gaol", 14, 171, 178–9
Wilde, Sir William, 45, 71, 73, 75, 99, 103
Wilkinson, John, 1

Yeats, W. B., 14, 99, 100, 112, 119
Yeo, Eileen, 81
Young Ireland, 97, 98, 100, 103
Young, Arthur, 26, 35, 38

Milton Keynes UK
Ingram Content Group UK Ltd.
UKHW022303260724
445936UK00017B/149